Application Acceleration and WAN Optimization Fundamentals

Ted Grevers, Jr.
Joel Christner, CCIE No. 15311

D1303551

Cisco Press

800 East 96th Street
Indianapolis, Indiana 46240 USA

Application Acceleration and WAN Optimization Fundamentals

Ted Grevers, Jr., Joel Christner

Copyright © 2008 Cisco Systems, Inc.

Published by:
Cisco Press
800 East 96th Street
Indianapolis, IN 46240 USA

Printed in the United States of America

First Printing July 2008

Library of Congress Cataloging-in-Publication Data

Grevers, Ted.

  Application acceleration and WAN optimization fundamentals / Ted Grevers, Jr., Joel Christner.

     p. cm.

  ISBN 978-1-58705-316-0 (pbk.)

  1. Wide area networks (Computer networks) I. Christner, Joel. II. Title.

  TK5105.87.G73 2007

  004.67--dc22

2007021688

ISBN-13: 978-1-58705-316-0

ISBN-10: 1-58705-316-0

Warning and Disclaimer

This book provides foundational information about application acceleration and WAN optimization techniques and technologies. Every effort has been made to make this book as complete and as accurate as possible, but no warranty or fitness is implied.

The information is provided on an "as is" basis. The authors, Cisco Press, and Cisco Systems, Inc., shall have neither liability nor responsibility to any person or entity with respect to any loss or damages arising from the information contained in this book or from the use of the discs or programs that may accompany it.

The opinions expressed in this book belong to the author and are not necessarily those of Cisco Systems, Inc.

Trademark Acknowledgments

All terms mentioned in this book that are known to be trademarks or service marks have been appropriately capitalized. Cisco Press or Cisco Systems, Inc., cannot attest to the accuracy of this information. Use of a term in this book should not be regarded as affecting the validity of any trademark or service mark.

Corporate and Government Sales

The publisher offers excellent discounts on this book when ordered in quantity for bulk purchases or special sales, which may include electronic versions and/or custom covers and content particular to your business, training goals, marketing focus, and branding interests. For more information, please contact: **U.S. Corporate and Government Sales** 1-800-382-3419 corpsales@pearsontechgroup.com

For sales outside the United States please contact: **International Sales** international@pearsoned.com

Feedback Information

At Cisco Press, our goal is to create in-depth technical books of the highest quality and value. Each book is crafted with care and precision, undergoing rigorous development that involves the unique expertise of members from the professional technical community.

Readers' feedback is a natural continuation of this process. If you have any comments regarding how we could improve the quality of this book, or otherwise alter it to better suit your needs, you can contact us through e-mail at feedback@ciscopress.com. Please make sure to include the book title and ISBN in your message.

We greatly appreciate your assistance.

Publisher: Paul Boger

Cisco Representative: Anthony Wolfenden

Executive Editor: Karen Gettman

Development Editor: Dayna Isley

Copy Editor: Bill McManus

Editorial Assistant: Vanessa Evans

Composition: ICC Macmillan, Inc.

Proofreader: Karen A. Gill

Associate Publisher: Dave Dusthimer

Cisco Press Program Manager: Jeff Brady

Managing Editor: Patrick Kanouse

Senior Project Editor: San Dee Phillips

Technical Editors: Jim French, Zach Seils, Steve Wasko

Book and Cover Designer: Louisa Adair

Indexer: Tim Wright

Americas Headquarters
Cisco Systems, Inc.
170 West Tasman Drive
San Jose, CA 95134-1706
USA
www.cisco.com
Tel: 408 526-4000
800 553-NETS (6387)
Fax: 408 527-0883

Asia Pacific Headquarters
Cisco Systems, Inc.
168 Robinson Road
#28-01 Capital Tower
Singapore 068912
www.cisco.com
Tel: +65 6317 7777
Fax: +65 6317 7799

Europe Headquarters
Cisco Systems International BV
Haarlerbergpark
Haarlerbergweg 13-19
1101 CH Amsterdam
The Netherlands
www-europe.cisco.com
Tel: +31 0 800 020 0791
Fax: +31 0 20 357 1100

Cisco has more than 200 offices worldwide. Addresses, phone numbers, and fax numbers are listed on the Cisco Website at **www.cisco.com/go/offices**.

About the Authors

Ted Grevers, Jr., is the solution manager of the Cisco Managed Media Solution (C-MMS) for the Cisco Video/IPTV Systems Test and Architecture (C-VISTA) team, focused on Cisco service provider customers. The C-MMS offering provides live streaming media and on-demand content delivery to cable high-speed data subscribers, adding QoS to DOCSIS service flows, ensuring an enhanced quality of experience. Ted joined Cisco via the SightPath acquisition in early 2000 as a systems engineer. The SightPath acquisition became the foundation for the Cisco Content Networking product offering with the Content Engine (CE) and ultimately the Wide Area Application Engine (WAE). Shortly after the acquisition, Ted transitioned to the Content Networking Business Unit in 2001 as a technical marketing engineer and then became manager of technical marketing in 2002. Currently attending Framingham State College, Ted is completing his undergraduate degree. Milford, MA, is home to Ted, his wife, and three children.

Joel E. Christner, CCIE No. 15311, is the manager of technical marketing within the Application Delivery Business Unit (ADBU) at Cisco. Joel and his team are responsible for the technical marketing aspects associated with the Cisco Application Networking Services (ANS) advanced technology products including Cisco Wide Area Application Services (WAAS) and Application and Content Networking Services (ACNS). These responsibilities include creating white papers, presentations, training, competitive analysis, and collateral; enabling sales; and driving product requirements and strategic direction with the product management team. Before joining the ADBU, Joel was a member of the storage networking advanced technology team within Cisco. Joel is a graduate student at Columbia University working toward a master's degree in computer science. He holds a bachelor of science degree in electronics engineering technology. Joel lives with his wife in San Jose, CA.

About the Technical Reviewers

Jim French, CCIE No. 4074, has more than 9 years of experience at Cisco, 13 years of experience in information technologies, and more than 13 years of experience fathering his wonderful son Brian. Jim has held the position of Cisco Distinguished System Engineer since early 2003 and holds CCIE and CISSP certifications. Since joining Cisco, he has focused on routing, switching, voice, video, security, storage, content, and application networking. Most recently, Jim has been helping customers to decrease upfront capital investments in application infrastructure, reduce application operational costs, speed application time to market, increase application touch points (interactions), increase application availability, and improve application performance. Working with Cisco marketing and engineering, Jim has been instrumental in driving new features and acquisitions into Cisco products to make customers successful. Jim received a BSEE degree from Rutgers University, College of Engineering, in 1987 and later went on to attain an MBA from Rutgers Graduate School of Management in 1994. In his spare time, Jim enjoys family, friends, running, basketball, biking, traveling, and laughing.

Zach Seils, CCIE No. 7861, is a technical leader in Cisco Advanced Services Data Center Networking Practice. Zach's focus is the design and deployment of Cisco WAAS solutions for the largest enterprise customers with Cisco. He is also frequently engaged with partners and internal Cisco engineers worldwide to advise on the design, implementation, and troubleshooting of Cisco WAAS. He also works closely with the Application Delivery Business Unit (ADBU) on product enhancements, testing, and deployment best practices.

Steve Wasko is a consulting systems engineer in Cisco Systems Advanced Technology Data Center team. He works with Fortune 500 companies in the areas of application networking services and storage area networking. He has been with Cisco for two years. Steve's career has been focused around server-side operating systems and infrastructure networking for large corporations. Graduating in 1995 from Central Michigan University, Steve has spent time deploying client/server environments for 10 years with EDS, IBM, Microsoft, and Cisco. While at Microsoft, Steve was also a senior product manager for Microsoft's Windows Server Division. Steve's industry certifications include Cisco Storage Networking Solutions Design Specialist, Novell Certified NetWare Engineer (CNE), and Microsoft Certified Systems Engineer (MCSE).

Dedications

This book is dedicated to Kathleen, my wife, and our three wonderful children, Ella, Teddy III, and Garon.
—Ted Grevers, Jr.

This book is dedicated to my beautiful wife Christina, our family, and to our Lord and Savior Jesus Christ, through Him all things are possible.
—Joel Christner

Acknowledgments

From Ted Grevers, Jr.:

Call it a clan, call it a network, call it a tribe, call it a family. Whatever you call it, whoever you are, you need one.
—Jane Howard

This work could not have been completed without the support of my family. My wife, Kathleen, daughter Ella, and sons Teddy III and Garon each had their evenings and weekends without me, supporting the completion of this work.

To my wife, Kathleen, you were instrumental in creating focus time opportunities for me. Without your love and support, I would have gone insane trying to find a balance between family, work, and writing time. Thank you for being there for me. Without you, Chapter 1 would still be a blinking cursor on a blank page, and the kids would be running the house.

Ella, "Baby E," and Teddy, "Mein Theo," we have a lot of catch-up time ahead of us at the playground. Who wants to be the line leader? "Monsieur Garon," although you will be just a year old when this work is published, you've been kind to Kathleen and I during my many late nights of writing. Who would have thought that 4 hours of sleep would be such a wonderful thing? Thank you, babies.

If I were to choose one word to describe Joel Christner during the process of co-authoring this book, it would be "dedicated." I've never worked with anyone at Cisco as dedicated as you, Joel. Your dedication and commitment to excellence made co-authoring this book a joy. Joel, you are a rock star.

From Joel Christner:

I would like to first thank my wife, Christina. Christina, you have been patient, supportive, and loving through this entire process, and I cannot find the words or expressions to thank you enough.

I would also like to give special thanks to you, the reader, for purchasing and reading this book. Ted and I both hope you find it to be of value to you, and look forward to your feedback and comments on improving it.

I'd also like to give thanks to a few teams within Cisco. To the team within ADBU, you are all a blessing, and it has been an honor and a privilege to work with such an amazing, aggressive, quality-oriented, and customer-focused team. To the Data Center and Application Networking Services advanced technology teams, I thank each of you for doing an outstanding job and helping position Cisco as a leader in application networking services.

Numerous thanks to each of the technical reviewers, Steve Wasko, Zach Seils, and Jim French, for their countless hours in reviewing this book and helping me and Ted improve its quality, accuracy, and readability. You are all three a pleasure to work with, brilliantly insightful, and we appreciate everything you do and have done.

A tremendous thank you to the production team, Dayna Isley, Karen Gettman, Kristin Weinberger, and Christopher Cleveland. Thank you for helping to "shape the experience." Working with you has been great, and I look forward to doing it again very soon!

Last, and certainly not least, I'd like to thank my co-author Ted Grevers, Jr. Ted, working with you on this project has been great. I thank you for being a good friend, a mentor, and for giving me the opportunity to join ADBU and work under your guidance.

This Book Is Safari Enabled

The Safari® Enabled icon on the cover of your favorite technology book means the book is available through Safari Bookshelf. When you buy this book, you get free access to the online edition for 45 days.

Safari Bookshelf is an electronic reference library that lets you easily search thousands of technical books, find code samples, download chapters, and access technical information whenever and wherever you need it.

To gain 45-day Safari Enabled access to this book:

- Go to http://www.ciscopress.com/safarienabled

- Complete the brief registration form

- Enter the coupon code J5A8-DMAC-UXZ6-4VCT-GAAW

If you have difficulty registering on Safari Bookshelf or accessing the online edition, please e-mail customer-service@safaribooksonline.com.

Contents at a Glance

Contents

Icons Used in This Book

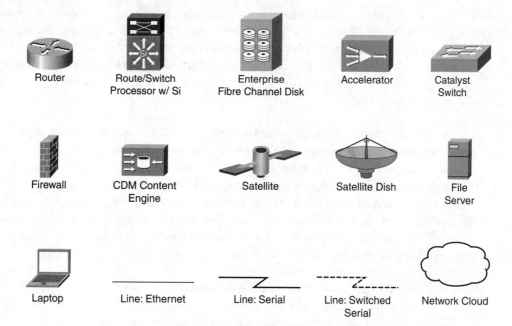

Command Syntax Conventions

The conventions used to present command syntax in this book are the same conventions used in the IOS Command Reference. The Command Reference describes these conventions as follows:

- **Boldface** indicates commands and keywords that are entered literally as shown. In actual configuration examples and output (not general command syntax), boldface indicates commands that are manually input by the user (such as a **show** command).

- *Italic* indicates arguments for which you supply actual values.

- Vertical bars (|) separate alternative, mutually exclusive elements.

- Square brackets [ ] indicate optional elements.

- Braces { } indicate a required choice.

- Braces within brackets [{ }] indicate a required choice within an optional element.

Foreword

Over the years, I have often taught myself a new technology by delving into the most complex aspects of the technology without first having a comprehensive understanding of the fundamentals. Inevitably, this leads to situations where I have to "double-back" and absorb some of the finer points of the underlying technology. I can't say for sure why I acquire knowledge this way, but I do know that having access to a trustworthy library of reference material goes a long way toward reducing the learning curve.

This book provides the first, most comprehensive coverage of WAN optimization and application acceleration technologies. Joel and Ted have done an excellent job of defining the business and technical challenges that many IT organizations face in supporting a globally distributed workforce. By leveraging their diverse backgrounds and experience, Joel and Ted have provided a unique perspective into the fundamental technologies that define this rapidly evolving market. And by taking a solution-centric approach, they are empowering the reader with the knowledge necessary to weave WAN optimization and application acceleration solutions into the fabric of today's complex IT infrastructures.

Businesses are just beginning to understand the potential of WAN optimization and application acceleration solutions. As these solutions take on an increasingly relevant role in the scalability and efficiency of the IT infrastructure, understanding the fundamental technologies will be invaluable. I would recommend *Application Acceleration and WAN Optimization Fundamentals* to anyone interested in learning the key concepts from two pioneers in this industry. I know this will be an important reference in my library.

Zach Seils
AS Technical Leader
Data Center Networking Practice
Cisco Systems, Inc.

Introduction

IT organizations face a number of increasing pressures to increase productivity, improve application performance, provide infrastructure conducive to global collaboration, improve posture toward data protection and compliance, and minimize costs across the board. These pressures come largely as a result of initiatives to increase availability and resiliency in times of an "always on" business driven by the Internet, natural disasters, acts of war, and increasing competition. The challenge is that the corporate workforce continues to become more global, and the characteristics of WANs are dramatically different from those of LANs. Simply consolidating infrastructure provides better support for global collaboration, cost reduction, and better posture toward data protection and compliance, but does so at the cost of performance and productivity. Adding servers to the infrastructure potentially can improve performance but does so at the cost of capital and operational expenditure, data protection, and complexity.

Application acceleration and WAN optimization are powerful technologies incorporated into accelerator solutions that are designed to help IT professionals intelligently deploy, in central managed facilities, an infrastructure that provides performance metrics for remote users that foster productivity, job satisfaction, and global collaboration. Accelerator solutions enable high-performance access to remote information such as files, content, video, rich media, applications, and more. These solutions can help IT organizations satisfy requirements from users, management, and regulatory bodies simultaneously.

Goals and Methods

The application acceleration and WAN optimization market is becoming increasingly relevant in today's IT climate because of the immediate and tangible benefits that such solutions provide to IT organizations. With such a dynamic market being born before our eyes, the authors realize that a book dedicated to defining the underlying and foundational technologies found in these solutions is necessary to better equip corporations with the information needed to not only understand product capabilities but also make informed decisions. *Application Acceleration and WAN Optimization Fundamentals* outlines the use cases and foundational technologies that are so vital to application acceleration and WAN optimization solutions.

After reading this book, you will understand why application acceleration and WAN optimization solutions are relevant and what business value they provide. You will also understand what techniques are employed by the majority of the solutions available today, and have insight into how many of these solutions are designed. While each vendor's implementation is unique, and this book simply cannot scale to discuss all of the implementations, the concept discussed in this book and purpose discussed of each implementation remains constant, as an example of how the foundational components are designed and interact with other components within the solution.

Who Should Read This Book?

This book is intended for anyone who is interested in learning about the foundational components of application acceleration and WAN optimization, including IT directors, network managers, application infrastructure engineers, and systems engineers. It is assumed that you have a high-level understanding of the end-to-end application architectures and protocols found within many enterprise and commercial companies. It is also assumed that you understand basic networking principals, including routing, switching, quality of service (QoS), and network monitoring. Unlike other books that dive into the abyss of device- and version-specific implementation guidelines and configurations, this book focuses on the technologies at large, looking at the numerous components that comprise a WAN optimization and application acceleration solution at a technology architecture level.

How This Book Is Organized

Although this book could be read cover to cover, it is designed to be flexible and allow you to easily move between chapters and sections of chapters to cover just the material that you are most interested in.

This book has seven chapters covering the following topics:

- Chapter 1, "Strategic Information Technology Initiatives," introduces the challenges faced by IT organizations and business at large, setting the tone for the relevance and importance of WAN optimization and application acceleration solutions.

- Chapter 2, "Barriers to Application Performance," builds upon the first chapter and examines what are the fundamental barriers to application performance in WAN environments and the need for a holistic solution to application performance.

- Chapter 3, "Aligning Network Resources with Business Priority," discusses how the network is the platform that touches all aspects of an organization and why it serves as the foundation for an infrastructure conducive to application performance.

- Chapter 4, "Overcoming Application-Specific Barriers," discusses how accelerators can work within the context of specific application protocols to improve user performance and efficiency over the WAN while minimizing bandwidth consumption. These topics, along with those presented in Chapter 5, are commonly viewed together as application acceleration.

- Chapter 5, "Content Delivery Networks," examines how accelerators can be leveraged to ensure that the right information is available in the right location at the right time through intelligent acquisition and distribution of information among accelerators throughout the network.

- Chapter 6, "Overcoming Transport and Link Capacity Limitations," examines application-agnostic techniques for improving application performance and efficiency over the WAN through integration at the transport layer. These topics include compression, data suppression, and transport protocol optimization and are commonly referred to as WAN optimization.

- Chapter 7, "Examining Accelerator Technology Scenarios," shows four scenarios of how WAN optimization and application acceleration solutions have provided benefit to four customer environments.

The book concludes with two appendixes:

- Appendix A, "Common Ports and Assigned Applications," serves as a quick reference guide for ports that are commonly used in today's diverse network environment.

- Appendix B, "Ten Places for More Information," provides links to external locations on the Internet to help you further your knowledge on the topics discussed in this work.

This chapter includes the following topics:

- Managing Applications

- Managing Distributed Servers

- Facing the Unavoidable WAN

- Changing the Application Business Model

- Consolidating and Protecting Servers in the New IT Operational Model

CHAPTER 1

Strategic Information Technology Initiatives

Organizations, companies, and governments have been using a distributed workforce for hundreds of years to more effectively reach a target audience, regional market, or geographic territory. Today, with advances in information technology, larger companies must compete in a global economy, which results in a workforce that is distributed globally. Supporting the applications that the distributed workforce must access to perform their daily tasks to drive productivity, revenue, and customer satisfaction has become a major business-impacting factor. Although this book does not address the process of employee management in a distributed workforce environment, it does address the IT aspects that directly impact the ability of employees to function efficiently in a distributed workforce environment.

This chapter introduces fundamental concepts related to applications, distributed servers, and wide-area networks (WAN) in a distributed workforce environment. It also explains how IT departments have had to modify their business models to support a distributed workforce.

Managing Applications

Software applications have become critical to an employee's productivity in today's workplace, driving greater competitive advantage and improving key business metrics. Utility applications are those that are pervasive across all employees in an enterprise (or subscribers in a service provider network). Utility applications generally include e-mail, file, print, portal, search, voice, video, collaboration, and similar applications.

Applications are no longer limited to simple word processing or spreadsheet applications. Critical business tools now range from the simple web browser to applications that support functions such as e-mail, video on demand (VoD), database applications, and streaming media. Applications, with the exception of Voice over IP (VoIP) and streaming media, now drive the majority of traffic that traverses most WAN connections today in the enterprise. These applications evolved from a centralized client/server model to a distributed architecture, which now includes client workstations, personal digital assistants (PDAs), printers, remote desktop terminals, and even telephones connecting over a broad array of WAN infrastructure possibilities.

Although maintaining a distributed workforce has many benefits, such as having knowledgeable employees closer to customers, these benefits cannot be realized without facing a list of challenges. Acquisitions, mergers, outsourcing, and diverse employee responsibilities are all contributors that force IT organizations to deal with a distributed workforce. Acquisitions and mergers create a unique set of challenges because common application platform "religions" need to be agreed upon, and the demands of corporate communication increase. Outsourcing creates not only network security concerns, but also several application-level challenges that require access to applications that might be housed in a corporate data center across potentially distant security boundaries. Lastly, diverse employee responsibilities create unique branch challenges, based on the role and expected output of each employee within a remote branch location.

In each of the previously mentioned scenarios, application performance becomes harder to effectively maintain as the distance between the user and applications grows. As network links increase to span larger geographies, so does the amount of latency due to the amount of time needed to transmit data from point to point across the network. Coupling the limitations of physics with application inefficiencies, commonly called *application chatter*, leads to exponentially slower response times than what would be encountered on a local-area network (LAN). While bandwidth capacity might continue to increase for such long-distance connections, applications and content continue to become more robust and rich-media centric. The need for greater bandwidth capacity will always outpace the capacities currently available. These variables, and many others, impact the overall performance of not just the application, but also the employee.

If you ask a network administrator why a specific application runs slowly in the remote branch office, he might say it is the application itself. If you pose the same question to an application manager, she might say it is the network that is causing slow application performance. Who is right in this situation? Many times, they are both right. This section describes testing new applications in the work environment and reducing application latency as methods of improving the usability of applications in a distributed environment.

Testing New Applications

Most enterprises have a structured testing model for the introduction of a new application into the work environment. Many times, the new application is written to meet an enterprise customer's business objective: process the data input by the user, and save the processed data in a defined location. New application testing typically occurs within the customer's controlled lab environment. A common test configuration includes a couple client workstations, a server, and a switched network environment. This type of testing environment proves the application's offering abilities but many times does not demonstrate the limitations the application brings to the end user who is based in a remote branch office on the other side of a slow WAN link. In many cases, these limitations are not discovered until a production pilot, or if the application is deployed en masse.

Figure 1-1 shows a simple application test environment, which includes an application server, switch, and two clients.

Figure 1-1 *Simple Application Test Environment*

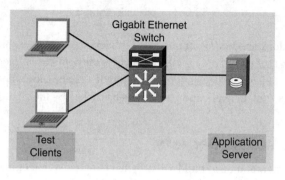

Reducing Application Latency

Application vendors are aware of many of the limitations created in a distributed workforce environment. To reduce application latency, many have introduced a set of features enabled on local workstations specific to each of the client applications, such as application caching. Some vendors provide applications that require software to be loaded on the client workstation prior to launching the application on the workstation.

Client-based application caching is not enough to overcome the obstacles that are introduced when accessing centralized applications and the associated data over the WAN. Although application caches do aid in the overall performance for a given user, they do not address all of the limitations imposed by application inefficiency, physics, the exponential increase in need for capacity, and the growing geographically distributed workforce.

Two applications common to the distributed workforce are Microsoft Outlook and Internet Explorer. Both applications allow the user or application administrator to define a certain amount of client disk space for application caching. The application cache on the client workstation operates independently of the application server that hosts the data the client is requesting, providing a better-performing application experience.

Microsoft Outlook retains a copy of the user's mailbox on the user's local disk storage. A local copy allows for the application to access all of the user's mail locally. On-disk access reduces the application's frequent reactive dependency on the WAN; Outlook seeks new mail periodically, appending the new mail to the locally cached copy of the user's mailbox.

Microsoft Internet Explorer supports configurable storage and location options for cached Internet and intranet content. The browser cache stores copies of any objects that do not contain header settings that prohibit the caching of objects for later use. Commonly cached objects include graphics files, Java objects, and sound files associated with web pages. A cached object is effective only if the object is requested two or more times. Users and application administrators have the option of increasing or decreasing the amount of space allowed for cached content, ranging from as little as 1 MB to as much as 32 GB of on-disk storage.

In Microsoft Outlook and Microsoft Internet Explorer, application caching is effective only for the application being cached and only for the user where the application caching is configured. Access to any content or object that does not reside within the client's local application cache must traverse the WAN. Not all application traffic can be cached by the client's local application cache.

Managing Distributed Servers

In the 1990s, it was common to build a distributed network architecture that involved deployment of application-specific or function-specific servers in each of the locations where users were present. High-speed WAN connectivity was considered very expensive by today's terms, often involving connectivity at rates less than 512 kilobits per second (kbps). To allow for efficient access to applications and common, shared storage for collaboration and other purposes, distributed servers located in branch offices became commonplace, as illustrated in Figure 1-2. Having distributed servers creates several challenges for the IT organization, including a difficult path toward implementing reliable and secure data protection and recovery, timely onsite service and support, and efficient, centralized management.

Protecting Data on Distributed Servers

A common method for protecting data on distributed servers is to leverage a form of direct-attached tape backup or shared tape backup in each of the locations where servers are present. Tape cartridges have been used for years as a common and trusted form of data protection. As a common practice, third-party services, or even a local employee, will take the tape(s) offsite after each backup has been completed. Although this is a trusted method, tapes can be stolen, misplaced, or lost in transit, or can become defective. Furthermore, some employees might not feel the same sense of urgency about manually taking tapes offsite, which might lead to some or all of the tapes never actually leaving the location.

As an alternative to tape backups, centralized backups have been used, but at a cost that impacts the WAN itself. Although it is not uncommon to run centralized backups over the WAN via third-party applications, data transfer mechanisms such as the File Transfer Protocol (FTP), or host-based replication implementations, these models call for a reliable and high-capacity WAN connection. Such means of protecting data perform best if the WAN is in a state of low utilization, such as can be found if there are no other business transactions taking place, commonly after hours. Even in scenarios where the amount of WAN capacity is high and link utilization is low, performance might suffer due to other causes such as server limitations, latency, packet loss, or limitations within the transport protocol.

Figure 1-2 *Traditional Distributed Server Architecture*

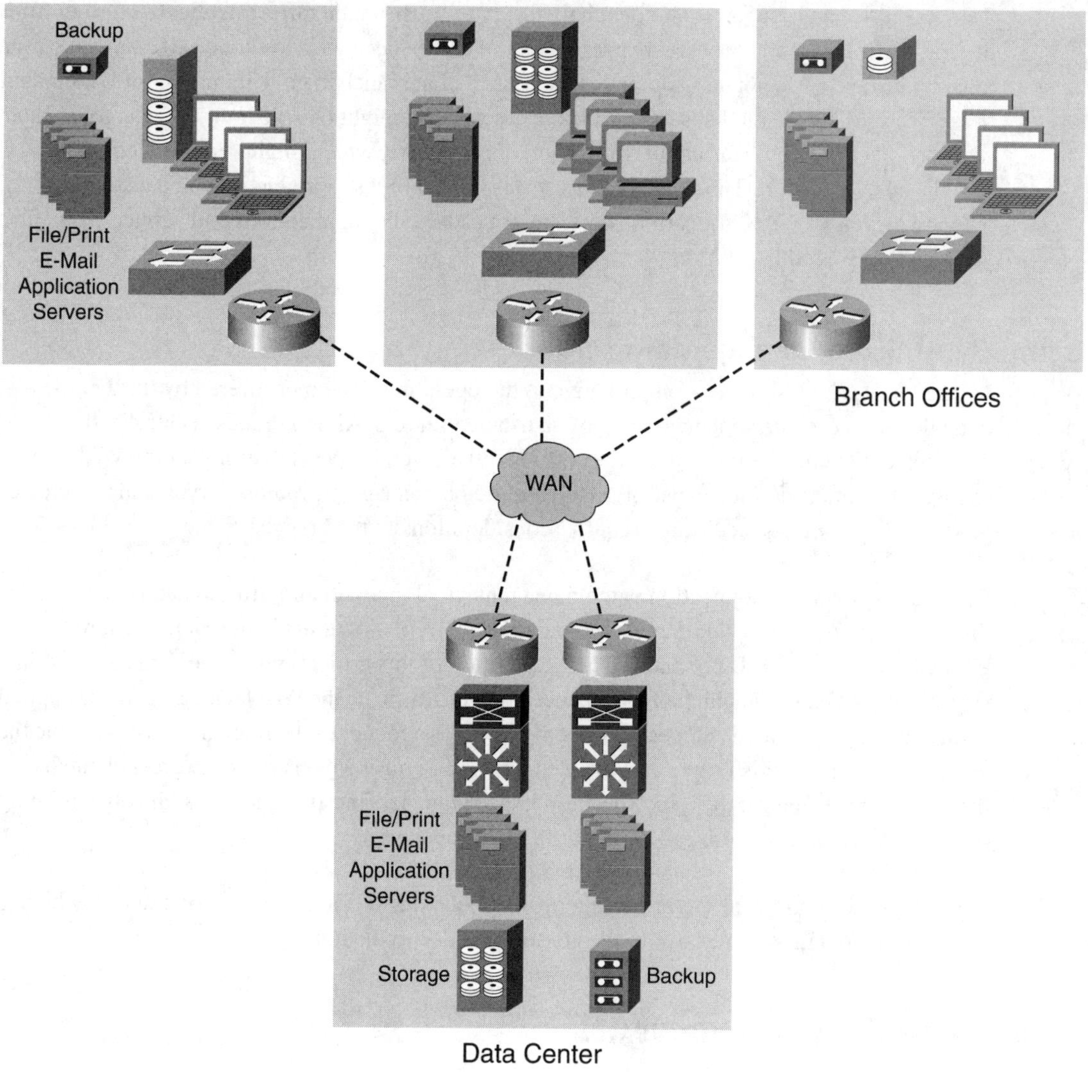

Centralized data protection is driven by a variety of forces including lower cost of management and less capital investment. Another key driver of centralized data protection is regulation initiated by government agencies or compliance agencies within a particular vertical. These regulations include Sarbanes-Oxley (SOX) and the Health Insurance Portability and Accountability Act (HIPAA).

Providing Timely Remote Service and Support

Remote service and support is another challenge with a distributed infrastructure; the further from the corporate data center the asset resides, the more costly the asset is to support. If a branch server fails, for instance, it is not uncommon for the users in that branch to go without access to their data or applications hosted on that server. In some cases, users might be able to make changes to their workstations to access information from another repository, which might require them to be introduced to the WAN. This can have disastrous impact on user productivity and also cause increased levels of WAN utilization, which might cause other applications and services using the WAN to suffer as well.

Using Centralized Management Methods

Several products exist today—either native to the operating system or offered by third parties—that allow for centralized management of distributed servers. Although these centralized management methods are effective, they still involve several aspects that impact the WAN. In some cases, remote desktop capabilities are required to manage the remote server, and this creates WAN traffic, as well as additional security considerations in the branch.

Operating system and application patch management, along with antivirus signature file distribution, can create a significant amount of WAN traffic, ranging from several hundred kilobytes to over 100 MB per patch. The distribution of this critical traffic needs to be timed in such a way that it does not impact the business-related traffic on the WAN. Once a patch is applied to an operating system, the process commonly involves a reboot of the branch server to enable the changes. The problem is further exacerbated when such mechanisms for software and patch distribution are extended to include desktop image management. In these cases, the objects being transferred over the network can be multiple gigabytes in size.

Alternatives to centralized server management include onsite administration of patches, which is often considered more expensive to the corporation due to the human factors involved.

Facing the Unavoidable WAN

Nearly all remote locations today have some form of network connection that connects the location to the data center or an intermediate location such as a regional office. This connection, commonly a WAN connection in the case of a remote office, carries all traffic to the data center and beyond via fiber, cable modem, DSL, satellite, metro Ethernet, or other interconnect technology. Today, WAN traffic comprises more than just file server access, file transfer, data protection, and e-mail message transmissions; business and personal Internet traffic, streaming media, printing, management, enterprise applications, and thin client sessions all traverse the same shared WAN connection. Although the WAN now has to support traffic that might not have been planned for in the past, all of this traffic needs to share this connection. In this way, the reliance of the IT organization on the network continues to increase over time, and the demands placed on the network increase as well.

In today's business model, many times the users, and the applications and content needed by the users, dictate what services the WAN supports. The web browser, for example, was traditionally seen as a non-business-critical application on the user desktop. Some operating systems used to support the full removal of the web browser. Today, the web browser is one of the first applications a user launches after logging into the workstation. The web browser is now the portal into business-critical applications such as customer relationship management (CRM), enterprise resource planning (ERP), and document collaboration applications, and to personal destinations such as e-mail hosting sites and web logs, known as "blogs."

As more and more applications transition from client/server to browser based, and as application vendors continue to standardize applications on web-based protocols such as the Hypertext Transfer Protocol (HTTP) and Extensible Markup Language (XML), the dependency of the web browser will only increase within the corporation. This is one form of traffic that will call for a significant amount of awareness and optimization when planning for the future.

Most traditional business functions rely on protocols that are more client/server centric. The Common Internet File System (CIFS) protocol is one of many widely used and accepted protocols for reading, writing, transferring, or otherwise manipulating content stored on a file server share. CIFS is commonly recognized as a protocol that has a lot of overhead in terms of client and server transactions, and is recognized by many enterprises as costly to WAN links, but necessary to support the needed business transactions and productivity functions when file shares are centralized.

Changing the Application Business Model

In light of the challenges discussed in this chapter so far, IT organizations have begun turning to new ways of solving complex infrastructure, productivity, and performance issues. A new class of networking technologies called *application acceleration* and *WAN optimization* helps to overcome many of these obstacles. These technologies are deployed on devices called *accelerators*, which reside at strategic points in the network—typically one or more exist on each end of a WAN connection—and employ advanced compression, flow optimization, latency mitigation, and other techniques to improve performance and minimize bandwidth consumption.

These devices are fundamentally changing the application business model and IT at large, as they enable centralization and consolidation of resources while ensuring performance service levels. As such, remote users are able to work with remote servers, applications, data, and more and receive performance that is similar to that of having the infrastructure in the same office. In short, accelerators help to mitigate the performance challenges presented by the WAN and ensure more efficient and effective utilization of network resources.

Accelerators and the foundational technologies that they employ are the topic of the remainder of this book and will be examined in more detail in later chapters.

The first step, prior to deploying accelerators, in transforming the way enterprise applications and service infrastructure are deployed and managed and optimizing networks to support business-critical application traffic is to have full awareness of how the network, in particular the WAN, is being used. Several utilities are available today to analyze and categorize the traffic that traverses a network. Utilities ranging in cost from freeware to multiple millions of dollars provide deeper inspection and granular examination of traffic flows.

These utilities help application and network administrators understand how to ensure that the network is provisioned in such a way that packet handling is aligned with business priority and application requirements (discussed at length in Chapter 3, "Aligning Network Resources with Business Priority"). These utilities also help application and network administrators understand what traffic needs to be addressed when considering a solution leveraging accelerators. Each application that traverses the WAN reacts differently to an accelerator, so understanding what traffic is crossing the network will help to determine which applications can be optimized and which ones will better function without optimization or require no optimization at all.

After determining which applications can be targeted for optimization, consider how the client uses these applications. Business applications utilize several different methods of interaction, including client to server, thin-client to server, and web-based sessions. Also included in this consideration should be any protocols that are natively leveraged by the operating system to map to remote resources, such as the Common Internet File System (CIFS), the Network File System (NFS), the Messaging Application Programming Interface (MAPI), and remote-procedure call (RPC)-based services.

In some cases, removing servers from branch locations and centralizing the applications, storage, and management in the data center will prove to be not only possible, but also more cost effective and efficient when combined with the addition of an accelerator solution. Leveraging an optimized WAN will allow branch locations to reduce their overall operating and capital expenses while maintaining the overall user experience in the branch, and allow for a greater level of control over the traffic that traverses the WAN.

Consolidating and Protecting Servers in the New IT Operational Model

Already burdened with the challenges of providing access to content, applications, and services for the growing geographically dispersed workforce, IT organizations are also faced with a conflicting challenge: controlling capital and operational costs across the enterprise while enabling an "always-on" infrastructure.

Companies sell into hypercompetitive markets that are driven by the explosion of the Internet, efficiencies in supply chaining, diminishing consumer prices and profits, and the entrance of larger profit-centric organizations into historically niche markets. Managers are now treating IT organizations as profit and loss centers, controlling expenses in the same way that other departments within an enterprise organization control their expenses.

Looking at infrastructure deployments globally, IT organizations quickly realize that the choice to move to a distributed server model globally has fulfilled the need of many initiatives, such as enabling productivity through high-performance access to local infrastructure resources. It has, however, also created a nightmare of a capital and operational expenditure model that, in the new economy, must be controlled. Enter server consolidation.

Server Consolidation

Servers and the associated infrastructure deployed in distributed locations, particularly remote branch offices, comprise arguably the largest cost center for any IT organization that operates within a distributed, global enterprise. Having a local server infrastructure for applications, content, and collaboration does certainly provide remote users with the access and performance metrics they need to drive productivity and revenue, but also requires many costly capital components, data protection, and management resources. Examining the remote branch office server infrastructure more closely reveals that most offices have a plethora of services and applications running on remote servers to provide basic networking functions and interfaces to revenue-producing corporate applications. Such services and applications could include the following:

- **Network access services:** Dynamic Host Configuration Protocol (DHCP), Domain Name System (DNS), Windows Internet Name Service (WINS), and Microsoft Active Directory (AD) enable user workstations to become addressable on the network, identify and resolve other network resources, and provide login and security services.

- **File and print services:** CIFS and NFS for file sharing and local spooling and management of print jobs enable collaboration, data storage, record keeping, and productivity.

- **E-mail and communication services:** Simple Mail Transfer Protocol (SMTP), Post Office Protocol v3 (POP3), Internet Message Access Protocol (IMAP), MAPI, and a variety of call control, VoIP, and other telephony applications provide the foundation for employee communication within the organization and abroad.

- **Data protection services:** These applications, including Symantec Veritas NetBackup, EMC Legato, Connected TLM, and others, enable the transfer of data from network nodes to be stored as a backup copy for compliance or recovery purposes.

- **Software distribution services:** Applications such as Microsoft Systems Management Server (SMS), Novell ZENworks, or Symantec's Software Download Solution allow IT organizations to distribute patches for operating systems and applications to ensure proper operation and security.

While the prices of servers might continue to fall, the costs of server management and data storage management are increasing. Each server deployed requires a number of costly components that, when examined as a solution, dwarf the capital cost of the server and associated components themselves. These costly components include the following:

- **Server hardware and maintenance:** A server for the remote branch office costs approximately $1000 but can be as high as $10,000 or more. Purchasing a maintenance contract from the server vendor ensures fast replacement of failed components and potentially onsite troubleshooting but is generally accompanied by a price tag of $500 or more per year for the first three years and might increase year over year, thus making server replacement an attractive solution as the age of the server increases.

- **Data storage capacity:** Each server needs a repository for the operating system, applications, and data that will be used by remote branch office users. For smaller sites that require no redundancy, a single disk might be used, but for medium and large branch offices where redundancy and performance are required, data storage might involve multiple disks within the server chassis (also known as direct-attached storage, or DAS) using Redundant Array of Independent Disks (RAID) technology. Many medium and large branches require capacity that goes beyond what the server itself can hold, dictating the need for costly external storage or dedicated storage infrastructure such as network-attached storage (NAS) devices or storage area networking (SAN) components. The cost of remote branch office storage can range from a few hundred dollars to tens of thousands of dollars or more.

- **Data protection hardware:** Data stored on client workstations and servers must be protected, and copies must be kept for long periods of time. For the small remote branch office, a single tape drive attached to the server might suffice, but for offices with larger data storage requirements, external tape subsystems, including automation and libraries, might be required. Such solutions can range in price from a few hundred dollars to tens of thousands of dollars.

- **Data protection media and management:** Costly tape media is required when using tape as a form of data protection. Some government regulations require that corporations retain copies of their data for longer periods of time; organizations will find that they need to have as much as ten times the disk storage capacity or more simply to hold archived copies of protected data to meet such regulations, requiring a large number of tapes. Furthermore, these tapes might be vaulted offsite for additional protection.

■ **Server operating system and maintenance:** Operating systems for servers range from zero cost (freeware) to $1000 or more, depending on the vendor and functions provided. Purchasing a maintenance contract or support contract from a server operating system vendor can be even more expensive than the server hardware maintenance contract. Adding to the costs, monthly patch management and related operating system costs increase the administrative staff's direct involvement and costs associated with their department's operating expense budget.

Alongside these components are a number of equally costly capital expenses that must be undertaken, including the cost of applications and application support, antivirus software and support, and management tools. When coupled with the operational costs incurred by having to manage the server infrastructure, including full-time, part-time, or contract IT resources, many organizations find that the first-year cost of a single server, including capital expenditure, can be $50,000 or more. Second- and third-year expenses, which do not include the majority of the original capital expense (with the exception of additional storage capacity and tape media), can be $35,000 or more per server. For an enterprise with 100 branch offices or more, with two servers in each branch, this adds up to a first-year investment of $5 million and a total three-year investment of $12 million.

Simply consolidating server infrastructure into one or more managed data centers is an attractive option. While this eliminates the need for deploying, managing, and maintaining the remote office servers, this creates two much larger problems:

■ Remote branch office users are subject to a dramatic change in information and application access. In a utopian environment where WAN bandwidth were unlimited and physics (and, more specifically, the speed of light) could be defeated, perceived user performance would not change noticeably. The reality is that WANs do not behave like LANs because they do not share the same characteristics (discussed in Chapter 2, "Barriers to Application Performance"), and application performance quickly degrades.

■ Supporting these centralized services requires greater WAN capacity. Many WAN connections run at nearly full utilization, driven by the increasing richness of content and value provided by deploying telephone communications (VoIP) using existing network connections.

Solutions such as application acceleration and WAN optimization can fill the gap between performance and consolidation while also ensuring that network capacity utilization is controlled and effectively used, thereby improving performance for accessing applications and services that are already centralized while also maintaining performance levels of services that are being centralized from the remote branch office. With these technologies in place, IT organizations can safely remove many of these high-cost items from the remote branch office infrastructure, replacing them with lower capital- and operational-cost components such as accelerators, without impeding upon the ability of the remote branch office worker to be productive and drive revenue. An example of an accelerator deployment is shown in Figure 1-3.

Figure 1-3 *A Centralized Deployment Leveraging Accelerators*

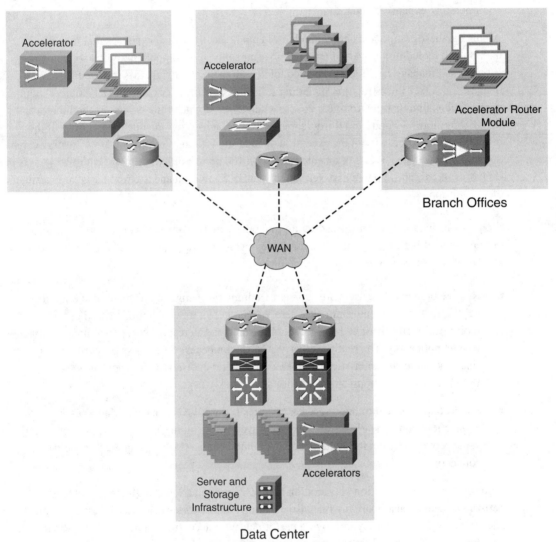

Compliance, Data Protection, Business Continuity, and Disaster Recovery

Compliance, data protection, business continuity, and disaster recovery have become priorities for IT organizations in the last decade, in particular due to acts of war, natural disasters, scandalous employee behavior (financial, security, and otherwise), and regulations from government or industry bodies. IT organizations of today have additional pressure on them to ensure that every byte of data is protected, secured, and replicated to a distant facility in real time (synchronous) or near real time (asynchronous) to ensure that transactions relative to key business applications, communications, or even basic productivity applications are recoverable:

■ **Synchronous replication:** Used for business-critical tier-1 applications, data, and infrastructure. Provides the ability to guarantee data coherency to the last successfully completed transaction. Generally bound to small geographic areas due to transmission latency and bandwidth requirements, typically a metropolitan area. Used primarily for hot sites, where recovery times need to be minimal.

■ **Asynchronous replication:** Used for less-critical applications or for longer-distance replication where transmission latency and bandwidth prohibit synchronous operation. Enables replication of data across a larger geography but might compromise coherency, as the replica site might not have received the latest transactions. Used primarily for warm or cold sites, where recovery times can take longer.

Meeting coherency challenges is next to impossible. With a distributed server infrastructure, the distance separating the IT personnel chartered with the responsibility of data management is commonly combined with reduced technical expertise and differences of opinion surrounding priority of such tasks. For example, IT resources chartered with data protection tasks in remote branch offices might treat data protection management as a repetitive annoyance. (Swapping tapes and rerunning failed backup jobs might not be the most enjoyable of responsibilities.) IT resources chartered with data protection tasks in the data center see data protection as a business-critical job function and generally take great strides to ensure its success.

Data Protection and Compliance

Server consolidation enables the cost-savings metrics discussed in the previous section and also allows IT organizations to better meet data protection requirements and regulation from industry or government bodies more effectively. Not only is it good practice to keep copies of data to use for recovery purposes, many industries and agencies are mandated to do so and must adhere to strict guidelines. Having fewer silos of data in fewer locations means fewer pieces of data need to be protected, which translates into better compliance with such regulation.

A side benefit of server consolidation is that fewer redundant copies of data need to be kept, and global collaboration across multiple locations can be safely enabled, thereby mitigating version control and data discrepancies in most cases. For example, assume that a company has 100 branch offices, each with two servers and 250 GB of total storage capacity per remote location. If the storage capacity at each location is 50 percent utilized, each location has approximately 125 GB of data that needs to be protected. If each site has even 20 GB of data that is common among each of the locations (an extremely conservative estimation), 2 TB of data storage capacity is wasted across the enterprise—not only on disk, but also on tape media housing the backup copies. Alongside having wasted capacity due to redundancy, approximately 12.5 TB of disk capacity is unutilized. Other, less commonly measured resources will also benefit from server consolidation, such as processor utilization, memory consumption, and network interface utilization. Figure 1-4 illustrates storage utilization in a distributed infrastructure.

Figure 1-4 *Low Utilization and Stranded Capacity*

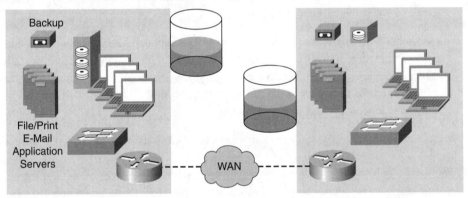

By collapsing this infrastructure into the data center, redundant copies of data can be safely eliminated. Higher levels of efficiency can be gained, because data can be stored on shared arrays, which in turn enables capacity planning efforts and capital purchases to be amortized. The need to overprovision a remote branch office server with excess capacity that goes largely unutilized is nearly eliminated. Expert-level, experienced, and well-trained data center IT staff using enterprise-class data protection software and hardware can manage the protection of the data, ensuring that backup windows are better managed, fewer operations fail, and failed operations are corrected.

Figure 1-5 illustrates an efficiently designed network, using accelerators for storage consolidation and data protection. Within the illustration, an automated backup process has been centralized to the data center, eliminating the need for "human" intervention.

Figure 1-5 *High Utilization, High Efficiency, and Lower Costs*

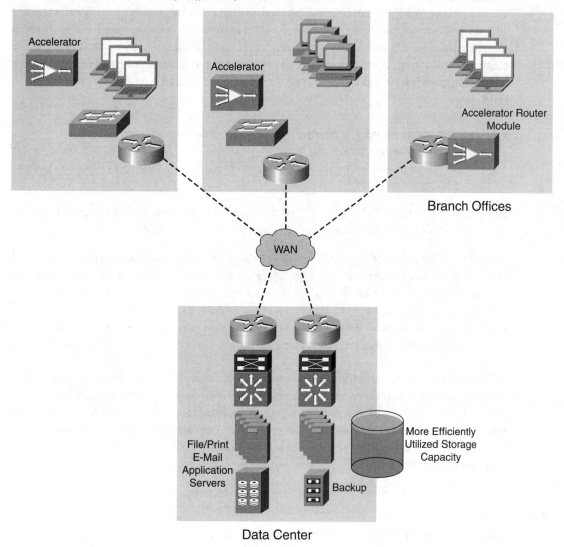

With fewer silos of data, a smaller number of data protection components need to be purchased and maintained, including tape drives, tape libraries, and expensive tape media, which again lowers costs.

Business Continuance and Disaster Recovery

Business continuance and disaster recovery planning are becoming commonplace in today's enterprise, driven particularly by both compliance (as mentioned in the previous section) and the overarching threats presented by malicious attackers (inside and outside), natural disaster, and terrorist attacks. While business continuance and disaster recovery are two mutually exclusive and adjacent business initiatives, they are often coupled together to provide a more holistic approach to ensuring that businesses can survive in the presence of a disastrous scenario through articulate contingency planning, effective system recovery processes, service failover, and routing of application traffic and workload. Business continuance and disaster recovery are defined as follows:

- **Business continuance:** The ability of a business to continue operations in the event of a disaster. This requires that systems be readily available, in an active (hot site), standby (warm site), or offline (cold site) mode to assume responsibility when primary systems are rendered unavailable.

- **Disaster recovery:** The ability of a business to recover business-critical data, applications, and services after a disastrous event has taken place.

Both of these initiatives rely not only on well-documented and tested processes, but also on the availability of data, infrastructure, and personnel to run business-critical applications. To ensure that data and infrastructure are readily available, many organizations have deployed secondary (or tertiary) data centers that have facilities and hardware necessary to resume operation. Data can be replicated from the primary data center(s) to the secondary or tertiary data center(s) via synchronous or asynchronous methods to ensure different levels of recoverability and continuity.

With a consolidated server infrastructure, organizations are better positioned to implement more effective business continuance and disaster recovery solutions. Less server infrastructure is required and fewer silos of data must be replicated to distant data centers. Accelerators can even be deployed to improve the throughput and efficiency of replication by minimizing bandwidth consumption, enabling better utilization of available network capacity, and ensuring that the replicated data in the secondary site is more coherent to the data stored in the primary site.

Summary

Transitioning the IT business model from distributed to centralized will bring many enterprises a higher degree of control over their resource utilization and improve manageability, while also reducing the overall capital and operating expenses associated with managing a distributed server, application, and storage infrastructure.

Application acceleration and WAN optimization solutions help poise organizations for initiatives such as server consolidation and meeting regulatory compliance by overcoming WAN conditions to enable consolidation without compromising on performance. Accelerators not only enable consolidation and improve performance for applications that are already centralized, but also ensure that remote-user performance expectations for services that were initially distributed are maintained once that infrastructure is centralized. Such technologies help to improve overall user productivity and organizational posture relative to meeting business objectives and driving revenue. With a consolidated server, application, and storage infrastructure, IT organizations find themselves operating in a new model. Accelerators create uncompromising efficiency, positioning the WAN to meet the demands of the global workforce, government regulations, data protection needs, business continuance, and disaster recovery.

This chapter includes the following topics:

- Networks and Application Performance

- Application and Protocol Barriers to Application Performance

- Operating System Barriers to Application Performance

- Hardware Barriers to Application Performance

CHAPTER 2

Barriers to Application Performance

Why are many organizations now faced with the challenge of centralizing distributed server and storage infrastructure? Given the complexities and costs associated with managing such distributed infrastructure, one would assume that servers, storage, and data protection would have been deployed centrally to begin with. Unfortunately, many factors exist that can quickly diminish performance when users access applications, files, content, or other services across a WAN. These factors are often not encountered in a LAN or even a campus but are exacerbated when the network in question is a WAN, due to its many unavoidable characteristics such as bandwidth, latency, and packet loss. Furthermore, applications continue to become more robust and feature rich, which places additional demand on the network and drives complexities in software design and protocol usage. In summary, many networks are not good places for applications to operate, and many applications and the underlying protocols are not designed to function well on many networks.

With these barriers to performance in place, many organizations are forced to deploy difficult and costly to manage devices at the enterprise edge to provide performance and service levels that meet the needs of the remote user. If such performance and service levels could not be met, employee productivity and job satisfaction would plummet, causing corporate revenue and productivity goals to not be achieved. New technologies found in accelerator products help to overcome these barriers by allowing organizations to deploy infrastructure centrally without compromising remote-user performance expectations.

This chapter examines the characteristics of networks today and how these characteristics directly impact the performance of applications and services. This chapter also examines how application and protocol inefficiencies directly contribute to degraded performance on a network.

Networks and Application Performance

The primary goal of an application is to allow two nodes to transfer and manipulate information over an internetwork. Given that networks today are varied and might be hub and spoke, hierarchical, and can span the world, many aspects of the network can have a direct impact on the ability of an application to exchange information among communicating nodes.

Many commonly used applications today are designed, developed, and tested by software vendors in controlled lab and production environments. In these "utopian" environments, nodes that are exchanging application data are deployed relatively close to one another, typically attached to a LAN switch and in the same subnet and address space. Such environments do not always represent the model that enterprise organizations follow when deploying these applications to enable a business process, for the following reasons:

- Bandwidth is virtually unlimited. Fast Ethernet or Gigabit Ethernet is used as an interconnect between nodes in the development environment.

- Close proximity yields low latency. Having nodes adjacent to one another means data can be exchanged at very high rates because network transmission delays and serialization delays are low.

- Network congestion or contention is unlikely. With high bandwidth and low latency, encountering contention for network resources is unlikely unless the application server being tested is not bound in any way by hardware limitations. The bottleneck is generally shifted to the application server due to lack of hardware capacity, including processing power, memory, and overall efficiency of the application.

Figure 2-1 shows an example of a utopian test, development, and lab environment, which does not adequately reflect network conditions encountered in today's enterprise WAN.

Figure 2-1 *Utopian Test, Development, and Lab Network*

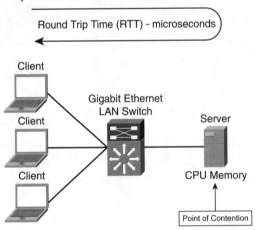

The reality is that today's enterprise WAN presents a significant bottleneck to application delivery, one that is large enough to drive most organizations to deploy costly distributed infrastructure in favor of centralization. When an application is deployed in a WAN environment, the efficiency and performance found in a utopian test, development, and lab environment are not present. Figure 2-2 summarizes the performance challenges encountered when deploying applications that are accessed by remote users over a WAN.

Figure 2-2 *Application Performance Barriers in a WAN*

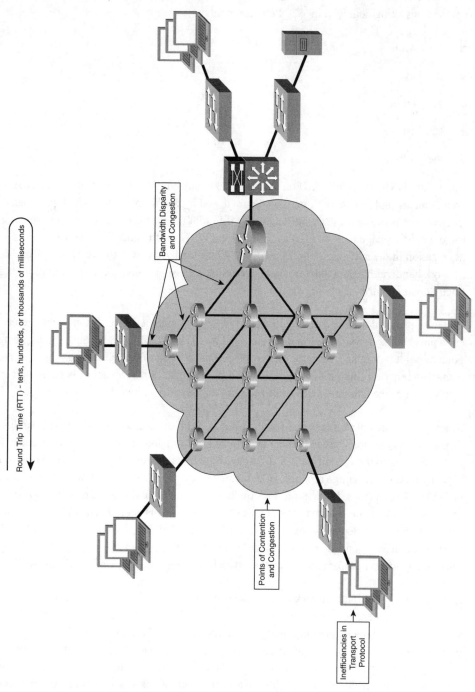

Network and transport factors such as the following directly impact the performance of applications being deployed in WAN environments:

- Bandwidth

- Latency

- Throughput

- Congestion

- Packet loss

Bandwidth is virtually unlimited on the LAN segments but limited and finite on the WAN. This creates a bandwidth disparity that must be managed by the WAN router, which provides the interconnect between these two dramatically different networks. Furthermore, intermediary routers must manage bandwidth disparities in the WAN. With bandwidth disparities and aggregation in the network, network nodes and intermediary devices must contend for available network bandwidth, causing bandwidth starvation, loss of packets, and retransmission of data. Each directly contributes to poor application performance.

Distance, protocol translation, and congestion yield high latency. The distance between two endpoints results in transmission delays caused by the speed of light, because moving data from point to point within an internetwork takes a certain amount of time. Routing among networks using different data link protocols introduces significant serialization delay, because data must be received, unpacked, and then repacketized onto the next-hop network.

Congestion causes packet loss and retransmission. With the previously mentioned bandwidth disparities, congestion increases under periods of load, causing devices to manage transmission of data according to the capacity and utilization of the links it is directly connected to. With large-capacity mismatches, large amounts of data must be queued, and only a finite amount of data can be held in these queues. Device interface queues become full, causing no new data to be accepted until data in the queue is transmitted. During this time, data is stalled and stuck in the queue, waiting to be forwarded to the next hop toward its intended destination, where it will likely encounter congestion again. Each of these "network rest stops" introduces latency and variability into the application performance equation, which can degrade performance dramatically.

Each hop within an internetwork must manage transmission of data from one node to the next. Internetworks that have loads equal to or greater than the capacity of any hop within the network will experience congestion at that point within the network. In these cases, the amount of data is greater than the capacity of the next segment. When a segment reaches its capacity, the data that is trying to traverse that segment must be held in an interface queue until capacity on the next segment becomes available. Packet loss results in a lack of acknowledgment from the receiving node, causing the originating node to retransmit data from the retransmission buffer. The application might incur delay before continuing due to situations such as this.

Packet loss and retransmission cause transport protocol throttling. Connection-oriented transport protocols such as the TCP are able to adapt to WAN conditions and throttle the application process according to the conditions encountered in the network. In the case of TCP, a packet loss event can result in a 50 percent decrease in the amount of data that can be sent at a given time. In the case of the User Datagram Protocol (UDP), which is connectionless and provides no means of guaranteed delivery, the application on the receiving node must be aware of such a loss of data and request retransmission when necessary. Most applications that rely on UDP and require guaranteed delivery of data implement their own mechanism for flow control and means of adapting to network conditions. Given the disparity in application and transport protocol reaction to congestion, this can create additional complications in terms of the amount of congestion in intermediary network devices. When a transport protocol throttles an application and contains its ability to transmit data, application performance is impacted because less data can be sent at a given time.

Connectionless transport protocols rely on the higher-layer protocols to implement flow control and reliable delivery. Mechanisms and characteristics are built into the application process itself if guaranteed delivery is required.

Transport protocols handle WAN conditions inefficiently. Throttling application throughput is only one of the performance-limiting factors associated with transport protocols. For connection-oriented transport protocols, such as TCP, new connections must undergo a search, called *TCP slow-start*, to identify the available network capacity. This search involves analysis of successful round trips at the beginning of a connection to identify the network capacity. This search can take a large number of round trips, and the application performance is very limited until the search is completed. Once the search is completed, the connection is able to enter a steady-state mode known as congestion avoidance (or congestion management), where the connection is able to leverage the capacity discovered in the search.

During congestion avoidance, the connection becomes reactive to network conditions and adjusts throughput according to ongoing network congestion and loss events. These reactions are quite dramatic and the subsequent returns to maximum levels of throughput are quite slow, thus degrading application performance over the WAN.

Application vendors recently have begun implementing design and test considerations to address the application performance barriers presented by the network that sits in between the communicating nodes and the transport protocol being employed. Each of the challenges previously listed will be examined in more detail in the following sections.

Bandwidth

Bandwidth is the amount of data that can be passed along a communications channel in a given period of time. Specifically, each message that is exchanged between two nodes communicating on a network requires that some network capacity, or bandwidth, be available to allow the movement of information between the two nodes.

In a LAN environment where nodes are connected to the same switch or in a campus network where nodes are connected within proximity to one another, available bandwidth is generally much higher than that required by the two communicating nodes. However, as nodes become spread across a larger, more complex internetwork, network oversubscription might be encountered, or points of aggregation within the network might be encountered. These two factors have a significant impact on application performance, because the point of oversubscription or point of aggregation must effectively throttle transmission from attached networks and negotiate access from the higher-capacity network to the lower-speed, oversubscribed network.

Figure 2-3 shows multiple layers of oversubscription. Assuming each node is connected with the same data-link interface type and speed (for this example, assume 100-Mbps Fast Ethernet), the four client workstations contend for the available capacity between the access switch and the distribution switch. The three access switches must contend for available capacity between the distribution switch and the server. All 12 of the client workstations must contend through these oversubscribed links for access to the server itself.

Figure 2-3 *Oversubscription at Various Points Within the Network*

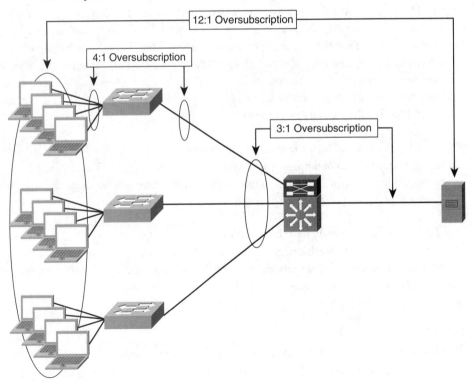

Assuming fairness between equally prioritized connections, each client would receive only approximately 8 percent of the server's network capacity, and this does not take into consideration the overhead associated with application, transport, or network layer mechanics.

This problem is compounded in WAN environments where the oversubscription or aggregation might be dramatically higher. In the case of a WAN, not only do multiple network nodes contend for access to available bandwidth, but the available bandwidth is many orders smaller than that by which the node is communicated to the LAN. In this way, not only does the network element need to manage access to the smaller bandwidth link, but it must also handle the pacing of traffic onto the node through queuing.

Figure 2-4 shows multiple locations each with multiple client workstations. These client workstations are connected by the same data-link interface type and speed as the servers and switches (for this example, assume 100-Mbps Fast Ethernet). The routers in this example connect to the LAN in each location and also a point-to-point T1 (1.544 Mbps) circuit. Not only do the client workstations in each of the remote offices have to contend with 4:1 oversubscription to the router, but the bandwidth disparity in the network also introduces another layer of oversubscription: 67:1 (100 Mbps / 1.544 Mbps).

Figure 2-4 *Oversubscription in a WAN Environment*

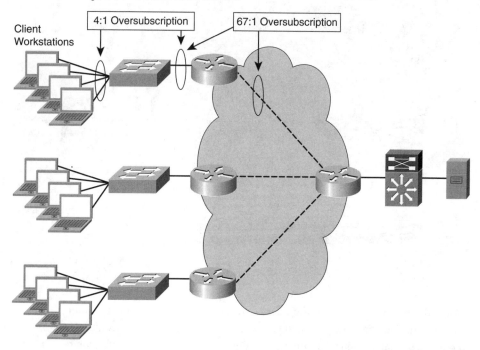

Assuming fairness between equally prioritized connections, each client would receive only approximately 25 percent of the WAN capacity, which equates to 384 Kbps, or roughly 1/260, of the link speed to which the client is attached to the LAN. This also assumes that there is no overhead associated with the application protocol, transport protocol, and network protocols being used.

The performance challenges created by bandwidth disparity, oversubscription, and aggregation can quickly degrade application performance. Not only are each of the communicating nodes strangled because their flows are negotiated onto a lower-speed link, but the flows themselves remain strangled even when returning to a higher-capacity link, as shown in Figure 2-5. From the perspective of the server, each of the clients is only sending small amounts of data at a time (due to network oversubscription and bandwidth disparity). The overall application performance is throttled because the server can then only respond to the requests as they are being received.

Figure 2-5 *Performance Impact of Bandwidth Disparity: Client to Server*

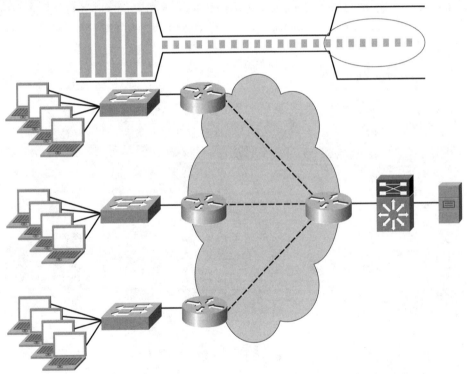

When the server responds to the client, the same challenges are encountered, as shown in Figure 2-6. Potentially large amounts of data can be sent from the server when it services a user request. This data, when set in flight, encounters the neighboring router, which is managing the bandwidth disparity, and the data is trickled over the network based on the capacity available to the flow. From the perspective of the client, the server is only sending small amounts of data at a time (due to network oversubscription and bandwidth disparity).

Figure 2-6 *Performance Impact of Bandwidth Disparity: Server to Client*

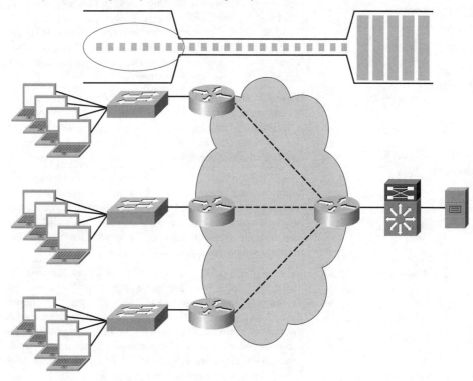

The prior examples assume a perfect world where everything works as advertised and overhead is unheard of. The reality is that application protocols add overhead to message exchanges. Transport protocols add overhead in the form of segmenting, window management, and acknowledgment for guaranteed delivery. Network and data link protocols add overhead due to packetization and framing. Each of these consumes a noticeable amount of network capacity and can be classified as control information that only serves the purpose of helping data reach the distant node, reassembling data in the correct order, and informing the application on the distant node of the process that is being attempted.

This process of exchanging application data using a transport protocol over an internetwork with potentially many segments between communicating nodes directly follows the Open System Interconnection (OSI) reference model, which is outlined in Table 2-1.

Table 2-1 *Open System Interconnection Reference Model*

OSI Layer	Description
Application (7)	Provides services directly to user applications. Because of the potentially wide variety of applications, this layer must provide a wealth of services, including establishing privacy mechanisms, authenticating the intended communication partners, and determining if adequate resources are present. This layer is also responsible for the client-to-server or peer-to-peer exchanges of information that are necessary from the application perspective.
Presentation (6)	Provides data transformation and assimilation guidelines to provide a common interface for user applications, including services such as reformatting, data compression, and encryption. The presentation layer is responsible for the structure and format of data being exchanged between two application processes.
Session (5)	Establishes, manages, and maintains connections between two nodes and manages the interaction between end systems. The session layer is not always implemented but is commonly helpful in environments where structured communications are necessary, including web conferencing, collaboration over the network, and environments that leverage remote procedure calls or named pipes.
Transport (4)	Insulates the upper three layers—5–7— (commonly bundled together as an "application layer") from the complexities of Layers 1–3 (commonly bundled together as a "network layer"). The transport layer is responsible for the exchange of datagrams between nodes over an internetwork. The transport protocol commonly implements either a connection-oriented transmission protocol that provides guaranteed delivery (such as TCP) or a connectionless protocol that does not provide guaranteed delivery (UDP).
Network (3)	Establishes, maintains, and terminates network connections. Among other functions, standards define how data routing and relaying are handled. Packets are exchanged between two nodes that are attached to an internetwork when each has an internetwork address that can be reached directly or through a routed infrastructure.
Data link (2)	Ensures the reliability of the physical link established at Layer 1. Standards define how data frames are recognized and provide necessary flow control and error handling at the frame level. Frames are exchanged between two nodes that are on a common shared medium.
Physical (1)	Controls transmission of the raw bitstream over the transmission medium. Standards for this layer define such parameters as the amount of signal voltage swing, the duration of voltages (bits), and so on.

The application reads and writes blocks of data to a socket interface, which abstracts the transport protocol itself from the application. The blocks of data vary in size based on the application and the amount of memory allocated to the socket buffers. Application data blocks are generally 1 KB to 64 KB in size, and in some cases can be larger or smaller. Notice that an application data block is measured in bytes and not bits, as from the perspective of an application it is simply reading or writing block data to or from a buffer in memory.

The transport protocol is then responsible for draining data from the socket buffer into the network layer. When the data is written to the socket buffer by the application layer, the socket interacts with the transport protocol to segment data into datagrams. These datagrams are sized with the knowledge of the network transmission capacity (based on a search, discovery, or predefined parameter if using rate-based transmission protocols). For connection-oriented transmission protocols such as TCP, control information such as source and destination ports is attached along with other information, including cyclic redundancy check (CRC)/checksum information, segment length, offset, sequence number, acknowledgment number, and other flags. Most other transport protocols, reliable or not, provide additional data that helps to identify the application process on the local and distant nodes, along with checksum information to provide some means of guaranteeing data integrity and correctness, as well as other flow-control parameters.

The transport protocol manages both the drainage of data written to socket buffers into segments of data exchanged on the network and the extraction of data received from the network into socket buffers to be read by a local application. When data has been read from the socket buffer and processed by TCP (it is ready to be handled by the network layer), it is packetized by the network protocol (in this case, IP), where a header and trailer are added denoting the source and destination network address on the internetwork. Other information might be included such as version, header length, type of service, fragment identification, header checksums, protocol, options, and other flags.

The network protocol (generally IP) then sends the packet to be framed at the data link layer (generally Ethernet), where yet another header and trailer are added denoting the source and destination address of the next adjacent recipient on the subnet (router) and other flags. Each of these layers commonly adds checksum or CRC data to ensure correctness of data.

Figure 2-7 shows the overhead associated with application data traversing the OSI model.

When the distant node receives the packets, the reverse process begins in order to reassemble the application data block. In many cases, as much as 20 percent or more of network bandwidth can be consumed by forwarding, routing, segmentation, and delivery guarantee-related overheads. To put it simply, the WAN, which introduces a massive bandwidth disparity, coupled with the overhead just described in this section, is not an environment conducive to high levels of application performance.

Figure 2-7 *Framing, Packetization, Segmentation, and Application Layer Overhead*

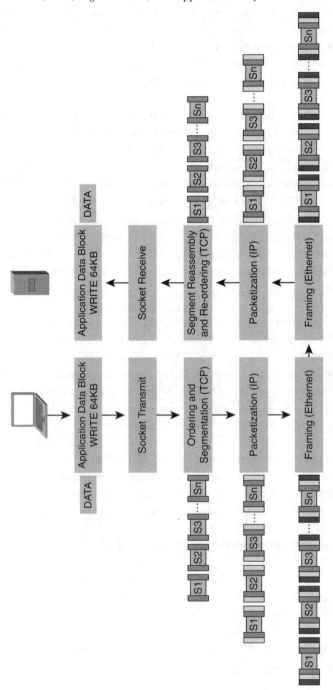

Latency

Historically, many IT organizations have simply added bandwidth capacity to the network to enable higher levels of application performance. In modern-day networks where bandwidth capacities are exponentially higher than those of the past, extra bandwidth might still erroneously be seen as the end-all fix for application performance woes. The metrics of the network have largely changed, and in many cases, the bottleneck to application performance has been shifted from the amount of bandwidth available in a network. Other aspects of the network must now also be examined to fully understand where barriers to application performance lie. Latency is another aspect that must be carefully examined.

Latency is the period of apparent inactivity between the time the stimulus is presented and the moment a response occurs, which translated to network terminology means the amount of time necessary to transmit information from one node to the other across an internetwork. Latency can be examined in one of two ways:

■ *One-way latency*, or *delay*, is the amount of time it takes for data to be received by a recipient once the data leaves a transmitting node.

■ *Roundtrip latency*, which is far more complex and involves a larger degree of layers in the communications hierarchy, is the amount of time it takes not only for data to be received by a recipient once the data leaves a transmitting node, but also the amount of time it takes for the transmitting node to receive a response from the recipient.

Given that the focus of this book is directly related to application performance over the network, this book focuses on the components that impact roundtrip latency.

Communication between nodes on an internetwork involves multiple contiguous layers in a hierarchy. Each of these layers presents its own unique challenges in terms of latency, because they each incur some amount of delay in moving information from node to node. Many of these layers add only trivial amounts of latency, whereas others add significant amounts of latency. Referring to the previous section on bandwidth, you see that application data must traverse through the following:

■ A presentation layer, which defines how the data should be structured for the recipient

■ A session layer (for some session-based protocols), which defines a logical channel between nodes

■ A transport layer, which manages the delivery of data from one application process to another through an internetwork, and segmentation of data to enable adaptation for network transmission

■ A network layer, which provides global addressing for nodes on the internetwork and packetization of data for delivery

■ A data link layer, which provides framing and transmits data from node to node along the network path

■ A physical layer, which translates framed data to a serial or parallel sequence of electronic pulses or lightwaves according to the properties of the physical transmission media

Many of these processes are handled at high speeds within the initiating and receiving nodes. For instance, translation of framed data to the "wire" is handled in hardware by the network interface card (NIC). Packetization (network layer) and segmentation (transport layer) are largely handled by the NIC in conjunction with the CPU and memory subsystem of the node. Application data, its presentation, and the management of session control (if present) are also handled largely by the CPU and memory subsystem of the node. These processes, with the exception of managing guaranteed delivery, tend to take an amount of time measured in microseconds, which does not yield a significant amount of delay.

In some cases, systems such as servers that provide services for a large number of connected application peers and handle transmission of large volumes of application data might encounter performance degradation or scalability loss caused by the management of the transmission protocol, in most cases TCP. With TCP and any other transport protocol that provides connection-oriented service with guaranteed delivery, some amount of overhead is encountered. This overhead can be very small or very large, depending on several factors, including application workload, network characteristics, congestion, packet loss, delay, and the number of peers that data is being exchanged with.

For each connection that is established, system resources must be allocated for that connection. Memory is allocated to provide a buffer pool for data that is being transmitted and data that is being received. The CPU subsystem is used to calculate sliding window positions, manage acknowledgments, and determine if retransmission of data is necessary due to missing data or bad checksums.

For a system that is handling only a handful of TCP connections, such as a client workstation, this overhead is minimal and usually does not noticeably impact overall application performance. For a system that is handling a large number of TCP connections and moving large sums of application data, the overhead of managing the transport protocol can be quite significant, to the tune of consuming the majority of the resources in the memory and CPU subsystems due to buffer space allocation and context switching.

To fully understand why TCP can be considered a resource-intensive transport protocol and how this translates to latency, let's examine TCP in detail.

Understanding Why TCP Adds Latency

First, TCP is a transport protocol that provides connection-oriented service, which means a connection must be established between two nodes that wish to exchange application data. This connection, or socket, identifies ports, or logical identifiers, that correlate directly to an application process running on each of the two nodes. In this way, a client will have a port assigned to the application that wishes to exchange data, and the server that the client is communicating with will also have a port. Once the connection is established, application processes on the two connected nodes are then able to exchange application data across the socket.

The process of establishing the connection involves the exchange of control data through the use of TCP connection establishment messages, including the following:

- **TCP SYN:** The TCP SYN, or synchronize, message is sent from the node originating a request to a node to which it would like to establish a connection. The SYN message contains the local application process port identifier and the desired remote application process port. The SYN message also includes other variables, such as sequence number, window size, checksum, and options. Such TCP options include the Maximum Segment Size (MSS), window scaling, and Selective Acknowledgement (SACK). This message notifies the recipient that someone would like to establish a connection.

- **TCP ACK:** The TCP ACK, or acknowledge, message is sent in return from the receiving peer to the originating peer. This message acknowledges the originating peer's request to connect and provides an acknowledgment number. From here on, the sequence number and acknowledgment number are used to control delivery of data.

TCP connections are bidirectional in that the two nodes are able to exchange information in either direction. That is, the originating peer should be able to send data to the receiving peer, and the receiving peer should be able to send data to the originating peer. Given that information needs to be exchanged in both directions, a SYN must be sent from the originating peer to the receiving peer, and an ACK must be sent from the receiving peer to the originating peer. To facilitate transmission of data in the reverse direction, the receiving peer will also send a SYN to the originating peer, causing the originating peer to respond with an ACK.

The SYN and ACK messages that are exchanged between peers are flags within a TCP datagram, and TCP allows for multiple flags to be set concurrently. As such, the process of exchanging SYN and ACK messages to establish a connection is simplified, because the receiving peer can effectively establish a connection in the reverse path while acknowledging the connection request in the forward path.

Given that the SYN and ACK flags can be set together within a TCP datagram, you will see a message called a SYN/ACK, which is the receiving node acknowledging the connection request and also attempting connection in the reverse path. This is used in favor of exchanging separate SYN and ACK control datagrams in the reverse direction.

Figure 2-8 illustrates the process of establishing a TCP connection.

Figure 2-8   *TCP Connection Establishment*

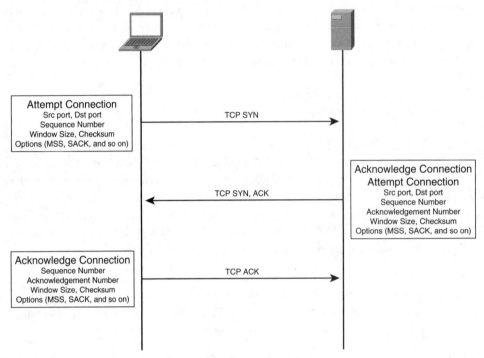

Now that a connection has been established, application processes can begin exchanging data. Data exchanged between application processes on two communicating nodes will use this connection as a means of guaranteeing delivery of data between the two nodes, as illustrated in Figure 2-9.

Second, TCP provides guaranteed delivery. Providing guarantees for delivery involves not only acknowledgment upon successful receipt of data, but also verification that the data has not changed in flight (through checksum verification), reordering of data if delivered out of order (through sequence number analysis), and also flow control (windowing) to ensure that data is being transmitted at a rate that the recipient (and the network) can handle.

Each node must allocate a certain amount of memory to a transmit buffer and a receive buffer for any sockets that are connected. These buffers are used to queue data for transmission from a local application process, and queue data received from the network until the local application process is able to read it from the buffer. Figure 2-10 shows how TCP acts as an intermediary between applications and the network and manages movement of data among data buffers while managing the connection between application processes.

Figure 2-9 *Applications and TCP Connections*

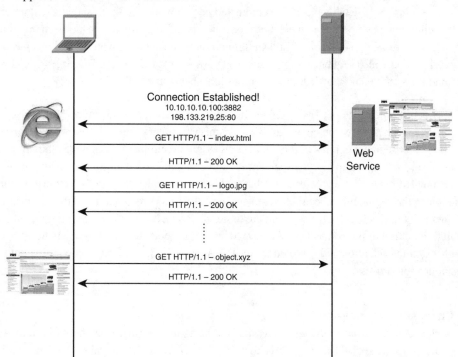

Figure 2-10 *TCP Transmit and Receive Buffers*

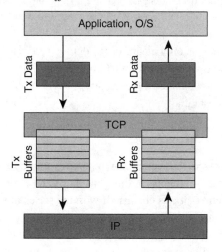

ACK Message

Each exchange of data between two connected peers involves a 32-bit sequence number (coordinating position within the data stream and identifying which data has been previously sent) and, if the ACK flag is set, an acknowledgment number (defining which segments have been received and which sequence is expected next). An ACK message acknowledges that all segments up to the specified acknowledgment number have been received.

For each segment that is transmitted by an originating node, a duplicate copy of the segment is placed in a retransmission queue and a retransmission timer is started. If the retransmission timer set for that segment expires before an acknowledgment number that includes the segment is received from the recipient, the segment is retransmitted from the retransmission queue. If an acknowledgment number is received that includes the segment before the retransmission timer expires, the segment has been delivered successfully and is removed from the retransmission queue. If the timer set for the segment continues to expire, an error condition is generated resulting in termination of the connection. Acknowledgment is generated when the data has passed checksum verification and is stored in the TCP receive buffer, waiting to be pulled out by the application process.

Checksum Verification

Each exchange of data between two connected peers involves a 16-bit checksum number. The recipient uses the checksum to verify that the data received is identical to the data sent by the originating node. If the checksum verification fails, the segment is discarded and not acknowledged, thereby causing the originating node to retransmit the segment. A checksum is not fail-safe, however, but does serve to provide a substantial level of probability that the data being received is in fact identical to the data transmitted by the sender.

The TCP checksum is not the only means of validating data correctness. The IPv4 header provides a header checksum, and Ethernet provides a CRC. As mentioned previously, these do not provide a fail-safe guarantee that the data received is correct but do minimize the probability that data received is incorrect substantially.

Data Reordering

As each segment is received, the sequence number is examined and the data is placed in the correct order relative to the other segments. In this way, data can be received out of order, and TCP will reorder the data to ensure that it is consistent with the series in which the originating node transmitted the data. Most connection-oriented transmission protocols support some form of sequencing to compensate for situations where data has been received out of order. Many connectionless transmission protocols, however, do not, and thus might not even have the knowledge necessary to understand the sequencing of the data being sent or received.

Flow Control

Flow control is the process of ensuring that data is sent at a rate that the recipient and the network are able to sustain. From the perspective of an end node participating in a conversation, flow control consists of what is known as the *sliding window*. The sliding window is a block of data referenced by pointers that indicates what data has been sent and is unacknowledged (which also resides in the retransmission buffer in case of failure), and what data has not yet been sent but resides in the socket buffer and the recipient is able to receive based on available capacity within the window.

As a recipient receives data from the network, the data is placed in the socket buffer and TCP sends acknowledgments for that data, thereby advancing the window (the sliding window). When the window slides, pointers are shifted to represent a higher range of bytes, indicating that data represented by lower pointer values has already been successfully sent and written to the recipient socket buffer. Assuming more data can be transmitted (recipient is able to receive), the data will be transmitted.

The sliding window controls the value of the window size, or win, parameter within TCP, which dictates how much data the recipient is able to receive at any point in time. As data is acknowledged, the win value can be increased, thereby notifying the sender that more data can be sent. Unlike the acknowledgment number, which is incremented when data has been successfully received by a receiving node and written to the recipient socket buffer, the win value is not incremented until the receiving node's application process actually extracts data from the socket buffer, thereby relieving capacity within the socket buffer.

The effect of a zero win value is to stop the transmitter from sending data, a situation encountered commonly when a recipient's socket buffer is completely full. As a result, the receiver is unable to accept any more data until the receiver application extracts data from the socket buffer successfully, thereby freeing up capacity to receive more data. The network aspects of flow control are examined in the later section, "Throughput." Figure 2-11 shows an example of how TCP windows are managed.

The connection-oriented, guaranteed-delivery nature of TCP causes TCP to consume significant resources and add latency that can impair application performance. Each connection established requires some amount of CPU and memory resources on the communicating nodes. Connection establishment requires the exchange of control data across the network, which incurs transmission and network delays. Managing flow control, acknowledging data, and retransmitting lost or failed data incur transmission and network delays.

Figure 2-11 *TCP Sequence, Acknowledge, and Window Values*

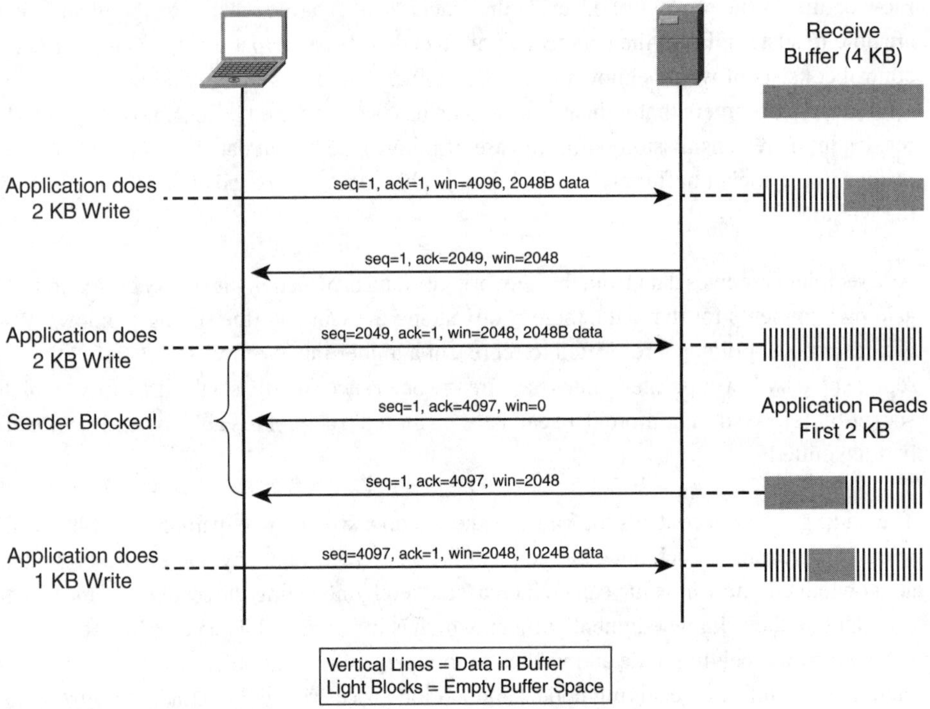

Receive
Buffer (4 KB)

Application does ---- seq=1, ack=1, win=4096, 2048B data
   2 KB Write

   seq=1, ack=2049, win=2048

Application does ---- seq=2049, ack=1, win=2048, 2048B data
   2 KB Write

Sender Blocked!   seq=1, ack=4097, win=0   Application Reads
                                              First 2 KB

   seq=1, ack=4097, win=2048

Application does ---- seq=4097, ack=1, win=2048, 1024B data
   1 KB Write

Vertical Lines = Data in Buffer
Light Blocks = Empty Buffer Space

Understanding How Other Protocols Add Latency

How do other transport protocols fare compared to TCP? Other transport protocols, such as UDP, are connectionless and provide no means for guaranteed delivery. These transport protocols rely on other mechanisms to provide guaranteed delivery, reordering, and retransmission. In many cases, these mechanisms are built directly into the application that is using the transport protocol.

While transport protocols such as UDP do not directly have the overhead found in TCP, these overhead-inducing components are often encountered in other areas, such as the application layer. Furthermore, with a transport protocol that does not have its own network-sensitive mechanism for flow control, such transport protocols operate under the management of an application and will consume as much network capacity as possible to satisfy the application's needs with no consideration given to the network itself.

Understanding the Physics Aspect of Latency

Although the transport layer can certainly add incremental amounts of latency due to connection management, retransmission, guaranteed delivery, and flow control, clearly the largest impact from the perspective of latency comes from physics. Put simply, every network connection between two nodes spans some distance, and sending data across any distance takes some amount of time.

In a complex internetwork, a network connection might be between two nodes but span many intermediary devices over tens, hundreds, thousands, or tens of thousands of miles. This delay, called *propagation delay*, is defined as the amount of time taken by a signal when traversing a medium. This propagation delay is directly related to two components:

- **Physical separation:** The distance between two nodes

- **Propagation velocity:** The speed at which data can be moved

The maximum propagation velocity found in networks today is approximately two-thirds the speed of light (the speed of light is 3×10^8 m/sec, therefore the maximum propagation velocity found in networks today is approximately 2×10^8 m/sec). The propagation delay, then, is the physical separation (in meters) divided by the propagation delay of the link (2×10^8 m/sec).

For a connection that spans 1 m, information can be transferred in one direction in approximately 5 nanoseconds (ns). This connection presents a roundtrip latency of approximately 10 ns.

For a connection that spans 1000 miles (1 mile = 1600 m), or 1.6 million meters, information can be transferred in one direction in approximately 8 ms. This connection presents a roundtrip latency of approximately 16 ms.

For a satellite connection that spans 50,000 miles (1 mile = 1600 m), or 80 million meters, information can be transferred in one direction in approximately 400 ms. This connection presents a roundtrip latency of approximately 800 ms.

These latency numbers are relative only to the amount of time spent on the network transmission medium and do not account for other very important factors such as serialization delays, processing delays, forwarding delays, or other delays.

Serialization Delays

Serialization delays are the amount of time it takes for a device to extract data from one queue and packetize that data onto the next network for transmission. Serialization delay is directly related to the network medium, interface speed, and size of the frame being serviced. For higher-speed networks, serialization delay might be negligible, but in lower-speed networks, serialization delay can be significant. Serialization delay can be calculated as the size of the data being transferred (in bits) divided by the speed of the link (in bits). For instance, to place 100 bytes of data (roughly 800 bits) onto a 128-kbps link, serialization delay would be 6.25 ms. To place 100 bytes of data onto a 1-Gbps link, serialization delay would be 100 ns.

Processing Delays

Processing delays are the amount of time spent within a network node such as a router, switch, firewall, or accelerator, determining how to handle a piece of data based on preconfigured or dynamic policy. For instance, on an uncongested router, a piece of data can be compared against a basic access list in under 1 millisecond (ms). On a congested router, however, the same operation might take 5 to 10 ms.

The forwarding architecture of the network node impacts processing delay as well. For instance, store-and-forward devices will wait until the entire packet is received before making a forwarding decision. Devices that perform cut-through forwarding will make a decision after the header is received.

Forwarding Delays

Forwarding delays are the amount of time spent determining where to forward a piece of data. With modern routers and switches that leverage dedicated hardware for forwarding, a piece of data may move through the device in under 1 ms. Under load, this may increase to 3 to 5 ms.

Understanding Application Protocol Latency

The sum of all of these components (physics, transport protocols, application protocols, congestion) adds up to the amount of perceived network latency. For a direct node-to-node connection over a switch, network latency is generally so small that it does not need to be accounted for. If that same switch is under heavy load, network latency may be significantly higher, but likely not enough to be noticeable. For a node-to-node connection over a complex, hierarchal network, latency can become quite significant, as illustrated in Figure 2-12.

Figure 2-12 *Network Latency Between Two Nodes*

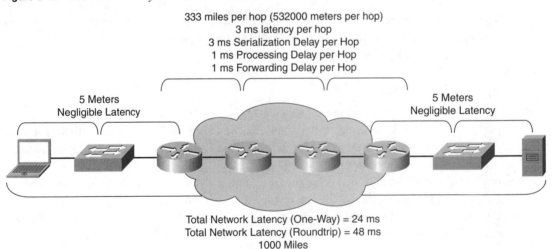

This latency accounts for the no-load network components in the path between two nodes that wish to exchange application data. In scenarios where intermediary devices are encountering severe levels of congestion, perceived latency can be dramatically higher.

With this in mind, you need to ask, "Why is latency the silent killer of application performance?" The reason is quite simple. Each message that must be exchanged between two nodes that have an established connection must traverse this heavily latent network. In the preceding example where the perceived roundtrip network latency was 48 ms, we must now account for the number of messages that are exchanged across this network to handle transport protocol management and application message transfer.

In terms of transport protocol management, TCP requires connection management due to its nature as a connection-oriented, guaranteed-delivery transport protocol. Establishing a connection requires 1.5 round trips across the network. Segment exchanges require round trips across the network. Retransmissions require round trips across the network. In short, every TCP segment sent across the network will take an amount of time equivalent to the current network delay to propagate.

To make matters worse, many applications use protocols that not only dictate how data should be exchanged, but also include semantics to control access, manage state, or structure the exchange of data between two nodes. Such application protocols are considered "chatty" or said to "play network ping-pong" or "ricochet" because of how many messages must actually be exchanged before a hint of usable application data is exchanged between the two nodes.

Take HTTP, for example, as illustrated in Figure 2-13. In a very basic web page access scenario, a TCP connection must first be established. Once established, the user's browser then requests the container page for the website being viewed using a GET request. When the container page is fully transferred, the browser builds the structure of the page in the display window and proceeds to fetch each of the embedded objects listed in the container page. Oftentimes, this is done over one or two concurrent TCP connections using serialized requests for objects. That is, when one object is requested, the next object cannot be requested until the previous object has been completely received. If the browser is using a pair of TCP connections for object fetching, two objects can be transferred to the browser at any given time, one per connection. For a website with a large number of objects, this means that multiple GET requests and object transfers must traverse the network.

In this example, assuming no network congestion, packet loss, or retransmission, and that all objects are transferable within the confines of a single packet, a 100-object website using two connections for object fetching over a 100-ms network (200-ms roundtrip latency) would require the following:

- 1.5×200 ms for TCP connection 1 setup (300 ms)

- 1×200 ms for the fetch of the container page (200 ms)

- 1.5×200 ms $\times 2$ for TCP connections 2 and 3 setup (600 ms)

- 50×200 ms for the fetch of 100 objects using two connections (10 sec)

Figure 2-13 *Application Protocol Latency*

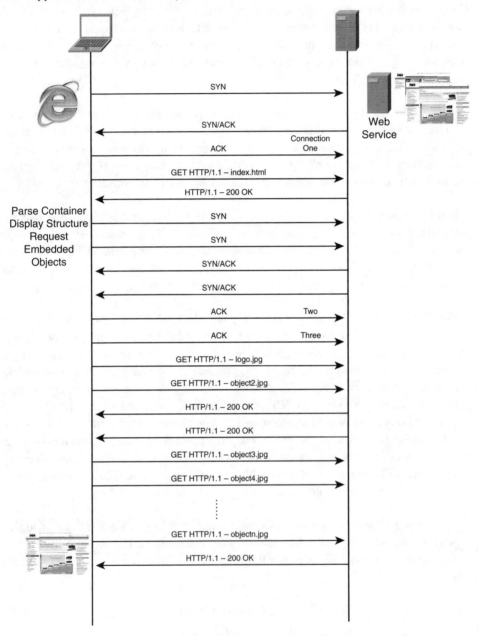

The rendering of this website would take approximately 11 seconds to complete due to the latency of the application protocol being used. This does not account for network congestion, server response time, client response time, or many other very important factors. In some cases, based on application design or server configuration, these objects may already be cached on the client but require validation by the application protocol. This leads to additional inefficiency as objects that are stored locally are verified as valid and usable.

HTTP is not the only protocol that behaves this way. Many other application protocols are actually far worse. Other "ping-pong" application protocols that require extensive messaging before useful application data is ever transmitted include the following:

- **Common Internet File System (CIFS):** Used for Windows file-sharing environments

- **Network File System (NFS):** Used for UNIX file-sharing environments

- **Remote Procedure Call (RPC):** Used extensively by applications that rely on a session-layer, including e-mail and collaboration applications such as Microsoft Exchange

More details on application protocol inefficiencies will be discussed later in this chapter in the "Application Protocols" section.

Throughput

The previous sections have examined network capacity (bandwidth) and latency as network characteristics that deteriorate application performance over the WAN. The third most common performance limiter is throughput. Throughput, or the net effective data transfer rate, is impacted by the following characteristics of any internetwork:

- **Capacity:** The minimum and maximum amount of available bandwidth within the internetwork between two connected nodes

- **Latency:** The distance between two connected nodes and the amount of time taken to exchange data

- **Packet loss:** The percentage of packets that are lost in transit due to oversubscription, congestion, or other network events

Network capacity is the easiest challenge to identify and eliminate because it relates to application performance over the network. With network capacity, the amount of throughput an application can utilize will never exceed the available capacity of the smallest intermediary hop in the network. For instance, assume a remote branch office has Gigabit Ethernet connectivity to each of the workstations in the office, and the router connects to a T1 line (1.544 Mbps). On the other end of the T1 line, the WAN router connects the corporate headquarters network to all of the remote sites. Within the corporate headquarters network, each server is connected via Gigabit Ethernet. Although the client in the branch office and the server in the corporate headquarters network are both connected by way of Gigabit Ethernet, the fact remains that they are separated by a T1 line, which is the weakest link in the chain.

In this scenario, when user traffic destined to the server reaches the network element that is managing the bandwidth disparity (that is, the router), congestion occurs, followed by backpressure, which results in dramatically slower application performance, as shown in Figures 2-5 and 2-6 earlier in the chapter. The same happens in the reverse direction when the server returns data back to the client. In this simple case, adding WAN bandwidth may improve overall user throughput, assuming the available bandwidth is indeed the limiting factor.

For congested networks, another way to overcome the challenge is to examine traffic flows that are consuming network resources (classification), assigning them a relative business priority (prioritization), and employing quality of service (QoS) to provision network resources for those flows according to business priority.

Network capacity is not, however, the limiting factor in many cases. In some situations, clients and servers may be attached to their respective LAN via Gigabit Ethernet and separated via a T1, and upgrading from a T1 to a T3 provides little if no improvement in throughput. How can it be that an organization can increase its bandwidth capacity in the WAN by an order of magnitude without providing a noticeable improvement in application performance? The answer is that the transport protocol itself may be causing a throughput limitation.

From earlier sections, you know that TCP consumes system resources on each communicating node, and that there is some overhead associated with TCP due to transmit and receive buffer management, flow control, data reordering, checksum verification, and retransmissions. With this in mind, you can expect that you will pay a performance penalty if you are to use a transport protocol that guarantees reliable delivery of data. However, there are larger issues that plague TCP, which can decrease throughput of an application over a WAN.

First, TCP does not require a node to have explicit understanding of the network that exists between itself and a peer. In this way, TCP abstracts the networking layer from the application layer. With a built-in mechanism for initially detecting network capacity (that is, TCP slow start), TCP is safe to use in almost any network environment. This mechanism, however, was designed over 20 years ago when network capacity was minimal (think 300-bps line). Although extensions to TCP improve its behavior, only some have become mainstream. The remaining extensions are largely unused.

Second, TCP not only has a built-in mechanism for detecting initial network capacity but also has a mechanism for adapting to changes in the network. With this mechanism, called *congestion avoidance*, TCP is able to dynamically change the throughput characteristics of a connection when a congestion event (that is, packet loss) is encountered. The way TCP adapts to these changes is based on the algorithms designed over 20 years ago, which provide safety and fairness, but is lacking in terms of ensuring high levels of application performance over the WAN. At the time of TCP's inception, the most network-intensive application was likely Telnet, which hardly puts a strain on even the smallest of network connections.

To summarize these two mechanisms of TCP—slow start and congestion avoidance—that hinder application performance over the WAN, remember that slow start helps TCP identify the available network capacity and that congestion avoidance helps TCP adapt to changes in the network, that is, packet loss, congestion, or variance in available bandwidth. Each mechanism can directly impact application throughput in WAN environments, as discussed in the following sections.

What is TCP slow start and how does it impact application throughput in WAN environments? TCP slow start allows TCP to identify the amount of network capacity available to a connection and has a direct impact on the throughput of the connection. When a connection has first been established, TCP slow start allows the connection to send only a small quantity of segments (generally, up to 1460 bytes per segment) until it has a history of these segments being acknowledged properly.

The rate at which TCP allows applications to send additional segments is exponential, starting from a point of allowing a connection to send only one segment until the acknowledgment of that segment is received. This variable that is constantly changing as segments are acknowledged is called the *congestion window*, or *cwnd*.

When a packet-loss event is encountered during the TCP slow start phase, TCP considers this the moment that the network capacity has been reached. At this point, TCP decreases the congestion window by 50 percent and then sends the connection into congestion avoidance mode, as shown in Figure 2-14.

Figure 2-14 *TCP Slow Start*

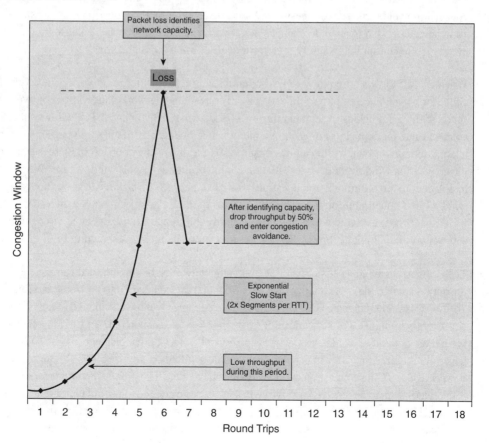

The congestion window, along with the maximum window size, determines the maximum amount of data that can be in flight for a connection at any given time. In fact, the *lesser* of the two (congestion window vs. maximum window size) is considered the maximum amount of data that can be in flight, unacknowledged, at any given time. For instance, if a packet-loss event is never encountered, the connection will not exit the TCP slow start phase. In such a scenario, the amount of network capacity is likely very high and congestion is nearly nonexistent. With such a situation, the TCP throughput will be limited by the maximum window size or by other variables such as capacity in the send and receive buffers and the latency of the network (how quickly data can be acknowledged).

TCP slow start hinders application throughput by starving connections of precious bandwidth at the beginning of their life. Many application transactions could occur in a relatively small number of roundtrip exchanges, assuming they had available bandwidth to do so. While TCP is busy trying to determine network capacity, application data is waiting to be transmitted, potentially delaying the entire application. In this way, TCP slow start *extends* the number of roundtrip exchanges that are necessary to complete a potentially arbitrary operation at the beginning of a connection.

The other mechanism of TCP that can have a negative impact on application performance is congestion avoidance. TCP congestion avoidance allows a TCP connection that has successfully completed slow start to adapt to changes in network conditions, such as packet-loss or congestion events, while continuing to safely search for available network capacity.

Whereas TCP slow start employs an exponential search for available network bandwidth, TCP congestion avoidance employs a linear search for available network bandwidth. For every successfully acknowledged segment during TCP congestion avoidance, TCP allows the connection to increment its congestion window value by one additional segment. This means that a larger amount of bandwidth can be consumed as the age of the connection increases, assuming the congestion window value is less than the value of the maximum window size. When packet loss is encountered during the congestion avoidance phase, TCP again decreases the congestion window, and potential throughput, by 50 percent. With TCP congestion avoidance, TCP slowly increases its congestion window, and consequently throughput, over time, and encounters substantial throughput declines when packet loss is encountered, as shown in Figure 2-15.

TCP congestion avoidance is not an issue on some networks, but on others it can have a sizeable impact on application performance. For networks that are considered to be "long and fat," or "LFNs" (also called elephants), TCP congestion avoidance can be a challenge to ensuring consistently high levels of network utilization after loss is encountered. An LFN is a network that has a large amount of available network capacity and spans a great distance. These LFNs are generally multiple megabits in capacity but tens or hundreds of milliseconds in latency. From the perspective of TCP's congestion avoidance algorithm, it can take quite some time for an acknowledgment to be received indicating to TCP that the connection could increase its throughput slightly. Coupled with the rate at which TCP increases throughput (one segment increase per successful round trip), it could take hours to return to maximum link capacity on an LFN.

Figure 2-15 *TCP Congestion Avoidance*

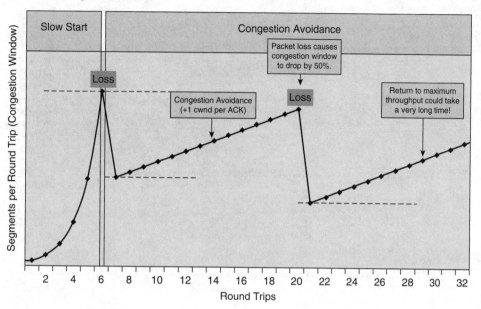

As mentioned in the previous section, a node's ability to drive application throughput for a TCP-based application is largely dependent on two factors: congestion window and maximum window size. The maximum window size plays an important role in application throughput in environments where the WAN is an LFN. By definition, an LFN has a large capacity and spans a great distance. An LFN can potentially carry a large amount of data in flight at any given time. This amount of network storage capacity, the amount of data that can be in flight over a link at any given time, is called the *bandwidth delay product (BDP)* and defines the amount of data that the network can hold.

The BDP is calculated by multiplying the bandwidth (in bytes) by the delay (round trip). For instance, a T1 line (1.544 Mbps = 190 KBps; note that lowercase *b* is used for *bits* whereas uppercase *B* is used for *bytes*) with 100 ms of delay has a BDP of approximately 19 KB, meaning only 19 KB of data can be in flight on this circuit at any given time. An OC3 line (155 Mbps, 19 MBps) with 100 ms, however, has a BDP of approximately 1.9 MB. As you can see, as bandwidth and delay increase, the capacity of the network increases.

The BDP of the network is relevant only when the nodes using the network do not support a maximum window size (MWS) that is larger than the BDP itself. The client's maximum amount of outstanding data on the network can never exceed the smaller of either cwnd or MWS. If the BDP of the network is larger than both of these values, then there is capacity available in the network that the communicating node cannot leverage, as shown in Figure 2-16. Even if cwnd were to exceed the MWS, it would not matter, because the smaller of the two determines the maximum amount of outstanding data on the wire.

Figure 2-16 *BDP and MWS*

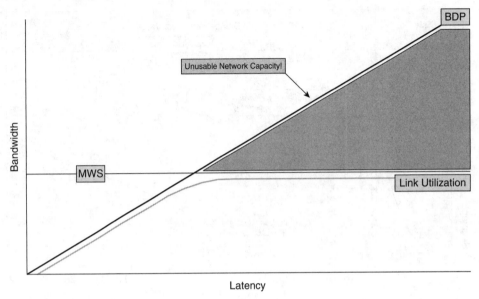

Bandwidth, latency, packet loss, and throughput intertwine with one another to determine maximum levels of application throughput on a given network. The previous sections examined the factors that directly impact application performance on the network. The next section examines other factors outside of the network infrastructure itself, including hardware considerations, software considerations, and application considerations, that can also have a significant impact on application performance and stability.

Application and Protocol Barriers to Application Performance

The performance of an application is constantly impacted by the barriers and limitations of the protocols that support the given application and the network that resides between the communicating nodes. Just because an application performs well in a lab does not always mean it will perform well in a real-world environment.

As discussed earlier in this chapter, protocols react poorly when introduced to WAN conditions such as latency, bandwidth, congestion, and packet loss. Additional factors impact application performance, such as how the common protocols consume available network bandwidth and how traffic is transferred between devices. Furthermore, other application performance barriers can be present in the endpoints themselves, from something as basic as the network card to something as complex as the block size configured for a local file system.

Application Protocols

Network latency is generally measured in milliseconds and is the delta between the time a packet leaves an originating node and the time the recipient begins to receive the packet. Several components exist that have a negative impact on perceived network latency.

Hardware components such as routers, switches, firewalls, and any other inline devices add to the amount of latency perceived by the packet, because each device applies some level of logic or forwarding. As discussed in the previous section, network characteristics such as bandwidth, packet loss, congestion, and latency all have an impact on the ability of an application to provide high levels of throughput.

Protocols that are used by applications may have been designed for LAN environments and simply do not perform well over the WAN, not because of poor application or protocol design, but simply because the WAN was not considered a use case or requirement for the protocol at the time. This section examines a few protocols and their behavior in a WAN environment, including CIFS, HTTP, NFS, and MAPI.

CIFS

CIFS sessions between a client and file server can be used for many functions, including remote drive mapping, simple file copy operations, or interactive file access. CIFS operations perform very well in a LAN environment. However, given that CIFS was designed to emulate the control aspects of a shared local file system via a network interface, it requires a high degree of control and status message exchanges prior to and during the exchange of useful data. This overhead, which is really due to how robust the protocol is, can be a barrier to application performance as latency increases.

As an example, accessing a 1.5-MB file over the network that resides on a Windows file server requires well over 1000 messages to be exchanged between the client and the server. This is directly related to the fact that CIFS requires the user to be authenticated and authorized, the file needs to be found within the directory structure, information about the file needs to be queried, the user permissions need to be verified, file open requests must be managed, lock requests must be handled, and data must be read from various points within the file (most likely noncontiguous sections).

CIFS is a protocol that has a high degree of application layer chatter; that is, a large number of messages must be exchanged to accomplish an arbitrary task. With protocols such as CIFS that are chatty, as latency increases, performance decreases. The combination of chatty applications and high-latency networks becomes a significant obstacle to performance in WAN environments because a large number of messages that are sent in a serial fashion (one at a time) must each traverse a high-latency network.

Although TCP/IP is a reliable transport mechanism for CIFS to ride on top of, latency that is introduced in the network will have a greater impact on CIFS performance, because the CIFS protocol is providing, through the network as opposed to being wholly contained within a computer, all of the semantics that a local file system would provide.

CIFS does support some built-in optimization techniques through message batching and opportunistic locks, which includes local caching, read-ahead, and write-behind. These optimizations are meant to grant a client the authority necessary to manage his own state based on the information provided by the server. In essence, the server will notify the user that they are the only user working with a particular object. In this way, the CIFS redirector, which is responsible for transmission of CIFS messages over the network, can respond to its own requests to provide the client with higher levels of performance while offloading the server. Although these techniques do provide value in that fewer messages must be handled by the origin server, the value in a WAN environment is nullified due to the extreme amounts of latency that exist in the network.

HTTP

For Internet traffic that uses HTTP as a transfer mechanism, several factors contribute to latency and the perception of latency, including the following:

- Throughput of the connection between the client and server

- The speed of the client and server hosts themselves

- The complexity of the data that must be processed prior to display by the client

Intranet web traffic is generally much more dynamic than traditional client/server traffic, and Internet traffic today is much more dynamic than it was 10 years ago. With the introduction of Java and other frameworks such as Microsoft's .NET, the client browser is empowered to provide a greater degree of flexibility and much more robust user experience.

Along with the capabilities provided by such frameworks, the browser is also required to process and render a larger amount of information, which may also increase the burden on the network. Although Internet browsers have matured to include functions such as local caches, which help mitigate the transmission of locally stored objects that have been previously accessed, the browser still cannot address many of the factors that contribute to the perception of latency by the user.

For objects embedded within a web page, the browser may be required to establish additional TCP connections to transfer them. Each TCP connection is subject to the roundtrip latency that natively exists between the client and server in the network, and also causes resource utilization increases as memory is allocated to the connection. Negatively adding to an already challenged protocol, the average Internet web page is populated with a significant number of small objects, increasing the number of TCP connections required when accessing the web page to be browsed and the number of roundtrip exchanges required to fetch these embedded objects.

In a network environment with several users located in a remote branch sharing a common WAN link, browser caching aids in improving the overall performance. Browser caching does not, however, address the limitations created by the fact that every user must request his own copy of content at least once because he is not sharing a common repository. Compounding the number of users across a limited-bandwidth WAN link adds latency to their browsers' ability to receive requested HTTP data. Application response times increase, and network performance declines predictably.

The most common browser, Microsoft Internet Explorer, opens two TCP connections by default. Though HTTP 1.1 supports pipelining to allow multiple simultaneous requests to be in process, it is not widely implemented. As such, HTTP requests must be serially processed over the two available TCP connections.

A typical web page is composed of a dynamic object or container page and many static objects of varying size. The dynamic object is not cached, whereas the static objects may be locally cached by the client browser cache or perhaps an intermediate public cache. In reality, even the static objects are often marked noncacheable or immediately expired because the application owner either is trying to account for every delivery or has at some point experienced problems with stale objects in web caches.

The application owner's knee-jerk reaction was to immediately expire all objects allowing the client to cache an object but then force the client to issue an If-Modified-Since (IMS) to revalidate the objects' freshness. In this case, a web page with 100 objects that may be cached in the client browser cache would still have to IMS 100 times over two connections, resulting in 50 round trips over the WAN. For a 100-msec RTT network, the client would have to wait 5 seconds just to revalidate while no real data is traversing the network.

By nature, HTTP does not abide by any given bandwidth limitation rules. HTTP accepts however much or little bandwidth is made available via the transport layer (TCP) and is very accepting of slow links. Consider that a web browser will operate the same if connecting to the Internet via a 2400-bps modem or a 100-Mbps Ethernet card, with the only difference being the time required to achieve the same results.

Some HTTP implementations are forgiving of network disruption as well, picking up where the previous transmission was disrupted. The lines that separate an application from the traditional browser have been blurring over the past several years, moving the browser from an informational application to the role of critical business application. Even with the evolution in role for the web browser, HTTP still abides by its unbiased acceptance of the network's availability.

With the transition of many core business-related applications from client/server to HTTP based, some applications use client-based software components while still using HTTP as the transport mechanism. With the vast success of Java, application infrastructure can be centralized, yet, segments of the application (such as applets) can be distributed and executed on the remote user workstation via his web browser. This benefits the application and server in two ways:

- The server processes less of the application.

- Processor-intensive efforts can reside on the client's workstation.

Following this model a step further, it is common for only the database entries to traverse the network and for any new Java applets to be distributed to the client as needed. The client continues to access the application via the local Java applets that are active in their browser. The applet remains available until the browser is closed or a replacement applet is served from the application server. This process works very well when the client has the Java applet loaded into the browser, but getting the initial Java applet(s) to the client consumes any bandwidth made available to HTTP during the transfer.

Many web-accessible database applications are available today and are commonly tested in a data center prior to their deployment within the corporate network. As previously shown in Chapter 1, "Strategic Information Technology Initiatives," the testing of new applications commonly takes place within a lab and not in a network environment that mirrors a full production remote branch. If a branch location has 20 users, each requiring access to the same application, that application must traverse the shared WAN link 20 times.

Testing of applications that use an actual production branch may not test the application and WAN to their fullest capacity, that is, all users simultaneously within the branch. Some applications may load in seconds when tested in a lab with high-speed LAN links connecting the client, but when tested over a WAN link with 20 simultaneous users sharing the common WAN link, it could take 30 minutes or more for the same application to become available to all users in that branch.

Due to the forgiving nature of HTTP, the loading of the application becomes slow to the user but does not time out or fail the process of loading. Branch PCs commonly have slow access in the morning, because applications must be loaded on workstations, and other business-critical functions, such as e-mail and user authentication, traverse the network at the same time. HTTP does not care about what else is happening on the network (TCP does), as long as the requested content can eventually transfer to the client's browser.

FTP

Many network administrators consider the FTP a "necessary evil." Legacy applications and logging hosts commonly use FTP for simple, authenticated file transfers. FTP is viewed as a simple solution but with a potential for a major impact. Everything from the NIC of the server to the WAN link that the traffic will traverse is impacted by the manner in which FTP transfers content. FTP can disrupt the ability to pass other traffic at the same time an FTP transfer is taking place. By nature, FTP consumes as much bandwidth as possible during its transfer of content, based on what TCP is allowed to consume. FTP tends to use large data buffers, meaning it will try to leverage all of the buffer capacity that TCP can allocate to it.

Precautions exist within many operating systems and third-party applications that allow the administrator to define an upper limit to any given FTP transfer, preventing congestion situations. FTP is not fault tolerant and, by nature, is very unforgiving to disruptions. In many cases, a network disruption requires that the file be retransmitted from the beginning. Some application vendors have written client and server programs that leverage FTP as a control and data transfer protocol that allow for continuation of a failed transfer, but these mechanisms are not built into FTP as a protocol itself.

NFS

NFS, which was originally introduced by Sun Microsystems, provides a common protocol for file access between hosts. NFS provides read and write capabilities similar to CIFS, but NFS is stateless in nature whereas CIFS is extremely stateful. This means that the server requires use of idempotent operations, that is, each operation contains enough data necessary to allow the server to fulfill the request. With CIFS, the server knows the state of the client and the file and can respond to simple operations given the known state.

Since the acceptance of NFS by the Internet Engineering Task Force (IETF), vendors such as Microsoft, Novell, Apple, and Red Hat have adopted the NFS protocol and implemented a version into their server and client platforms.

Although the standards are clearly defined to implement NFS, there are currently three common versions of NFS that all have different abilities and create and react differently to latency challenges introduced on the network. NFS version 2 (NFSv2) leverages UDP as a transport layer protocol, which makes it unreliable in many network environments. Although some implementations of NFSv2 now support TCP, NFSv3 was more easily adopted due to its native support of TCP for transport.

NFS is similar to CIFS in that a physical location within a file system is made accessible via the network, and clients are able to access this shared file system as if it were local storage. NFS introduces some challenges that are similar to those of CIFS, including remote server processing delay when data is being written to the remote host, and sensitivity to network latency when data is being read from or written to a remote host.

For file transfers, NFS generally uses 8-KB blocks for both read and write actions. NFS impacts more than just the network; NFS also impacts the CPU of the server, disk throughput, and RAM. There is a direct parallel between the volume of data being transferred via NFS and the amount of server resources consumed by NFS.

Fortunately, vendors such as Sun have implemented bandwidth management functionality, allowing for NFS traffic flows to be throttled for both incoming and outgoing traffic independently of each other. If bandwidth management is not applied to NFS traffic, as with other protocols, the client application will consume as much bandwidth as allowed by the transport protocol. As network speeds become faster, file sizes will trend toward becoming larger as well. NFS has been used by applications as a transport for moving database and system backup files throughout the network, requiring that traffic management be planned in advance of implementing the NFS protocol.

The ability to control NFS traffic on the WAN will aid administrators in preventing WAN bottleneck slowdowns. Much like CIFS, if 50 users in a remote office each need a copy of the same file from the same mount point, the file must be transferred across the network at least once for each requesting user, thereby wasting precious WAN bandwidth.

MAPI and Remote Procedure Calls

MAPI provides a common message exchange format that can be leveraged in client/server and peer-to-peer applications. MAPI is commonly used as a standardized means of exchanging data over another protocol such as a Remote Procedure Call (RPC). For instance, Microsoft Exchange uses MAPI for the structuring of messages that are exchanged using remote-procedure calls (RPC). Although not all vendors' implementation of MAPI may be the same, not to mention the use of the protocol that is carrying data (such as RPC), several applications use MAPI to dictate the way messages are exchanged.

Throughput of many client/server applications that leverage MAPI, such as Microsoft Outlook and Exchange, which use MAPI within RPC, decreases by as much as 90 percent as latency increases from 30 ms to 100 ms. As e-mail continues to become an increasingly important enterprise application, poor performance of e-mail services within the network is generally brought to the attention of network administrators faster than other poorly performing business-critical applications. The majority of this decline in application performance is directly related to bandwidth, latency, throughput, and the inefficiencies of the protocol being used to carry MAPI message exchanges.

Microsoft's use of MAPI and RPC differs between Exchange Server 2000 and Exchange Server 2003. Traffic patterns between the two different server versions differ from the perspective of network traffic due to the introduction of cached mode in Exchange Server 2003, when used in conjunction with the matching Microsoft Outlook 2003 product. When Exchange 2003 and Outlook 2003 are combined, cached mode allows for the majority of user operations to be performed locally against a "cached copy" of the contents of the user's storage repository on the server. In essence, cached mode allows a user to keep a local copy of his storage repository on the local PC. This local copy is used to allow operations that do not impact data integrity or correctness to be handled locally without requiring an exchange of data with the Exchange server. For instance, opening an e-mail that resides in the cached copy on the local PC does not require that the e-mail be transferred again from the Exchange server. Only in cases where updates need to be employed, where state changes, or when synchronization is necessary do the server and client actually have to communicate with one another.

E-mail vendors such as Lotus, with its Domino offering, support compression and other localization functions as well. Lotus recognizes that allowing less traffic to traverse the WAN between the client and server will improve application performance for its users.

Although compression reduces the overall volume of data that traverses the network, e-mail protocols are still very sensitive to latency and packet loss. When operating on networks that are subject to a predictable amount of traffic loss, e-mail may not function at all, making services appear as if they are offline. Most e-mail applications have a default interval of 60 seconds for synchronization between the client and server. With such offline synchronization, traffic is greatly reduced once the e-mail client has sent and received all of its messages and has synchronized the local cached copy. However, if the amount of data that needs to be synchronized to the server is large and transfer of this data extends beyond the synchronization window, it could be quite difficult for a client to catch up. Similar to file-sharing protocols, if 50 users in a remote office each received a copy of the same e-mail with the same 5-MB attachment, that 5-MB attachment would be transferred across the network once per recipient, consuming large amounts of network capacity.

Network Stability

The networks of today are much more stable than they were 10 years ago. As bandwidth capacity has continued to increase, so has the amount of memory and hardware capacity of the devices (routers and switches) that direct traffic on private and public networks. With this increase in network capacity and network element hardware, packet loss is far less noticeable in the enterprise network and very rare across the public Internet, primarily because the bottlenecks have shifted away from the network.

Network stability is still a key factor in today's networks as some networks transition from Fast Ethernet (100 Mbps) to Gigabit Ethernet (1000 Mbps), or even to 10-Gigabit Ethernet (10,000 Mbps). Traffic at these speeds will traverse a router or switch that needs to accommodate not just the traffic of one client to one server, but potentially from hundreds or thousands of nodes.

Several components impact overall stability of the network, including each of the network elements (routers, switches, firewalls), wireless access points, cabling, and more. For outsourced or managed WAN environments, network stability also includes a service provider plan and its network offerings that connect the data center and remote branch location, including any optional redundancy or service level agreements (SLA).

An unreliable network has an impact on more than just the data that traverses the network. Factors that cannot be as easily monitored or calculated, such as employee morale, can cost an enterprise in ways that cannot be forecasted. Employees who depend on an unreliable network may avoid certain applications, or look to alternative methods to get a job done if they do not feel that they can efficiently or, more importantly, reliably perform their required daily tasks. In some cases, the employees may just refuse to do their jobs, because they do not feel that they have adequate tools available to complete their assigned tasks. As mentioned in Chapter 1, sometimes the application is to blame for poor performance, and in some cases the network is to blame. In this case, the network is to blame if stability is impacted to the point that users cannot get to the tools they need to be productive and drive revenue.

As an example, consider how your mobile wireless provider's network impacts the usage patterns of your personal mobile phone. Your mobile phone is dependent on an accessible network to allow you to make or receive calls. In your daily travels, you will find over the course of time that certain areas have unreliable cellular coverage. During your travels through those areas, you will disconnect from the cellular network either intentionally prior to the service disruption or unintentionally when you unknowingly enter the poor service area. Data networks and applications share many similarities. If your daily responsibilities call for you to access several applications, one of which has extremely poor performance, you will approach the usage of that one application differently than you do the others. If that one application resides in a data center that is a long distance away over an oversubscribed and unreliable network, then both the application's and employee's performance will suffer.

Identifying Network Components

Understanding network infrastructure and network management is the first step in venturing to assess and manage application performance over the network. If you do not know how your network is designed and implemented, you will not be in a position to effectively monitor and manage your network or the applications that use it. Take the time to understand your network topology, and be sure to become familiar with each component, including the following:

- The make and model of routers, switches, firewalls, server load-balancers, and other network elements currently in use at each location.

- The version of operating system and licensed features that are in use on each of the network elements.

- The interface number and type, as well as any assigned IP address information of each interface and node.

- The interface configuration, including speed and duplex. Interfaces should either negotiate properly with the peer device or be hard-coded to the correct configuration to ensure consistency.

Identifying Non-Network Components

Similarly, become familiar with each of the non-network components that have an impact on application performance, including these:

- The make and model of client laptops, desktops, and servers

- The version of operating system and the licensed features that are in use on each of these

- The applications that are installed and how they are configured

■ Service packs, hotfixes, and device drivers that are installed

■ The network connectivity (speed, media, network configuration) for each of these nodes and their location within the network (campus, remote office, VPN user)

From the network and non-network information, an administrator can easily identify how his network is configured, as well as where to take action if an outage is observed.

Understanding the Health of Network Devices

The next step in understanding the network's impact on application performance is to know the limits of your network. Every router, switch, network card, and cable has a capacity limit. If the limiting factor is not the speed of the interface, it could be the CPU or memory utilization of each device that the traffic must traverse.

A router or switch that is running at capacity may drop an excessive number of packets (that is, become a point of congestion). If aggregation and oversubscription are not planned appropriately, packet loss and queuing delays could have a significantly adverse effect on the performance of applications traversing that device.

Network switches are commonly designed with inherent oversubscription. For instance, a switch that supports 24 ports of 1000-Mbps traffic per port may not have an adequate backplane capacity to support 24 ports under full load. Understanding the limits of a router, switch, firewall, or other network element will help identify potential bottlenecks in the network. Adequately sizing network infrastructure components will help prevent network stability issues and better guarantee higher levels of application performance.

Several monitoring utilities exist today that allow you to monitor all aspects of a router or switch. Monitoring utilities range from simple shareware tools to monitoring and reporting systems that cost millions of dollars. The following sections describe SNMP-compliant managers and syslog.

SNMP

Routers and switches that support network management and monitoring via the Simple Network Management Protocol (SNMP) should be configured to report to an SNMP-compliant manager, because this will aid in providing visibility into the overall health of each of the devices. SNMP monitoring will inform an administrator of a device that exceeds a configured threshold, generates specific warnings, or triggers alerts. If a defined threshold such as CPU utilization is exceeded, the stability of the network may be at risk due to a device that cannot support or scale beyond its current workload.

SNMP supports several functions that help secure and stabilize the monitoring information that is provided by the network routers and switches. Functions include the ability to encrypt and authenticate the requests that the router or switch must respond to.

Although SNMPv1 is the most commonly implemented version, versions 2c and 3 provide additional levels of protection that help deter network threats from snooping around the network. Table 2-2 provides a simplistic overview of SNMP version differences.

Table 2-2 *SNMP Version Differences*

Version	Authentication	Encryption	Security
1	No	No	No
2c	No	No	Yes
3	Yes	Yes	Yes

Syslog

In addition to SNMP, syslog can be used to monitor system-related events, which can prove useful in many network environments. Syslog tracks just about every event that occurs on the network, depending on the level of visibility desired by the network administrator. If an application is suspect in the stability or performance of a given network, implementing syslog may help in tracking down specific suspect events. Also, depending on what information you are tracking on the network, there may be legal implications that protect the employee's rights. Syslog will help in understanding network traffic patterns, and in a way that helps determine if there are application or network failures being observed on the network.

Obtaining Vendor-Specific Performance Validation Test Results

Many network vendors today have results of performance validation tests and may make these available to customers. This information may not be publicly available due to the sensitive nature of the data. Most vendors make this information available upon request, and understanding how each device in your network behaves will help you to know what the observed limits are and how to deploy accordingly. For example, deploying a router that cannot meet the packets per second requirement or that has insufficient resources may not scale to meet the needs of the location it connects to.

Establishing a Redundancy Plan

One of the most important factors in network stability is the redundancy plan. Redundancy planning and implementation can be leveraged at any place within the network, ranging from the data center application servers to the remote branch WAN connectivity or even the LAN switch. With the intelligence that exists in today's infrastructure components, redundancy has become easier to implement. Although items such as redundant WAN connections and the associated routers can be costly, the technology exists today to allow for near-immediate failover with granular control over which applications are allowed to take advantage of the alternate WAN connectivity.

Take the time to consider the options that exist when considering redundancy in the network. Proper planning is the key to providing network access that is scalable, reliable, and stable for the remote user. In most cases, the cost of downtime is far greater than the cost of redundancy.

Stabilizing the Client and Server Network Connections

The client and server also are large factors in network stability and application performance, starting with the connection point to the network, the NIC. For all devices, if the client or server network connection is not stable (because of improper device drivers, faulty network cards, bad cables, or a poorly implemented or misconfigured TCP/IP stack, for example), then the network will appear to lack stability and application performance will suffer.

The device driver selected by the operating system may not always be the most appropriate, accurate, or current. Ensuring that servers, client workstations, and their respective NICs are operating in the most efficient and stable manner will impact the stability of the LAN and WAN directly. The stability of the network offers no value if the server or client devices cannot reliably transmit data through it. There is a possibility that the operating system's default driver selection will lead to packet loss or a network interface exhibiting intermittent functionality. The host operating system may not be equipped to communicate the lack of functionality to the administrator.

Operating System Barriers to Application Performance

The impact the clients and servers play in perceived network stability and application performance does not stop with the connection to the network. Several factors exist that are commonly not taken into consideration when looking at the performance of an application. These factors include the operating system itself, which hosts the application, and the hardware platform, which hosts the operating system and other I/O functions.

Proper selection of the application host server's hardware and operating system components improves the overall performance and efficiency of the application. A poorly tuned application server will have a negative effect on the application's performance and functionality across the WAN.

Configuring a server to run "optimally" requires a significant amount of research and can have a large overall impact on application performance. This section describes operating systems and offers guidance as to what aspects of the system should be examined to enable better levels of application performance. The next section describes the hardware.

Microsoft Corporation

In the data center, Microsoft offers several different editions of the popular operating system Windows Server 2003 R2. The operating system and third-party device drivers must be compatible with the hardware platform, which must explicitly support the operating system.

The purpose of the server must be taken into consideration when selecting the correct operating system and processor combination (32-bit or 64-bit, Intel or Advanced Micro Devices [AMD]). Selecting a processor and operating system combination that is not compatible will reflect in the performance results of the application, and ultimately the perceived performance at the client.

NOTE Microsoft offers multiple flavors of the Windows Server 2003 operating system: Standard Edition, Enterprise Edition, and Datacenter Edition. Consult Microsoft's website (http://www.microsoft.com) for the latest product information regarding each of these editions and any changes specific to each edition's product features.

To ensure that the system administrator selects only quality components, Microsoft provides the Windows Hardware Quality Labs (WHQL) certification. The WHQL certification, which is written by hardware manufacturers and device driver authors, provides a framework for driver development and hardware quality standards. Leveraging the WHQL certification will help in determining a suitable hardware platform to host a Microsoft Windows Server 2003 operating system.

Microsoft offers several resources to system administrators who are seeking to optimize Microsoft products, including server platforms. One of the most popular resources is Microsoft TechNet (http://technet.microsoft.com). TechNet provides administrators with access to numerous tuning guidelines for operating systems and file systems and focused topic areas such as file server scalability and performance. Additional resources offer detailed steps for tuning the server's network, memory, processor, software configurations, and registry.

To help address application performance, Microsoft offers the Windows Server 2003 Scalable Networking Pack, which provides three key advancements to the Windows Server 2003 operating system:

■ TCP Chimney Offload

■ Receive-side Scaling (RSS)

■ NetDMA

TCP Chimney Offload

TCP Chimney Offload is Microsoft's software implementation that directly supports TCP Offload Engine (TOE) NICs. The subject of TOE is discussed later in this chapter, in the section "Network Interface Cards." TCP Chimney Offload, when combined with a Microsoft-approved TOE, allows for a stateful offload of traffic from the operating system to the TOE NIC. This mitigates the need for the server CPU to spend cycles managing TCP connections. Instead, it can focus on application-centric efforts such as serving web pages, files, or database content.

Receive-Side Scaling

Receive-side Scaling addresses the common challenge of load allocation to a single processor within a multiprocessor server. A single network processor in a server handles all network traffic. For servers that have high utilization levels and multiple processors, one processor will commonly show a high level of utilization, while other processors will not receive network traffic. When RSS is implemented on the server with supported NICs, all inbound network traffic is load-balanced across all recognized processors, allowing for additional network traffic to be accepted by the server.

NetDMA

NetDMA is the third offering of the Windows Server 2003 Scalable Networking Pack. NetDMA requires supporting hardware, which optimizes data flow through a server. NetDMA reduces the dependency on the server's processor to manage moving data between the network adapter and application buffers within the server's RAM. NetDMA, through supporting hardware that optimizes data flow through a server, manages the memory data transfer processes, enabling the server's processor to be allocated to other application-related functions.

Sun Microsystems

Sun Microsystems (http://www.sun.com) offers hardware and operating system platforms for the data center. All Sun Scalable Processor Architecture (SPARC) powered server platforms support the Solaris operating system. Sun also supports AMD powered server platforms, which adds support for Red Hat Linux, Microsoft Windows, and EMC VMware operating systems.

Sun Microsystems server hardware platforms range from a single processor to 128 processors per server. Sun includes support for the AMD Opteron 64-bit processor on some platforms; Sun's implementation of the Opteron processor has been qualified under Microsoft's WHQL certification program for the Windows 2003 Server operating system for both 32-bit and 64-bit implementations.

Sun Microsystems provides the Hardware Compatibility List (HCL) to assist system administrators in determining if their hardware platform is based on supported components against a specific operating system version. It is important to note that Solaris is not limited to Sun Microsystems branded hardware. Sun operating system compatibility certifications exist on many mainstream and blackbox server platforms as well. Hardware support ranges from an endorsed "Sun Certified" to "Reported to Work," which implies that a component has been observed as working in a system running a specific operating system. Keep in mind that just because a component works with the operating system does not always mean that its functionality is optimal to an application.

Sun offers several resources for administrators who are faced with tuning or optimizing their server. Sun BluePrints OnLine offers administrators with Sun-specific best practices, based on real-world administrator experiences. Each best practice outlines a specific problem and provides a clearly identified solution. Additional Sun Microsystems resources include the BigAdmin program, which offers discussion forums, as well as hardware and software informational submissions by system administrators. BigAdmin offers a structured format, viewable by logical subjects such as networking, performance, and product installation.

Red Hat

Red Hat (http://www.redhat.com) offers two versions of the Enterprise Linux operating system for data center computing, Linux AS and Linux ES. Red Hat is an operating system vendor that supports an array of processor platforms, including Intel Corporation's Itanium 2 and x86, AMD's EM64T, and select IBM POWER series servers. For application hosting, the Linux AS operating system platform is more common to the data center than the Linux ES operating system, providing a more robust platform for hosting of database and customer relationship management (CRM) type applications.

When selecting Red Hat Linux as an operating system platform, several decisions must be well planned prior to a purchase from a selected hardware vendor. First, the performance and expectations of the application server must be determined. Once the server expectations have been defined, the proper version of the operating system and corresponding hardware must be selected. Not all platforms support the same maximum quantity of RAM per server, ranging from 64 GB to as much as 8 TB. The number and type of processor, either 32-bit or 64-bit, must be taken into consideration when planning an application server, with vendor-defined limits ranging from as few as 8 processors to as many as 64 processors per server. Some platforms have theorized support for as many as 512 processors per server platform.

To make the selection of hardware easier for the administrator, Red Hat offers its Hardware Catalog of certified and compatible hardware. Certified hardware is broken down into classifications of server or workstation. For servers, each named product includes a list of supported operating system platforms. As an example, the IBM eServer xSeries 336 is listed as a certified and supported platform. Red Hat certifies that this platform has been approved to operate the x386 and x86_64 base operating systems. The Hardware Catalog assists in determining which platforms are supported by a given vendor if existing hardware supplier relationships exist for an enterprise buyer. As with all data center–related purchases, any given platform should be fully tested prior to being placed into a production environment.

Red Hat provides several resources for optimization and tuning of the Linux AS and Linux ES operating systems. Red Hat's administrator documentation provides suggestions for tuning the Linux operating system's kernel, which include command-line references, scripts, and proper procedures for user and group permissions. Red Hat offers an administrator's exam specific to system monitoring and performance tuning based on a course that focuses on capacity planning and performance tuning. These types of resources will aid administrators in recognizing performance trends in their application servers, as well as offer guidance in suggested platform changes.

Interestingly, many administrators will compile their own applications for their servers, which is where the application tuning process begins. Tuning of the compiler will not provide optimal application results; the application code itself must be written to perform in an optimal manner. Administrators must have access to the application authors in the event that changes must be made to the source code.

For database applications, tuning must be done in several locations, including the operating system, file system, and the database application itself. Many database applications require extensive use of raw and defined file systems that host the database. For the database to perform optimally both on the server and to the end client, the kernel, the underlying file system, disk and partition configurations, and the amount of physical RAM in the server are all considered. The amount of installed physical RAM may also impact the exact size of any disk swap partition or virtual swap files that must be created.

Hewlett-Packard

Hewlett-Packard (http://www.hp.com) offers several different server platform product lines and a proprietary operating system called HP-UX. In addition to supporting HP-UX, the Hewlett-Packard server platforms support other operating systems, such as Microsoft Windows Server 2003, Novell Corporation's NetWare, Red Hat Linux, and many more.

Server platforms offered by Hewlett-Packard range from small dual-processor servers, which support either the Intel Corporation's Xeon series processor or the AMD Opteron series processor, to multiprocessor data center servers supporting as many as 128 processors.

The HP-UX UNIX operating system has entered its 11th generation, offering an operating system platform for the 9000 and Integrity series servers from Hewlett-Packard, which are its elite data center servers.

Hewlett-Packard supports all major operating systems used today in the data center. The broad array of operating systems adds to the complexity of selecting the correct operating system and hardware platform to develop an optimal host server. Hewlett-Packard produces one of the supported operating systems, HP-UX 11i. This UNIX operating system supports application hosting, in both custom and off-the-shelf types. HP-UX, like other UNIX operating systems, may require the administrator to take measures to optimize not just the operating system, but also the actual compiled code that will reside on the server.

HP-UX includes software compilers that may require tuning or optimizations prior to touching the code that will be compiled into executable software. Leveraging a compiler produced by Hewlett-Packard may produce more predictable results than using a third-party or open-source compiler.

Leveraging a compiler produced by Hewlett-Packard also allows access to Hewlett-Packard's support offerings, if problems or incompatibilities are discovered. Ensuring that the HP-UX compiler is a current version may also improve the performance of the compiler, providing faster compile results.

When focusing on the HP-UX UNIX operating system, maintaining a current patch state for the operating system optimizes how the server's operating system operates. Applying all patches to an operating system may not be required, but maintaining patches related to memory paging, file system I/O, and network traffic has a direct impact on the optimization of the server.

The HP Caliper performance analyzer provides performance-related statistics of applications running on HP-UX and Linux operating systems. The HP Caliper analysis tool is offered free for HP-UX users and noncommercial Linux users. Commercial Linux users must pay a license fee to test with this analysis tool.

Additional server optimization resources are available on Hewlett-Packard's website. Available white papers illustrate how to write and optimize software written in various programming languages. Although not all programmers may work for the ultimate owner of the application, the suggestions and free utilities provided through the Optimization and Performance Tuning section enable application developers to monitor system utilization when applications are written or tested.

IBM

IBM (http://www.ibm.com) offers a broad array of 32-bit and 64-bit servers. These servers support operating systems offered by vendors such as Microsoft and Red Hat.

Select servers include the POWER5 series processor that is designed to specifically support operating systems such as IBM AIX 5 and Red Hat Linux in the data center. Entering its 20th year, AIX is a UNIX operating system whose strengths are found primarily in the data center. IBM server platforms running under AIX 5 support a range of 2 to 64 processors per server.

IBM offers a wide array of enterprise servers, which support processors such as AMD Opteron, Intel Pentium D, and Xeon series processors. Larger servers will support processors such as the IBM POWER5 and POWER5+ series processors.

When selecting the proper processor and operating system combination, consult IBM's hardware and software compatibility matrix. Compatibility matrices are provided for various Microsoft operating systems, easing the selection process based on business need.

Tips and tricks to aid in optimization of the operating system, as well as common database applications that run on IBM servers, are available via several different sources. IBM Redbooks offer suggestions and guidelines for tuning hardware, AIX operating system parameters, and specific database applications. Redbooks are excellent administrative resources, because they are written with the system and database administrators in mind.

Hardware Barriers to Application Performance

This section looks into the hardware components more specifically to outline how each of these subsystems directly impacts application performance.

Central Processing Unit

There are several factors to take into consideration when selecting a processor. As the CPU speed war continues, competition will only benefit your applications and their performance. The continual evolution of processors will make selecting the correct processor continually more difficult, as the processor becomes more and more sensitive to the operating system it has to support.

Each processor is rated by several variables, including processor cache capacity, front side bus speed, dual-core support, hyper-threading support, and 32- and 64-bit support. This section explains each of these components, outlining the benefit that each brings to application performance.

Cache Capacity

Layer 2 and Layer 3 caches reside in the processor chip. These caches accelerate the processor's ability to receive data. Processors today support caches that range in size from 1 MB to 24 MB or larger. Typically, the larger the processor's cache, the faster the processor will function in a server that runs under high utilization.

Frequently accessed data, which would typically be held in the server's RAM memory, may be partially or entirely stored in the processor's cache memory to reduce the latency of data lookups. The processor will always check its local cache before checking with the server's installed RAM.

Front Side Bus Speed

The front side bus is a significant factor in the server's ability to move data about the server. The numerical rating of a server's front side bus designates at what speed the processor can transfer data to other devices, including RAM and I/O cards (such as those attached via PCI or other interconnect). The speed rating of a server's front side bus will directly correlate into how quickly the server can pass data between its components; this distribution of data has a direct impact on the server's ability to process and serve data to clients, thereby impacting application performance overall.

Dual-Core Support

A dual-core processor is simply a single processor chip that contains two processors that can work in parallel. A common benefit of a dual-core processor is that the individual processors will each have their own primary cache, or Level 1 cache. The traffic of the individual processors will pass through a common Level 2 cache, or secondary cache, allowing the individual processor instances to share a common cache. The dual-core, shared-cache architecture provides a faster processor response time for both processors within the same chip.

Because no direct dual-core support is built into operating systems, the support must be built into the applications that use the server's processors. To produce an application that will optimally perform on a dual-core server, the application vendor must be aware of the processors installed within the server to support the available resources offered by the dual-core processor. Figure 2-17 illustrates the shared L2 cache architecture of the dual-core processor.

Figure 2-17   *Dual-Core Processor*

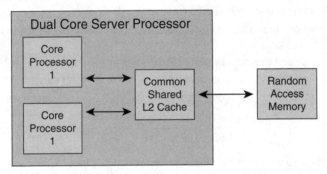

Hyper-Threading

Hyper-threading and Super-threading are offerings that are specific to processors manufactured by Intel Corporation. Hyper-threading allows a single processor to appear as if two separate processors exist. Super-threading allows a thread, or thread of execution, to be shared with a processor that has available thread resources.

For servers, hyper-threading is best taken advantage of by applications that are aware of and support hyper-threading, although the operating system may or may not need to be aware of the processor's ability. Hyper-threading support must exist in the BIOS and chipset of the server to take advantage of a hyper-thread-capable processor. Intel has combined the dual-core and hyper-threading capabilities in some of its more powerful processor offerings.

Support for 32-Bit and 64-Bit Architectures

Some processors support a 32-bit architecture, whereas others support a 64-bit architecture. As operating systems evolve toward a greater array of 64-bit support, applications must also support the ability to communicate with a 64-bit processor. Applications that are written specifically to support the 32-bit server architecture may operate in a diminished capacity when run on a 64-bit architecture, because the server must emulate the 32-bit architecture.

In the case of database applications, overall performance improves if the database application was compiled specifically to support a 64-bit architecture. Database application performance improves due to the ability to better support multitasking and the ability to transfer larger blocks of data among components within the server.

Proper selection of the server's operating system will depend on which processor has been installed in the server. 128-bit processors will be the next numerical evolution of the server processor.

Random Access Memory

Memory selection for servers is a constantly evolving process. Although naming is very similar between types, the performance and capabilities differ significantly. Common server memory implemented today includes double-data-rate (DDR), synchronous dynamic random-access memory (SDRAM), double-data-rate two (DDR2), and double-data-rate three (DDR3). Proper memory selection not only is critical to the performance of the server but also directly impacts the server's ability to stage, alter, and distribute data throughout the bus efficiently.

Although not as common as other types of memory, the DDR SDRAM memory type still exists in servers today. This, the slowest of the DDR RAM types, is considered legacy memory by today's standards. As a foundation for understanding how DDR memory is rated, consider DDR-266 memory as an example. The first "D" implies that the clock rate of the memory is doubled. For a server that operates with a 133-MHz front side bus, DDR chips will operate at 266 MHz. Taking this example to the next step, PC-2100 DDR-SDRAM, a popular-speed memory for early Intel Xeon servers, requires the same 133-MHz bus, leveraging multiple DDR memory chips rated at 266 MHz. PC-2100 DDR-SDRAM has an overall throughput rating of approximately 2.1 GBps.

DDR2 SDRAM utilizes nearly the same calculation process as DDR memory, with the exception that the 2 implies that the original DDR clock speed is doubled. Using the same example as with DDR-266 SDRAM, DDR2-533 SDRAM would be 133-MHz memory chips, clocked at 266 MHz, then doubled again, to 533 MHz. DDR2-533 chips are based on the same 133-MHz bus speed as DDR-266. Following through on the example, DDR2-533 chips would be required for PC2-4200 SDRAM, with an approximate throughput of 4.2 GBps.

DDR3 SDRAM is expected to be the next generation of SDRAM. The 3 in DDR3 implies that the clock rate and overall throughput of the SDRAM has been doubled, not tripled. In the example of the 133-MHz bus, the calculations would be as follows: 133-MHz memory would be double-clocked to 533 MHz and then doubled to 1066 MHz. DDR3-1066 would be the rating of the chips, with an approximate throughput of 1.06 GBps per chip. DDR3-1066 chips would be applied toward the PC3-8500 SDRAM, allowing for an ultimate throughput of approximately 8.5 GBps.

Table 2-3 compares the speed differences and throughput ratings of a broad array of memory options available today, and into the near future.

Table 2-3   *SDRAM Comparison*

Bus Speed	DDR	DDR2	DDR3 (*future)
100 MHz	Chip: DDR-200 Module: PC-1600 Throughput: 1.6 Gbps	Chip: DDR2-400 Module: PC2-3200 Throughout: 3.2 Gbps	Chip: DDR3-800 Module: PC3-6400 Throughput: 6.4 Gbps
133 MHz	Chip: DDR-266 Module: PC-2100 Throughput: 2.1 Gbps	Chip: DDR2-533 Module: PC2-4200 Throughput: 4.2 Gbps	Chip: DDR-1066 Module: PC3-8500 Throughput: 8.5 Gbps
166 MHz	Chip: DDR-333 Module: PC-2700 Throughput: 2.7 Gbps	Chip: DDR2-667 Module: PC2-5300 Throughput: 5.3 Gbps	—
200 MHz	Chip: DDR-400 Module: PC-3200 Throughput: 3.2 Gbps	Chip: DDR2-800 Module: PC2-6400 Throughput: 6.4 Gbps	—

Disk Storage

The spinning disk is inevitably going to be the choke point for application performance in many server environments, as information is exchanged between the server bus and magnetized areas on a spinning platter. Typical storage deployments have changed radically over the past 30 years, starting with consolidated storage deployments (mainframe centric) toward distributed computing with captive storage (onset of open systems computing) and back to a consolidated storage deployment model (open systems with storage networking).

During the rapid proliferation of distributed servers with captive storage, each node had its own directly attached storage capacity, also known as direct-attached storage (DAS). With the onset of storage area networks (SANs), which enable consolidation of storage capacity onto a storage array device that can be logically provisioned and shared through a networking fabric, many organizations find themselves collapsing storage infrastructure once again to simplify deployment, control costs, and improve utilization and efficiency.

DAS can be as simple as a single disk within the server chassis or multiple disks within a dedicated unintelligent external chassis (just a bunch of disks, or JBOD), or as complex as a directly attached dedicated array using Redundant Array of Independent Disks (RAID) technology. With DAS, storage is completely captive to the server it is connected to and can be connected to that server using a number of storage interconnects, including Small Computer Systems Interface (SCSI), Serial Attached SCSI (SAS), serial advanced technology attachment (SATA), or Fibre Channel.

SANs provide logically the same function as DAS with the exception that the disk (physical or virtual) being accessed is attached to a network and potentially behind a controller that is managing disks that are accessible to other nodes on that network. With SAN-attached storage, disk capacity appears to the server as DAS but is managed as a provisioned amount of capacity on a shared array, accessible through a high-speed network such as Fibre Channel.

Network-attached storage (NAS) is similar to SAN in that storage capacity is made accessible via a network. NAS, however, does not provide a server with a physical or logical disk to perform direct operations against. With NAS, a file system is made accessible via the network, and not a physical or logical disk. This means that accessing information on the shared file system requires that it be accessed through a file system protocol such as CIFS or NFS.

Each of these types of storage interconnect have strengths and weaknesses. For instance, with DAS, the upfront cost is minimal, but longer-term management costs are extremely high, especially in dynamic environments where capacity may need to be repurposed. SAN, on the other hand, has a very high upfront cost but far lower long-term costs in terms of management and data protection. NAS generally has a lower initial cost than SAN but is commonly more expensive than DAS. As clients that access NAS for storage pool access utilize network file system protocols such as CIFS and NFS, NAS is generally less applicable in certain application environments. For instance, in database application environments where the server attempts to leverage its own file system or make direct calls against a physical volume, NAS may not be the best fit due to the abstraction of the file system protocol that must be used to access the capacity.

So how does this impact application performance? Simple. The slowest component in the path of an application is typically the spinning disk on the client and the server. If the storage subsystem is adequately sized and configured, application performance will still be dependent on the speed of the rotating disk, but the characteristics of how data is accessed may be changed to improve performance. For instance, some levels of RAID provide higher levels of data throughput than others, while some merely provide an added level of data redundancy without providing much of an improvement to overall throughput.

RAID implementations remain one of the most popular options for in-server and direct-attached storage because of their performance, price point, and simplicity to implement and support. In arrays attached to SANs, RAID is commonly used behind the disk controller to provide performance and high availability. Table 2-4 shows the characteristics of commonly used RAID levels.

Table 2-4 *Commonly Used RAID Levels*

Hardware Disk Implementation	Pro	Con	Throughput	Storage Capacity	Performance Limitation
JBOD	1:1 storage capacity, no wasted space	No redundancy, low performance	Low	Equal to sum of all disks	Without additional software configuration, operations are not spread across spindles as it would be with RAID.
RAID0	Speed	No redundancy	Excellent	Equal to sum of all disks	Data is striped across all spindles, which provides very high levels of performance.
RAID1	Full 1:1 redundancy	Limited capacity	Good	Equal to half of overall disk capacity	Data must be written to two disks at the same time to provide redundancy.
RAID5	Speed and redundancy	Write penalty associated with parity calculation	Good	Equal to sum of all disks minus one disk	Parity information and data are both striped across all spindles, and each write operation requires parity calculation.

In many enterprise environments, RAID levels are abstracted from servers because storage capacity is deployed in a SAN. It is important to note, however, that some applications prefer to use spindles that are configured for a certain RAID level. For instance, an application that needs a volume with extremely high availability characteristics would most likely prefer to use a RAID-1 protected volume. An application that is performing a large number of reads from disk would prefer RAID-5, because multiple spindles could be used concurrently for read operations. An application that is constantly writing data may prefer RAID-0, because of its ability to stripe data across spindles without performance penalty.

With some subsystems, RAID levels can even be mixed to provide the best of both worlds. For instance, RAID 10 provides mirroring across equal-sized stripe sets. In this way, it provides 1:1 redundancy of the entire stripe set, and stripes read and write data across the spindles within the stripe set.

When choosing a storage interconnect, it is important to examine the performance characteristics. Many servers deployed today are still using legacy SCSI technology that limits maximum disk performance to 20 MBps or less. SAS and Fibre Channel are the more commonly used storage interconnects available today, as described in the next sections.

Serial Attached SCSI (SAS)

Serial attached SCSI (SAS) is the next generation of SCSI interconnect where communication with the drives occurs in serial, not parallel, between the controller and attached drives. With serial operation, clock rates can be increased due to minimized cross-talk, which also enables greater distances to be achieved.

SAS disk drives and controllers are the result of 20 years of learning from traditional SCSI storage devices. SAS controllers allow drives to be attached in either RAID or JBOD configurations, just as traditional SCSI allowed. RAID configurations of SAS-capable disks can produce throughput ratings of up to 3 GB per second, aiding in affordable and optimal application access.

Fiber Channel

Fiber Channel (FC) attached storage is commonly connected to the server via Lucent connectors (LCs) embedded within a small form-factor pluggable (SFP) optical adapter, such as a PCI host bus adapter (HBA). HBAs have throughput ratings of up to 4 Gbps and have become reasonably priced to implement in the data center.

FC HBAs are manufactured to support either 32-bit architectures, 64-bit architectures, or both, when interfacing with the PCI bus. This allows application performance to take advantage of a combination of an operating system and processor that may already be 64-bit enabled. If a server is already operating in 64-bit mode, it is advised to implement FC with a 64-bit-capable adapter as well.

FC HBAs are commonly supported by operating systems such as Microsoft Windows Server 2003, Red Hat Linux, and Sun Solaris. Furthermore, FC HBAs generally support direct connection to a disk subsystem (DAS) or to a Fibre Channel fabric (SAN) to access a provisioned portion of a shared array. Interestingly enough, SCSI command sets are most commonly used on top of FC interconnect.

Figure 2-18 examines how current-generation storage interconnect compares to legacy storage interconnect. This table clearly articulates the performance differences that can be found with newer-generation technology.

Figure 2-18 *Comparing Storage Interconnect Throughput*

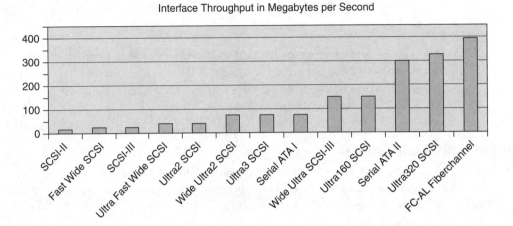

Along with examining aspects such as CPU subsystem, memory subsystem, and storage interconnect, the file system configuration should also be examined for its impact on application performance.

File System Considerations

A file system facilitates the storage needs of an application, housing any data that the application or server itself cannot hold in physical RAM. A file system is a creation of its parent, the operating system. File systems maintain many unique characteristics, including physical block size requirements, file and partition size limitations, and, occasionally, specific configurations defined by a given application. When installing an application onto a new server, the administrator must take the application's needs into consideration; not all default file system values will support optimal application performance.

Solaris

Solaris uses blocks in a consecutive manner for a logical method of disk space allocation. Applications such as Solaris Volume Manager can be used to configure and optimize a server's file system. There are two common types of file system: a raw I/O file system and the UNIX File System (UFS). Solaris 8 and later releases allow for database applications to be run directly from the UFS partition, with very good performance.

Solaris block sizes are 4 KB and 8 KB, allowing for data to be written to blocks in smaller incremental sizes. For 4-KB block sizes, data may be written in 512-B, 1-KB, 2-KB, and 4-KB fragment sizes. For 8-KB block sizes, data may be written in 1-KB, 2-KB, 4-KB, and 8-KB fragment sizes. To check the current block size configuration of a server, execute the command given in Example 2-1 as the super user or administrator of the server.

Example 2-1 *UNIX Block Size Command Output*

```
# df -g
/               (/dev/dsk/c0t0d0s0 ):    8192 block size     1024 fragment size
/proc           (/proc            ):     512 block size      512 fragment size
/etc/mnttab     (mnttab           ):     512 block size      512 fragment size
/dev/fd         (fd               ):    1024 block size     1024 fragment size
/tmp            (swap             ):    8192 block size     8192 fragment size
```

Database application vendors offer guidelines for configuring an application server's file systems to operate optimally with their application. If the disk block sizes are 4 KB, and the fragment sizes are configured to utilize 4 KB each, then buffering and memory utilization will be improved, because the amount of data that needs to be passed to disk is identical to the size of the block being written. In this way, data does not need to be manipulated or otherwise shaped to match the block size of the file system. The same rule applies to 8-KB blocks and 8-KB fragment sizes, allowing for fewer read operations prior to writing data to a specific block on the disk.

Using the **forcedirectio** option allows for data writing that spans several blocks to occur as a single I/O event. This allows database applications to bundle together events scheduled to be written to disk.

CAUTION   Although using the **forcedirectio** options does allow writes to occur faster to disk, it does bypass caching options for the file system. Some database applications are dependent on file system caching to improve overall database application performance. Implementing the **forcedirectio** option should not be done without consulting the application vendor or author.

Microsoft Windows Server 2003

Microsoft Windows Server 2003 defaults to 4-KB allocation units within the NTFS file system. Several functions of the NTFS are dependent on the 4-KB allocation unit, such as disk compression. Any other size will impact the ability to enable compression, which may not improve overall server performance on an application server.

Disk partitions of 2 GB to 2 TB utilize the 4-KB application unit by default. To change the default allocation unit size of Windows Server 2003, the Disk Management snap-in is required to change a disk's partition properties. Once an application is installed on a server and the partition housing the database is created, you should not change the allocation unit size. Any time an administrator attempts to change the allocation unit size, the disk partition must be reformatted. Reformatting will eliminate all data within the altered partition. Windows Server 2003 supports allocation unit sizes up to 64 KB in size.

HP-UX

For HP-UX, there are three common file systems, VxFS (Veritas File System), UFS (UNIX File System), and HFS (Hierarchical File System). All three of these file systems have different characteristics for their block size allocation parameters. For example, VxFS, which has a default block allocation unit size of 1 KB, supports a maximum of 8 KB per allocation unit. HFS defaults to 8 KB per block, allowing for several different options at the time the disk partition is created, ranging from 4 KB to 64 KB in size.

It is common for database applications running under an HP-UX operating system to leverage 8-KB block sizes for their file systems. 8 KB is a recommended block size for applications such as Oracle 11i and SAP. 8-KB block sizes are ideal for large transactions on the server, whereas smaller block sizes are most appropriate for database applications that call for a significant amount of random access. In the case of Oracle and other database applications, the application itself must be configured to match the disk block size for optimal and efficient application performance.

The 64-KB block sizes are viewed by many as the optimal disk allocation size for both HFS and JFS, with HFS supporting 8-KB fragment sizes, and JFS having no fragment support. These sizes may not be optimal for the application's database on the server, requiring the application vendor or author to be consulted to validate which file system format and block size should be implemented at the time of the server installation.

Linux

Red Hat Linux supports three commonly deployed operating systems:

- ext2

- ext3

- ReiserFS

Each file system has characteristics that are critical to database application performance. Areas such as block size, maximum file size supported, journaling, and maximum supported partition size all become factors when selecting the proper Linux file system.

The second extended file system (ext2) is considered the benchmark of Linux file systems. Although ext2 is supported by many database applications, ext2 is not considered to be suitable by some vendors due to a lack of journaling. Journaling is a process in which a segment of the actual disk is used to store a temporary copy of the data prior to being written to the actual data partition specific to the disk. In the event of a disk failure, any disk access intentions are read from the journaling section of the disk, allowing the system to recover after power is restored to the server.

ext2 supports a maximum partition size of 4 TB, allowing for a maximum file size within the 4-TB partition of 2 TB. The ext2 file system also supports block sizes ranging from 1 KB to 4 KB.

The ext2 file system is considered to be more efficient in terms of disk utilization than ext3, nearly eliminating the need for the use of any defragmentation tools.

The third extended file system (ext3) shares many commonalities with the ext2 file system. The primary differences can be classified as the support of journaling, as well as a method to change the file system and partition sizes of existing partitions. Journaling has been added to ext3, using a section of disk that is separate from the general data storage section of the disk.

ext3 supports three different levels of journaling:

- **Journal:** Supports the writing of both the metadata and file content to the journaling space prior to writing it to the usable data space of the disk

- **Writeback:** Differs from journal in that only the metadata is written to the journaling space of the disk

- **Ordered:** The ext3 default writes the data to the disk prior to writing the metadata to the journaling segment of the disk

Each level of journaling provides the application server increased storage reliability. Although file systems that support journaling may be a requirement, it does have a minor impact on the performance of the storage, requiring some data to be written to the disk twice. ext3 file systems do not require utilities to defragment storage to optimize disk block usage.

ReiserFS is the latest file system supported by Red Hat Linux. ReiserFS is a journaling file system, much like ext3 but supports additional features. The ReiserFS file system supports a maximum partition size of 16 TB and a maximum file size of 8 TB per file. For block sizes, the ReiserFS file system supports only a 4-KB block size, which is optimal for applications that leverage files of 4 KB or smaller. Some database applications do not support the ReiserFS file system, which may be a concern when large file support must exceed the 2-TB limit of the ext2 and ext3 file systems.

The differences in file system limitations across several operating system vendors are illustrated in Table 2-5.

Table 2-5 *File System Differences*

File System	Maximum File Size	Maximum Volume Size	Block Journaling	Meta-Data Journaling
ext2 (1-KB block)	16 GB	2048 GB	No	No
ext2 (2-KB block)	256 GB	2048 GB	No	No

continues

Table 2-5 *File System Differences (Continued)*

File System	Maximum File Size	Maximum Volume Size	Block Journaling	Meta-Data Journaling
ext2 (4-KB block)	2048 GB	2048 GB	No	No
ext2 (8-KB block)	2048 GB	2048 GB	No	No
ext3 (1-KB block)	16 GB	2048 GB	Yes	Yes
ext3 (2-KB block)	256 GB	2048 GB	Yes	Yes
ext3 (4-KB block)	2048 GB	2048 GB	Yes	Yes
Ext3 (8-KB block)	2048 GB	2048 GB	Yes	Yes
ReiserFS 3.6	17 TB	17 TB	Yes	Yes
NTFS (4-KB block)	16 TB	16 TB	No	Yes
NTFS (64-KB block)	16 TB	256 TB	No	Yes
NTFS (dynamic volume)	16 TB	64 TB	No	Yes
JFS (512-KB block)	8 EB	512 TB	Yes	No
JFS (4-KB block)	8 EB	4 PB	Yes	No

The Reiser4 file system, which has not yet been merged into the Linux operating system, has added some unique enhancements to the Linux file system. Disk block sharing allows a block that may not have been completely filled to share space with other files. Block sharing will allow for significantly better disk space utilization. Reiser4 also introduces a new concept of journaling, termed the *wandering log*. Wandering logs change the method of the initial write of file data during the journaling process, allowing data to be written anywhere in the data portion of the disk. If data is written throughout the disk, data defragmentation may be required to optimize the Reiser4 file system. The Reiser4 file system is too new to be supported by major application vendors and will require support of the Linux kernel prior to becoming supported by application vendors.

Some database applications require an alternative to traditional disk partitions that use a formatted file system. These applications use raw I/O disks or raw partitions. Eliminating the traditional barriers of file systems, raw I/O is written to a specific disk, array, or host. When using raw I/O, the application does not allow for the same type of disk administration as a traditional operating system managed partition, and is commonly managed by the database application. Raw I/O partitions are commonly faster than operating system formatted partitions, because there is less operating system overhead managing the raw partitions or disks. Raw I/O partitions are typically specified as a requirement by the application, and not the operating system. Management of the data that resides in the raw I/O partition is commonly a function of the database application.

Network Interface Cards

There are two common methods to improve the performance of the NIC. These methods involve offloading of the network traffic from the processor of the server, and allowing hosts to place data directly into other hosts' memory. The TCP/IP Offload Engine (TOE) and remote direct memory access (RDMA) acceleration methods are supported today by many operating systems. These methods allow for improved network performance without creating an increased workload on the server's processor, bus, or physical RAM.

RDMA is a process that occurs over TCP/IP. In RDMA's simplest form, one TCP/IP device has access to a second TCP/IP device's physical RAM over TCP/IP. This process allows data to be sent directly to the second device's physical RAM. As network speeds have increased beyond 1 Gbps to 10 Gbps, they introduce challenges to the server's processor: the network is becoming faster than the processor. With the intelligence built into an RDMA-supporting Ethernet network adapter, the card can process much of the traffic, placing the payload directly into the physical memory of the server.

A NIC that supports RDMA is referred to as an RNIC. RNICs do not require changes to the operating system or TCP/IP stack on the server, but operating system support may be directly required to support RDMA functions in a server. Some database application vendors have written support for RDMA directly into their applications, allowing for improved TCP/IP performance within the application server.

A TOE allows for TCP/IP traffic to be processed by the network card, instead of passively handing the TCP/IP traffic workload to the server's bus and processor. A TOE is commonly implemented on a wide array of NIC vendors' products, including Intel, QLogic, and 3Com. With the exception of Red Hat Linux, most server operating systems recognize the TOE implementation in their operating system TCP/IP stack.

Figure 2-19 illustrates the difference in CPU involvement when a network card that is TOE enabled is introduced into a supporting server and operating system. Notice that the use of a TOE can minimize the amount of system resources necessary to manage TCP connections with connected nodes.

Figure 2-19 *TOE and System Resource Utilization*

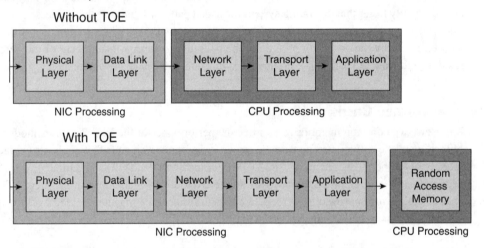

TOE-enabled NICs bring additional benefit to many applications because the workload of handling TCP/IP is moved from the server CPU and memory to the card. In this way, applications that are data-access intensive, such as Internet SCSI (storage over IP), see performance improvement due to faster handling of network data. Web servers and application servers also benefit from a TOE, due to the nature of TCP-based application protocols, such as HTTP, CIFS, and NFS, and streaming media traffic.

Summary

This chapter investigated several barriers to application performance, including the network, the traffic that traverses the network, and the hosts that reside on the network. Bandwidth, oversubscription, aggregation, and network utilization directly control the amount of data that can traverse a network connection. Other factors introduce an indirect control, including packet loss, latency, and the transport protocol.

Applications will continue to evolve into areas that will constantly test the resources of a given network and any attached resources. Servers, workstations, file systems, and underlying supporting operating systems are all items that impact the performance of a given application. Optimal application performance requires that administrators be aware of all aspects of their infrastructure, including the overall network topology, intermediary devices, and endpoints. Knowing your network, and key aspects of a network, is critical in spotting areas where application performance could be compromised.

This chapter includes the following topics:

- Viewing Network Utilization

- Employing Quality of Service

- Understanding Accelerator Control Features and Integration

CHAPTER 3

Aligning Network Resources with Business Priority

The first step in overcoming network barriers to enabling high-performance access to remote files, content, applications, and data over the WAN is to ensure that the resources of the WAN are aligned with the appropriate business priority. By aligning network resources with business priority, you can ensure that specific applications that are critical to the business are given the appropriate levels of bandwidth and response time in terms of network transmission throughput. These factors are, of course, limited by the capabilities of the physical network itself.

Aligning network resources with business priority allows IT organizations to identify network consumers, prioritize traffic accordingly, and apply policy. For instance, an IT organization may want to make sure that Voice over IP (VoIP) calls are guaranteed a minimum of 30 percent of the available bandwidth capacity on the WAN (based on the bandwidth per call and the number of expected calls), and ensure that unsanctioned Internet traffic never consumes more than 10 percent of available bandwidth capacity.

Furthermore, policy may also dictate that intermediary network devices handle traffic such as VoIP, which is sensitive to network latency and jitter, in such a way as to accommodate their low-latency requirements (for example, low-latency queuing and interleaving). To do this, IT organizations must first employ network visibility mechanisms to identify traffic on the network, followed by network control mechanisms to ensure that applications are given the right level of service on the network.

IT organizations need to determine which applications are using the network, how the network is being used, and how much of the network each consumer or application should consume. Many IT organizations find that a large percentage of their network bandwidth is consumed by unsanctioned applications, such as instant messaging, peer-to-peer file sharing, or general web surfing. When bandwidth capacity is added to the network, many IT organizations find that only a fraction of the additional capacity goes to the applications that were in need of the extra capacity, and the remainder provides more capacity for those using unsanctioned applications, thereby wasting the majority of the expenses incurred to upgrade the network.

Leveraging visibility to enable classification, prioritization, and control helps to ensure that network resources are aligned with business objectives and that applications and consumers receive the level of service from the network that they need. Employing such policy is a good practice for traditional network implementations and is foundational to employing accelerator devices, which can integrate and leverage these technologies as well.

Because many authoritative resources focus on technologies such as quality of service (QoS), Network Based Application Recognition (NBAR), NetFlow, and other features, this chapter serves as an overview to these technologies relative to how you can employ them to align network resources with business priority and application requirements. The latter part of the chapter provides an introduction to accelerators and how you can deploy them in conjunction with these value-added network services to provide end-to-end acceleration, control, prioritization, and visibility.

Viewing Network Utilization

Many network administrators today still do not know what type of traffic is consuming network capacity, what the top applications are, and who the top talkers are. Most routers, switches, and other network devices today include feature sets that provide network administrators with the information necessary to examine how the network is being used. Some of these feature sets provide real-time analysis of network utilization, and others provide a historical view of network utilization. Both types of data enable the network administrator to prove and establish a baseline for network utilization.

This section examines two commonly used mechanisms, NetFlow and NBAR, for viewing network utilization characteristics at a very granular level. Once collected, this data is useful to network administrators not only to get a better grasp on how the network is being used, but also to choose relative priority among applications, data, and nodes that consume network capacity.

NetFlow

NetFlow is a set of instrumentation tools, pioneered by Cisco, that allows network administrators to characterize network operation and utilization. NetFlow was developed and patented by Cisco in 1996 as NetFlow version 1. NetFlow v1 provided basic characterization of flows based on the common 5-tuple (source and destination IP addresses, source and destination TCP ports, and IP protocol).

NetFlow has evolved into a more robust system of flow characterization, NetFlow v5, which is the most commonly used version of NetFlow today. NetFlow v6 added additional details related to encapsulation. NetFlow v7 provided extensions to support the Catalyst 5000 family switch with a NetFlow feature card (NFFC) installed. NetFlow v8 provided enhancements necessary to enable router-based aggregation. Router-based aggregation allows the router to group multiple traditional flows together, thereby minimizing router resource utilization.

NetFlow v9, the latest version of NetFlow at the time of this writing, provides a flexible and extensible export format. NetFlow v9 (RFC 3954) accommodates new NetFlow-supported technologies such as IP Multicast, Multiprotocol Label Switching (MPLS), Network Address Translation (NAT), and Border Gateway Protocol (BGP). Given the widespread adoption of NetFlow, NetFlow v9 became the foundation for the IP Flow Information Export (IPFIX) standard, which can be found as RFC 3917.

NetFlow allows network administrators to have visibility into the network, which is necessary to better understand the following:

- **Applications and network utilization:** Enables network administrators to examine a history of traffic flows to determine how many flows exist between connected nodes and the amount of bandwidth capacity being utilized between them.

- **Overall network capacity consumption:** Allows network administrators to better understand how much of the network is being utilized holistically to determine if additional capacity is required to support productivity and business-critical applications.

NetFlow is primarily used for baselining application requirements and network utilization for the purpose of determining what configuration of prioritization and control should be employed. NetFlow can also be used to assess the impact of changes to the network, assess network anomalies, identify security vulnerabilities, provide facilities for charge-back and bill-back, diagnose network performance problems (such as bandwidth "hogs"), and access monitoring. Given the focus of this book on application performance, these capabilities of NetFlow are not discussed.

NetFlow operation involves two key components:

- A NetFlow-enabled device
- A NetFlow collector

NetFlow-Enabled Device

A NetFlow-enabled device (which includes most routers and switches), when configured, keeps a cache of IP flows that have traversed that device. An IP flow is a series of packets with matching packet attributes. An IP flow generally includes five attributes and up to a maximum of seven attributes, as follows:

- **Source IP address:** The source IP address within the packet being transmitted

- **Destination IP address:** The destination IP address within the packet being transmitted

- **IP protocol number and type:** The protocol as defined by the IP packet header (that is, TCP, UDP, ICMP, or others)

- **Source port:** The source port number of the Layer 4 header

- **Destination port:** The destination port number of the Layer 4 header

- **Type of service (ToS) identifier:** The bits tagged within the type of service, or ToS, byte within the IP header, denoting priority

- **Router or switch interface:** The interface at which the packet from the flow was received

When packets with matching attributes are identified on an interface configured for NetFlow, they are grouped internally by the NetFlow device and counters are generated and maintained against the matching packets. This information is stored in a NetFlow cache and contains details about each of the identified flows and counter data related to those flows. Furthermore, additional information can be gathered about these flows, including:

- **Timestamps:** Help to determine the longevity of the flow to provide analysis and summarization of traffic and network utilization based on the time of day

- **Next-hop information:** Includes the next-hop IP address and routing protocol–specific information such as the BGP autonomous system (AS)

- **Subnet mask:** Used to determine the network that the flow is related to

- **TCP flags:** Bits contained within the TCP header that identify handshakes and other signaling, including synchronization and resets

You can examine this information in real time using a device's CLI or GUI, which is helpful in troubleshooting and examining real-time utilization. You also can configure the device to export flows in the cache that have terminated to a node on the network (typically a PC or a server) that is configured to receive export packets containing NetFlow data, commonly called a *NetFlow collector.*

NetFlow Collector

Exporting terminated flows (that is, when a TCP connection is torn down) to a NetFlow collector is helpful because it not only enables long-term retention of statistics related to previously seen flows for offline analysis, reporting, and baselining, but also removes the need for the network device itself (that is, a router or switch) to maintain this data long-term, thereby ensuring precious NetFlow device resources are kept relatively free. These flows are exported to the NetFlow collector using UDP packets and typically contain information for 30 to 50 flows at a time.

Figure 3-1 shows the process of NetFlow collection on a router with export to a collector. Figure 3-2 shows a more granular view of the data collected by NetFlow.

Figure 3-1 *NetFlow Collection and Export*

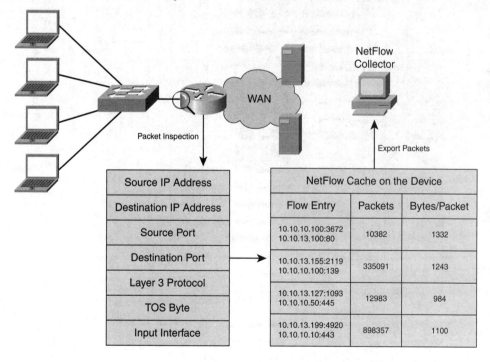

Figure 3-2 *Data Collected and Exported by NetFlow*

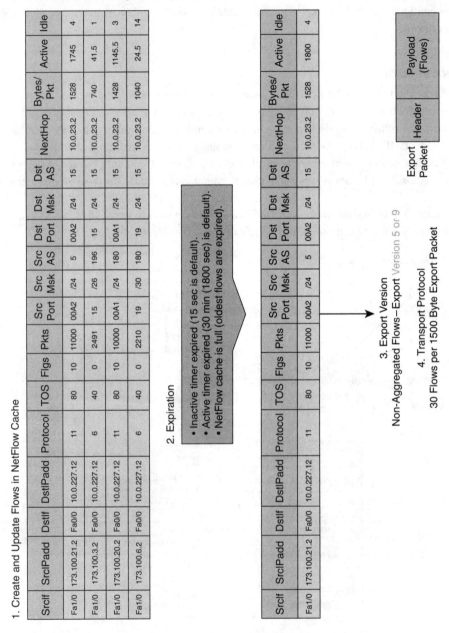

Many applications exist that allow for in-depth and thorough analysis of NetFlow data, including products from Cisco, CA, Hewlett-Packard, InfoVista, NetQoS, and many others. These applications are helpful in analyzing the data presented by NetFlow and correlating the data into various reports, including these:

- **Top talkers:** The nodes that consume the most bandwidth

- **Top applications:** The applications that consume the most bandwidth

Many of these applications also couple other mechanisms for analyzing performance metrics such as Simple Network Management Protocol (SNMP) polling, remote monitoring (RMON), and traffic analysis using port mirroring. For example, Figure 3-3 shows a report generated using NetQoS SuperAgent that provides insight into who the top talkers on a given network are.

Figure 3-3   *Top Talkers Report (Source: NetQoS)*

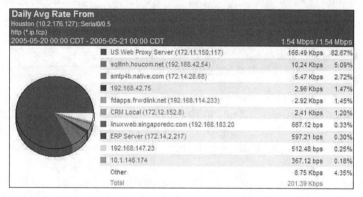

Figure 3-4 shows another report generated by NetQoS SuperAgent that displays the top applications found on the network.

Figure 3-4   *Top Applications Report (Source: NetQoS)*

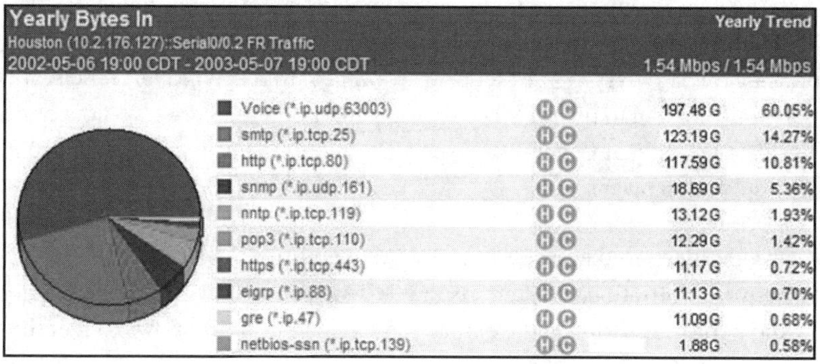

Figure 3-5 shows a NetQoS SuperAgent report that displays network utilization trends over a 4-hour period, and a breakdown of which applications were identified during each sample period. More information about NetQoS can be found at http://www.netqos.com.

Figure 3-5 *Network Utilization Report (Source: NetQoS)*

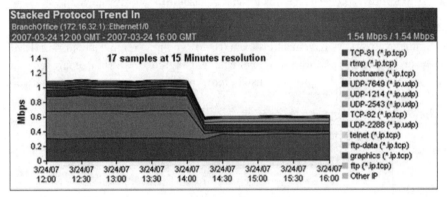

With the information provided by NetFlow, network administrators can begin to fully understand how the network is being utilized, which applications are consuming network resources at what time of day, and which nodes are consuming the most available network capacity. Then, they can begin the process of classification and prioritization.

For more information on Cisco IOS NetFlow, including a detailed technical overview, visit http://www.cisco.com/go/netflow.

Network Based Application Recognition

NBAR is another mechanism that network administrators can employ on network devices such as routers or switches to automatically discover application protocols and collect statistics. You can use NBAR in conjunction with NetFlow to provide a more granular view of specific applications that are using the network. While NetFlow examines primarily Layer 3 (network) and Layer 4 (transport) information to quantify network consumption on a flow-by-flow basis, NBAR examines data not only at Layer 4 (transport layer, port identification), but also all the way up to Layer 7 (application layer).

NBAR provides deep packet inspection (DPI) capabilities to classify and quantify application-specific network utilization. This means that NBAR can go beyond examination of traditional IP address and port information and examine the payload of traffic flows to identify the application that is being transported across the network. This allows NBAR to uniquely classify and differentiate application traffic within a shared connection (for instance, a print job within a remote desktop session). Figure 3-6 shows a comparison of NBAR and NetFlow in terms of which aspects of network traffic each can examine.

Figure 3-6 *NBAR and NetFlow*

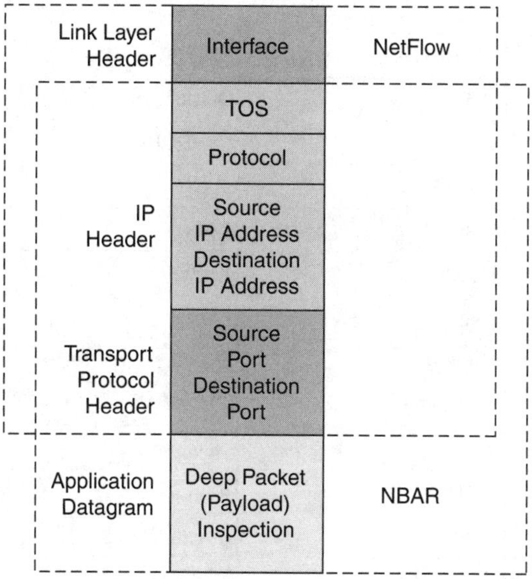

Link Layer Header	Interface	NetFlow
IP Header	TOS	
	Protocol	
	Source IP Address Destination IP Address	
Transport Protocol Header	Source Port Destination Port	
Application Datagram	Deep Packet (Payload) Inspection	NBAR

While both NetFlow and NBAR provide flow identification at Layer 3 and Layer 4, each provides a different set of capabilities that are useful to a network administrator who wishes to align network resources with relative business and application priority. NetFlow is helpful in tracking the longevity of flows on the network and providing the data necessary to analyze network utilization characteristics. NBAR provides administrators with an application-based view rather than a network-based view, yielding insight into which applications are actually the consumers of the available network resources. NBAR is used not only for visibility into application flows traversing a network, but also to provide traffic classification necessary to employ QoS actions.

NOTE The following list summarizes applications that NBAR is able to recognize. For more information on Cisco IOS NBAR, including a detailed technical overview, visit http://www.cisco.com/go/nbar.

Enterprise Applications	Security and Tunneling	Network Mail Services	Internet
Citrix ICA	GRE	IMAP	FTP
pcAnywhere	IPINIP	POP3	Gopher
Novadigm	IPsec	Exchange	HTTP
SAP	L2TP	Notes	IRC
Routing Protocols	MS-PPTP	SMTP	Telnet
BGP	SFTP	**Directory**	TFTP
EGP	SHTTP	DHCP/BOOTP	NNTP
EIGRP	SIMAP	Finger	NetBIOS
OSPF	SIRC	DNS	NTP
RIP	SLDAP	Kerberos	Print
Network Management	SNNTP	LDAP	X-Windows
ICMP	SPOP3	**Streaming Media**	**Peer-to-Peer**
SNMP	STELNET	CU-SeeMe	BitTorrent
Syslog	SOCKS	Netshow	Direct Connect
RPC	SSH	Real Audio	eDonkey/eMule
NFS	**Voice**	StreamWorks	FastTrack
SUN-RPC	H.323	VDOLive	Gnutella
Database	RTCP	RTSP	Kazaa
SQL*NET	RTP	MGCP	WinMX
Microsoft SQL Server	SIP	**Signaling**	
	SCCP/Skinny	RSVP	
	Skype		

Employing Quality of Service

The previous section presented two means of examining the network to gather a fundamental understanding of how the network is being used. This information forms the foundation from which you can make decisions about how to align network resources to accommodate the relative priority of applications and hosts that are using the network. This information is also important to ensure that the network is configured in such a way that it provides the appropriate levels of handling and control based on application and business requirements.

Using information gathered through NetFlow or other mechanisms (for instance, network analysis modules or accelerators with monitoring capabilities, both of which generally provide similar reporting capabilities), network administrators can then define what levels of service need to be applied to different types of traffic and how this data should be handled. These same tools also serve as a means of validation after such policies have been implemented within the network to verify that the application requirements and business priority definitions are being met.

Without QoS, best-effort handling is provided to all flows on the network, thereby introducing the possibility that noncritical traffic may delay or block the service of business-critical traffic or traffic from applications that have sensitivities to network characteristics such as latency or loss. With best-effort handling, all traffic is considered equal, as shown in Figure 3-7. In this figure, peer-to-peer sharing consumes all the available network resources, leading to bandwidth starvation for the applications that need precious WAN bandwidth to drive user productivity. Such situations could quickly lead to employee frustration with business applications, loss of revenue, poor morale, and job dissatisfaction.

Figure 3-7 *Networks with Best-Effort Delivery—No Quality of Service*

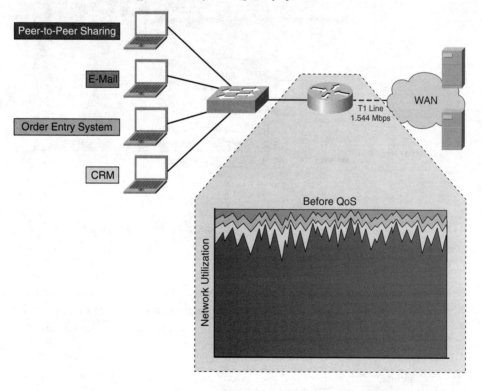

With QoS configured, appropriate handling can be provided to traffic flows based on classification and priority. As shown in Figure 3-8, the result is that the business-critical applications that demand bandwidth and service on the network are unimpeded even when unsanctioned traffic is present. In this example, peer-to-peer sharing is shown as being permitted, and it should be noted that such applications could be blocked altogether.

Figure 3-8 *Networks with Quality of Service*

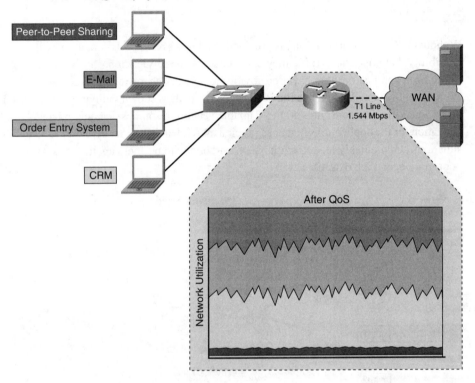

> **NOTE** Figure 3-8 shows peer-to-peer sharing as permitted, however, this traffic could be blocked rather than permitted.

With QoS in place, network administrators are able to better allocate available network capacity to those applications that need it the most. This allocation of network resources with business priority helps to ensure precious network capacity is used by sanctioned applications, thereby encouraging user productivity.

The QoS architecture is built around a behavioral model that comprises the following four key functions, each of which is outlined in the following sections. These functions provide the facilities necessary to align network resources with business priority and application requirements.

■ **Classification:** Identifies application and traffic flows on the network. Once identified, further action and specific handling can be applied to the flow.

- **Pre-queuing:** Includes operations that are performed against flows prior to consuming network device (router or switch) resources such as queues. The operations include dropping packets (undesirable flows), traffic conditioning (policing), and marking relative priority on the packets themselves.

- **Queuing and scheduling:** Enforce priority of selected packet streams through the use of configurable queuing mechanisms, such as high-priority handling of delay-sensitive traffic, selective delay of lower-priority traffic during periods of congestion, traffic conditioning (shaping), and enforcement of bandwidth allocation.

- **Post-queuing:** Improves link throughput using optional operations such as packet compression, header compression, and link fragmentation and interleaving (LFI).

The behavioral model provides the facilities necessary to align network resources to business priority and to optimize user productivity over the network. Figure 3-9 shows an example.

Figure 3-9 *QoS Behavioral Model*

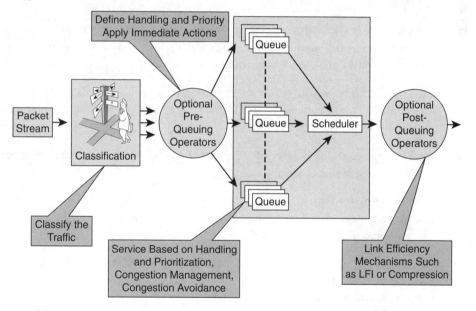

Packet Classification

Packet classification allows a network device (such as a router, a switch, or even an accelerator) to partition network traffic into multiple priority levels or classes of service based on a variety of match conditions. These match conditions help the network device to differentiate flows from one another based on packet, flow, or application characteristics. With regard to the QoS behavioral model, as packets enter a device, they undergo classification such that the device is able to discern what application the flow represents and how to appropriately handle that traffic. This serves as the foundation by which a device can provide differentiated service among equal or unequal flows.

Most network devices provide an array of match conditions that can be used to examine traffic for purposes of classification. The most common classifiers include the following:

- **Access control lists (ACL):** ACLs (standard, extended, or otherwise) allow for explicit permission or denial of a packet to be matched based on the match conditions defined within the ACLs as parameters. These match conditions include IP protocol number, routing protocol parameters, ICMP, IGMP, source or destination IP address, source or destination TCP or UDP port assignment, and more. Some of these characteristics can be used as match conditions without the use of an ACL. These match conditions are the most frequently used, as they cover nearly the entire set of Layer 3 and Layer 4 parameters used by a packet or flow.

- **MAC address:** The link layer addresses contained in the frame being examined by the network device can be used as a match condition for classification.

- **VLAN identifier:** The VLAN ID of a tagged frame can be used as a match condition to identify which VLAN a packet was received on. This allows for differentiated handling of packets and flows based on VLAN.

- **Input interface:** The interface that the packet was received from on the network device itself can be used as a match condition. This allows for differentiated handling of packets and flows based on the physical interface being used.

- **Previous DSCP/ToS settings:** Previously marked differentiated services code point (DSCP) bits within the type of service (ToS) field can be used for packet classification for packets received by the network device.

- **Class of service:** The class of service (CoS) bits previously marked within a link layer header can be used as a means of classification.

- **Packet length:** The length of the packet received can be used as a classifier. For instance, it may be desirable to classify small packets and large packets to adjust the way the network device handles packets based on their size.

- **NBAR:** NBAR is used not only for protocol discovery and to identify which applications are found on the network, but also to provide classification for those applications. NBAR, when used for classification, can provide standard Layer 4 classification (based on port identification) or Layer 7 classification (by examining the payload of a packet).

Pre-Queuing Operators

Once packets have been classified, the next set of functions in the QoS behavior model, pre-queuing operations, are employed. Pre-queuing operations are employed before queue capacity in the network device is consumed. Pre-queuing operations ensure that queue capacity is used only by those application flows that are sanctioned on the network. Pre-queuing operations can also result in the marking, or coloring, of packets, which allows the network device itself, along with any upstream intermediary network device that uses the same coloring scheme, to correctly understand the relative priority and handling requirements of the packets being received. In addition to packet marking, pre-queuing operations include packet dropping and policing.

Packet Marking

Packet marking involves the manipulation of a 1-byte (8-bit) field within the IP packet header called the type of service, or ToS, byte. Network devices use this byte of data to determine the relative priority and handling requirements of incoming packets. The ToS byte contains data for one of two widely adopted mechanisms:

- Integrated Services (IntServ)

- Differentiated Services (DiffServ)

In either case, a series of bits is flagged within the ToS byte to identify the relative priority and handling requirements of the packet. Accurate handling of marked packets can be ensured only when adjacent devices are in agreement about how packets are handled based on their marking. Figure 3-10 shows the IP packet header containing the ToS byte.

Figure 3-10 *IP Packet Header Containing ToS Byte*

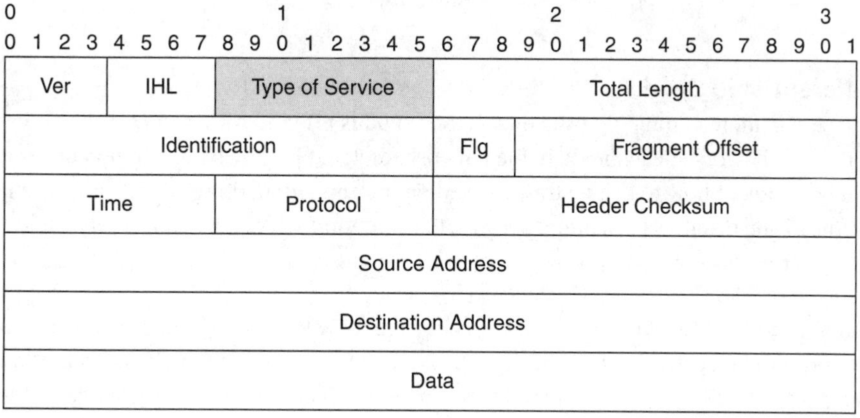

Integrated Services

IntServ is commonly referred to as *hard QoS* due to its ability to set flags related to reliability, bandwidth, and latency and also its reliance on the Resource Reservation Protocol (RSVP) to signal and reserve the desired QoS for each flow in the network. IntServ uses the first 3 bits of the ToS byte for IP Precedence (priority) and the remaining 5 bits to define the need for maximum reliability, throughput, minimum delay, and cost. The first 3 bits used by IntServ represent up to eight levels of relative priority. Table 3-1 shows the defaults for these levels, with the lower values representing lower levels of priority.

Table 3-1   *Integrated Services Priority Levels*

Binary	Decimal	Priority Level
000	0	Routine
001	1	Priority
010	2	Immediate
011	3	Flash
100	4	Flash override
101	5	Critical
110	6	Internetwork control
111	7	Network control

IntServ requires configuration of intermediary network devices and end nodes, and as such can be seen as a complex end-to-end system to configure in light of its capabilities. Network utilization can increase slightly due to the overhead of refreshing the end-to-end QoS policy and maintenance of state information at each network device in the path, which hinders scalability. Due to the complexity of implementing IntServ, many organizations have chosen to implement DiffServ as a less complicated alternative. However, given IntServ's robust capabilities, it is still considered the strongest solution for providing end-to-end QoS.

Differentiated Services

DiffServ is more commonly used than IntServ and is referred to as *soft QoS* due to its reliance on per-hop behaviors at each node in the network, dictated largely by a common understanding and configuration of how to handle traffic based on the applied marking. The result is far less network overhead and resource utilization, because the configuration can remain largely static and does not require constant synchronization.

Furthermore, bandwidth and handling do not need to be requested from each node within the network. Rather, predefined per-hop behavior dictates the handling of classified traffic at each hop. In this way, DiffServ is often referred to as the more efficient and more scaleable end-to-end QoS model when compared to IntServ. Unlike IntServ, which uses 5 bits of the ToS byte for signaling and control flags, DiffServ does not use control flags, thereby allowing it to consume a larger quantity of bits within the ToS byte and providing a greater degree of differentiation. DiffServ uses 6 bits of the ToS byte, thereby allowing for up to 64 differentiated levels of traffic. Although 64 differentiated levels of traffic is significant, many enterprise organizations commonly use 8 or fewer. On the other hand, most service providers offer only four differentiated levels of traffic.

DiffServ uses the ToS byte in such a way that it provides backward compatibility with IntServ implementations. The first 3 bits are used as a class selector and the next 3 bits are used to assign drop precedence. Note that in any case, per-hop behaviors may differ for each intermediary node in the network path between two communicating hosts, and as such, this should be understood in advance. For instance, organizations that use a managed WAN from a service provider may be able to negotiate appropriate handling of packets marked in a certain way within the provider cloud.

For more information on DiffServ, visit: http://www.cisco.com/en/US/tech/tk543/tk766/ technologies_white_paper09186a00800a3e2f.shtml.

Traffic Policing

Traffic conditioning is another pre-queuing operation that can be performed on traffic. Traffic conditioning is a mechanism that can selectively drop incoming traffic to ensure an appropriate level of bandwidth consumption through a network device such as a router. This is commonly called *policing*.

Policing helps to ensure that the amount of data a device such as a router receives does not exceed the physical capacity of the next-hop link. Policing is commonly used in conjunction with shaping, but the two differ significantly.

Policing enforces a strict bandwidth capacity for traffic that is entering a router queue, thereby ensuring that the amount of traffic in queue does not exceed the capacity of the next-hop link or the configured policy. Traffic entering the router queue that exceeds this rate is immediately dropped. For flows that use TCP as a transport, detection of a lost segment is used as an indicator by the transmitting node that congestion has been encountered, and the sender adjusts the transmission rate accordingly.

Shaping, on the other hand, which is described in more detail in the next section, allows the incoming packets to enter the device queues even if the packets are received at a rate higher than that of the next-hop link or configured policy. The queue itself is then serviced according to the capacity of the next-hop link or configured policy. In this way, shaping queues packets rather than immediately dropping them, assuming the queue capacity is large enough to hold the incoming packets. Figure 3-11 examines the use of policing as a means of traffic conditioning.

Again, pre-queuing operators have three purposes: to mark classified traffic appropriately to ensure that it is handled properly throughout the network by intermediary network devices; to drop unnecessary or excess traffic; and to conform application flow throughput so that it does not consume more network capacity than allocated or physically available.

Figure 3-11 *Using Policing for Traffic Conditioning*

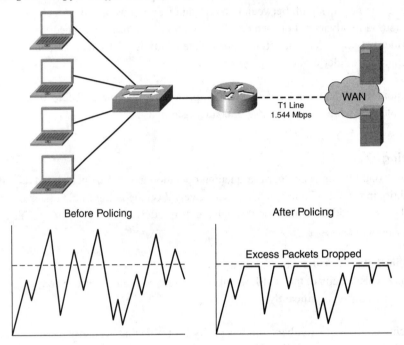

Queuing and Scheduling

Once traffic has been classified (identified) and pre-queuing operators have been applied (policing, dropping), the router then queues traffic for service onto the next-hop link. *Queuing* is defined as the way a node temporarily stores data while waiting for system resources to become available to act upon that data. The queues within the network device are serviced based on the configuration of the router and link speed. This layer of the QoS behavioral model ensures that the router services packets according to the application demand and business priority. Furthermore, this layer ensures that packets are forwarded in such a way that network capacity is more efficiently used.

As packets enter a queue, the router must schedule the service of those packets. Queuing and scheduling go hand in hand: one function temporarily holds data while waiting for resources (queuing), and the other determines when the data is to be serviced and how (scheduling). Other functions are also applied during queuing and scheduling, including shaping, congestion management, and congestion avoidance.

Not all packets are created equal, and neither are the applications that cause packets to be exchanged between end nodes. Some applications are more sensitive to network conditions and QoS metrics than others. Applications use different means of exchanging data, and the architecture of process-to-process data exchange may cause applications to behave differently under different network conditions. For instance, interactive voice and video traffic, which is transported by an unreliable transport such as UDP, is considered sensitive to link quality and changes in network service level. In this way, interactive voice and video quality can be compromised by not forwarding packets in a timely fashion, or by allowing the transmission of these flows to be delayed (congestion) due to the transmission of other flows on the network.

Furthermore, the quality of the data being received (that is, the sound of the other person's voice on the other end of the phone call, or the stream of video and audio that is being examined, for example) might be compromised if too many packets are lost in transit. In many cases, voice and video encoding can accommodate a reasonable amount of loss through predictive algorithms; however, these types of data are commonly classified and marked as requiring high-priority and low-latency handling to ensure that the sound of the other person's voice or the image being viewed is not compromised during congestion scenarios.

Other applications that are transactional in nature commonly use TCP as a transport (for reliability) and might not be as sensitive to packet loss or jitter but can be impacted by delays in servicing the packets within the network. This type of data will likely need to be classified as requiring low-latency handling as well. Less-sensitive applications that commonly use bulk movement of data over reliable transport protocols, such as file transfers or e-mail, may need to be handled with lower priority and serviced in such a way that the performance of transactional applications and the quality of interactive communications protocols are not compromised.

The following multiple levels of queuing are available, each providing a different type of service to packets that are queued:

- First in, first out (FIFO)

- Priority queuing

- Weighted fair queuing (WFQ)

The following sections describe each queuing mechanism as well as traffic shaping.

FIFO Queuing

Most networking devices implement a basic FIFO queuing mechanism. FIFO queuing places packets from all flows entering a common interface into a common queue. As packets enter interfaces in a serial fashion, the first packet received is also the first packet that is serviced.

Using FIFO queuing provides no means of QoS, because there is no differentiation of packets or flows. With FIFO queuing, a large bulk data transfer that is sharing a router interface with other application flows may quickly compromise the interface's queues, causing service starvation for other applications on the network. For instance, an interactive voice call between two users across the network could be impacted if another user is transferring a large file to a file server through the same router interface. FIFO generally is implemented only on high-speed interfaces, because the likelihood of congestion is far less than on a low-speed interface.

Priority Queuing

Priority queuing is a technique that allows multiple queues to be used and assigns each queue a relative priority. Priority queuing ensures that traffic entering a high-priority queue is always serviced before traffic waiting in a lower-priority queue, and provides the level of service needed to ensure that high-priority traffic (such as internetwork control and voice conversations) is serviced first.

The drawback with priority queuing is that higher-priority traffic always takes precedence and is serviced first, which could lead to starvation, or blocking, of flows waiting in lower-priority queues should a large number of high-priority conversations exist. This can create performance challenges for applications that are assigned to lower-priority queues, because they simply do not receive an adequate level of service from the network. In some cases, priority queuing is automatically configured with a bandwidth maximum to ensure that other queues are not starved.

Figure 3-12 shows an example of priority queuing.

Figure 3-12 *Priority Queuing*

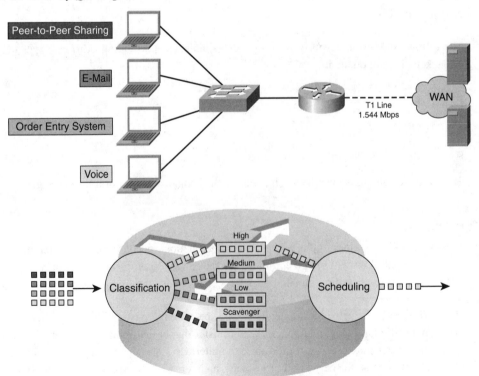

Weighted Fair Queuing

Weighted fair queuing overcomes the issue of lower-priority queue starvation by allowing each of the queues to be assigned a weight. This weight identifies the amount of service that the queue can consume. Configuring a queue to consume only a portion of the available service allows the scheduler to provide some level of service to packets in lower-weight queues even if there are still packets waiting in the higher-weight queues.

Figure 3-13 illustrates an example of WFQ. Comparing Figure 3-12 and Figure 3-13 shows how WFQ can overcome the challenges with priority queuing starvation to ensure some level of fairness among packets that are queued.

Figure 3-13   *Weighted Fair Queuing*

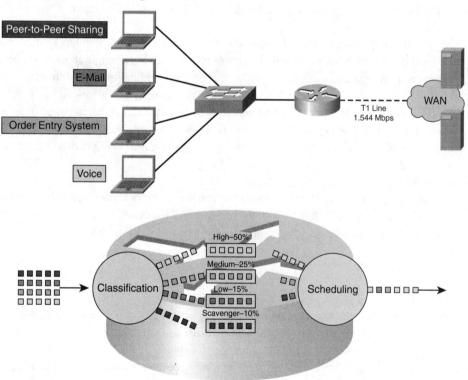

WFQ can be extended using "classes." By using match criteria such as identified protocol, input interface, or granular ACLs, traffic can be queued in a weighted fair fashion based on the class that the packets are matched with.

Bandwidth can be assigned to each of the classes to ensure that flows consume network capacity only up to the specified limit. These queues can also be limited in terms of the number of packets that are held in queue. When a queue defined for a particular class of traffic becomes full, either packets at the tail can be dropped from the queue to allow additional data to be queued (the dropped data may require retransmission by the end node) or weighted random early detection (WRED) can be used to drop packets based on the configured drop policy and markings that exist within the ToS byte of the packet. This allows the router to selectively control how much data is held in the queue based on the drop policy, in an effort to mitigate queue congestion and network congestion by throttling the transmission source by means of packet loss.

Referring to Chapter 2, "Barriers to Application Performance," when packet loss is detected by a node using a connection-oriented, reliable transport protocol such as TCP, it triggers a decrease in transmission throughput. Likewise, with the router selectively dropping packets before and during periods of congestion, end-node applications using protocols such as TCP as a transport are proactively throttled to mitigate larger-scale congestion problems. In this way, the transmission protocol is said to be normalizing around the available network throughput.

Other forms of queuing exist, and many network devices allow multiple levels of queuing to be intermixed. This allows network administrators to provide very configurable service policies for converged networks that carry voice, video, transaction applications, and other types of data through a common and shared infrastructure. For instance, hierarchical queuing employs a combination of queuing architectures concurrently. An example of hierarchical queuing is where low-latency queuing mechanisms such as priority queuing are used for latency and loss-sensitive applications such as voice and video, and class-based WFQ is used for interactive applications.

With hierarchical queuing, the network device can use the right form of queuing based on application requirements while providing the flexibility necessary to ensure adequate levels of service for all applications. Such a compromise can be met only when using hierarchical queuing architectures.

Traffic Shaping

Traffic shaping, also known as rate limiting, is applied as part of the queuing and scheduling subsystem of a network device. Traffic shaping is used to smooth the output flow of packets leaving a queue in order to control the amount of bandwidth that is consumed by a particular flow or class. As described in the previous section, traffic policing is used to drop incoming packets when a specified rate has been exceeded. Traffic shaping, however, allows the packets exceeding the specified rate to be received, assuming the queue has capacity. With traffic shaping, the servicing of the queue is done at a rate equal to the configured policy or the next-hop link. In this way, traffic shaping does not drop packets unless queue capacity is exceeded; rather, it throttles the servicing of the queue according to policy or network capacity.

Figure 3-14 provides an example of traffic shaping. Notice that, compared to Figure 3-11, traffic shaping allows packets exceeding the configured rate to be queued and serviced, whereas policing simply drops the packets.

Figure 3-14   *Traffic Shaping*

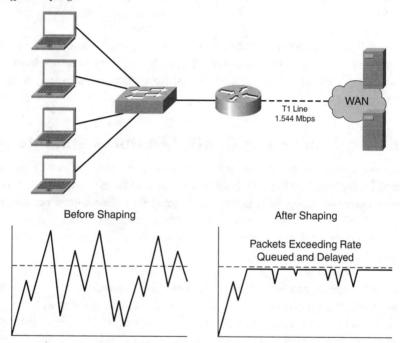

Post-Queuing Optimization

Traffic that has been released from a queue by the scheduler according to queuing policy and shaping then passes through a series of post-queuing optimizations. Post-queuing optimizations help to ensure optimized delivery of packets across the network by interleaving packets from small flows with packets of larger flows and also by compressing packet headers.

Although localized queuing and scheduling certainly can overcome the issue of localized latency, jitter, and loss for interactive applications such as voice and video, upstream device queues can still pose a threat to this traffic because the link will be shared with other applications that transfer in bulk and use larger packets. Furthermore, the links on upstream devices may also be points of aggregation for a larger number of locations, thereby exacerbating the problem. Upstream network devices that employ queuing may delay smaller packets even if the appropriate level of queuing and service has been deployed on the first network device that receives them.

Link fragmentation and interleaving (LFI) is a means by which a router or other network device can fragment larger packets from applications that transfer in bulk (such as file transfers and print jobs) such that smaller packets from interactive voice applications can be interleaved. This allows upstream devices to receive a fair mix of packets from both types of applications and minimizes the opportunity for larger packets to potentially delay the service of smaller packets for higher-priority interactive applications.

You can also employ packet header compression to minimize the amount of capacity consumed on the network by overhead data such as packet headers, which can comprise an especially high percentage of overall data given that these interactive applications are using particularly small packet sizes.

Understanding Accelerator Control Features and Integration

The previous sections in this chapter outlined a few of the many key network technologies that you can employ to help understand how the network is used and to effectively align network resources with the relative business priority of the applications that consume those network resources. Put simply, by gaining a firm understanding of how the network is used and then implementing an appropriate set of control and manageability services, the administrator can establish the foundation for an application optimized network.

All accelerator devices and technologies have some form of posture toward the functions that are implemented within the network: accelerators either work in conjunction with these functions, or, they can defeat these functions. The introduction of accelerator technology can be either disruptive or complementary to the functions deployed in intermediary network devices. The posture of accelerators relative to the features in the network that are used for visibility and control is largely dictated by the way optimization services are implemented in the accelerators themselves and also by the way in which accelerators are introduced and integrated into the network.

The following section examines the primary purpose of an accelerator and the functionality that it provides. The subsequent sections examine how accelerators are integrated into the network and how optimization services are implemented.

Overview of Accelerator Technology

Network accelerators provide a combination of functions to help improve the performance of applications over a network. These functions help to mitigate many of the performance-limiting factors in enterprise networks today such as those discussed in previous chapters: bandwidth disparity, congestion, packet loss, and latency, among other things.

For many applications, the level of acceleration provided when accessing applications and data over a WAN where accelerators are deployed is similar to that found when accessing the same applications and data over a LAN. Thus, accelerators not only help to improve the performance of user access to data and applications that are already centralized and accessed over a WAN but also provide performance levels necessary to enable the centralization of resources that are commonly deployed in a distributed fashion.

With accelerator technology, IT organizations are able to more confidently deploy centralized applications and infrastructure while also enabling the consolidation of a broader array of services into fewer locations to better meet data protection, compliance, cost, and management requirements without compromising the levels of performance that users require to be productive. Accelerators accomplish this monumental task by employing functionality in two key areas, WAN optimization and application acceleration, each of which will be explained in great detail in the upcoming chapters.

WAN Optimization

WAN optimization is a set of services that overcomes the performance limitations caused by transport protocols, network conditions, and network utilization. The three most common WAN optimization services employed by accelerators include

- TCP optimization

- Data suppression

- Compression

Many accelerators offer WAN optimization capabilities beyond these three services. This book examines only these three services because they commonly provide the foundational services for WAN optimization.

TCP Optimization

TCP is particularly challenged in WAN environments due to the connection-oriented, guaranteed-delivery behavior of the protocol. Furthermore, TCP generally has only a limited amount of memory capacity assigned to each connection, meaning only a small amount of data can be in flight at a given time. Many of the limitations of TCP are self-imposed by the nodes that are exchanging data; that is, off-the-shelf operating systems have limited TCP stacks that do not help facilitate high-performance transmission of data over a WAN.

Figure 3-15 shows how TCP can be latency sensitive and inefficient in terms of retransmission when packet loss is encountered. As the figure shows, TCP exponentially increases throughput. In environments with high latency, it could take a considerable length of time before a large amount of data could be transmitted per network round trip. When the loss of a packet is detected, TCP is forced to retransmit the entire set of data contained within the window that experienced the loss, leading to inefficiency of network utilization and poor performance.

Figure 3-15 *TCP Challenges*

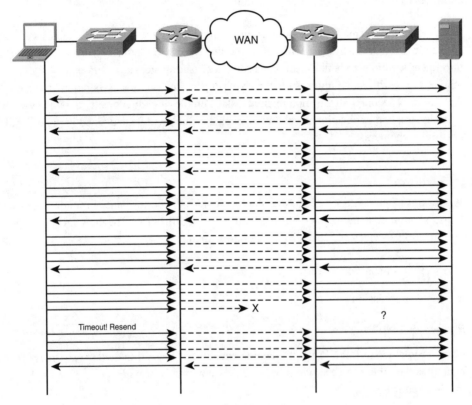

TCP optimization capabilities help TCP applications better utilize the existing network by overcoming limitations imposed by network latency, bandwidth, packet loss, and the TCP stack itself. Many of these services are implemented as part of a TCP proxy, which allows the accelerator to temporarily buffer data on behalf of clients and servers so that high throughput and reliability are achieved over the WAN.

TCP optimization commonly consists of the following optimizations:

- **Virtual window scaling:** Allows the WAN bandwidth to be more effectively utilized by the connection by increasing the window size. This allows a much larger amount of data to be outstanding and unacknowledged in the network at any given time.

- **Loss mitigation:** Enables more intelligent retransmission and error-correction algorithms to ensure that the impact of packet loss is minimized.

- **Advanced congestion avoidance:** Changes the behavior of transport protocols to enable better packet-loss recovery handling and bandwidth scalability.

Figure 3-16 illustrates an accelerator architecture where a TCP proxy is implemented. Notice that each of the accelerator devices terminates the adjacent TCP connection. In this way, the accelerator provides localized handling of TCP data with the adjacent client or server. By buffering TCP data locally and managing optimized connections between accelerator peers, unruly WAN conditions can be handled by the accelerator on behalf of the adjacent client or server, thereby shielding them.

Figure 3-16   *TCP Proxy and TCP Optimization*

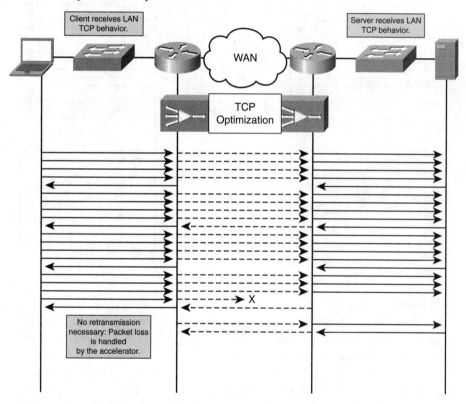

In contrast, Figure 3-17 illustrates an accelerator architecture that does not use a TCP proxy. As shown in the figure, the accelerator is unable to locally buffer TCP data and manage WAN events such as packet loss on behalf of the adjacent client or server. In this way, the client and server do not experience a LAN-like TCP behavior, as is experienced when using accelerators that implement a TCP proxy.

Figure 3-17   *Accelerators Without TCP Proxy*

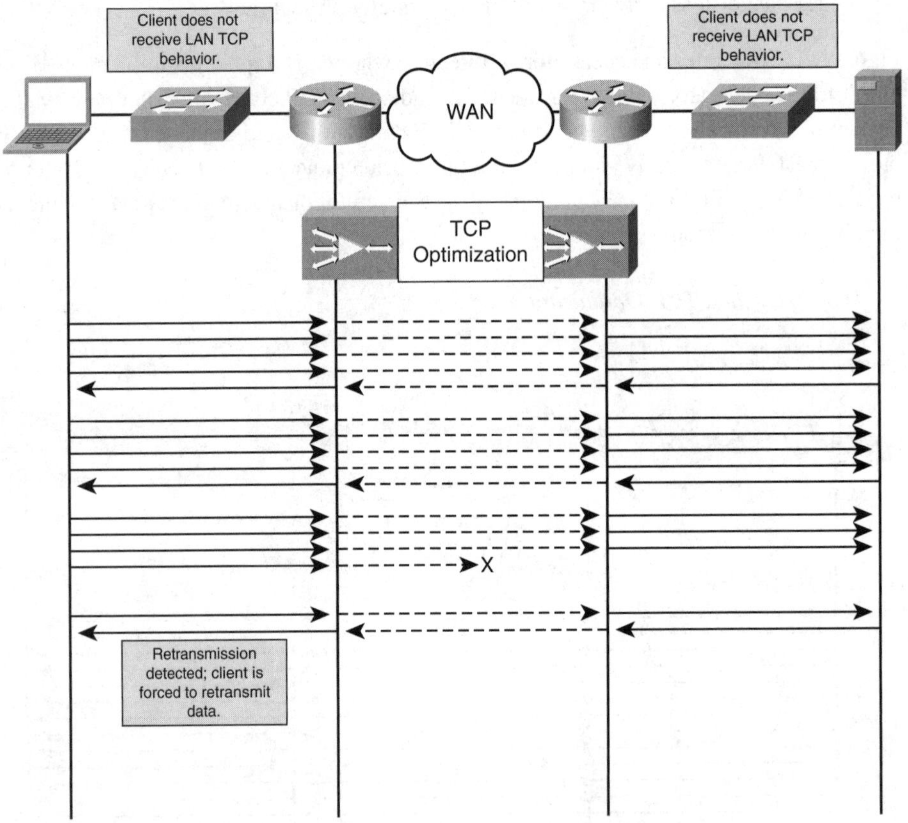

Data Suppression

Data suppression is a function of WAN optimization that allows accelerators to eliminate the transfer of redundant data across the network, thereby providing significant levels of throughput and bandwidth savings. Data suppression is a means by which accelerator devices can keep a repository of previously seen patterns of data. When a redundant pattern of data is identified, the redundant pattern can be replaced by a unique identifier. This unique identifier is a representation of the original pattern of data and references a block of data found in the distant accelerator's memory or disk repository. This unique identifier, when seen by the distant accelerator, is used as an instruction to locate the original block of data, which is subsequently added to the message in place of the unique identifier that was received. In this way, a unique identifier that is very small in size can be used to replace an arbitrarily large amount of data in flight.

Data suppression is commonly called *codebook compression* because each of the two accelerators maintains a compression history (unique identifiers and previously seen patterns of data) called a codebook that allows them to mitigate transmission of redundant data patterns. In many cases, this codebook can be implemented using capacity in both memory (high performance for the most frequently seen patterns and identifiers) and disk (lower performance, but allows the accelerator to maintain a very long compression history). These codebooks can also be implemented in a hierarchical fashion; that is, a single, unique identifier can be used as an instruction to reference multiple disparate blocks of data, providing even higher levels of compression. Data suppression is discussed in more detail in Chapter 6, "Overcoming Transport and Link Capacity Limitations."

Compression

Compression is similar to data suppression in that it minimizes the amount of data that must traverse the network. Whereas data suppression uses a codebook to minimize the transmission of redundant data, traditional compression employs algorithms that scour data within a window (that is, a packet, or within a connection for session-based compression) to find areas for consolidation (see Figure 3-18).

Figure 3-18 *Data Suppression and Compression*

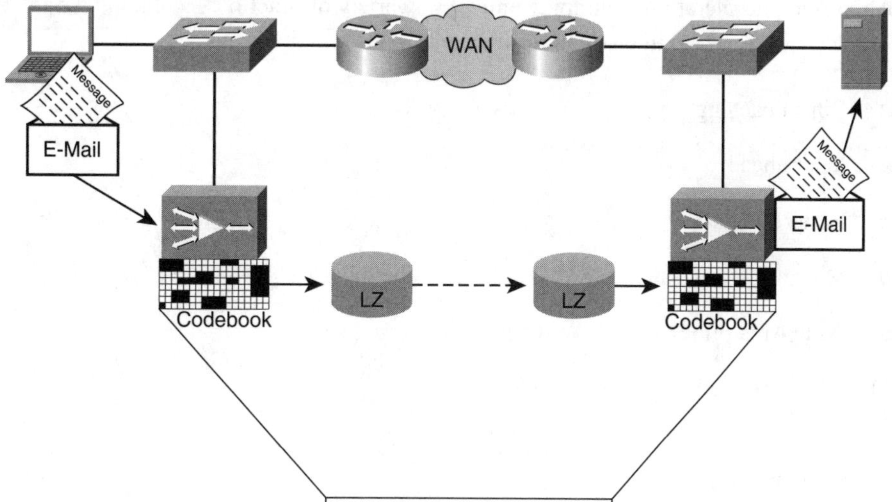

Synchronized Codebook	
Identifier	Data String
A1001	The Quick Brown Fox
A1002	Jumps Over The
A1003	Lazy Dog
A1004	A1001+A1002
A1005	A1003+A1004

Compression is very helpful in that the first transfer of a data pattern may not be seen as redundant by the data suppression library but may be compressible. In those cases, compression will help minimize the amount of bandwidth consumption for the first transmission of a given data set. In many cases, the unique identifiers generated by data suppression technologies for redundant data patterns are compressible, so the transmission of redundant data patterns will not only be redundancy-eliminated, but also be compressed to provide additional bandwidth savings and throughput improvements.

Application Acceleration Functions

WAN optimization is designed to help make the network a better place for applications to live but does little to nothing in terms of actually changing the behavior of applications to make them perform better over a network. Application acceleration complements WAN optimization in that application protocol–pecific optimizations are applied to overcome the performance-limiting behavior associated with the application protocol itself. When application acceleration and WAN optimization are used together, the network becomes a better place for applications to live (because transmission of redundant data is minimized, data is compressed in flight, and transport protocol behavior is improved and made more efficient), and applications perform better on the network.

Application acceleration commonly employs a variety of functions, including the following, which are designed to improve performance in some way:

- Object caching

- Read-ahead

- Write-behind

- Message prediction

- Wide Area File Services (WAFS)

The following sections describe each function.

Object Caching

Accelerators that provide application acceleration may provide object caching to help minimize bandwidth consumption, reduce the impact of latency, and improve user performance. The intent of an object cache is to allow an accelerator (also known as a *cache*) to retain a local copy of objects that have been requested using a specific application or protocol when it is safe to do so. Should the object be requested again, and the object is verified to be identical to the copy on the server (also called an *origin server*), it can be safely served to the requesting user assuming the application requirements for freshness and state have been met. These application requirements may include that the user has successfully authenticated to the server (or domain, for instance), the user is authorized to use the object (permissions are configured to allow the user to open the object), and the appropriate state is applied to the object on the origin server (for instance, a file lock for files being accessed on a mapped network drive).

Object caching is similar to data suppression in that the redundant transfer of an object is mitigated. The key difference between the two, however, is that object caching removes the need for the object to be transferred across the network in any form (redundancy eliminated or otherwise), whereas data suppression minimizes the bandwidth consumption when the object is transferred across the network.

When coupled together, the two provide a high-performance solution for objects that are both read and written. For instance, in an environment where a large object that is cached has been accessed, the performance when opening the object is accelerated significantly. Should the object be changed and written back to the server, the data suppression capabilities will be employed to provide high levels of compression for the transfer of the object back to the origin server.

Caching can also be coupled with content delivery networking capabilities (also known as *prepositioning*), which allows an accelerator's cache to be proactively populated with objects that the user may need to access. This is particularly helpful for environments with large object requirements, such as software distribution, patch management, CAD/CAM, medical imaging, and engineering, as it helps to improve performance for the first user access of that object. Prepositioning and content delivery networking are discussed at length in Chapter 4, "Content Delivery Networks."

Accelerators that provide application acceleration and caching also provide an additional benefit: offloading the origin server from having to manage user requests and transmission of information. By allowing the accelerators to become object-aware and respond to object data requests when safe to do so, a smaller quantity of requests must traverse the WAN through the core accelerator and to the origin server. This means that the origin server sees fewer requests, providing higher levels of scalability in existing server and application infrastructure (see Figure 3-19).

Figure 3-19 *Accelerator Object Caching*

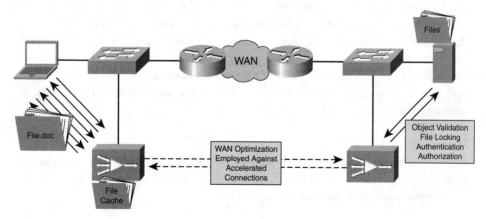

Additionally, accelerators that provide object caching for application protocols in addition to data suppression internally isolate object data from compression history. Architecturally, this allows the capacity of the two storage repositories to be managed separately rather than together. This provides significant value in that large objects, such as service pack files, hotfixes, CAD/CAM objects, medical images, and more, can be prepositioned to the edge of the network. With an isolated storage repository for these objects, any network traffic burst that causes the compression history to be overwhelmed with new data will not have an impact on the objects that are cached in the object cache. In this way, when a user begins a large backup of his home movie and picture archive across the WAN to a data center NAS device, the service pack files that were prepositioned to the accelerator will remain uncompromised in the object cache for future use.

Read-Ahead

While object caching provides improved performance for objects that are accessed multiple times, many objects are accessed only one time or are accessed in such a way that prohibits caching. Accelerators commonly implement application-specific read-ahead algorithms as a complement to caching to improve performance in scenarios where caching is not possible or otherwise cannot be employed due to state.

Read-ahead allows the accelerator to examine application requests and incrementally request additional segments within the object from the origin server on behalf of the user. This allows the accelerator to stage data that the user may request in the future. Data that is "read ahead" by the accelerator may be retained temporarily to be used should the user actually request that data. Read-ahead can also be used to more aggressively populate an object cache when an object is accessed for the first time or if the object in the cache is deemed out of date when compared to the object on the origin server.

Although read-ahead provides value in terms of improving user experience, it can create additional workloads on the origin server if not coupled with an edge-side object cache. In such cases where accelerators do not provide caching at the edge, every request is treated in the same way that a cache miss (object not in cache) would be treated in a scenario where accelerators that do provide an object cache have been deployed. Each request would be accompanied by a large number of read-ahead requests, thereby creating incremental workload on the server itself. Accelerators that provide object caching along with other application acceleration techniques such as read-ahead provide the best balance between server offload and performance improvement.

Figure 3-20 shows how read-ahead can be used to prefetch data on behalf of the user. This figure shows the read-ahead capabilities of an accelerator when either object caching is not being employed on the accelerator, or, object caching is being employed but the object is not in the cache (cache miss) or the object cannot be cached safely.

Figure 3-20 *Accelerator Read-Ahead*

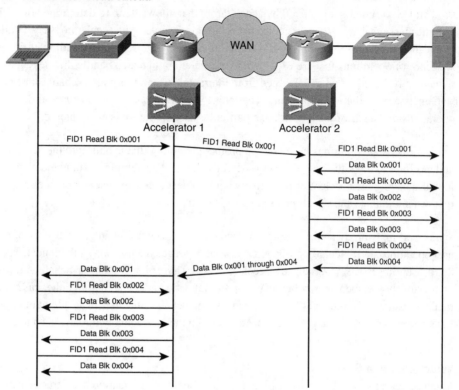

Write-Behind

Write-behind is a function that an accelerator applies within an application protocol to locally handle and acknowledge a write request coming from a user. This helps to mitigate the transmission latency of the data contained within the write operation, because the accelerator makes the client believe that the data has been received. When using write-behind, the accelerator must also ensure that the data is actually written to the origin server. In many cases, accelerators only implement write-behind optimizations that are safe and recoverable should network connectivity be lost or connections be destroyed.

Many application protocols provide a built-in write-behind mechanism that is granted to a user under certain circumstances. For instance, with the Common Internet File System (CIFS) protocol, certain opportunistic locks permit the user to perform write-behind operations locally. In such a case, the user is able to respond to his own write requests and flush the data periodically to the server. Many accelerators leverage protocol mechanisms such as this to ensure a safe implementation of optimization.

Message Prediction

Prediction is a function employed by accelerators that allows them to determine how to handle a specific message that has been received from a user or a server. The accelerator may handle certain application messages in a static fashion based on a preconfigured understanding of the order and sequence of operations that are expected. The accelerator can also handle the messages dynamically, based on what is learned from interactive user and server exchanges. For instance, static message prediction allows an accelerator to programmatically issue an additional set of operations on behalf of the user when a particular user operation is encountered.

Static message prediction is based on the protocol handling that is built into the accelerator logic and has little to do with what the user is actually doing. An example of static message prediction includes having the accelerator proactively apply object locks against an object of a specific type when the first object lock in a sequence is seen.

When working with dynamic message prediction, the accelerator maintains a history of previous user operations and calculates probability of what messages the user may submit next. The result of this probability assessment is that the accelerator issues a set of operations on behalf of the user based on previously seen behavior rather than on programmatic understanding. In either case, message prediction allows the accelerator to issue requests on behalf of the user in an attempt to mitigate the transmission latency of the predicted messages when the user actually initiates such a request.

Wide Area File Services

Many accelerators that provide caching as a component of application acceleration can also be used to implement a form of disconnected mode operation for certain application protocols. Disconnected mode allows the accelerator to act on behalf of the server that the user is attempting to access during periods of time when the network between the user and the server is severed and the resource is otherwise not accessible. For file server shares, this is commonly referred to as Wide Area File Services (WAFS).

Although WAFS generally refers to the application acceleration components that help improve performance over the WAN for interactive file server access, WAFS also refers to the ability to provide file services to the enterprise edge, even when the WAN is down. In disconnected mode of operation, the accelerator acts as a full proxy for the origin server and provides some level of access to the cached objects based on previously seen access control entries or statically defined security parameters.

For some accelerator solutions, WAFS refers to the broader set of services that needs to be provided to the enterprise edge beyond file services, including print server capabilities, authentication and login, and other infrastructure services. For the purposes of this book, WAFS is considered part of the larger set of application acceleration capabilities that is provided by accelerators.

Integrating Accelerators into the Network

To understand how accelerators coexist with the foundational network technologies for visibility, control, and resource alignment, it is also important to understand how accelerators integrate into the network. Integrating accelerators includes deploying accelerators and delivering to the accelerator traffic that should be optimized or needs to be unoptimized. In essence, deploying an accelerator requires that traffic somehow be given to the accelerator, and that the traffic optimized by the accelerator somehow be delivered to the distant accelerator on the other side of the WAN. This integration can be achieved physically or logically and can leverage network-integrated or nonintegrated mechanisms.

Physical Integration

Physical integration refers to the ability of an accelerator to be deployed directly into a pre-existing network device. This allows IT organizations to collapse the number of devices necessary in the physical infrastructure, which helps to minimize costs related to management, support, and power.

In most cases, physical integration refers to integration directly into the router using modules that have accelerator capabilities. With physical integration, the network device could use an integration protocol such as Web Cache Control Protocol (WCCP) or Cisco Policy Based Routing (discussed in the next section, "Logical Integration"), or another mechanism for routing traffic through the onboard accelerator.

In other cases, physical integration refers to integration of the accelerator directly between the WAN router and the LAN switch using a network card that supports fail-to-wire operation. This mode of physical integration, commonly referred to as *physical inline*, allows the accelerator to be deployed directly in the network path, and removed from the network path virtually should a failure occur. This is accomplished using the fail-to-wire network card, which physically closes the connection between the two network cables if a software, hardware, or power failure is encountered.

With physical inline, the accelerator sits physically between the WAN router and the LAN switch and sees all traffic traversing that connection. Physical inline provides the simplest, yet least elegant, means of integrating an accelerator into a network architecture, because it requires changing of cables and generally lacks the same levels of scalability and high availability as provided by other integration mechanisms such as WCCPv2 (discussed in the next section). Physical inline also poses the risk that a failure condition encountered by the device that is not recognized by the inline card hardware or driver might not immediately trigger a fail-through condition on the card, thereby preventing network traffic from passing through the device.

Figure 3-21 shows an example of deploying an accelerator as an integrated module within a branch office router.

Figure 3-21 *Physical Integration Using Router-Integrated Network Modules*

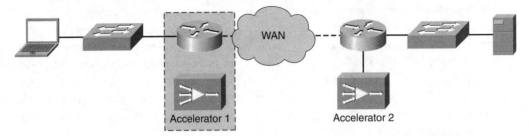

Figure 3-22 shows an example of deploying an accelerator physically inline between the branch office LAN switch and router.

Figure 3-22 *Physical Integration Using Physical Inline*

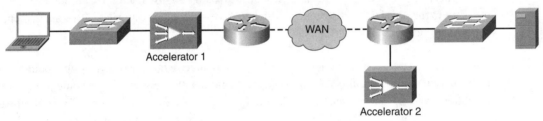

Logical Integration

Logical integration, also called *network interception*, refers to the use of networking protocols, features, or devices to ensure that traffic is routed through the accelerator in such a way that optimization and de-optimization can be applied to those traffic flows. The three most common means of logical integration through network interception include the following:

- Web Cache Control Protocol version 2 (WCCPv2)

- Policy Based Routing (PBR)

- Interaction with a dedicated or shared load-balancing device such as a server load balancer (SLB)

Web Cache Control Protocol v2

WCCPv2 is a control protocol that allows a WCCP child device such as an accelerator to connect with a network device such as a router, also known as a *WCCP server*. The result of this connection is that the accelerator notifies the network of the types of traffic it is able to handle so that the network device can intercept traffic (remove it from the normal forwarding path) and forward that traffic to a WCCPv2 child device if the specified type of traffic is encountered. The router maintains a service group of accelerator devices and balances the distribution of workload across the devices within that service group.

WCCPv2 supports up to 32 routers and 32 child devices being joined within the same service group, which allows for near-linear scalability and performance increases as additional accelerator devices are joined into the service group. WCCPv2 also provides fail-through operation; if no service group child devices are present, traffic is not intercepted and is serviced by the router without any form of redirection. With WCCPv2, devices can be dynamically added to or removed from service groups with little to no interruption of service. Because WCCPv2 provides off-path integration, scalability, and load-balancing, it is considered the most desirable architecture for integrating accelerators into a network location.

Figure 3-23 shows an example of how accelerators are deployed within a location where WCCPv2 is configured.

Figure 3-23   *WCCPv2 and Accelerators*

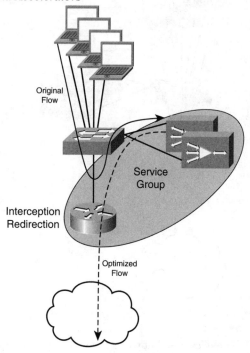

Policy Based Routing

Policy Based Routing (PBR) is a mechanism implemented in network devices such as routers that allows network administrators to apply a policy to how specific types of traffic should be routed through the network based on something other than the destination IP address. PBR can use access lists or other match conditions to identify traffic that should be routed through the policy route along with the next-hop router through which the traffic should be forwarded.

Using accelerators with PBR allows network administrators to treat the accelerator as a next-hop router for traffic flows that are candidates for optimization. PBR can also be used in conjunction with network availability management mechanisms, such as IP service level agreements (IP SLAs) or Cisco Discovery Protocol (CDP) neighbor adjacency verification, to track the availability of the accelerator as a next-hop router. If no accelerators are available, the policy route is considered invalid because the next-hop router (in this case the accelerator) is not reachable or available on the network. In such a case, the flow is not routed through the accelerator and is instead routed using the entries in the routing table.

Figure 3-24 shows an example of how accelerators can be deployed as next-hop routers when using PBR.

Figure 3-24 *Policy-Based Routing and Accelerators*

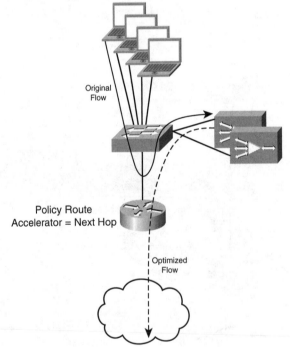

Server Load Balancing

Server load balancer (SLB) devices, also known as Layer 4 or Layer 7 switches, can also be used to integrate accelerator devices into the network. SLB devices can inspect traffic traversing the network and load-balance flows against one or multiple managed accelerators in a farm. SLB devices are typically deployed as an appliance but in many cases can be deployed in an integrated form factor within existing network devices such as data center switches. SLB devices commonly handle flow management and load balancing in hardware, which enables the greater levels of scalability and performance that are required in the enterprise data center.

Many SLB devices offer features beyond server load balancing, including better server scalability and security. This is accomplished through security protocol offload (allowing the SLB to manage SSL termination, encryption and decryption), TCP connection management, application acceleration functionality (complementary to accelerator functionality), and application firewall functionality. SLB devices can scale a farm of accelerators to hundreds of nodes if necessary, supporting multiple gigabits of throughput and millions of TCP connections.

Figure 3-25 shows an example of an intelligent switch with integrated server load-balancing capabilities being used as a means of integrating accelerators transparently into a data center network.

Figure 3-25 *Server Load Balancers and Accelerators*

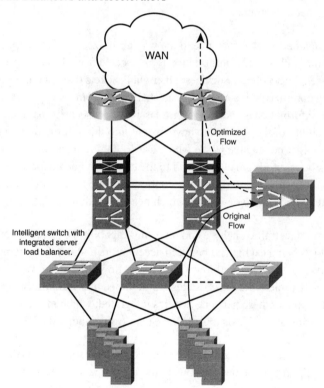

Architecture of Accelerator Services

All accelerator devices (and acceleration technology in general) have some posture to services deployed in the network. These network services include any action that can be performed against network packets and flows, including network visibility, monitoring, end-to-end performance analysis, control, prioritization, security, and other functionality. The architecture of accelerators and the underlying technology largely determines the ability of the acceleration solution to either interoperate with or break such features. This posture is primarily determined by the level of transparency provided by the underlying accelerator architecture.

Nontransparent Accelerators

Nontransparent accelerators are designed to optimize traffic that has been redirected to it and explicitly forward the optimized traffic to a statically defined or dynamically discovered peer through an explicit connection to that peer accelerator. In this way, the accelerator knows about its peer either through some form of automatic discovery or through a previously applied configuration. Packets leaving an accelerator that is applying optimization are explicitly destined to the distant peer accelerator.

With nontransparent accelerators, due to the way optimized traffic is explicitly forwarded to the peer accelerator, packet header information is obfuscated from the network. The network sees only packets between the accelerator devices rather than packets that contain header information about the flow being optimized. This might present challenges from a network feature perspective where packet header information is used for traffic classification, security, path selection, or anything that relies on the ability of the network to have insight into this information. For instance, QoS classification might not be able to see which user is communicating with which server or which application is being used. This might lead to the configured behavior of policing, queuing, or shaping being defeated. Similarly, any preconfigured policy routes or optimized routes will not be able to differentiate flows to determine which network path to use.

As another example, traffic analysis and reporting capabilities, including NetFlow, might be able to see only flows being exchanged between accelerators and not the communication between the client and server. In this way, NetFlow would export flows that are between accelerators, rendering the NetFlow data useless. Because of these limitations, many nontransparent accelerators are designed with some of these network features integrated, which may require operational changes to have monitoring and analysis tools receive data from another device.

Figure 3-26 elaborates on how a nontransparent accelerator solution can directly impact the ability of features configured in the network due to the loss of packet header visibility.

Transparent Accelerators

Transparent accelerators use similar metrics as nontransparent accelerators to identify peer devices on the other end of the network (automatic discovery or static configuration) but do not manipulate packet headers for data in flight. This helps to ensure compatibility with features that are deployed in the network that require visibility of packet header information for classification, prioritization, security, route selection, and more, as shown in Figure 3-27.

Figure 3-26 *Nontransparent Accelerators*

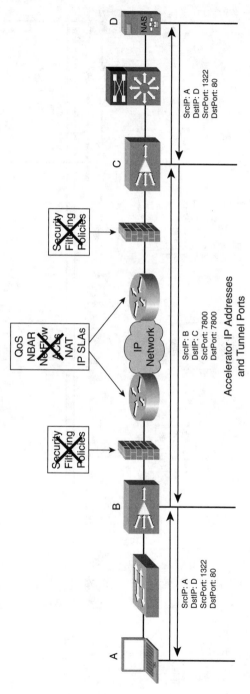

Figure 3-27 *Transparent Accelerators and Compatibility with Network Features*

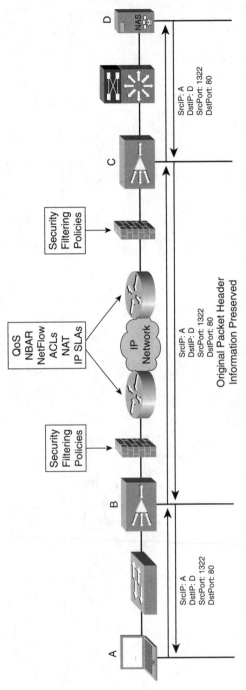

Figure 3-28 shows how a transparent accelerator solution retains packet header data that is critical to ensuring compatibility with existing network functions.

Figure 3-28 *Transparent Accelerators and Preservation of Packet Header Information*

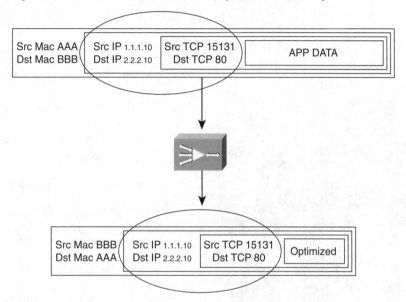

Summary

Features deployed in networking devices such as QoS, NetFlow, and many others allow IT organizations to align network resources in a way that is conducive to application business requirements. This helps to ensure that the right level of service and resources is supplied to the right application. Having a network that is configured to align network resources and handle traffic according to business and application requirements serves as the foundation and framework for ensuring that the network is optimally utilized for application performance.

Accelerators can improve performance of business applications, but you must first ensure that the physical network resources are aligned with application and business requirements. For instance, transparent accelerators preserve information necessary to allow the network to provide granular control of bandwidth consumption, control network flows through security implementations, select the most optimal network path, and provide detailed and granular data about network utilization. The network serves as the foundation through which all network traffic flows and is positioned uniquely to provide granular control and resource allocation because it is the common interconnect for application infrastructure. The accelerator solution architecture should be considered carefully to ensure that it is compatibile with this foundation.

This chapter includes the following topics:

- Understanding Application-Specific Acceleration

- Application-Specific Caching

- Web-Based Database Applications

- Read-Ahead

- Message Prediction

- Pipelining and Multiplexing

CHAPTER 4

Overcoming Application-Specific Barriers

Accelerators are generally able to provide optimization at two distinct layers. The first layer of optimization is application-agnostic, otherwise referred to as WAN optimization, which consists of transport protocol optimization and compression (discussed in Chapter 6, "Overcoming Transport and Link Capacity Limitations"). WAN optimization is primarily employed to overcome conditions caused by or otherwise encountered in the WAN, including latency, bandwidth constraints, and packet loss, as well as conditions caused by lower-performing implementations of transport protocols on end nodes.

The second layer of optimization is functionality that interacts with or otherwise improves behavior of the application layer itself, also known as application acceleration. Most accelerators provide a combination of WAN optimization and application acceleration, as well as content distribution, as described in Chapter 5, "Content Delivery Networks," which can also be considered a form of application acceleration. Application acceleration capabilities interact within the context of specific applications and application protocols to improve performance for users accessing applications and content over a WAN, including protocol-specific behaviors such as pipelined or multiplexed transactions.

Application acceleration (application-specific) and WAN optimization (application-agnostic) are two separate layers of optimization that commonly coexist on the same accelerator device and leverage one another. When combined, application acceleration and WAN optimization can overcome a host of challenges that plague application performance in WAN environments.

Simply put, accelerators make the WAN a place that is conducive to application performance and make application protocols perform better over networks. This chapter examines how accelerators make application protocols perform better over networks by examining optimization techniques that minimize the impact of bandwidth and latency, including reactive and proactive acceleration techniques including caching, read-ahead optimization and pre-fetching, write-behind optimization, video stream splitting, message prediction, pipelining, and multiplexing. The optimizations discussed in this chapter, as well as the Content Delivery Network (CDN) capabilities discussed in Chapter 5, serve as a foundation for application-specific acceleration. These techniques combine with the WAN optimization principles found in Chapter 6 to form the foundation of accelerator solutions, which help ensure networks provide the performance levels necessary to enable high-performance access to centralized applications, data, and content in a global infrastructure environment.

Understanding Application-Specific Acceleration

Application-specific acceleration refers to mechanisms employed at the application layer within an accelerator to mitigate application latency, improve data transfer times, and provide disconnected service in the event of network disruption. The level of application-specific acceleration applied to a specific application is directly dependent on the application and protocols themselves and what can be done within the confines of correctness, coherency, and data integrity.

Some application protocols are robust and complicated, requiring a large degree of message exchange, or chatter, between nodes. Such protocols might be feature rich and robust but yield poor performance over the WAN when not using some form of acceleration. In many cases, applications that depend on these protocols dictate that you deploy infrastructure to support those applications in remote office locations to provide adequate levels of performance. Deploying infrastructure in such a distributed manner can overcome performance limitations of applications that rely on protocols that do not perform well over the WAN but also leads to dramatically higher capital costs and IT management expenditure.

Application acceleration can be categorized into two primary types: reactive acceleration and proactive acceleration. Reactive acceleration refers to the behavior employed by an accelerator device when a specific type of stimulus is seen. These are behaviors and functions that are implemented upon encountering a specific request from a given user. Proactive acceleration, on the other hand, refers to the behavior employed by an accelerator device based on administrator configuration. With proactive acceleration, accelerators may be preconfigured with instructions on how to handle specific data types, specific messages or requests, or specific protocols, and on which sets of data to proactively distribute throughout the fabric of accelerators. Both of these approaches work cohesively and in conjunction with WAN optimization to ensure significant performance improvements for users accessing files, content, and applications over a WAN.

Application-Specific Caching

Caching is a method commonly used in computer and networking systems to help compensate for I/O requests that are performance bound to the slowest device in the processing path. Caching refers to the introduction of an intermediary buffer between two devices within a processing path, where the intermediary buffer can retain a copy of data found in the slower device, albeit at a much smaller capacity.

For instance, caching is employed between the CPU of a personal computer or server and the main memory, which acts as primary storage. Although we commonly consider main memory to be high performance, main memory is dramatically slower than the CPU itself, as well as the CPU registers. By introducing a cache between the CPU and main memory, content fetched from memory can be stored authoritatively in the cache and retrieved from there by the CPU (as opposed to paying the performance penalty of fetching the data directly from memory), because the cache has performance characteristics that are more similar to those of the CPU registers as compared to the system's main memory. This helps to dramatically improve performance of applications running on a PC or server. Similarly, caches are commonly used in other areas of a system, including the disk subsystem, which provides far greater levels of throughput and better response times as compared to continually fetching data from the mechanical disk drives.

Similar to how caching is deployed within a PC or a server, *application-specific caching* can be deployed as a function within an accelerator in the network to allow that accelerator to maintain local copies of previously requested objects (reactive) or objects that have been distributed to the accelerator by way of administrative configuration (proactive). This minimizes the number of requests for objects and corresponding objects that require transmission over the low-speed network. Along with providing performance improvements, application-specific caching also helps to offload other accelerators in the network path to the origin server and provides a significant amount of workload reduction on the origin server itself, as it no longer has to serve redundant copies of data. This section examines caching in detail along with how content is managed and object validity is preserved.

Advantages of Application-Specific Caching

The process of caching objects accessed by a target protocol, or employing other optimizations (discussed later in the chapter in sections such as "Read-Ahead" and others), is considered an application-specific process. For application-specific acceleration that includes caching, protocols such as HTTP, HTTPS, and Common Internet File System (CIFS), or even streaming media protocols such as Real-Time Streaming Protocol (RTSP), become the cache's primary processing objective. An application-specific cache stores not only the intercepted objects, but also any related metadata and directory information associated with the location of the object. By maintaining a repository of previously accessed objects and the associated metadata, the accelerator is in a position to determine not only the validity of cached objects, but also the safety in employing optimizations against object requests or other operations.

An application-specific cache within an accelerator offers more than just copies of cached objects that traverse its network interfaces. First, the process of caching a specific piece of content during the initial request places the content in the accelerator memory and disk. Second, the content must be stored in a location that is quickly accessible in the event that a subsequent request is received by the accelerator. Lastly, in the event of a request for content that exists on the accelerator, the accelerator must be able to validate the freshness of the given object prior to serving the object to the requesting user, while also ensuring that application semantics such as authentication and authorization are preserved. This is done to ensure that data is not served to a user when the data has been changed or the user is not allowed to access it. Each of these steps allows an application-specific cache to interoperate with the requesting user, origin server, and application in the interest of accelerating object requests over the target protocol.

Application-specific caches are useful to any requesting user whose request traverses a target protocol. The accelerator's ability to intercept the protocol messages exchanged between a requesting user and the origin server is inspected and compared against requests that may have traversed the accelerator previously. Once validated, each reactively stored object is served over the LAN and is delivered in a more efficient manner than if it were served by an origin server located across the WAN, thereby mitigating the performance penalty of the WAN for the majority of the transaction. Although the requesting user might not know that his request was intercepted and processed by an accelerator, his object request has been satisfied faster than a remote origin server could respond and transferred more quickly than the WAN could possibly handle. The ability to speak the application protocol allows application and network administrators to implement application-specific caching with little to no changes on the origin server or client.

The four entities that benefit the most from an application cache are the user, the WAN, intermediary accelerators, and the origin server itself. The user experiences a noticeable improvement in performance when requesting objects that are accelerated by an accelerator, because the majority of the workload is done locally on the LAN at near-LAN speeds as opposed to the WAN. With application-specific caching, less data needs to traverse the WAN. This directly translates into bandwidth savings on the WAN and also minimizes the amount of traffic that must be handled by any intermediary accelerators that are deployed in the network between the accelerator closest to the user and the origin server. Similarly, the origin server will likely see a substantial decrease in the number of requests and amount of application I/O it must service, thereby allowing increased levels of scalability with existing origin server infrastructure. In this way, accelerators that provide application acceleration and object caching as a component of a performance-enhancing solution not only improve user performance, but also offload the network and the origin server dramatically while maintaining content freshness, validity, and correctness.

Cache Validation and Content Freshness

An accelerator that provides application-specific caching validates content items stored on its disks at the time it receives a request that matches the properties of an item that is stored in the cache. Cached content validation prevents stale content from being served to any requesting user and ensures compatibility with existing security semantics and correctness from an application protocol perspective. Content validation is a function that is required of an accelerator that performs application-specific caching, and the next paragraph demonstrates why it is required.

To demonstrate the impact of serving stale content to a requesting user, consider the business impact of an out-of-date payroll spreadsheet being served to an accountant who is requesting the spreadsheet from the payroll server. The spreadsheet, which is hosted on the origin server, might be several minutes or hours newer than what the accountant has obtained if an application cache does not check the spreadsheet's freshness. Any last-minute changes that do not exist in the outdated spreadsheet might cause an employee to receive an incorrect paycheck. As another example of the importance of cache validation, suppose that an employee of the corporation checks his online banking statement via a web browser. Unknowingly, the employee might be served a cached record of a banking statement that belongs to another employee of the corporation. Or, the information that was just served from the application cache might have been cached the previous day, leading the employee to believe that an account has more or less in it than what is actually there.

Each application dictates how an accelerator that is providing application-specific caching should validate content items that have been cached, to maintain coherency and correctness. Each validation method involves protocol interaction between the client and the origin server, which the accelerator is able to intercept and leverage for the purposes of validating cached objects based on stored metadata and origin server responses. Accelerators that perform application-specific caching must adhere strictly to protocol and application semantics and must use existing protocol and application messages as a means of validating the freshness of cached objects. Although the behavior of an accelerator that has an application-specific cache might be different on a protocol-by-protocol or application-by-application basis (each has its own requirements and methods of validation), the conceptual process of cached object validation remains the same. Every request intercepted by the accelerator with the application-specific cache will be parsed and associated with any matching local cached content. The content that already resides on the application-specific cache's disks is then compared to the content that is provided as part of the response by the origin server.

Each method of object validation within an accelerator with an application-specific cache must have the ability to natively communicate with the origin server as needed and exchange information specific to the application and the content item that requires validation. For protocols such as HTTP and HTTPS, a generic web application cache inspects the origin server's response to a client's proxied request, comparing the text within the header to the header information recorded from the previous request that placed the content into the cache's storage. For CIFS file server traffic, which has no inherent freshness metrics built into the protocol, each object accessed must first be checked against the origin server to examine whether or not the object has changed based on time stamps, size, or other version-control mechanisms.

The two levels of freshness check implemented for requests follow:

- **Strict content coherency:** The object must be validated directly against the origin server by the accelerator.

- **Nonstrict content coherency:** The object can be validated based on responses sent to the user by the origin server.

The CIFS protocol, for instance, dictates the use of a strict coherency check because it does not natively include information within message exchanges that defines the coherency of the content being accessed. Furthermore, with CIFS, users from potentially many locations have the ability to apply read and write functions to the content stored on the origin server. With CIFS, it must be assumed that the object could possibly have been edited since the previous access. CIFS also provides metrics for collaboration and multiuser access, which means that an accelerator with CIFS caching and acceleration capabilities must be able to accommodate such scenarios. Given the possibility of multiuser access scenarios, the accelerator must be prepared to dynamically adjust the level of caching and optimization applied to object interaction based on what can be done safely and without violation of the correctness requirements of the protocol. The accelerator must also take ownership of content validation and leverage this information as part of its adaptive optimization model.

Protocols such as HTTP and HTTPS commonly employ nonstrict coherency and cache validation because information about content validity is commonly carried in protocol messages that are exchanged between clients and servers. HTTP and HTTPS are commonly used in a unidirectional request and response form, meaning that the content that is served is generally not edited at the edge of the network, with the exception commonly being collaborative workspaces and web-enabled document management applications. Protocols such as HTTP and HTTPS can rely, and commonly have relied, on tags contained within messages exchanged between nodes to determine the freshness of content stored in the application-specific cache.

Some accelerator protocol caching functions can be configured to completely bypass the function of cache freshness validation, but this type of configuration exposes the client to the risk of accessing stale content from the application-specific cache. This kind of configuration is common with HTTP and the Internet, where bandwidth savings are more important than freshness. If an administrator applies freshness validation bypass settings to a caching device, the administrator must have detailed information specific to the application and its content provided to clients.

Figure 4-1 illustrates nonstrict coherency where an accelerator employing application-specific caching is able to examine client and server message exchanges to understand content validation periods. This figure shows an example of a cache hit (top portion of the example) and a cache miss (bottom portion of the example). Any data exchanged between the user and the origin server that traverses the accelerator is a candidate for optimization through compression, flow optimizations, and other WAN optimization capabilities.

Figure 4-1   *Cache Validation with Nonstrict Coherency*

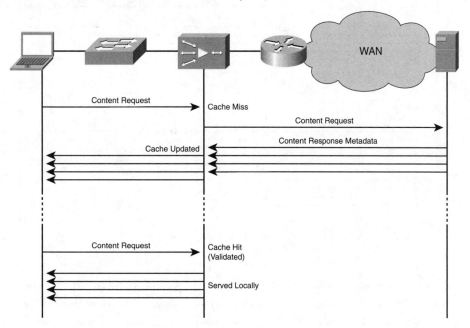

Figure 4-2 illustrates the strict coherency model, where an accelerator employing application-specific caching is not able to examine client and server message exchanges to understand content validation periods. For these applications and protocols, the accelerator must validate the content against the origin server using other means such as time stamps or other version-control methods. This figure shows an example of a cache miss (top portion of the example) and a cache hit (bottom portion of the example). Any data exchanged between the user and the origin server that traverses the accelerator is a candidate for optimization through compression, flow optimizations, and other WAN optimization capabilities.

The next sections will examine caching and optimization in more detail relative to CIFS, HTTP, HTTPS, and SSL/TLS.

Figure 4-2 *Cache Validation with Strict Coherency*

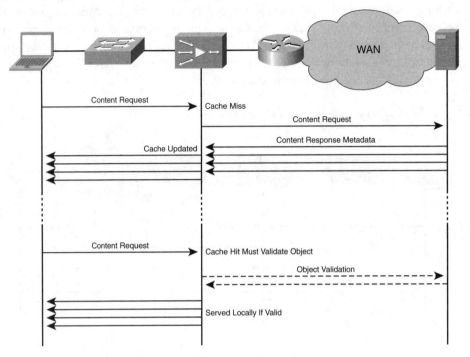

CIFS

File-related content that traverses a WAN link over CIFS can range from just a few bytes to several gigabytes in size. CIFS, which is most commonly used between Microsoft Windows–based clients and servers, provides a protocol for accessing named pipes, network resources, and file shares. Given that CIFS works to make portions of a local file system accessible via a network, file system semantics must be supported over the network between client and server. As such, the CIFS protocol is rather robust, providing over 100 different types of messages that can be exchanged, spread over ten or more different dialects (protocol versions).

An accelerator that provides CIFS acceleration and caching for CIFS must be aware of how clients and servers negotiate the dialect to be used and how to handle the different types of messages that are exchanged between client and server. Some messages can be safely suppressed or otherwise handled locally by the accelerator, without compromise to data integrity or coherency. Other messages are so critical to data integrity and coherency that they must be handled in a synchronous fashion by the origin server, and the accelerator must be prepared to accelerate delivery of such messages to the server. Because CIFS is not dictated by published protocol standards, an accelerator must also be prepared to handle messages that are structured in a way that it does not understand and gracefully pass them through to ensure support for vendor-specific implementations that deviate from others.

When an accelerator with CIFS caching and acceleration capabilities resides in the path of the client to server session, several WAN traffic reduction benefits and performance improvements will be realized, including these:

■ The number of messages exchanged between the client and server will be greatly reduced, because the accelerator can safely minimize the amount of chatter that must be exchanged over the WAN. This helps to improve response time to the client, minimize the amount of work that must be performed by the origin server, and negate the penalty of WAN latency on user performance.

■ The file on the server that is accessed by the client can be captured and cached by the application-specific cache if it is safe to do so. This allows the accelerator to mitigate the need to transfer files across the WAN that have been previously accessed, assuming that the user is authenticated and authorized and the object in cache is successfully validated against the origin server.

The most important aspect of a cache is its ability to store entire objects or portions of objects that are usable at an application layer. This stored copy becomes the primary source of benefit when implementing an application-specific cache; the content does not need to be served by the origin server a second time if validation and freshness requirements are met, which also translates to a reduction of the number of bytes that must be served over the potentially low-bandwidth and high-latency WAN. The realized benefits of an application-specific cache increase with each additional request received for a piece of content that already resides within the cache and can be validated as coherent when compared to the copy on the origin server. The benefits of the cache's ability to re-serve any given piece of cached content can be tracked linearly, based on the number of requests that are processed and serviced following the initial caching of content.

In addition to the reduction in the number of requests that must traverse the WAN, the CIFS messaging overhead is also significantly reduced by the application-specific cache and protocol optimization. Some messages might not be required to traverse the WAN for a client to successfully acquire a given piece of content or search a directory, while others require message exchanges with the origin server. For instance, an accelerator may have performed a read-ahead function (as discussed in the "Read-Ahead" section later in this chapter) and temporarily stored the results of the read-ahead data for use by a user. A request for this data may be satisfied locally, thereby removing the need to send the user's read request to the origin server.

Many accelerators that optimize CIFS also prefetch large amounts of information about the directory structure and stage this data at the edge of the network. If a user browses a directory structure, the directory traversal data may be served out of the accelerator if it is considered valid. Most accelerators that optimize directory traversal use a very short window of validation on directory traversal data (for example, 30 seconds) to allow directory updates to be received by the user in a timely fashion.

It is those messages that do not need to communicate with the origin server that the application-specific cache will interpret and terminate or otherwise respond to locally at the accelerator. Messages that are critical to data integrity, security, or state, however, must traverse the WAN to ensure compliance with CIFS object freshness and protocol semantics. Such messages include those that provide protocol negotiation, user authentication, user authorization, file locking, file open requests, and write operations. These messages can, however, be optimized through WAN optimization techniques that operate in an application-agnostic manner, including compression, flow optimization, and loss mitigation.

CIFS natively creates a tremendous amount of overhead traffic in native client to server exchanges. In many instances, a seemingly simple operation such as a file open of a 1-MB document might require that over 500 messages be exchanged between the client and the server. In a WAN environment, the maximum throughput that can be achieved is directly impacted by the amount of total network latency and is easily calculated as the number of messages multiplied by the latency per operation.

For instance, in a 100-ms roundtrip WAN, 500 messages being exchanged can lead to upwards of 100 seconds of latency to open a simple document. With CIFS acceleration and CIFS caching, clients benefit from the elimination or reduction of certain types of overhead traffic and potentially the elimination of the redundant transfer of requested files. Reducing the amount of latency experienced by the client during client to server exchanges will improve the overall perceived performance of a given application, file transfer, or other operation. Coupling the accelerator's capabilities to accelerate the protocol (mitigate latency and minimize bandwidth consumption) with WAN optimization capabilities (discussed in Chapter 6), accelerators can help to improve performance over the WAN to the degree that remote office file servers can be consolidated into a centralized data enter.

Many accelerators rely on a built-in CIFS capability called the *opportunistic lock*, which is a message sent from the server that can effectively relay the state of a file in question to an end user. The original intent of the opportunistic lock was to enable the client to, when determined safe to do so by the server, leverage optimizations built into the CIFS redirector on the client. These optimizations include client-side read-ahead, write-behind, and other types of operations including local open and lock handling. All of these not only help to improve the client experience, but also minimize the workload on the origin server. In a way, this same information about state is leveraged by accelerators to determine how "safe" it is to apply a specific optimization or set of optimizations to a file that has been requested, and file caching is one of those optimizations. In essence, most accelerators maintain CIFS protocol semantics and apply only a level of optimization that is safe based on what the origin server says the state of the file is and, furthermore, based on what the origin server allows a client to do on his own. In this way, the accelerator is able to employ additional optimizations that work in concert with the capabilities that the server permits the client to utilize.

Opportunistic locks and standard locks are also used to inform any clients requesting a file that the requested file is already in use by another client. The level of access in multiuser, concurrent access, collaborative types of scenarios is largely dependent upon another security mechanism called a *share mode*, which determines whether or not multiple users have privileges to read, write, delete, or otherwise manipulate a file while someone else is accessing that same file. From the perspective of an accelerator, these state relay messages (authentication, authorization, locking, and others) must not be handled locally and must be passed to the origin server synchronously. This is to ensure full compliance with protocol correctness, content freshness, and security. For instance, if a user accesses a file on a CIFS file server, whether accelerators are optimizing the session or not, and another user is already accessing that same file, the server must notify the requesting user that the file is unavailable for read-write access, as shown in Figure 4-3. Some applications permit multiuser concurrent access scenarios and might permit users to have read privileges to certain areas of the object and read-write privileges to other areas that are not in use.

Figure 4-3 *CIFS Notification of File in Use*

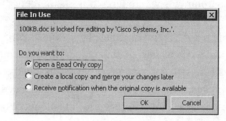

There are three types of opportunistic locks in the latest CIFS dialect:

- **Batch:** A batch opportunistic lock involves a client accessing a file on a CIFS file server with complete and unrestricted access. When a batch opportunistic lock is provided to the client, the client is allowed to make any changes to the content that his privileges allow, including local open, close, read, and write operations. The batch opportunistic lock is considered the least restrictive opportunistic lock a client can be provided, as it provides the client with the most freedom to perform operations locally.

- **Exclusive:** An exclusive opportunistic lock, as with a batch opportunistic lock, informs the client that he is the only one to have a given piece of content open. Like the batch opportunistic lock, many operations, including open, close, read, and others, can be performed against the local client cache. The primary difference between exclusive and batch is that with an exclusive opportunistic lock, the server must be updated synchronously with any changes made to the state of the file (contents of the file or attributes of the file).

- **Level II:** The Level II opportunistic lock informs the requesting client that there are other users who already have access to the file, but none has changed the contents or state of the object. In this case, the client may perform local read operations against the file and its attributes from the local client cache, but any other requests must be sent to the server synchronously. The level II opportunistic lock is considered the most restrictive opportunistic lock but still provides the client with the ability to perform many of the operations locally, thereby providing better performance than a standard lock, which requires *all* messages to propagate synchronously to the server.

An application-specific cache for CIFS within an accelerator will commonly intercept requests over the standard TCP ports used by CIFS—TCP/139 and TCP/445 and many can be configured to accelerate CIFS on non-standard ports if necessary, which is not common. The main purpose of a CIFS application-specific cache is to minimize bandwidth consumption and improve response times for requested content or file transfers. The larger the objects stored in the application-specific cache, the faster the response times will be to any clients who request previously cached content, as compared to accessing the same object over the native WAN. Accelerator-based CIFS caching is useful in environments where file server consolidation is desired, especially environments where large files are present, because the performance provided by the accelerator is similar to that provided by a local file server. Accelerators with CIFS caching and acceleration are equally useful in environments where large objects are being used.

System administrators often use CIFS to distribute large objects across the network. Some of the more common applications that leverage large content objects include computer-aided design/computer-aided manufacturing (CAD/CAM) applications. The objects that these applications create might be as small as a few hundred kilobytes to as large as several hundred megabytes or gigabytes. Applications that focus on graphics and imaging involve a significant amount of detail and, thus, the objects in use consume a tremendous amount of storage capacity. With increased image resolution requirements, the amount of disk usage consumed increases as well. Medical applications that involve imaging consume large amounts of disk storage depending on the type of imaging being done. Enterprise network administrators also commonly leverage CIFS to distribute software updates, operating system patches, or entire operating system images. It is common for these applications to rely upon CIFS drive mappings to a central server in the data center (or a local software distribution server that can then be consolidated once accelerators are deployed).

Each of these large distribution jobs tax the WAN for each request. Regardless of the file's purpose, an application-specific cache stores the object when safe to do so and can potentially serve it locally, thereby mitigating unnecessary transfer. For environments that require interactive read-write operations against large files, such as CAD/CAM applications, software development applications, and others, CIFS acceleration and caching can leverage the accelerator's WAN optimization components (discussed in Chapter 6) along side object caching to further improve performance of both read and write operations over the WAN.

For CIFS, the accelerator intercepts and examines each message that is transferred between the client and server. The accelerator determines where the client and server are in their message exchange and what function is being performed, which enables the accelerator to make intelligent decisions on how to process and optimize the conversation. While observing the traffic between hosts, the accelerator can safely eliminate some messages after determining that they are not required by the origin server.

Beyond the messaging resides the requested file itself, which is evaluated within a process different from the CIFS messaging. Each file that traverses the accelerator may or may not be stored on the accelerator's local disks depending on the level of optimization that the accelerator can safely apply. For content that is stored on the accelerator's disks, the content might be whole content objects or portions of a given piece of content. A whole content object does not need to be received at the accelerator for the accelerator to successfully cache or serve the portions of traffic that traverse it. If a request arrives at the accelerator, the application-specific cache will deterministically serve the content that is stored on its disks to the client when safe to do so and fetch any missing portions of the partially cached object from the origin server. The application-specific cache will proactively read ahead of the client's request to fetch the content missing from the partial cache. Overall, this dual method of content fetch and serve will improve the performance to the user and dynamically populate the remaining portions of the partially cached file's missing data.

An application-specific cache might cache only portions of a given file based on the needs of the requesting application; a partially cached file does not demonstrate a faulty application-specific cache. Figure 4-4 illustrates a partially cached object being served from the accelerator's cache, while the accelerator is acquiring any missing segments of the content from the origin server.

Figure 4-4 *Logical Partial Object Cache Serve*

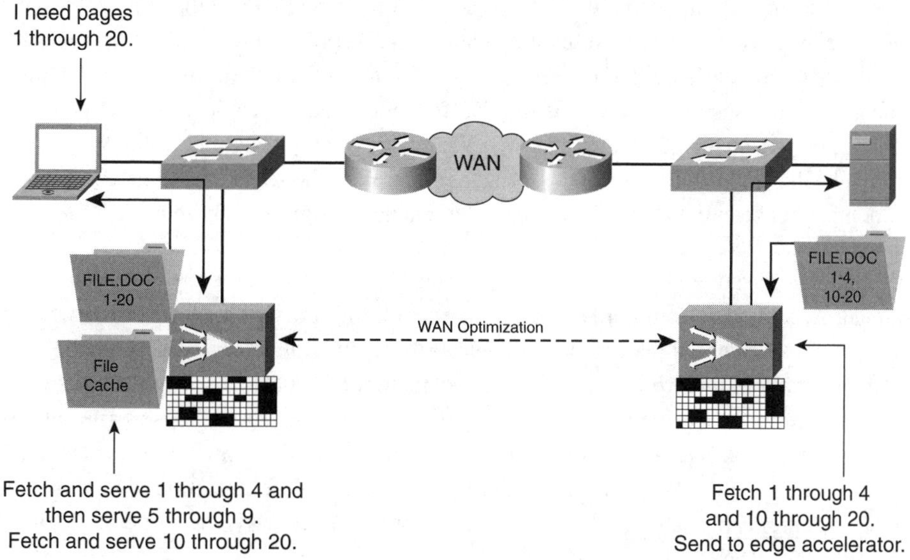

I need pages 1 through 20.

FILE.DOC 1-20

File Cache

WAN

WAN Optimization

FILE.DOC 1-4, 10-20

Fetch and serve 1 through 4 and then serve 5 through 9.
Fetch and serve 10 through 20.

Fetch 1 through 4 and 10 through 20.
Send to edge accelerator.

Caching and read-ahead functionality combine to provide a dramatic performance improvement when accessing objects over the WAN. For content requests that can be served locally, the accelerator can respond to data requests when doing so is safe. For content requests that cannot be satisfied by the accelerator, the accelerator can choose to apply additional optimizations such as read-ahead, discussed later in the chapter, to proactively fetch a larger degree of an object, which helps to satisfy future requests for portions of the object locally.

When CIFS requests arrive at the accelerator, cached content is not served to the requesting client until the accelerator has performed validation and it has been deemed safe to do so. The validation process is dependent on a number of factors, including the state of the opportunistic lock supplied to the client and verification with the origin server that the object has not changed. The process of determining the file's coherency is automated and subject to the origin server's proper delivery of state and response to inquiries from the accelerator. In any scenario, the origin server will always own the state of the data, thereby ensuring that in hybrid accelerated and nonaccelerated environments where users access from remote locations with accelerators and locations without accelerators, the security, safety, and freshness characteristics are identical with or without the presence of an accelerator that is optimizing or caching CIFS data.

As noted earlier, when an application-specific cache receives a request for content that already partially exists within the cache's storage, the accelerator may generate additional read requests on behalf of the client to acquire the remaining portions of the partially cached file. The application-specific cache will recognize the pattern created by a client requesting a series of small content reads for a larger content item. Once this pattern has been observed, the application-specific cache will initiate read-ahead requests for the remainder of the content item prior to the actual client's request for the remaining data. Several applications exhibit the trait of smaller data reads, ultimately building to request an entire file. When operating in this default mode, the application-specific cache transitions from content request cache misses to content request cache hits proactively. To the requesting client, the overall throughput of the WAN appears dramatically faster in the presence of accelerators. With the read-ahead requests having been pipelined between the accelerator and server, latency is significantly reduced.

Optimizations gained by the accelerator are not limited just to the process of caching or read-ahead. Accelerators commonly also provide pipelining for user write requests when safe to do so, which is discussed later in this chapter. Prior to an application-specific cache's implementation, the origin server would receive write requests directly from the client. When the write requests are intercepted by an application-specific cache, these writes are batched by the application accelerator when applicable, allowing for the writes to be pipelined and streamlined over the WAN. In many cases, write requests are also filtered against the known contents of the cached object to ensure that unnecessary write operations need not traverse the WAN.

When writes are made to the origin server directly by the client, each write requires the origin server to provide acknowledgment to the client for each operation. When writes are sent to a server with accelerators in the network, the accelerator can make a determination, based on safety, on whether or not optimization can be applied that would allow the accelerator to generate acknowledgments on behalf of the server. These acknowledgements allow the accelerator to temporarily buffer data while managing the process of transferring the writes on behalf of the user to the origin server in a more write-optimized fashion. Figure 4-5 illustrates the process of automated write responses from the accelerator to the server.

Figure 4-5   *Accelerators and Write-Back Optimization*

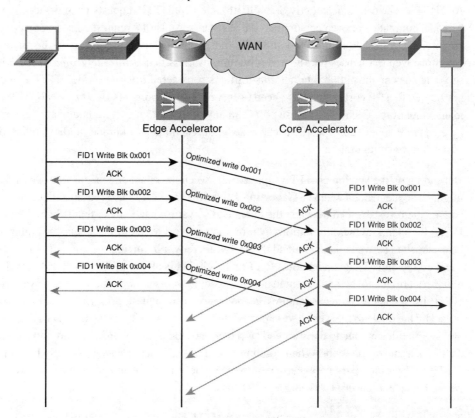

Many accelerators employ acceleration capabilities for file access protocols other than CIFS, such as the Network File System (NFS) for UNIX environments. The concepts of file protocol acceleration are largely similar to the concepts of acceleration that can be provided to other file access protocols and other application protocols in general. The primary differences among them are the structuring of the messages and the way state is maintained. CIFS, for instance, is an extremely stateful protocol, whereas NFS is stateless and requires that all operations be idempotent. Regardless of the file system protocol in use, an accelerator that performs acceleration and object caching must be employed in a way that preserves data integrity and coherency.

HTTP

The HTTP application-specific cache functions of an accelerator allow for reactive caching of objects that are requested through on-demand HTTP content requests. To appropriately intercept HTTP traffic via traditional caching, the accelerator must have the ability to natively speak the HTTP protocol. Although HTTP and the secured HTTPS share the same foundational transfer methods, HTTPS is treated differently by accelerators. Session encryption is the primary difference between the protocols, and some accelerators can become a *man-in-the-middle* through a process of decryption, optimization, and re-encryption. Any responses served locally are re-encrypted, and any requests that must be sent upstream are re-encrypted to maintain security semantics.

An HTTP cache can transparently or explicitly intercept HTTP requests from devices such as personal computers or even personal digital assistants. An HTTP request consists of a connection commonly established over TCP port 80. From a client to a given origin server, the majority of enterprise web traffic uses port 80 and is commonly classified as *intranet traffic*. If the origin server resides on the public Internet, this traffic is considered *Internet* traffic. HTTP requests are not limited to TCP port 80 but have been observed on TCP ports 8000, 8001, 8080, 3128, and many other ports. Each one of these ports and any other custom port number can be intercepted by the HTTP application-specific cache based on predefined port number understanding or administrator configuration.

Depending on the version of HTTP supported between the client and origin web server, requests might be sequential, as with HTTP version 1.0 traffic. HTTP 1.0 also requires that a new TCP connection be established between the client and server for each object that is being requested. HTTP 1.1 addresses these limitations by providing support for multiple concurrent connections to be established between the client and the server, thereby minimizing the amount of time that is spent establishing TCP connections. Request pipelining is also supported with HTTP 1.1, although it might not be implemented in some specific web-server or application-server instances. HTTP 1.0 sequential requests require a response for each request, prior to the next request being issued by the client to the web server after establishing a new TCP connection. HTTP 1.0 requests are very inefficient, due to the start and stop nature of the protocol and the start and stop use of TCP as a transport protocol. When combined with a WAN that has a significantly high latency, HTTP 1.0 becomes extremely inefficient to the requesting client and can present a severe performance bottleneck.

Traditional application-specific caches rely on HTTP headers or relative time values to determine the freshness validity of a given piece of content. When a client initiates a request for content from an origin server, through an accelerator with HTTP caching and protocol acceleration, the accelerator first checks the object cache to see if the content already resides within storage. If the content does not exist in storage, the accelerator forwards the request upstream toward the origin server to fetch the content and update the local object cache. When the origin server responds to the request, a copy of the content is served to the user while simultaneously updating the local object cache with the object itself. At this point, the object may be a candidate for use upon receipt of a subsequent request.

If the content already resides in the application-specific cache, the accelerator initiates an HTTP If-Modified-Since (IMS) request to the origin server, checking the date, time, and entity tag, or "ETag," properties of the content on the origin server within the response header. If the date, time, or ETag properties have changed at the origin server, the server provides the updated content to the accelerator. To prevent the serving of stale content from the accelerator's cache, newer content will always be acquired, stored, and served to the requesting client. Example 4-1 illustrates the common structure of an HTTP response header that the accelerator will inspect to determine object validity.

Example 4-1   *Common HTTP IMS Response*

```
NameValueDelimHTTP Status Code: HTTP/1.1 200 OK
Date:Thu, 09 Nov 2006 03:51:20 GMT
Server:Apache/2.0
Last-Modified:Mon, 02 Oct 2006 03:02:18 GMTETag:"345"Accept-Ranges:bytes
Content-Length:837
Content-Type:image/gif
Connection:Close
```

When an HTTP application-specific cache is combined with compression and other optimization techniques such as read-ahead, the overall traffic that traverses the WAN between a core accelerator and edge accelerator is significantly minimized. Although many web servers today apply gzip or DEFLATE compression to served objects, a cache still bases its decisions on the header properties provided by the web server. Many times, the objects served by the web server contain data patterns that the accelerator can leverage through data suppression algorithms, as discussed in Chapter 6. An object served from a web server might contain patterns that the core and edge accelerators have already recorded, eliminating the traffic patterns found within the response to the client's HTTP GET. When combined, HTTP caching, read-ahead, transport optimization, compression, and data suppression provide a vast improvement to the requesting user's web experience.

HTTPS

Although similar to HTTP, HTTPS adds security through encryption to the transfer of content between a client and web server. Unless the accelerator is able to actively participate in the session with the use of a valid key and certificate, the accelerator can provide only WAN optimization components. Both in-session (man-in-the-middle) and out-of-session (TCP flow optimization only) optimization services provide performance improvements to the end user. To provide a greater degree of optimization for HTTPS traffic, accelerators that are participating in the optimization of such flows must either be preloaded with the keys necessary to decrypt encrypted flows or be able to participate in the secure session establishment as a man-in-the-middle using single-sided key distribution and session keys (as opposed to private keys).

To establish a successful HTTPS session between a client and server, the two hosts must establish a secure session based on a successful exchange of certificates and keys. If the negotiation process of the certificate and key cannot be established, the attempt to establish an HTTPS session fails. With a failed HTTPS session, content is not transferred between the origin server and requesting client, and the client must reattempt the certificate and key negotiation or seek an alternative method of access to the origin server.

For accelerators to actively participate in and optimize an HTTPS session, the accelerators in the network path between the client and the server must have access to the proper certificates and keys needed by the origin server. HTTPS certificates and keys must be administratively applied to the accelerators prior to the first secure session traversing the accelerator.

Alternatively, accelerators may employ techniques that allow for single-sided distribution of keys to the data center accelerators and leverage the session establishment and session keys to participate in the encryption and decryption of traffic. In this way, the data center accelerator must become an SSL proxy on behalf of the origin server and may also use its own encryption between the user and itself, as opposed to using the server's encryption. This type of deployment, which minimizes the distribution of keys outside of the data center, may also create complications in environments with client keys.

Once keys have been distributed to an accelerator, the accelerator can then safely inject itself into the message exchange through the process of decryption and re-encryption. When an accelerator is actively a part of the HTTPS session and receives HTTPS traffic, the secure traffic is first decrypted. After the traffic is decrypted, the accelerator has visibility to the clear-text data being exchanged between the user and the server. With clear-text data visibility, the accelerator can then parse the data for any cacheable content or requests that can be optimized and employ any optimizations that are safe to employ for that particular request.

For content requests that cannot be satisfied locally, the request and any optimized requests are passed through WAN optimization components such as compression and data suppression (discussed in Chapter 6) and then encrypted and sent upstream toward the origin server through the optimized transport. For content requests that can be satisfied locally, the accelerator can fetch the requested object from the local object cache and apply the encryption necessary to serve the object to the user. Other forms of optimization, such as read-ahead and pre-fetching, are employed in a similar fashion. Figure 4-6 illustrates the data flow of an accelerator that is an active participant in an HTTPS session between a client and server.

The next section takes a more in-depth look at SSL and Transport Layer Security (TLS) and how accelerators that provide optimization for encrypted traffic interact with these security layers.

Figure 4-6 *Accelerator with HTTPS Certificate and Key*

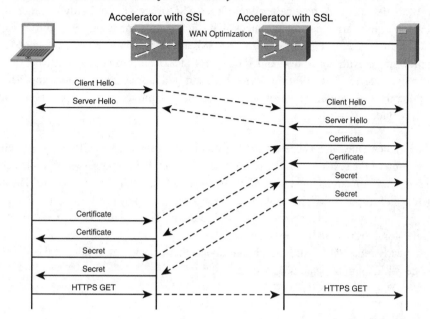

Secure Sockets Layer

Secure Sockets Layer (SSL) is a cryptographic protocol. This protocol provides session-layer encryption for users and servers to ensure that exchange of application traffic over the network is done in an encrypted manner. For HTTP, SSL provides secured browsing access to targeted hosts that have been configured to support the SSL protocol at the application server. Although SSL can be used for a plethora of application protocols, HTTPS is the most common implementation of SSL and thus is the focus of this section. Not all web servers support SSL, nor do all web servers have SSL enabled, but SSL is becoming progressively more popular given customer security requirements and demands from regulatory bodies. SSL sessions create added requirements and workload on the server and client to properly encrypt and decrypt data, which impacts components such as the CPU and memory subsystems. In many cases, SSL can have an impact on performance given how compute intensive it can be, unless SSL processing is offloaded to a secondary processor, which may be installed as a PCI or PCI/X card within a workstation or server.

SSL has progressed to version 3.0, which offers encrypted authentication and communication between the client and server. When an accelerator is introduced in the path of an SSL session, the client establishes a session with and through the accelerator, which in turn provides the predefined credentials to the origin server.

For an accelerator to actively participate in an HTTPS session between a client and server, a hardware decoder card may be used to offload SSL processing to hardware, thereby nearly eliminating the performance bottleneck that is created by managing SSL in software on the CPU. Such hardware acceleration cards for SSL are intended to reside in an open PCI slot within an accelerator. Although external dedicated HTTPS decryption devices exist today, it is rare to find a dedicated SSL decryption device installed in a remote network location. Many can be found in the data center, however, and are typically deployed in existing server load balancing (SLB) devices.

When implemented in an accelerator, the SSL acceleration card handles the decryption and re-encryption of the session with the requesting client and the origin server. Without such a card present, these functions must be handled by the accelerator CPU and software. The accelerator itself is still responsible for establishing the session setup, key exchanges, and any negotiations required during the establishment of the SSL session. The use of an active SSL card in an accelerator does not completely eliminate the need for added resources at the accelerator but does greatly reduce the processing requirements that consume resources at the accelerator device while optimizing an SSL session.

Transport Layer Security

Transport Layer Security (TLS) version 1.1 is the successor to SSL version 3.0. The primary differences between the two involve recent RSA enhancements to TLS 1.1 that did not exist in SSL 3.0. TLS 1.1 supports RSA, DSA, RC2, triple DES, AES MD2, MD4, MD5, and SHA algorithms. Depending on which is negotiated at the time a session is being established, a TLS 1.1 session might become an SSL 3.0 session. If HTTPS interception and SSL acceleration are enabled on an accelerator, and the required key and certificate have not been provided to the accelerator or are otherwise unavailable, the request transparently passes through the application-specific acceleration capabilities of the accelerator yet may still leverage the benefits provided by the WAN optimization capabilities between accelerator appliances to improve the performance of the connection.

Streaming Media: RTSP, HTTP, and Flash

Streaming media has become one of the most popular methods of corporate communication. Streaming media brings the presenter to his audience, taking the messaging contained within the streaming media to a more personal level with the viewer. The following four major contributors are foundational to the success of streaming media:

- Microsoft Corp., with its Windows Media Server and client-based Windows Media Player

- RealNetworks, Inc., with its Helix Server and client-based RealPlayer

- Apple, Inc., with its Darwin Stream Server and client-based QuickTime Player

- Adobe Systems, Inc., with its Flash Media Server and client-based Flash Player

Each of these streaming media vendors requires two common components: a server that provides content over the vendor's native transport protocol and a dedicated media player or browser plug-in installed on the client's computer to effectively decode and play back the media. From an application perspective, streaming media has taken a corporation's ability to communicate to a new level, bringing executive management to the employee.

The protocols used by each of the major streaming media vendors may be based on a protocol as basic as HTTP or may progress into other protocols, such as the Real Time Streaming Protocol (RTSP). To become an active participant in the streaming media event, an accelerator must have the ability to properly match an RTSP-based request to the proper instance of the streaming media server or proxy. Although HTTP sessions are a progressive download or unmanaged flow of content to participating clients, RTSP requires intelligent decision awareness at the streaming media–specific cache or server.

As discussed in greater detail in Chapter 5, there are two methods of delivering streaming media to the requesting client: video on demand and live streaming. Video on demand involves serving streaming media to a client reactively. The client's request is served by the delivery of content at either the beginning of the media or at a specified offset contained within the client's request to the accelerator. Access to content served as video on demand involves the client accessing a given predefined URL that points to a video file on a server. The target of this predefined URL may reside at an origin server or an accelerator.

Live streaming media is used within an enterprise network less frequently than video on demand is. Live streaming media involves much more planning and schedule synchronization. For an accelerator to participate within the flow of a live streaming media event, the accelerator commonly becomes the live stream's splitting point at the data center and edge of the network. The stream splitting process allows for the accelerator to acquire a single live feed from the media's server source and provide that single stream to multiple participating clients behind the accelerator. This method of splitting streams allows an accelerator to serve a large number of streams without requiring multiple copies of the same stream to traverse the WAN. A streaming-focused application-specific cache will not obtain a copy of the live event as it traverses the accelerator but merely facilitates the ability to distribute a single feed to multiple users simultaneously. Figure 4-7 shows how a small number of streams from an origin server can be used to serve live content to a large number of users.

When an accelerator that supports optimizations for RealNetworks, Windows Media, and QuickTime receives the initial RTSP request for content, it looks for the client's media player to be identified within the first eight transactions of the request. Once the accelerator has identified the client's media player, it routes the request to the proper streaming engine within the accelerator. For requests that require the accelerator to communicate across the WAN, the accelerator applies WAN optimization components such as transport protocol optimization to the TCP-based stream as it traverses the WAN. To the client of the live stream, the optimizations might not be as apparent as they are to the network administrator.

Figure 4-7 *Using Stream Splitting to Minimize WAN Bandwidth Consumption*

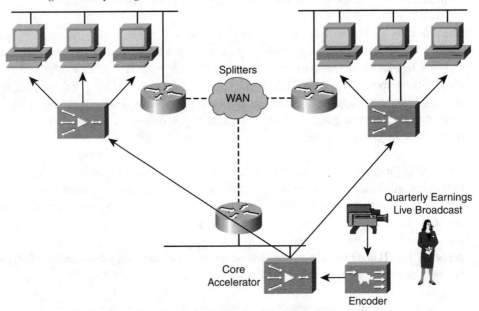

Video-on-demand content that has been prepositioned to the accelerator over protocols such as HTTP or CIFS, also leverages WAN optimization components while traversing the WAN. Although video content by nature is already compressed, repeated data patterns can be safely eliminated through data suppression when traversing the WAN, as discussed in Chapter 6.

Just as with other media accessed via the WAN, video-on-demand content is subject to the same risks of stale status and latent freshness. If the video-on-demand content is accessed over CIFS or HTTP, then the accelerator confirms that the content to be served is the absolute latest version available from the origin server. If the content is to be accessed over a native protocol such as RTSP, then the application accelerator first validates the freshness factor of the content with the origin server prior to its delivery to the requesting client.

For live streaming events, the concerns of content freshness do not apply; the live streaming event is delivered to participating clients at the exact time the content is being broadcast throughout the network. The accelerator may simply serve as a platform for optimized delivery through multicast or stream splitting to minimize bandwidth consumption on the WAN for a large number of remote viewers.

Web-Based Database Applications

Three of the most commonly used web-based applications found within the enterprise today include Oracle Corporation's Oracle and Siebel database, as well as SAP AG of Germany's SAP. Each of these applications has the following traits:

- The ability to allow client access to an application via a web browser as an alternative to or in conjunction with the deployment of a legacy desktop application that is preinstalled or installed on-the-fly

- A common authenticated HTTP access model, with the option to transition to HTTPS for added security

- The use of Java applets to generate the application within the client's web browser

- Potentially long wait times required of the user accessing the application, because large Java applets may be used and must be transferred from the database server to the client's web browser over the WAN

Web-based applications can be addressed by accelerators via two different models. The first involves the application-specific caching described earlier. Accelerators that perform application-specific caching of the protocols used by applications are able to keep a cached copy of objects, such as Java applets, that have been previously transferred. This allows the accelerator to minimize the redundant transfer of objects across the network. The second approach involves the use of the WAN optimization components provided by accelerators, which include transport protocol optimization (overcome packet loss, latency, and throughput), compression, and data suppression. This section illustrates both models, showing the benefits that each approach provides to these sample business-critical applications. Chapter 6 provides a more in-depth examination of the WAN optimization components in a more application-agnostic manner.

Oracle, Siebel, and SAP support the use of HTTP to provide simplified distributed access throughout a corporate network. The HTTP requests that are served by the database server to the requesting client carry several cache-friendly objects. Depending on how the database server is configured, the primary Java applet delivered to the client will be a JAR file, specifically the Jinitiator for Oracle clients. Siebel delivers Java applets and graphics objects while SAP uses JS, GIF, and CSS objects. Depending on the application and origin server configuration, objects served to the client may or may not be identified as cacheable content to a traditional HTTP cache.

When using HTTP acceleration and caching in an accelerator, three simple steps help identify how cacheable the application is:

Step 1   Enable the accelerator to intercept the client's requests made to the database server. This might involve special configuration changes on the accelerator, allowing the interception and application acceleration of traffic on nonstandard ports such as 8802. Many accelerators will automatically recognize ports that are commonly used by application vendors.

Step 2   Enable transaction logging on the accelerator. Transaction logs easily identify which types of content are already cacheable and which types are not.

Step 3   Gain access to a packet-capture or protocol analyzer application such as Ethereal or Wireshark, to inspect the HTTP responses of the object headers that traverse the network between the database server and client.

Once you have configured the accelerator with HTTP acceleration, including caching to intercept the client's database traffic, check the accelerator's statistics for any initial cache savings and compression savings. There is a possibility that no additional configuration changes will be needed on the accelerator, providing the simplest of implementations. Although unlikely, you might find that the server has no privacy or cache header parameters defined to prevent the HTTP cache within the accelerator from storing current requests and serving future requests.

When you are inspecting the transaction logs assembled by the accelerator, the client generating the test traffic must request the same database applets at least twice. If the user has requested a given object only once, there is no way to validate whether the cache was able to serve the object that might have been cached. Transaction logs help to quickly identify the filename and URL associated with the request as well as how the accelerator processed the requested content during the second request. Any transaction log entries that state that the second request was a MISS require additional network trace–based investigation by the administrator.

Many of the objects served by the dynamically generated pages are sourced from static, common URLs within the database server. For accelerators that implement standards-compliant forward caching for HTTP, such changes should be made at the server or data center load balancer, where applicable, to improve cacheability. If these changes are not made, other components such as data suppression (discussed in Chapter 6) will still provide potentially tremendous levels of optimization and bandwidth savings.

Some HTTP accelerators support the ability to override the unique headers defined by the server, including an Oracle database server. This type of configuration change is not generally recommended unless the person performing the configuration is intimately familiar with the application content and freshness requirements. In some instances, the Ethernet trace utility will identify which header variables have been set by the Oracle database server.

Knowing which headers prevent object caching aids the administrator in tuning the accelerator. When properly configured, an accelerator with HTTP acceleration capabilities can reduce database object traffic by as much as 90 percent or more and reduce response times by as much as 80 percent or more. A 90 percent reduction in bandwidth utilization and an 80 percent reduction in response time help to provide faster application access for employees, while reducing bandwidth consumption and overall server workload.

Some database applications serve their objects to clients who present a valid cookie during the transaction process. This cookie provides session information to the database server, which commonly includes information specific to the requesting client, or state of the overall business transaction that the client is attempting to perform. Cookies are based on previous transactions that have taken place with the database server. The actual cookie issued by the database server commonly has an associated expiration timer, preventing a session from being accessed at a later date. Although the use of cookies interferes with the actual caching process, cookies and intelligent web caching can be configured to work together properly. Cookies are unique to a specific user's session with the application and are easily identified within the header of a server's response to a client's GET request. By default, any content that has an assigned cookie is not reactively cached in preparation of future requesting clients.

If cookies have been defined by the database application server, or the database application, many accelerators with HTTP acceleration capabilities support configurability of a function that ignores the cookie variables defined within the header and forces the act of caching upon any cookie-related responses. Cookie bypassing does not break the cookies required by the database server to track client application status or database administrator monitoring abilities. Any bypassed cookie variables are transparently passed between the database application server and requesting client, with no disruption to the performance of the application.

Another trait infrequently found within browser-based database transactions is the use of *byte range requests*, sometimes known as *range requests*. Support for byte range requests is not a common requirement of most Internet web servers but has become a requirement of many database application servers. A byte range request made by a client to an application server is a request for a specific range of bytes within a larger object. To an intelligent accelerator, the entire object may never be provided to the clients that reside behind the intelligent cache, prohibiting the cache from storing the database server's response. To address this unique situation, the intelligent accelerator HTTP cache supports the ability to cache the byte range responses provided by the database server. Once the range has been stored by the cache, it becomes immediately available to future requesting clients.

Range requests and session cookies are not taken into consideration by an application-specific cache. The requests presented to the application server include any session cookies needed for a successful transaction with the database server. Range requests also traverse the application-specific cache, allowing for proper application functionality. It is not until the response from the database application itself is provided to the core accelerator that the responses are inspected for any previously known packet structures. The core accelerator provides any known signatures to the branch accelerator, while preserving any session information required by the database application.

When users attempt to access a database server that challenges them for valid credentials, one of two authentication methods may be applied:

- Database server hosted

- User domain based

One method involves the use of the passwords held within the database server. This method challenges the client during its initial HTTP session between the client and database server. This process places a dependency on the database server administrator to properly manage any credentials associated with access to the database application, as well as how the application interacts with any requesting clients. In-database authentication involves challenges over HTTP or HTTPS between the client and database server. If authentication is handled centrally, based on external authentication hosts, then the database application operates independently of any operating system–based authentication. Using external hosts, the operating system of the database server initiates a challenge to the requesting client prior to allowing access to the database application that resides on the server.

Regardless of the authentication method, the intelligent web cache supports the ability to cache authenticated content that has been provided by the database server. By default, client requests for authenticated content require the client to first provide valid credentials to the server's challenge. Once the client has provided valid credentials, the content is delivered to the client. The intelligent web cache will acknowledge that the content had required valid credentials at the time the object was stored in its cache, establishing that any future requests for the cached object will also require the authentication process to be completed successfully.

Figure 4-8 illustrates the traditional intelligent web-caching capabilities of accelerators with the database server in a central data center and requesting clients at remote branch locations.

Much of the object-based data served by a database application is sourced from static locations. These objects do not change. They are the Java applets required by the client to execute the application within the client's browser. These reoccurring object requests make an application-specific cache perform very well. Once the core accelerator has observed and identified an object served by the application server, the packets representing the database server's response become a signature or signatures. The dynamic content served by the database server is often a significantly smaller amount of data when compared to the Java-based applets required by the client's browser. Performance observed by the requesting client may be as high as ten times quicker than a nonaccelerated connection that would traverse the WAN.

Figure 4-8 *Accelerator Deployment for Web and Database Applications*

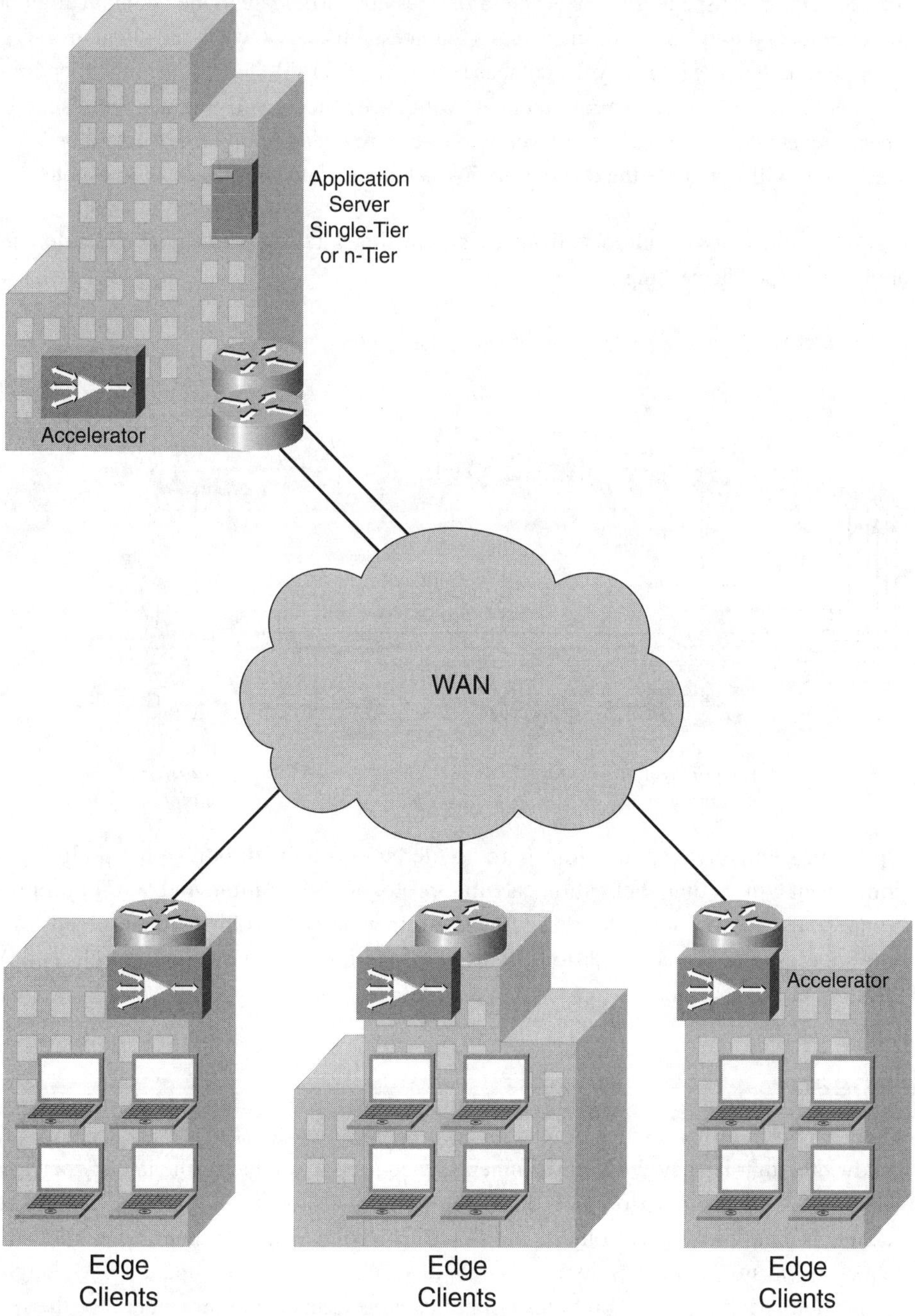

Accelerators with application-specific caching allow the authentication sessions to pass through the accelerator transparently. The accelerator does not participate in the authentication process, nor does it need to be aware of the actual session established between the client and server when the challenge is issued by the database server over HTTP. During the authentication process, the client and database server communicate with each other, qualifying the client's credentials. These credentials, as well as any server responses, are not stored by the accelerator. The accelerator will store only the content or any metadata related to the server's response.

Figure 4-9 illustrates a traditional database application with core and edge accelerators providing application-specific caching.

Figure 4-9 *Application-Specific Acceleration of Database Applications*

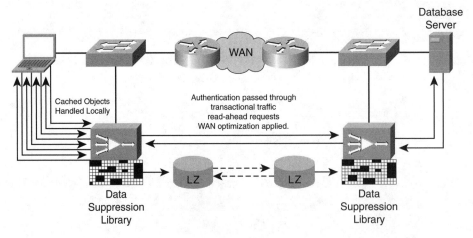

Optimizing enterprise applications with accelerators is done through a hierarchy of components, including application caching, protocol acceleration, and WAN optimization components. When combined, these functions provide bandwidth savings (object caching, data suppression, and compression), latency mitigation (object caching, acceleration), and throughput improvements.

Read-Ahead

Many applications use a series of read requests to fetch objects or data from a server. In low-bandwidth, high-latency WAN environments, each transaction incurs the latency penalty of the WAN and is subject to performance limitations introduced by the WAN. Application-specific caching is a means by which objects are stored locally on an accelerator during the first client request to ensure that objects do not need to traverse the network redundantly. Although application-specific caching provides a significant performance improvement for the second requestor of an object, it does little to improve performance for the first requestor and very little for the second user if the first requestor requested only part of an object.

Application-specific read-ahead is a technique that can be employed within an accelerator that is or is not performing caching for a specific application or protocol. Read-ahead examines incoming application or protocol read requests and augments the requests to either fetch a larger amount of data on behalf of the user or instantiate a larger number of read requests on behalf of the user. In essence, read-ahead tries to retrieve more data than the user is requesting. As the accelerator fetches a larger amount of data, thereby populating the compression history as well as the object cache, subsequent read operations that are made for data that has been read ahead by the accelerator can be serviced locally. In this way, read-ahead prevents the "back and forth" syndrome of read requests that occur between clients and servers.

When an application-specific cache has only part of an object stored in cache, or when an accelerator employs protocol acceleration that does not involve caching, there is a chance that a future request might seek an area of an object that has been used previously but was never requested. In environments where caching is present, the accelerator's application-specific cache begins serving the existing cached data to the client or his application while simultaneously requesting the remainder of the object from the origin server. In environments with accelerators where caching is not employed, the accelerator can still perform read-ahead optimization against the object and temporarily buffer the response from the origin server in an attempt to use the read-ahead data to satisfy a future client request. In such cases, the data is maintained only for a very short period of time and not persistently. An application-specific cache monitors for sequential read requests against a given object and then proactively reads ahead for the remainder of the content (or a larger sequential portion of the object) from the origin server if the client's read patterns persist. Read-ahead caching provides an intelligent method of demand-based content prepositioning onto the accelerator without additional configuration changes by the administrator.

The most efficient model of read-ahead application-specific caching involves two devices: a branch accelerator, which services the client's requests locally, and a core accelerator, which serves both as an aggregation point for several branch accelerators and a termination point for WAN optimization capabilities such as data suppression and transport optimization.

When requests are made for regions of an object that cannot be satisfied locally (cached object, or where read-ahead is a safe optimization to apply), the edge or core accelerator may initiate a read request on behalf of the user. These read requests, when issued by the accelerator, are used as a means of prefetching additional data on behalf of the user such that if the user submits a request for that data, it can be served by the accelerator.

Accelerators can commonly parse human-readable container pages, such as the index file used with HTML, to identify objects that a page viewer might request and to prefetch the objects before the user requests them. In the case of prefetching an object, a user might request a range of bytes from within an object, and the accelerator might submit a larger number of requests against the object on behalf of the user, as is common when accessing a file using the CIFS protocol through an accelerator system. Figure 4-10 shows an example of accelerator read-ahead when employed for segments within an object being accessed by CIFS.

Figure 4-10 *Read-Ahead Optimization for CIFS*

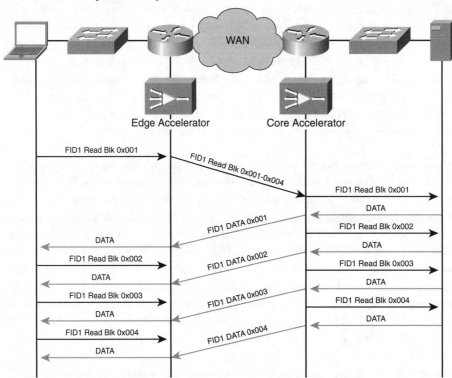

Figure 4-11 shows a similar example where the edge accelerator parses HTML container pages to issue read-ahead requests in a prefetch fashion. This type of read-ahead, based on container page parsing, can be implemented on either the core accelerator (as shown in Figure 4-11) or on the edge accelerator.

When read-ahead acceleration is actively processing client requests, the accelerators provide added intelligence to proactively fetch content and improve the application's performance. When monitoring the accelerator's performance, statistics such as request hits increase and request misses decrease. As the requesting client's application initiates gradual requests for a larger object, the WAN optimization components of the accelerator will likely begin to recognize the request and response data patterns and initiate requests on behalf of the client's application. As the data suppression compression library increases in capacity, the amount of actual compressed data that must traverse the WAN between the core and edge accelerators decreases.

Applications that rely on protocols that are sensitive to latency perform significantly better when leveraging read-ahead technology. When non-accelerated requests traverse the WAN, each individual request made by the requesting client or his application is subject to any roundtrip latency imposed by the protocol or network. Each one of the roundtrip requests adds to the overall response time of the given application. Many times, the latency issues can be safely mitigated at the edge through local protocol handling or through the accelerator's ability to serve requested content locally. Any content requests that cannot be served locally by the accelerator will prefetch via the edge accelerator's read-ahead functionality, reducing future latency in advance of the application's actual request for the data. This also, again, serves the purpose of populating the data suppression library on the accelerators, which will help improve performance as the library grows.

Figure 4-11 *Container Page Parsing and Object Prefetch*

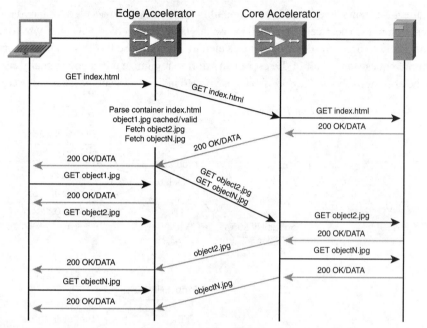

Many applications exist today that exhibit the trend of requesting smaller blocks of data from larger files. It is these specific applications that benefit the most from the read-ahead technologies that an accelerator offers for specific protocols.

Alternative methods to read-ahead caching involve prepositioning the target content. When content is prepositioned, the content distribution process benefits from the use of WAN optimization techniques provided by the accelerators, including compression and data suppression. Prepositioning of content eliminates the need for read-ahead acceleration, due to the intentional predistribution of target content to the edge accelerator object cache, which can also populate the data suppression library. Prepositioning should be considered for large batches of content that the administrator knows must reside at targeted edge accelerators, such as software distribution images or other large objects that are accessed in a collaborative fashion, such as CAD/CAM objects or software development files. Content request read-ahead caching will still continue to function, in conjunction with prepositioning, providing an optimal scenario for known and unknown content requests to an edge-serving accelerator. Content request read-ahead is particularly helpful in environments where the object being used has changed since the last preposition.

Message Prediction

The process of observing a client's messaging patterns and developing statistics on his application's habits becomes the foundation for an accelerator's ability to perform message prediction. With message prediction, the accelerator can begin to learn the patterns of interactive client object access and begin to predict which operations might occur shortly after a certain operation is seen. Once predicted, the accelerator may initiate a series of requests on behalf of the client based on previously exhibited behavior and probability.

Figure 4-12 shows an example of a probability table built by an accelerator based on previously seen operations. The accelerator can then use this table to proactively calculate what operations are most likely to occur in sequence. The accelerator can then use this information to proactively submit requests on behalf of the user in an effort to minimize the latency penalty caused by each of the operations should they need to be performed individually and in sequence over the WAN.

Figure 4-12 *Message Prediction and Probability*

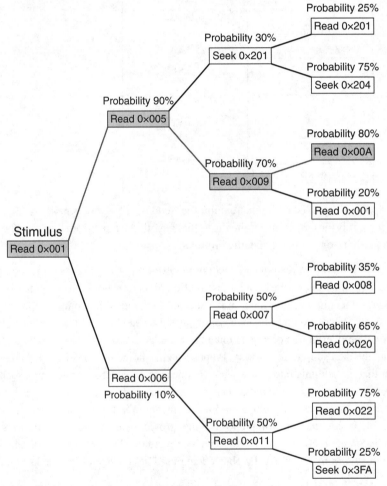

Message prediction tracks the message history of clients whose requests traverse a given edge accelerator and analyzes the recorded patterns for trends and probability. For an accelerator that employs message prediction, this process is performed automatically and on a per-application or per-protocol basis with no administrative intervention.

There are two primary benefits gained from message prediction:

- The accelerator begins to initiate client commands on behalf of the client, potentially beyond simple read-ahead, based on the probability learned from previous client interaction. Alternatively, this behavior may be programmatic and implemented in protocol acceleration functions within the accelerator.

- The accelerator begins to make intelligent predictions based on previous history and operations performed by the client's application, now making requests on behalf of the client's applications in predictable patterns. The response from these operations can be safely buffered at the edge device and used should the client actually make the request that was predicted by the accelerator.

The message prediction function of an accelerator initiates client application commands prior to the actual request by the client's application. The accelerator makes decisions based on an observed history of the client's request patterns, basing its decisions on previously exhibited behavior. The requests initiated by the accelerator, in advance of the client's request, might replace chatty CIFS communications between the client and origin server.

Another application for message prediction involves recognizing patterns in MAPI communications and improving the performance of the sessions between a client's mail reader and mail server. Message prediction can be applied in a generic manner but is commonly implemented as a programmatic function within accelerators today in a very protocol-specific and case-specific capacity.

Messages that are requested by the accelerator itself, on behalf of the requesting client, are staged at the client's accelerator. The response is stored temporarily, allowing the accelerator to safely respond to the user on behalf of the origin server should the predicted message actually be initiated by the client. Message prediction proactively initiates requests, which facilitates reduced latency for future client requests.

Pipelining and Multiplexing

When an application uses only a single connection between the client and the server, requests are commonly serialized over this connection, which can lead to an excessive amount of latency. This can easily translate into performance challenges for the user who is using this application. Many accelerators implement two features to overcome latency, called *pipelining* and *multiplexing*.

Pipelining refers to the process of sending multiple requests within a single TCP session, where a TCP socket remains open and multiple requests traverse the same common socket. With pipelining, multiple requests traverse the same connection in serial but can be sent without requiring that the previous request be satisfied. In this way, the performance exposure to roundtrip latency is greatly reduced. In some cases, requests can even be optimized beyond pipelining by batching multiple requests into a single round trip. Figure 4-13 illustrates a pipelined server response to a client request for three content objects.

Figure 4-13 *Pipelining HTTP Requests*

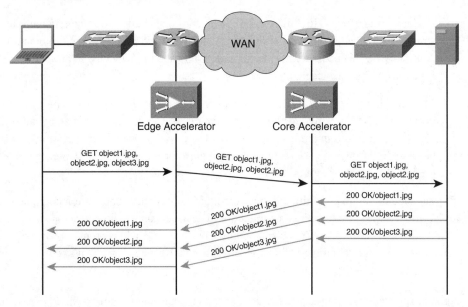

For some networks, a single pipelined session may not fully consume a WAN link, because other constraints exist such as the maximum window size and packet loss. Chapter 6 discusses these topics in detail. In such cases, multiple connections can be opened between the client and server (or between accelerators). This function is called multiplexing.

Multiplexing is commonly implemented in one of two ways. The most common, which is a client and server implementation, uses multiple connections and spreads requests across each of the connections. The other form of multiplexing, which is more commonly implemented in accelerators, uses packet distribution across multiple concurrent connections rather than request-based distribution across multiple concurrent connections. Multiplexing is an application-specific means of overcoming the performance limitations of the WAN and can be used in conjunction with the WAN optimization techniques described in Chapter 6.

Figure 4-14 illustrates multiplexed sessions between a core and edge accelerator, which are traversing a 45-Mbps WAN link.

When pipelining and multiplexing functions interoperate, the amount of data that is passed between devices is in a better position to leverage the full capacity of the WAN. As shown in Figure 4-14, both devices shared the same 45-Mbps WAN link. When the single pipelined session was traversing the WAN link, the fastest throughput the single TCP session could sustain was just over 6.5 Mbps. It was not until introducing multiplexing to the same network environment that the throughput increased to a full 45 Mbps of throughput from seven pipelined TCP sessions. The actual throughput observed by clients placing requests to their local accelerator will far exceed the actual WAN capacity limit until TCP stabilizes. All TCP requests received by any application-specific adapters on the accelerator will provide compression and other optimization to any qualifying traffic that is sent upstream over the WAN.

Figure 4-14 *Session Multiplexing*

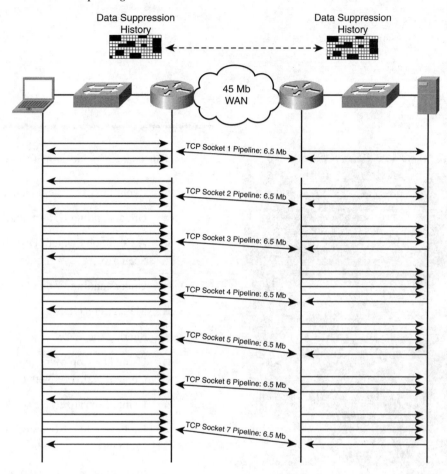

Summary

An accelerator that provides application-specific object caching, application protocol acceleration, and WAN optimization can provide a dramatic improvement in the performance of that application. Many accelerators provide acceleration components for the most commonly used applications, including Internet/intranet, file server access, streaming media, e-mail, and more. Application-specific acceleration and caching components are not necessarily focused on a given software product or application, but rather on the actual protocol that the application's sessions ride upon. When an accelerator has the ability to inspect and understand the actual application messages being exchanged, it has a strong posture to be able to apply application-specific acceleration to minimize the number of messages traversing an already latent WAN and save precious WAN bandwidth by mitigating the need to redundantly transfer previously requested objects. Application-specific acceleration and caching also provide significant performance improvement for the end user. These techniques are complemented by WAN optimization capabilities provided by the accelerator system, which are discussed in Chapter 6.

This chapter includes the following topics:

Content Delivery Networks

The content delivery network (CDN) is a collaboration of geographically distributed accelerators that are centrally managed. Collectively, the geographically distributed appliances are configured to serve one common goal: distribution of an identified set of content objects. A CDN facilitates core needs such as acquiring content from an identified source, distributing the content within administratively defined guidelines, and serving the content to a targeted audience.

In addition to the core functional areas of a CDN, enterprise-specific needs must be resolved. Provisioning for authentication, live and on-demand streaming media events, and client access methods must be coordinated with the network administrators and content owners in mind. Additionally, CDN appliances must adhere to predefined corporate control structures such as device management and monitoring. Finally, employee content consumption must be tracked, via transaction logging and system reporting.

This chapter begins by focusing on the dawn of the CDN in the early 1990s and its evolution into current-day functionality as a key component of an integrated WAN optimization and application acceleration solution. Today, CDNs support a vast array of native protocols, allowing them to seamlessly integrate into existing corporate portals and web sites. Topics such as client request authentication, live and on-demand streaming media, content acquisition, distribution, and delivery are all discussed in-depth. Additional topics such as accelerator function and proper placement within the network are discussed. Because some corporations already have desktop software management applications in place, their interaction capabilities with CDNs are explored. Tips, calculation tools, and guidance for administrators who are responsible for a CDN's successful implementation are provided to aid with future planning.

CDN technologies are an integral part of today's accelerator solutions. CDN, combined with application acceleration and WAN optimization functionality, helps to address the ever-changing demands of content owners and placement of their content items, while also improve access to applications and content over the WAN. This chapter will focus specifically on the CDN components of today's accelerator solutions.

Evolution of Content Delivery Networks

The CDN was introduced in the late 1990s, to improve the client experience by delivering web content locally and to offload the centralized web server farm. Prior to the CDN, software distribution and web servers were commonly centrally accessed, utilizing a star type topology with a web server as the hub to all requesting clients.

This model did not scale to the demand of the growing enterprise initiatives, prompting some web administrators to install mirrored copies of the web server in each remote branch. FTP or CIFS mappings were the method of transporting content to each server. It was common for administrators to script large FTP "batch jobs" to distribute content to each edge server. Some administrators took a more costly approach, distributing fully populated disk shelves to each of the remote offices on a monthly basis or mailing CDs for local personnel to load on the local systems. The batched FTP transfers were common for remote locations that supported WAN links that were of T1 or faster speeds, and disk shelve transport was common to enterprises that desired to move hundreds of gigabytes of content each month.

The challenge that many enterprises face, closely matches the growing trend for greater quantities of data and access to increased volumes of storage. However, WANs are limited by a legacy infrastructure that will take years to upgrade. As floppy disks led to the compact disc, and now the DVD, WAN connections are subject to the same expanding capacity needs. Content stored on web servers in the early 1990s was typically far smaller than content placed on servers in the late 1990s, and that content was smaller than content commonly found on web servers today.

Some of the challenges posed by traditional FTP transfer methods were the lack of fault tolerance, the protocol's sheer appetite for bandwidth, and the lack of firewall friendliness. FTP is very effective and most successful when used within the same data center between two hosts. Distribution via FTP does transfer specific content to edge locations, but not without the risk of requiring an entire file to be retransmitted in the event of a WAN outage. Even minor WAN disruptions might force the client's request to stop and require a restart of the file that was in transit. If the files are large, and the time window for the transfer is limited, the content might never complete its transfer within the allotted time frame. FTP is effective when little overhead exists but is unsuitable for the content delivery network.

Content owners have been known to ship single hard disks or even multigigabyte storage arrays to their remote locations, in support of distributing content. As one would expect, this process is very costly. Although shipping costs could be predictable on a month-by-month basis, shipping becomes a reoccurring operational expense that the corporation must account for. Shipping media adds significant security risks to the corporation, increasing the risk of losing its trade secrets and proprietary data. There is a chance that a storage device will be lost, stolen, or damaged in transit. Although portable media has increased in capacity and decreased in size over the years, the process of distributing physical media, including CDs and DVDs, poses the same risk as ever of data loss or theft. To the misfortune of shipping services and couriers worldwide, the process of shipping storage arrays or dedicated servers around the world can now be considered a process of the past.

Many organizations continue to distribute DVDs to their employees. These discs contain corporate messaging, sales initiatives, and even quarterly results. In one real-world case, a corporation had thousands of discs produced with messaging from the corporation's chief executive officer (CEO). One unpredictable challenge occurred after the media was recorded and distributed: the CEO resigned. In a real-world case such as this, a CDN would have enabled the content owners to remove only the CEO's portion of the media distributed over the corporation's network. Distributing physical media is costly and creates many risks that are now in violation of corporate security policies.

Understanding CDN Solutions

Content delivery networks have taken several different forms in the brief 10 years of their existence. Some vendors offer a pure appliance-based product, while others offer products that require special software or Java applets to reside on the client's desktop or web browser. There are several factors that must be considered when evaluating which technology is the most appropriate for the user's, network's, and administrator's needs. Throughout this chapter, comparisons are made between the more common "market approaches" provided by today's CDN vendors.

Management has several different responsibilities in a CDN, including managing each accelerator, managing the content that resides within the CDN, and monitoring and controlling content that is in the process of distribution throughout the network. Each of these aspects is subject to dynamics that include content owners with differing interests in common content. Content owners have their own set of business needs when a CDN becomes a shared resource for distributing content to edge locations. One of the benefits of the CDN is its ability to distribute selected content to differing locations. The concept of business-driven distribution becomes a key factor in determining what should be distributed and where selected contents' ultimate destination will be.

Content delivery networks extend the use of the origin web or media server's protocols closer to the requesting client. Delivering media via native protocols allows clients to interact with the content just as if they were connected to the origin media server itself. Content interaction may be with a given web portal or streaming media server for live or on-demand content. In the case of streaming media, the WAN creates barriers that limit how many users can simultaneously view a live broadcast. In some cases, if the broadcast can use multicast instead of unicast, additional users might be able to participate in the event, reducing the need for a CDN.

When content is prepositioned to an edge serving accelerator in the network, the user might access the content via its native protocol without realizing that he is actually accessing the content locally.

The user might be clicking a given URL on a central web server, yet all the server responses might be served from a local accelerator in their branch location. Local content serving is not subject to the same latency, bandwidth, and congestion factors associated with crossing the WAN. With edge serving accelerators supporting the protocols used by the origin web server, content can be delivered to the client without the client having any knowledge that the CDN and edge serving accelerator are in place.

With the introduction of CDNs, media owners gain distributed control of their "content," extending their grasp into the realm of flash media, executables, service patches, and beyond. Video owners leverage encoding rates that support full-screen video. Corporate communications mature from lightweight web pages to stunning portals. Teams that operate within a given enterprise obtain control of their media, sharing a resource that other teams have completely separate access to. Each group within the corporation now controls where its content will reside. Controls such as when the content will reside in a given remote location and when specific content will no longer be accessible by the employees in the remote location became new capabilities that would have never been realized by distributing content to a server in a remote branch. CDNs allow content administrators to control where content resides within a distributed network architecture.

All content delivery products today share many common functions. Each method allows the administrator to select the content that will be distributed to the edge location, supports a technology that will transport the target media to the edge location, and supports some form of management and monitoring function for the administrator. Outside of these core expectations, how each interoperates with the content servers and ultimately with the end user differs vastly. Understanding the business needs of the corporation and expectations of the content owner and network administrators is critical in determining which approach will provide the best overall solution for everyone. Two common content distribution methods are:

- Accelerator appliance devices

- Server and client software applications

A Common Content Distribution Scenario

Consider the following example: XYZ Corporation requires marketing, sales, and human resources (HR) content to be distributed to various locations throughout its global network. Some remote offices are exclusively sales focused. Marketing must distribute its content to select locations in the United States, Europe, and Asia. HR requires that its content reside in all global locations as part of its corporate policy, in the native language of any given remote location. Figure 5-1 illustrates how each group has vastly different content needs.

Although this example may seem common and somewhat simplistic, there are several levels of complexity to be addressed. This example represents a real-world model that is common in most globally distributed enterprises today, in which not all content is relevant to all remote locations.

Figure 5-1   *XYZ Corporation Content Needs*

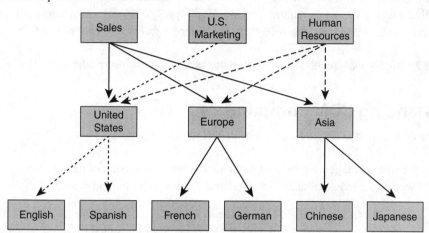

This scenario requires centralized management that must be accessible via Web browser by each of the interested parties. Each party does not need to see what the other groups are distributing, or even need to be aware of what the other groups' actual content items are. Although CDNs support a shared view of what each department is distributing, an isolated view is commonly more desired by each department. In addition, each group might have unique requirements of how content is accessed, and which protocols are to be used. To the system administrator, the distribution requirements are very different, focusing on the time of day of which the content should be distributed, and the amount of bandwidth each organization should be given access to during the distribution process.

The content distribution paths, or hierarchies, might be very different for each of the groups distributing their content. HR data must already be distributed to all locations, but documents written in English might not be appropriate for remote locations in Asia. Documents written in French might have no value to office locations in the midwest United States. These very factors drive the need for granular control and logical aggregation of content within a given organization. HR may have its CDN configured into regions, languages, or even a specific city, state, or country.

In addition to the distribution needs presented by the content owners themselves, infrastructure capabilities are a concern to the IT organization that supports the content owners' needs. The content owners must house their content somewhere on the corporate network, within a data center. The CDN enables the content owners' servers to offload the repetitive hosting of the content, thereby reducing overall utilization of the content owners' servers. Additionally, the IT organization supporting the WAN or satellite infrastructure benefits from the CDN's structured distribution model, which supports time-of-day and bandwidth considerations.

XYZ Corporation has invested heavily in a satellite network for many of its remote offices, due to the nature of its business; some locations are nowhere near an affordable broadband connection. In this case, some offices may use a satellite connection, while others may have a connection via their local cable operator, service provider, or telephone company. Proper selection of a content delivery network solution requires support for all types of network environment. Secure distribution is preferred when using "shared" Internet access connections.

XYZ Corporation's scenario will be revisited throughout the remaining sections of this chapter.

Understanding CDN Components

The three common device functions in a CDN are as follows:

- **Central management device:** Functions as the central point of management for all accelerator functions and content-related operations within the overall CDN.

- **Request routing device:** Manages the process of intelligent request routing. Any request for content under the control of the CDN is intelligently routed to the closest edge serving accelerator.

- **Content acquiring and edge serving accelerators:** Control the flow of content from its original web host to the end requesting client. The acquisition and edge serving accelerators are two separate devices, acting as parent (acquiring accelerator, located near the content server) and child (edge serving accelerator, located near the requesting user).

Software-based CDNs include four or fewer types of "host" configuration, depending on combined functionality:

- **Central management host:** Software configured on a dedicated server, defining the source content, time of day, and destination clients.

- **Content host:** A server or group of servers configured to serve predefined content to any software client applications.

- **Client application:** A software application or browser plug-in configured to listen to the central management host for time-of-day and content host directions. The client application commonly has awareness of other client applications installed on the same LAN.

- **Peering host:** A client application configured to request content on behalf of all other client applications on the same LAN, sharing the acquired content with all the other peers.

Within an appliance-based CDN, one central management device is deployed for overall CDN management, one request routing device is deployed to handle client requests, and a minimum of one content serving accelerator is deployed for content serving functions. For enterprise-grade deployments, redundancy is an option for every device and accelerator within the CDN. In a configuration that allows for each device to operate with a focused responsibility, scalability is increased. If a CDN requires that the central management device share responsibilities with a device that also touches managed content, the overall scalability of the CDN will be reduced. Due to the increased traffic that must pass through the management device, role-sharing central management devices, commonly found in software-based CDNs, experience reduced scalability. The same applies to devices that are responsible for intercepting content requests and redirecting the requests to the closest edge serving accelerator; if overhead is introduced to the request routing device, response times to the client will be slower. Figure 5-2 illustrates a standard content delivery networking architecture.

Today, service providers offer appliance and software-based services, allowing enterprise customers to deploy appliances into their customer enterprise branch locations. Service providers that manage a branch router for the enterprise now commonly offer a service to manage appliances and possibly the customer's content. Two common platforms include an appliance or a router-installed module solution that resides within the managed router itself. Some service providers resell turnkey CDN products to their customers, allowing the customers to own and operate the CDN on their own. Figure 5-3 illustrates a service provider's centralized control of a customer's network via its network operations center (NOC).

The alternative to a hardware-based solution is a non-appliance software-based solution, which in some cases is a service provider–hosted software solution. The component structure is very different from that of a hardware-based solution, with each client's computer being an active recipient of the solution. A server-based host used for management may also be the host that acquires and serves content to the edge clients. This server may employ a Microsoft Windows, Red Hat Linux, or UNIX-based operating system as its foundation.

With some software-based solutions, intermediary hosts may exist in the network to allow for the distribution of content; others require each client to communicate directly with the combined management and content server. As with any enterprise-grade product, content and management servers must offer a redundancy option, or the overall solution risks a single point of failure at its core. Figure 5-4 illustrates a sample software delivery model.

Figure 5-2 *Standard Component Architecture*

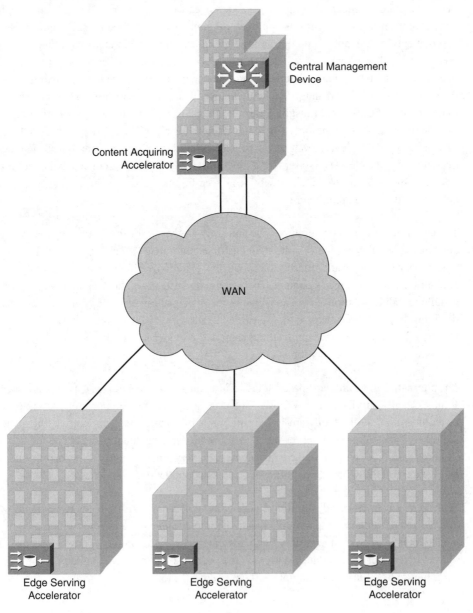

Central Management
Device

Content Acquiring
Accelerator

WAN

Edge Serving
Accelerator

Edge Serving
Accelerator

Edge Serving
Accelerator

Figure 5-3 *Service Provider Model*

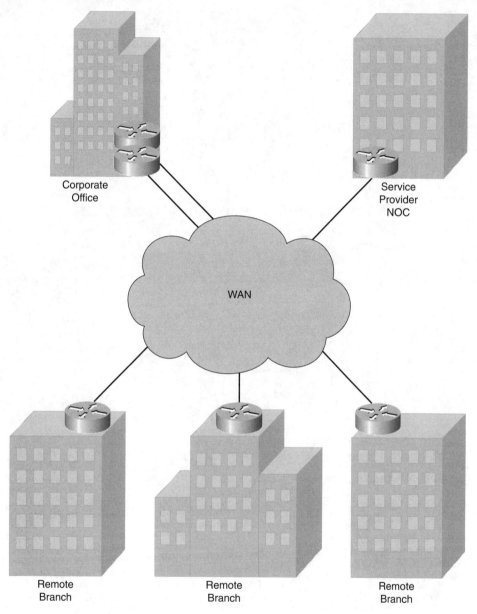

Figure 5-4 *Software Delivery Network*

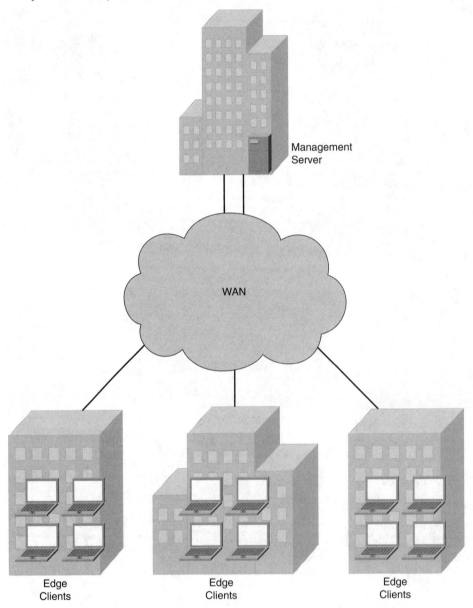

Managing a CDN

When managing a CDN, the content itself is only one of several areas that must be managed. Content-related devices, security, hardware health and state, network architecture, and usage statistics and transaction logs are all additional areas that must be "managed." The following subjects require administrative management, planning, and research:

- Target content identification

- Application and server protocol needs

- Suitable content acquisition methods

- Multiple platforms across distributed networks

- External costs

- Network mapping and usage planning

In many enterprises, the same person or organization does not manage each of these areas. The network or system operations team provides input to the owner of the content delivery team, or might require direct access to the CDN management console. The content owners themselves require access to and control over their content itself, because changes to corporate web portals might not happen at times that are most optimal to network operators.

Identifying Target Content

Effective content management begins with knowledge of the content items to be distributed. These target items will traverse the WAN as they travel to the network edge. Understanding the properties of the content items and how the origin server that hosts the content items operates is critical. Knowing the properties of the origin server allows the content administrators to properly configure their portion of the CDN to interoperate with fewer disruptions to the origin server owner.

Understanding Protocol Requirements

Some corporate policies might not allow content to be accessed by a protocol other than HTTP over SSL (HTTPS) or the Real-Time Streaming Protocol (RTSP), so the process of acquiring content from the origin server must comply with corporate policy, just as any client accessing content from the origin server must comply with corporate policy.

Continuing the earlier example of the XYZ Corporation, the marketing department posts all of its new product training content to a dedicated streaming media server. The training portal requires that the employee access the content with his desktop media player while accessing the corporate network. To retain control of the content, a digital rights management system has been employed, which will also help prevent media from being distributed outside of the company. In this case, the HTTP transport of streaming media would create a security risk to the content owner and corporation; HTTP is considered insecure, with control at risk of being compromised. Any URLs embedded within a stream could be easily identified while sniffing the traffic flow, for example.

The content administrator must determine which protocols corporate policy requires for content access. After identifying the access method specified by corporate policy, the content administrator can determine whether content acquisition can be done automatically or must be done manually as discussed in the next section. In most cases, HTTP is the most commonly implemented protocol for content acquisition. Authentication at the origin server provides content security, requiring authentication of the user or content acquiring accelerator.

Choosing Suitable Content Acquisition Methods

After the issues of content access and authentication have been addressed, the content administrator must then identify whether content acquisition may be a completely automated process or requires manual intervention. Automated content acquisition is the most common approach in today's CDNs.

For XYZ Corporation, HR documents reside on a dedicated server, within a dedicated directory. All content is accessible via HTTP and carries no unique restrictions; no user authentication is required to access these content items. HR places work safety reports on its web server at the end of each workday, making its new content creation and placement predictable.

For the content administrator responsible for HR content distribution, the easiest approach to distribution would be to configure the CDN to automatically scan the origin web server every evening for new content. A key benefit to a CDN is the ability to initiate the rediscovery process of a host at timed intervals. If HR were to produce new content as often as every few minutes, the CDN allows for configuration to automatically discover content just as quickly.

In some cases, content may be placed on an origin server at far less predictable intervals. In such cases, the administrator must initiate the discovery process manually, by accessing the central management device. If the CDN is a component of a broader content strategy within the corporation, application programming interfaces (APIs) might be used at a higher level within the network. Sending API calls to the CDN management platform allows the administrator to execute a manual discovery process.

To effectively manage the acquisition process, the content on the origin server must be identified and understood. There are two common approaches to targeting content in a CDN prior to acquisition:

- **"Crawl" or "spider" the server:** The crawl process allows the discovery process to be automated.

- **Explicitly identify each content item to be acquired and distributed:** The explicit URL method is commonly a much more manual process, requiring each item to be identified individually.

Both options have benefits and drawbacks, as described in the following sections.

Content Crawling

HTTP content crawling begins with the designation of a given content URL, which identifies where the content acquiring accelerator starts its discovery process. Just as many popular search engines start with a given URL and spider through any associated links, gathering content, the content acquiring accelerator does the same. The primary difference between the search engine and content acquiring accelerator is that the search engine gathers copies of all content, including HTML text, whereas the content acquiring accelerator gathers copies of only the embedded objects.

Content acquisition via the crawl method includes FTP and CIFS hosts as well. To acquire FTP content, the content acquiring accelerator must have credentials defined prior to accessing the target FTP server. Both the target FTP server host name and valid credentials are required, just as if a user were to access a given FTP server. Server identification and user credentials must be configured via the central management device, instructing the content acquiring accelerator when to crawl the host server, how often to recheck the host server, and how many directories deep from the root directory the content acquiring accelerator may go.

CIFS servers, such as a Microsoft Windows host, or UNIX servers operating Server Message Block (SMB), such as Samba, allow for CIFS content access. The content acquiring accelerator can acquire content via an explicit manifest file or via the crawl method of discovery. As with HTTP, HTTPS, and FTP, CIFS content acquisition supports the ability to define custom port numbers and username and password credentials for authenticated content access. CIFS acquisition also includes the option to define the username's domain if required by the CIFS server.

Some potential challenges are created by the crawl mechanism. The content administrator's knowledge of the content that resides on the origin server becomes critical to the success of an automated discovery system. If the administrator accidentally places an item on the server that should not be distributed, or that is excessively large, the content acquiring accelerator will automatically acquire and begin the distribution process of the unintentional content. CDNs allow for safeguards to be in place, limiting the automated crawl process to acquire only content that matches a given file extension, minimum or maximum file size, file creation date, or MIME type. Content acquisition flexibility is critical to effective administration. Figure 5-5 illustrates the logical method of content crawling.

Figure 5-5 *Crawl Discovered Objects*

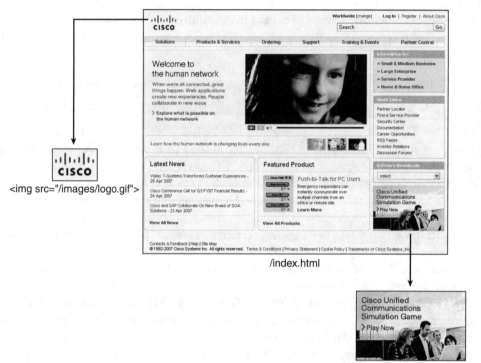

Explicit URL Specification

Explicit URL specification carries several benefits to the content administrator. Content portal vendors also benefit from the explicit URL method of content identification. With the use of an explicit manifest file, the content acquiring accelerator parses a predefined list of content URLs, acquiring strictly the content that is identified in the list. If a directory houses thousands of content items, and only ten items are identified within the manifest list, only the ten items identified will be acquired. Explicit manifest files guarantee to the content administrator that only specific content items will be acquired and distributed to the edge serving accelerator.

The manifest file may be hosted from any HTTP-, HTTPS-, or FTP-accessible source. It is critical to the content administrator that the list be accessed from a host that requires valid credentials prior to allowing access to the list. If a user inadvertently gains access to this list, the user will have visibility into every item targeted for distribution, as well as access to any login or password information included in the manifest file itself. A compromised list might provide the curious user access to a corporate announcement, time-sensitive marketing materials, or information about an upcoming event that might directly impact the user. To many enterprises, their employees pose just as much of a security threat as the outside world does to their corporate data. Example 5-1 lists five formatted entries from a sample manifest file.

Example 5-1 *Sample Manifest Text*

```
<CdnManifest>
<item-group
    server="cisco"
    ttl="1440"
    type="prepos" >
  <item src="images/logo.gif"/>
  <item src="images/wireless.gif"/>
  <item src="images/connected.gif"/>
  <item src="images/waas.gif"/>
</item-group>
</CdnManifest>
```

Third-party content portal vendors benefit from the use of the explicit manifest file as well. When the portal automatically creates the explicit manifest file for the CDN, the content acquiring accelerator can parse the portal-generated manifest file and acquire content automatically. For corporate communications, video on demand (VoD) recordings, e-learning materials, and HR policies are commonly created and added to the corporate servers on an ad hoc basis. Acquisition and distribution of the ad hoc content can be completely automated. The content acquiring accelerator can proactively scan for updates to the manifest file at timed intervals.

The CDN may also be instructed to check for an updated manifest file if the content portal application places an API call forcing the reparsing of the manifest file. For content portals that support API communication to CDNs, the content distribution process becomes a function that the portal owners do not need to be aware of. The acquisition and distribution process is automated, allowing job tasks to remain focused on the portal and the quality of the content provided within the portal.

Figure 5-6 illustrates an administrative host initiating an API session with a CDN, triggering the acquisition process. The externally initiated API session informs the central management device that a new manifest file is available. The central management device fetches the manifest file, passing it to the content acquiring accelerator. The content acquiring accelerator parses the new manifest file, fetching the content items listed within the manifest file.

Figure 5-6 *API-Initiated Acquisition*

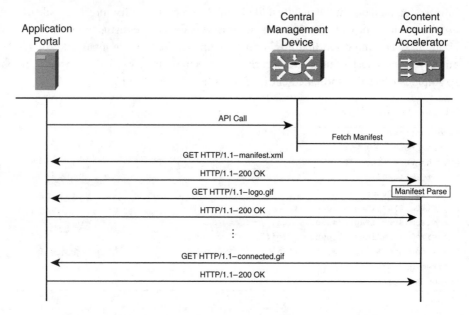

Managing Multiple Platforms Across Distributed Networks

Management of two or more platforms may require more than one administrator; as multiple platforms are introduced, an additional administrator per additional platform might be required. One administrator may be responsible for the CDN in general, one for the content functions on the CDN, and potentially one for each of the content portals that the CDN will access as a content source.

In large enterprises, individual media management teams are common. There may be one person representing HR and its portal, one for sales, and one for marketing. To smaller corporations, this may seem excessive, but to large corporations that have thousands of employees, the administrative staff might involve teams of people instead of one person. The more a CDN and portal can be automated, the easier the administrative staff's job will be, when a single point of contact manages content for a large department.

The ability to effectively and directly manage which content is to be distributed throughout the network requires planning, communication, and an understanding of the application to which the content is associated. Planning involves the content creator, the network administrators, and potentially those who oversee corporate policies. The content owner, CDN system administrators, and any parties interested in traffic that traverses the WAN must all be in communication with each other. Even in automated environments, each party having knowledge of what the others are doing enables each group to interoperate with fewer surprises. If a network outage is planned at the same time as the distribution of critical HR data, for example, this could significantly impact the corporation. Other systems may also be left at a disadvantage, such as the origin web server. If requests cannot be serviced by the edge serving accelerator, they will ultimately go to the origin file server.

It is not implied that CDN administrators should have infinite knowledge of how the application itself functions, but they must be educated on how the content they manage impacts the corporation. Administrators should have an understanding of the concepts that surround the application that users will access and what the application's role is within the corporation. If the CDNs' system administrators understand the application, they will be in a position to better manage the network and meet the content owners needs when a concern arises. If the application is something as simple as distributing a daily report, the report has a business value that content administrators must understand. Effective management of content distribution requires knowledge of the content and its value.

If networks were to involve a single data center, with no branch locations, distribution could be as simple as dragging and dropping content from one local server to separate local servers. Managing content distribution in small networks is just as critical as managing content distribution in a global organization. With today's distributed workforce, the distribution process has traditionally not been so simple. Content might traverse several different types of WAN technologies and cross multiple time zones during the replication process.

Distributed networks now follow geographic hierarchies, which provide an excellent reference point when determining how content should be distributed throughout a given network. Global enterprise networks span multiple countries, and a corporation might have in each country a network operations team that reports to the global headquarters of the corporation. To effectively manage and support content delivery in a global enterprise network, the regional data centers must be aware of any new technologies that reside in their regional data centers or remote branch offices.

Some administrators may take advantage of Multiprotocol Label Switching (MPLS) peer-to-peer distributed networks, eliminating the need for a hierarchical network topology. When an MPLS peer-to-peer network has been implemented, edge serving accelerators still service their native installed subnet, separate of any other subnet throughout the overall corporate network topology. Depending on the number of service providers used to create the overall peer-to-peer network, several hub-and-spoke CDN topologies might be created as a result. In a single MPLS peer-to-peer network, content distribution can occur via unicast or multicast broadcast, including the ability to apply QoS to the flows between the content acquiring accelerator(s) and edge serving accelerator(s). Although not a requirement of an MPLS network environment, QoS allows class-based queuing and weighted fair queuing of the CDN's distribution traffic, adding an additional level of traffic shaping and management.

The overall operation of the global CDN commonly remains within the corporate data center, but distributed regional data centers typically require access to the management console to monitor accelerators they have ownership of. Although management technologies such as the Simple Network Management Protocol (SNMP) allow for external probing of devices that reside in the network, any events that SNMP is not equipped to observe are commonly reported at the CDN management device. The ability to quickly identify a hardware or software fault in an edge serving accelerator that may reside 10,000 miles away from the corporate office reduces management's risk, and reduces downtime to the corporation.

Managing Costs

The cost of a network that uses a common service provider throughout the entire extended infrastructure usually is less than the cost of a distributed network that traverses multiple service providers. Although it is outside of the scope of the CDN system administrator to manage the infrastructure, he must be aware of the environment that supports his services. As one example, a U.S.-based corporation employed the services of three individual regional service providers. Although some service providers charge for bandwidth usage as a flat-rate price, this specific corporation used service providers that charged by measured usage. In an environment where bandwidth usage is the pricing model, distribution is most cost effective when content traverses the network only once. For the corporation that used three independent service providers, content distribution was costly because the content traversed two of the three providers' networks twice. Traffic billing occurred as the content was brought into the service provider's network and then out to the accelerators at the network's edge.

Understanding the network's topology and the cost model behind the network allows the CDN administrator to effectively manage the costs associated with the distribution of content. Although this U.S.-based corporation would have benefited from a single service provider instead of three different service providers, the costing would have become significantly higher if satellite-based networks were implemented. CDNs save on overall network bandwidth consumption and greatly reduce overall costs associated with client access to content. The network itself may always remain an expensive requirement of corporate success, regardless of the addition of a CDN.

CDN administrators must have access to announcements and the schedule for any LAN, WAN, and satellite outages. Outage and maintenance information help the content delivery manager to set delivery expectations with the content owners, reducing potential data outages and employee productivity losses at target locations. Not every network outage is planned, but scheduled events should be known by the CDN manager, to help maintain employee productivity and reduce financial loss.

Table 5-1 illustrates commonly used WAN technologies and their bandwidth offerings available today. Service provider offerings include traditional telecommunications rates, multiple service operator cable modem rates, and digital subscriber line (DSL) rates. Average price models are also shown for reference, but keep in mind that, as with any product, pricing will continually change.

Table 5-1   *Common WAN Offerings*

Commercial Service	Throughput Down	Throughput Up	Average Price (USD)
Cable modem, basic	4 Mbps	384 kbps	$60
Cable modem, premium	8 Mbps	1 Mbps	$160
DSL, basic	384 kbps	128 kbps	$50
DSL, premium	1.5 Mbps	786 kbps	$250
T1, branch	1.54 Mbps	1.54 Mbps	$550–$1200
T3, data center	45 Mbps	45 Mbps	$7500–$14,000

Usage Planning

To manage the distribution of content throughout an enterprise network, the network topology must be well understood. This includes a topology mapping of the WAN bandwidth between data centers and remote locations. If remote locations have secondary WAN connections, these too must be identified when planning the distribution topology of the CDN. Router configurations are beneficial for locations that employ secondary WAN connections, allowing for any additional configuration changes to be added to disable content delivery in the event of a failed primary WAN link. If a WAN outage requires that the secondary link be enabled, it is common to find that enterprises disallow content distribution to take place over their secondary WAN links. The already reduced throughput capacity of a secondary link might support only predefined business-critical applications.

With the affordable adoption of broadband services, many small branch locations now employ the offers of their local multiple service operator. Cable modems and digital subscriber lines are affordable connections that offer vast bandwidth improvements over legacy services such as fractional T1 connections. Internet connections that traverse the public Internet add security and content-protection challenges that the use of VPN-enabled routers have helped to address.

The CDN administrator must be aware of the "external" networking services provided by multiple vendors, because each service might offer a differing bandwidth rate. Some locations might support higher speeds than others. Differing speeds might allow content to be distributed to some locations faster than to others. For networks with differing WAN speeds, the ability to manage the distribution of content and the expectations of the content owners become important factors when structuring the support model of the CDN. It is common for administrators to define a flat-rate speed for all remote locations, regardless of their WAN's throughput capabilities.

The XYZ Corporation has offices in Asia, Europe, and the United States. Many of its U.S. locations are connected to the corporate network via major service providers. Some of the corporation's smaller branch offices use the local cable company's cable modem services. Some of the larger locations throughout the United States have satellite uplink capabilities, with access to 5 Mbps of downlink throughput. The corporate data center in New York City employs redundant T3 network connections to the Internet to support the aggregated connections of the United States, Europe, and Asia. In Europe, all remote offices use E1 connections that aggregate in London and then connect to the corporate data centers in the United States. Asia employs fractional T1s to the many manufacturing plants, with an aggregation point in Tokyo. Tokyo directly connects to the corporate data center in the United States. Although central management of the global network exists in the United States, regional management exists in London and Tokyo. Figure 5-7 illustrates a simple high-level master topology for the XYZ Corporation.

Figure 5-7 *XYZ Corporation WAN Topology*

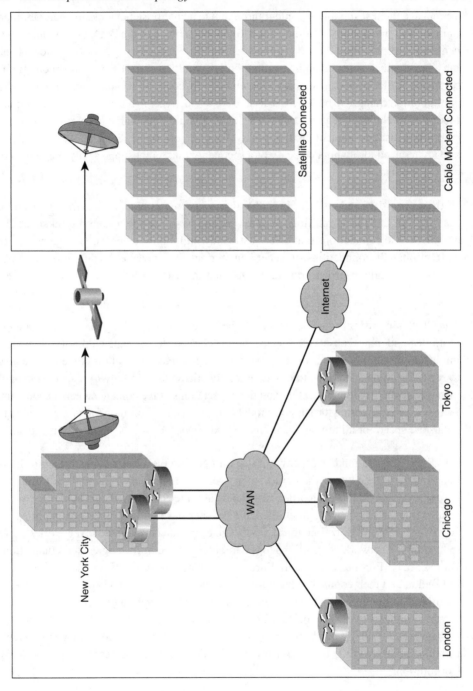

With the vast differences in WAN bandwidth offerings, the ability to effectively manage the distribution process requires some initial planning. For example, the distribution of a 10-MB file may take 53 seconds on a T1 throughput rated WAN connection. The same 10-MB file might take only 13 seconds when distributed to a remote location that has a 6-Mbps DSL connection. The introduction of cable and DSL services has broadened the remote-access options for corporations and created new expectations of content access performance by the employees who work in those connected offices.

It should never be assumed that remote locations that use public Internet-type connections are using a firewall, but if they are not, they should be. CDNs have the ability to pass traffic through firewalls, without disruption to other services. An edge serving accelerator that resides behind a firewall creates acquisition traffic that appears similar to web traffic created by the other clients that reside behind the firewall. Typically, no special considerations are required at the firewall to allow content delivery to take place through a firewall.

Sharing the WAN

CDNs share WAN bandwidth with other business-critical applications on the WAN. Many enterprises today that employ CDNs schedule the distribution process for nonbusiness hours in the remote branch. This prevents disruption of existing employee productivity, and utilizes the WAN at times when the network is least likely to be busy. With the exception of some administrators who execute remote backups of their distributed servers after hours, the WAN is commonly underutilized after hours.

In a perfect world, all remote office locations would have the exact same throughput, and content distribution would complete at exactly the same time for all locations. For the rest of the world, differing speeds, WAN disruptions, and other network traffic are all factors that must be accommodated. The central management device enables the system administrator to define policies that surround the bandwidth settings on a per-accelerator basis. Because bandwidth, time of day, and corporate events all impact how a WAN is utilized, the administrator must have the ability to manage accelerators individually, or via groupings. Bandwidth management is critical to the success of the CDN, and its administrator.

If bandwidth policies are defined to allow consumption of too much bandwidth, other business processes might suffer. If bandwidth policies are defined to allow consumption of too little bandwidth, the content might not be delivered in time for a corporate event or other business deadline. The process of defining and managing bandwidth variables is simple, but determining which part of the day or evening is most effective for distribution requires some research.

Some common network activities and data to investigate prior to defining the CDN's bandwidth policies include

- Data backup and replication operations configured to run after hours

- Desktop management applications in place, distributing content to branch PCs after hours

- Employee access to the Internet after hours

- Whether the WAN maintains continuous connectivity

- Network utilization trending statistics

- Maintenance schedules for the WAN

- Any WAN maintenance e-mail lists

- Any noncentralized PC imaging and software recovery procedures

Investigating the preceding network activities and data will enable the network, desktop, and CDN administrators to interoperate with fewer disruptions or disagreements. Each administrator has rightful access to the WAN, each with differing needs, demands, and challenges.

Server and client desktop backup operations commonly run after hours to avoid disrupting regular business flow. Backups could be as simple as an automated script that creates one large compressed file and *puts* the file via FTP to a host in the data center. Commercial software packages exist to perform the standard full, copy, incremental, and differential backup of a client or server. The backup process might consume the WAN connection during the entire after-hours period, depending on the volume of data to be backed up and the size of the WAN. Although CDNs are commonly one-way technology, the use of an accelerator will greatly reduce the effects of bandwidth consumed by traffic that traverses the WAN during legacy FTP transfers, and might also assist in WAN bandwidth for other backup products.

Using Desktop Management Suites with Content Delivery Networks

Application suites that provide direct control of the client's desktop environment are becoming more popular within the enterprise. These applications are not software-based CDNs but provide security, compliance, and delivery solutions. Many of these types of products leverage protocols such as CIFS or HTTP to distribute content to client desktops. Small desktop applications are installed on the client computer, allowing for centralized management of remote desktop devices. The application operates differently from how software-based content delivery products operate, focusing on the operating system and applications installed on the computer.

Desktop management suites do not compete with CDNs or accelerators, where software-based CDNs do. Desktop management suites keep their focus on allowing network and desktop administrators to control all desktop devices within the corporate network. There is little to no overlap between desktop management suites and software-based CDNs. Some of the more popular desktop management suites use protocols such as HTTP or CIFS for content distribution, protocols which operate natively on appliance-based content delivery devices and are recognized for optimization with accelerator appliances.

In environments that leverage a desktop management suite, the managed clients all communicate with a common server within the data center. When management of hundreds of computers applies, this model might operate with poor results over a WAN. Consider management of thousands of remote computers, and the use of content distribution appliances easily becomes justifiable. The CDN has the ability to acquire content from the desktop management server and preposition the content to edge locations throughout the network. When the managed client requests content, local request intercept or client redirection methods will guide the requesting desktop to the nearest serving appliance. When considering that several hundred computers may reside in a single remote location and a single service pack may consume over 100 MB of space, WAN resources should be required to transfer the file only one time. Once distributed to the remote edge serving accelerator, all desktops will obtain this update from their local edge serving accelerator.

Combining Solutions

Combining an existing desktop management suite with an accelerator or CDN will provide a significant improvement to the desktop management process. Combining a reliable distribution method with a proven desktop management suite will provide benefits to both administrative teams. The desktop management team will now know that their distribution traffic does not disrupt other business activities, and the CDN administrator will provide direct support to the desktop management team. Both can operate independently of each other, or the desktop management team can be given access to the central management device to coordinate its own distribution activities.

Some branch offices might have several client computers installed, requiring software updates to traverse the WAN independent of the other systems. This model is very inefficient and costly to the WAN's available resources. Desktop applications such as Microsoft Systems Management Server and Altiris Client Management Suite might apply software, patches, and upgrades to remote branch servers and workstations after hours, to prevent bandwidth contention. These applications might have access to branch systems only during hours when both the network is available and the remote systems are not active in a production environment. Unless patch management is applied locally to each edge system, access to the WAN becomes a requirement.

Combining Management Functions

If the software management system has to share bandwidth with the CDN, it may be most beneficial to integrate the software management system with the CDN solution. An alternative is to implement an accelerator solution in the branch office. The installation of a CDN will allow for a single transfer of the software updates, regardless of the number of clients and servers deployed in the remote branch.

Internet access during business hours is becoming an increasingly costly challenge to the corporation due to reduced employee productivity during normal work hours. Many network administrators have implemented URL filtering solutions in the core of the network to prevent employees from accessing the Internet during business hours. Some allow Internet access, but limit that access to only Internet sites that are deemed appropriate during business hours.

After-hours Internet access is becoming more popular, because employees enjoy the increased bandwidth offered by the corporation's network. Allowing after-hours Internet access also helps alleviate the spike in Internet access that many corporations observe during the midday lunch period. If after-hours Internet access is allowed, it should be known by the CDN administrator. Internet access is traffic that the CDN must interoperate with, even if the Internet access is not a business-critical use.

WAN traffic trending is the most valuable information a CDN administrator can have access to. These reports provide statistics and trends that are real-world usage patterns. Utilization and traffic flow reports confirm information that the network administrators provide, and occasionally uncover other traffic that network, server, and CDN administrators might not be aware of. If the resources exist within the data center to track and monitor network usage, even by protocol, applications or backups, new uses for the CDN may be uncovered, adding value to the corporation's investment.

Centralized accelerator management allows administrators to gain visibility into the underlying system that controls and houses prepositioned content. Accelerator management of the dedicated CDN is different from that of the distributed server management model. CDNs require management of not only the operating system that runs on the dedicated accelerator but might also go to a level that involves direct control of any content that resides on the edge serving accelerators. Centralized accelerator management, for the CDN, also requires a method to centrally administer any patches or system upgrades from a single secure console, due to the unification of the operating system and content delivery product itself.

To effectively manage an edge serving accelerator, its security properties, storage configurations, and how the accelerator will interact with the network environment, a centralized management platform is best. For CDNs, the central management device fulfills all device and accelerator-related management needs. Although SNMP-based solutions might offer limited control of an edge serving accelerator, an SNMP approach is a much more generic approach to a given device or accelerator's control needs. Centralized management that is secure will go far beyond what SNMP v2 and v3 support and will include a more diverse graphical interface. A purpose-built centralized management device will communicate with each edge serving accelerator securely, sending any new configuration and content instructions, while gathering health, content, and utilization statistics simultaneously.

Centralized device management allows for a lower level of control below what content administrators require, taking into consideration storage allocation, disk partitions that may be required, accelerator network settings, streaming media services, authentication, and access control lists (ACLs). Each of these settings will not require the content administrator's involvement, but will require proper configuration. As an example, if an enterprise-wide directory services administrator from the XYZ Corporation were required to apply a user-focused policy to each user's object in the network domain, it would be a repetitive process to do so for each employee's user ID. If an ACL were required for all content accelerators throughout XYZ Corporation's network, manually setting the ACL would be a very time-consuming process. Centralized accelerator management for remote edge serving accelerators allows for edge serving accelerators to be grouped for easier mass accelerator management, just as the principal of the user group aids administrators in configuring and controlling hundreds or thousands of user account properties.

Accelerator management of prepositioned storage-related settings for an edge serving accelerator involves discussions with the content owners themselves. Knowing how much content is to be prepositioned is required information, because any partitions related to prepositioned content must coexist with other disk needs as well. Knowing how long the content should coexist with newly added content is also required information for storage utilization purposes. Accelerator- and disk-related management might involve extended storage of transaction logs that are a result of content usage; this is a requirement for some corporations that have compliance regulations in effect. Accelerator management of CDNs that use partitions that support content caching and streaming media impacts how each edge serving accelerator's storage configuration is defined.

Establishing Storage Requirements

Some general rules exist for determining edge serving accelerator storage needs. The host operating system, cached content needs, streaming media content requirements, and transaction logging all become factors that must be known. In the process of investigating disk needs, consider the following content tendencies:

- Video-on-demand streaming media content traditionally requires the largest amount of storage per object.

- Web caching storage needs can be predicted based on usage trends, object sizes, and WAN connectivity.

- The host operating system will have a predefined storage requirement.

- Housing of content that is prepositioned requires an identifiable or controllable amount of storage space; the volume of content to be prepositioned is based on known objects.

- Transaction logs are commonly not held at the edge serving accelerator for more than 30 days.

Using Centralized Network Settings

Centralized management of edge serving accelerator network settings allows for an administrator to make changes to settings such as the accelerator's IP address, network mask, default gateway, or even the link speed of the physical network interface. By leveraging the proper centralized management method, network changes will not disrupt the overall process of content delivery, streaming media events, network upgrades, or access to the edge serving accelerators. If changes are made to an edge serving accelerator without applying the same changes to the centralized management device, the centralized management device might restore the edge serving accelerator's configuration to its previously defined settings.

An edge serving accelerator supports bandwidth settings of 10, 100, and 1000 Mbps, with full- and half-duplex settings per interface. If the switch that is used for the LAN is upgraded from 10 and 100 Mbps to 1000 Mbps, the edge serving accelerator's configuration might be changed centrally. Other settings, such as the maximum transmission unit (MTU) size and any ACL settings, are best applied centrally.

Although autosensing network interfaces make speed changes easier, some corporate environments do not allow for the use of autosensing network interface functionality. In rare instances, the autosensing negotiation process might not be compatible between a switch and a given client or host that has been installed into the network. If a system administrator requires access to an edge serving accelerator's configuration, access via the centralized management device allows them to interact with the CDN using the same controlled method used by other administrators.

Centralized control of a CDN requires awareness by many different business organizations. Depending on which organization controls a given function, multiple groups may be required to support the CDN's overall management functions. Organizational control will vary, including teams that manage content, network function, network security, and network stability. The following list identifies some of the functions controlled by differing organizations:

- Streaming media

- Authentication and authorization

- Access control lists

- SNMP

- Accelerator monitoring

- Edge serving accelerator control

Centralized Streaming Control

Accelerator management and live streaming media services are best managed in a centralized or group-based model, with VoD commonly leveraging static accelerator policies. Enabling streaming licenses commonly is applied to either new accelerators that have recently been added to the network or to all accelerators globally throughout the corporation. License keys often are lengthy and cumbersome and are best applied from a central management device.

The alternative to centrally applying licenses is to access the edge serving accelerator's command-line interface (CLI) and enter the configuration commands manually. The manual process is more prone to operator error, due to the less-streamlined process of keyboard interaction.

Accelerator configurations related to specialized live events, frequent streaming media bandwidth adjustments, and simultaneous session limits are all best handled via centralized accelerator grouping management; area commonalities such as remote users groups, and branch standardized LAN configurations can easily be managed as groups. To effectively deliver a live streaming event to large numbers of remote offices, nonstatic bandwidth changes may be required during the period of the live broadcast, or transitioning from unicast to multicast distribution for a given event.

The ability to centrally control each edge serving accelerator simultaneously will make the administration process significantly easier than accessing each edge serving accelerator locally, specifically when all accelerators must access a common stream source at exactly the same time. In situations that involve live broadcasts, the network administrators may commonly not be involved in the process, other than knowing that an event is pending. Content administrators and content delivery system administrators carry the majority of the responsibility for managing these events, calling in network administrators if an event fails to properly launch at a given remote location.

It is highly recommended that live events be tested several days in advance of the actual event, to ensure network stability. Pre-event testing is especially beneficial for multicast type broadcasts. Redundant streaming sources provide an added level of protection, allowing the CDN to access multiple sources as failover hosts. Prior to the actual live event's broadcast, many corporations will run a pre-event feed to ensure that all remote locations have adequate access to the event prior to the actual broadcast session. Actively monitoring and managing all edge serving devices during the test event, and prior to the actual event, will allow for any custom changes to be applied to edge serving accelerators before any business-impacting surprises arise.

Centralized Administration of Authentication and Authorization

Network administrators typically are responsible for accelerator management and user authentication and authorization policies. Content administrators must determine whether or not their content requires the enabling of access authentication for a given set of managed content.

The role of the content owner differs from the role of the CDN's edge serving accelerator, which the CDN administrator is responsible for.

Keeping job roles separate, the content owner requires that content requests will be secured behind a prompt for end-user credentials. The system administrator is responsible for the back-end authentication settings related to domain controllers, groups, and domains that facilitate the content owner's requirement. Each of these settings is configured at the accelerator level, with authentication impacting access to content, the accelerator itself, and the ability to actively configure and manage any accelerator in the CDN. Accelerator management and the ability to remotely manage an edge serving accelerator are functions that are controlled through credential-based validation.

System administrators commonly have a single defined standard for server-based content authentication. The most common methods are NTLM versions 1 and 2, HTTP basic, or an HTTPS form with a set cookie. The edge serving accelerator communicates with the authentication server's database via the LDAP, NT LAN Manager (NTLM), RADIUS, or TACACS+ protocol. For an edge serving accelerator to properly authenticate a user's credentials, a challenge is presented by the edge serving accelerator, to determine who the user is that is using the requesting computer. For some Microsoft Windows–based operating systems, the browser provides the user's credentials on behalf of the user, but only when NTLM is the authentication method used.

The XYZ Corporation has standardized on NTLM throughout its network, due to the dominance of Microsoft servers within the network. The edge serving accelerators have each been configured to direct authentication requests to specific hosts within the network. The system administrators require authentication from the CDN to prevent unauthorized access to content that is specific to different groups defined within their active directory domains.

When configuring the origin server that the user will access for the core HTML or ASP content, many times, the authentication challenge for content access will be issued by the origin server itself. In these cases, the edge serving accelerator might not need to be actively involved in the authentication process if the client must provide valid credentials just to gain access to the portal. This method of authentication is commonly referred to as *pass-through authentication*, where the edge serving accelerator plays a passive role in the passing of the credentials between the client and the origin server.

If a requesting client is accessing prepositioned content via an edge serving accelerator configured as a proxy, then the edge serving accelerator will issue an authentication challenge to the requesting client. Proxy configurations are described later in this chapter, in the section "Understanding Explicit and Transparent Proxy Modes." When the requesting client responds to the authentication challenge, the edge serving accelerator communicates with the configured external authentication host, to verify the credentials contained within the user's response. To the administrator of the CDN, the process of configuring authentication typically involves defining the external host or hosts and enabling the appropriate method of authentication.

The responsibilities of the content administrator and the CDN system administrator differ greatly from the perspective of user authentication. Content owners must only determine if authentication is required for their prepositioned content. The system administrators must configure and control the underlying authentication implementation to support the content owner's needs. Accelerator management of authentication-related functions is best handled at a central console, by targeting all accelerators collectively or by targeting groups of edge serving accelerators. It is very rare that each remote edge serving accelerator will have its own dedicated external authentication server; in situations where this is the case, each edge serving accelerator must be individually managed either via the central management device or via the edge serving accelerator's CLI.

Centralized Access Control List Administration

A less common method of content request control involves the use of ACLs. ACLs are most commonly applied to network routers and switches but are also supported by content networking accelerators. ACLs execute simple allow or deny type decisions against requests that pass through the edge serving accelerator. Decisions are imposed on content requests based on several factors, which include simple variables such as the source address or the destination address of the traffic passing through the edge serving accelerator. ACLs are not limited to just HTTP traffic, but are applied to a number of protocols. ACLs offer system administrators a level of control over IP, TCP, UDP, GRE, and ICMP traffic types.

For CDN administrators, the process of implementing ACLs should be done centrally. Accessing edge serving accelerators individually via a central management device is the best option for ACL management. Due to the differing subnet address ranges that might exist at each edge location, no two edge serving accelerators may be installed in the same subnet mask. ACLs applied to one edge serving accelerator might be valid for all requests that traverse a given edge serving accelerator, whereas misapplied ACLs might implicitly deny all requests due to no address matches. IP address–type ACLs are among the more basic types of ACLs that exist today.

Extended IP ACLs provide a greater level of control over and visibility into the requests that traverse an edge serving accelerator, by limiting the requests to which the edge serving accelerator will respond to only those that enter specific ports. In addition to the basics supported by ACLs, such as the source and destination IP addressing, extended IP ACLs take into consideration the source and destination ports within the request, specifically content-related ports such as 554, 1755, 21, 22, 80, and 8080. Source and destination port numbers can commonly be correlated to the application that the client may be requesting. When used properly within a corporation, streaming media leverages known port numbers. Nonbusiness-related streaming media requests may be blocked, if the edge serving accelerator does not recognize an approved client, server, and port number traversing the edge serving accelerator. The same accelerator management general rule that applies to basic IP ACLs also applies to extended IP ACLs: each edge serving accelerator may have been installed on a different subnet from where the other accelerators are installed, requiring differing ACLs for each edge serving accelerator.

Centralized SNMP Control

Accelerator management via SNMP is one of the most common methods for accelerator monitoring. Management via SNMP allows for visibility into each edge serving and content acquiring accelerator, including management and routing devices. At the first instance of a detected fault, or event, the edge serving accelerator has the ability to announce a *trap*. A trap is sent to an SNMP management host or station, which is a device that operates independently of the content delivery network. Many corporations implement SNMP management applications to allow for centralized monitoring of all network devices, including file servers and storage hosts.

SNMP supports three different versions: version 1, version 2c, and version 3. SNMP version 1 is the least common within the corporate network today, due to limitations in traffic security and authentication. The opportunity for unauthorized visibility into a given device is most likely due to version 1's "in the clear" model of communication. SNMP versions 2c and 3 are recommended over version 1, due to their inherent support for encrypted and authenticated communications.

SNMP monitoring is not a utility for content administrators; system administrators will have more interest in the information provided from SNMP management. Some of the more important information made available from SNMP monitoring includes disk-related data, such as read, write, and failure-related events. At a minimum, storage-related events should be tracked via SNMP, due to the storage-centric nature of the edge serving accelerator. Software and system events may be tracked from the central management device, but if storage-related events with a negative impact occur, the administrator must be made aware of the event at the soonest possible opportunity.

Centralized Monitoring

Management of the CDN's usage statistics, bandwidth savings, and transaction log generation are all topics that involve both the system administrator and the owner of the prepositioned content. Each topic potentially provides business-critical information. If the executive management of a corporation requires all employees to watch a designated video on demand to ensure procedural compliance, access to prepositioned media must be tracked. With the growing requirements for procedural compliancy, information consumption tracking is critical.

Enabling Transaction Logging

By enabling transaction logging, you can see how often a given piece of content is requested. If corporate messaging has no demand, the corporation is not effectively communicating with its employees.

Transaction logs provide statistics that aid content administrators in determining what types of content should or should not be distributed to remote locations of the network. Although it is common for transaction logs to be held for up to 30 days, some corporations require their transaction logs to be held for several years. If transaction logs must be held for periods of time greater than 30 days, it is recommended that the edge serving accelerator have the ability to export any self-created transaction logs to an external host. Using external hosts allows for adequate storage and aggregation of all edge serving accelerator statistics in a common, secure, and archived location.

Saving Bandwidth

Less important to content owners is the topic of bandwidth savings, an area that is commonly most interesting to executive management and network administrators. The value of the CDN will be associated with the savings created on the WAN. The return on investment will be closely monitored, focusing on bandwidth savings that the CDN creates.

For content that has been prepositioned to remote network locations, this information is easily quantified. Every time a given piece of content is requested, WAN bandwidth is saved. The content must traverse the network only once, and that is commonly during a time that has the least amount of network impact. Every request that occurs after the initial propagation is realized as immediate network savings. The information gathered within the transaction logs provides an exact numerical value of bytes served by the edge serving accelerator, and this number becomes the bandwidth savings value of each edge serving accelerator.

Centralized Edge Management

Operating system recovery, patch management, and device software management are the responsibility of the content delivery system administrator. These underlying device management obligations will not impact the content owner's responsibilities, and are viewed as system-related tasks. Unlike the model of distributed general-purpose file servers, server management may involve several teams, including content, application, and data owners.

Content delivery devices and their related accelerators are based on an operating system and appliance combination; true appliances use purpose-structured operating systems that are the foundation for a purpose-built content-hosting application. The concept of operating system patch management does not apply to the appliance model of accelerator operating system management. The most common method of host patch management is to apply an updated software image to the content accelerator.

The operating system used in an appliance-based model does not include many of the extras that are found within a generic operating system, including games, additional enabled ports, or non-content-related services. For example, the use of various ports and services on a dedicated appliance that supports ports related to Microsoft Windows host name resolution may interfere with legitimate client to server communications. Excessive ports and services become a security risk if left inadvertently active, and in some cases might interfere with other, non-content-related services.

The ability to centrally manage the software that resides on edge serving accelerators is critical to the success of the system administrator's role. Accelerator software management is not a function of the content administrator's job responsibilities, other than possibly coordinating the distribution of the software upgrade image itself. From the central management device, the acquisition, distribution, and scheduling of a software image upgrade can all be centrally controlled. CDNs support the ability to distribute their own images, without the need of compact discs or other portable media methods. In the event that software upgrades must be done locally, edge serving accelerator can leverage their local CD-ROM drive to source the software upgrade image. Flexible CDNs present several options to the system administrator, based on business needs and processes.

Understanding Content-Serving Protocols

Client content access of prepositioned content may involve more than just a web browser. Protocols such as CIFS, HTTP, HTTPS, FTP, RTSP, and TFTP are all common protocols in use in an active remote network branch. Each of these protocols is commonly tied to specific applications or devices within the network:

- **CIFS:** Microsoft Windows file access between Microsoft clients and servers, also supported by Linux clients and servers

- **HTTP:** Web browser access to Internet and intranet sites

- **HTTPS:** Secure web browser access to Internet and intranet sites

- **FTP:** File transfers between clients and servers, most commonly used in UNIX environments

- **RTSP:** Streaming media protocol, recognized by Microsoft, RealNetworks, and Apple

- **TFTP:** A standard protocol for file transfers to routers, switches, and other network devices

The following sections describe each protocol in greater detail.

CIFS

When used within a CDN, the CIFS protocol becomes a read-only access method at the network edge. Do not confuse the CDN's implementation of CIFS with the CIFS implementation found within an accelerator; accelerators allow for bidirectional access of content over the CIFS protocol. CDNs are a one-way distribution process; if content write access to an edge serving accelerator were allowed, a content mismatch between the edge serving accelerator and the origin server would exist.

CDNs have the ability to acquire content via CIFS and make the prepositioned content available via CIFS. Access to prepositioned content may be protected by user authentication, just as with other web-based protocols. Delivery of content that has been made available via a CIFS share should be compared to that of a network-accessible CD-ROM or DVD-ROM device, on which the user has access to the content only as read-only data.

CIFS distribution is very popular with enterprises that require the ability to distribute documents that have been converted to read-only formats, such as Adobe Corporation's Acrobat format. These documents might be corporate policies, customer records, or even images that the employee will never require write access to. CIFS-accessible content on the network appears just as any other file server access appears during network analysis.

Bandwidth throttling or throughput rate limiting of CIFS-accessible traffic is not common, due to the slow nature of the CIFS protocol and the amount of excessive overhead that is native to the protocol. Although CDNs support CIFS as an access method, a WAN optimizing accelerator will offer much better performance, with bidirectional content access as needed.

HTTP

HTTP is the most common access protocol used by clients of a CDN. HTTP is a one-way protocol at the network edge and is most commonly used by web browsers as an access application. HTTP is a very flexible and network-forgiving protocol, allowing for network disruptions, high latency, and slow-throughput environments.

The nature of HTTP allows for edge serving accelerators to impose throughput throttling at the edge without disrupting the ability for an application to function. Throttling is most important at the network edge if content objects are significantly large. A document may be several hundred megabytes in size and traditionally transfer very slowly over the WAN. This slow transfer disrupts the performance of the WAN, but has little effect on the performance of the LAN. If the same large file is requested from an edge serving accelerator that resides on the client's LAN, the high burst of traffic might be disrupting to the LAN. CDNs allow for maximum throughput ratings to be applied to HTTP to prevent LAN saturation.

HTTP traffic interoperates with other LAN traffic very well. If the network becomes saturated with other traffic, HTTP accepts what little network bandwidth is available. If the network has an inconsistent amount of available throughput throughout the day, the protocol just adapts to what is available. HTTP traffic commonly does not receive preferential treatment on the network, unless a quality of service (QoS) policy has been explicitly created for the content being distributed throughout the network.

To the benefit of HTTP, many applications have been written to take advantage of the protocol, outside of the web browsing software market. Desktop software and patch management applications commonly take advantage of HTTP, placing requests to their local edge serving accelerator for software and patch-related content. Database applications also leverage HTTP as a transport mechanism, due to the forgiving nature of the protocol and the ability to eliminate dedicated software-based applications from every accessing client. HTTP allows for distribution and access to nontraditional formats, such as spreadsheets, documents, and software applets. Throttling of these objects might become critical to the network administrator if LAN access becomes a limitation. Throttled content access will still perform at significantly faster rates than what may be available via the remote location's WAN connection.

HTTPS

HTTPS has become increasingly popular within enterprise and government networks. The selection and implementation of HTTPS is unique; protocol selection commonly involves predetermined technical business decisions. Content that has been acquired and prepositioned via HTTPS commonly involves sensitive corporate records, confidential data, or customer-related records. Unlike HTTP, HTTPS access requires a valid client certificate and key to gain access to the edge serving accelerator. Once a session has been established via HTTPS, any authentication and access control must be satisfied.

HTTPS should not be confused with other authentication methods; HTTPS is merely the access protocol. The traffic that traverses the LAN within an HTTPS session is encrypted, which prevents others on the network from "sniffing" and "inspecting" the traffic between the client and edge serving accelerator.

HTTPS offers many benefits, mostly security related. HTTPS requires valid server certificates and client keys to exist on the edge serving accelerator and requesting client. If the edge negotiation process fails between the two devices, then access to the accelerator is denied. Protocol negotiation occurs prior to the actual request for content.

There are two different methods of HTTPS implementation on an edge serving accelerator:

- Software based

- Hardware based

Software-based HTTPS decryption requires that the edge serving accelerator process the certificate and key negotiation within the accelerator's processor and RAM. As additional HTTPS sessions are established, additional system resources are consumed with each session. Software-based HTTPS processing is considered least efficient to the edge serving accelerator, with resource consumption increasing with each simultaneous connection.

Hardware-based HTTPS processing is considered more efficient than software-based decryption, due to the dedicated hardware components that process only HTTPS traffic. With a dedicated

HTTPS hardware component installed within the edge serving accelerator, the edge serving accelerator continues to have less-impacted processor and memory resources available.

With the growing adoption of HTTPS, applications must be ported from HTTP to HTTPS, and valid certificates of authority must be created for the application servers and edge serving accelerators. If a valid certificate is not available, the security and control of the content may be compromised. Transitioning from HTTP to HTTPS creates added potential costs to the corporation, although some corporations allocate additional funding for security-related functions. Enabling of software-based HTTPS processing does not incur any additional software costs to the CDN system administrator, because this functionality will already exist within the system.

FTP

FTP access of prepositioned content is very uncommon within the enterprise. FTP, by nature, is known to be nonfriendly to networks that have limited bandwidth. CDNs bypass the WAN limitations that FTP creates by acquiring the content from an FTP server and by distributing the content under the CDN's bandwidth and time-of-day control functions. Due to the traditional challenges imposed by FTP over the WAN, it is not common for enterprises to start using this protocol once the CDN has been implemented.

FTP distribution of content may be leveraged for some applications that still call for the protocol's usage. If an application that calls on FTP as its content transport is used, the content request might be intercepted by the edge serving accelerator, which would access the file locally. File servers that are accessible via FTP may be accessed by content acquiring accelerators for the process of content prepositioning to the network edge. The process is one-way when used with a CDN, not allowing files to be pushed back into the data center. If bidirectional FTP transfers are a requirement, then a WAN optimizing accelerator must be implemented.

Although the use of FTP within the corporate network still exists today, it is used less commonly than other protocols. UNIX systems and some legacy applications still use FTP today. Over the course of time, many of these applications are expected to evolve into using more common protocols such as HTTP and CIFS for file exchanges between the client and server, and between servers.

RTSP

The Real-Time Streaming Protocol is a streaming protocol implemented by Microsoft for its Windows Media Server, by Apple for its Apple Darwin Streaming Server (QuickTime), and by RealNetworks for its Helix Server. Although a standard exists today for this protocol, the implementations by each vendor differ enough to make each server and client function incompatible. For Microsoft's RTSP implementation, this protocol is the default protocol for streaming media for the current release of Windows Media Player. With the retirement of the MMS protocol, Microsoft has identified RTSP as the standard protocol for streaming media between a media server and client. Following Microsoft's lead, the same rule applies between an edge serving accelerator and requesting client's media player.

Although each vendor's products will continue to evolve into noncompatible inter-vendor solutions, each of the three vendors supports its own flavor of RTSP. All vendors have common minimum components to support RTSP, each component becoming a requirement within an enterprise network. Specification and management of the following components is commonly outside of the scope of the content delivery system administrator's duties, and is otherwise owned by the department overseeing the content creation:

- Content encoding requires appropriate encoder software and related software decoders or media players.

- Content encoding requires an encoder-compatible video encoder or capture card.

- A client player or browser plug-in is required for media playback.

In addition to the encoding process and any related hardware and software, content encoding should meet the following criteria:

- The content encode rate must be suitable for corporate playback on a client desktop.

- Digital rights management must be considered if the content must remain protected as a copyrighted asset of the corporation, limiting playback to authorized clients only.

- The end client software will commonly be a desktop media player, but many employees now carry their own portable media player hardware, which may utilize a nonstandard media player.

An encoder is a generic requirement for streaming media, but might not be the actual source of content for a CDN. A media server might exist between the encoder and content acquiring accelerator. In cases where the server is the encoder as well, then the content acquiring accelerator accesses the encoder as its content source. Matching CODEC are required for proper stream sessions to exist between the server and content acquiring accelerator. Unless the content is progressively downloaded via HTTP, the content acquiring accelerator must recognize the RTSP protocol and CODECs required by the media server or encoder. Native acquisition of RTSP content might be a security requirement, depending on the nature of the content and the security issue of media server exposure when streaming over HTTP. Protocol requirements at the encoder or server should carry down to the edge serving accelerator and the sessions that are exchanged with the end client media player.

The XYZ Corporation presently supports Microsoft Windows Media Player as the standard media player at every desktop. Prior to the deployment of the CDN, the network administrators had no way of providing a quality video experience over the corporate WAN. With the use of the CDN comes the ability to natively stream Windows Media content over RTSP, both live and prepositioned to the branch locations. Prior to the CDN deployment, streaming media tests proved poor results, with low-bit-rate streaming providing postage stamp–sized video at the client's media player. The prepositioned content now supports encode rates high enough to present full-screen video, with pause, fast forward, and rewind functions coming from the use of RTSP.

TFTP

Content delivery networks that support TFTP typically are used to deliver content to a client audience that does not include the traditional client computer. TFTP is most commonly used for uploading and upgrading software onto routers and switches. TFTP is not a common daily use protocol within an enterprise network, due to common transport of custom applications that require manual installation on each participating device. By definition, files that transfer via TFTP cannot exceed 32 MB in size. This limitation is defined as part of the protocol's standards, so CDNs follow this defined limitation. Some third-party applications allow for content larger than 32 MB to be transferred, but the CDN will not allow transfers to exceed the defined 32-MB standard.

Two common alternatives to TFTP are HTTP and FTP. Many newer routers and switches support software update transfers via these more common protocols. For routers and switches that require TFTP as the default transfer protocol, the CDN will support the distribution of the update images to the edge serving accelerators.

A router or switch that requires a TFTP-sourced upgrade image can request the content via TFTP from the edge serving accelerator. No content is pushed from the edge serving accelerator to the target router or switch device. The XYZ Corporation administrators will be using the TFTP serving function of their CDN to preposition software images for their routers and switches, allowing for centralized control of their global network. Previously, XYZ hired consultants to perform the software upgrades while on site at each remote branch location.

Streaming Media Live or On Demand

With streaming media, there are only two deployment scenario options: live streaming and video on demand (VoD). There are no alternatives to streaming media's current options. To aid with the quality of experience, QoS provides preferential treatment of streams that have originated from an edge serving accelerator. Streaming media players also include quality protection methods such as buffering to prevent disrupted media playback.

Live Streaming

Live streaming is typically more sensitive to network congestion than VoD streaming. Live streaming commonly involves the streams traversing the WAN, whereas VoD may only traverse the LAN. For live streaming, at least one stream must successfully traverse the WAN from the content acquiring accelerator to the edge serving accelerator. In the case where the live stream cannot traverse the WAN without loss, the end clients experience disrupted video streaming. When considering live streaming, the encode rate must be less than the smallest WAN link that the stream must traverse. If the encode rate exceeds the slowest link, the video playback will be disrupted, and appear as choppy, or create excessive client buffering.

Video on Demand

Video-on-demand playback of content that has been prepositioned will allow for higher encode rates to be used. The limitations imposed by the WAN are eliminated. A higher encode rate increases the overall LAN traffic if multiple users access the content at the same time and if the LAN experiences high volumes of traffic, is a non-switched (hub) environment, or operates at less than a 100 Mbps rating; then the streaming media playback performance may be degraded. Edge serving accelerators can limit the amount of streaming traffic introduced to the LAN, by limiting the number of sessions, limiting the maximum bandwidth per session, or capping the cumulative amount of bandwidth consumed in total. These settings are options to the system administrator. Unlike HTTP, streaming throughput cannot be throttled down to accommodate other traffic on the LAN; variable bit rate (VBR) encoding provides one form of control for network congestion. Any traffic that disrupts the flow of streaming media will likely disrupt the playback experience within the client's media player or browser plug-in, stepping down to a lesser encoding rate.

To the client, native protocol usage for VoD streaming facilitates the ability to utilize their media player's controls. For VoD, native controls allow the client to communicate with the edge serving accelerator and to properly handle client commands such as pause, fast forward, and rewind.

Other functions that improve the client's wait time for requested content include Fast Start and Fast Cache from Microsoft Windows Media Server. Fast Start allows the client's media player to begin playback immediately, reducing buffering times. Fast Cache populates the media player's cache as fast as the network will support the high-speed delivery of the content to the client's media player. The burst of Fast Cache preloaded content eliminates the potential for observed network disruption that might occur during traditional streaming to the client. Starting with the Windows Media Player version 9 release, Fast Cache and Fast Start functionality is supported. It is recommended that client PCs that are requesting content from an edge serving accelerator support a minimum of version 9 of Windows Media Player.

Authenticating Requests for Prepositioned Content

Content acquisition most commonly occurs over nonauthenticated sessions. If authentication is required for content acquisition, this requirement may be passed down through the CDN to the client requesting content from the edge serving accelerator.

The content administrator has several options when defining the properties that surround his content distribution settings. Enabling authentication for prepositioned content is handled differently from enabling traditional web cache authentication. For prepositioned content, the edge serving accelerator must have the ability to communicate with the origin server directly. The origin server must have the ability to authenticate requests for controlled content. The process of authentication is handled between the client and edge serving accelerator, with back-end communications and validation taking place between the edge serving accelerator and origin content server, or live streaming server.

The decision to enable authentication of prepositioned content is a matter of internal corporate policy. No two groups within a corporation may have the same policies, due to the nature of their content. If authentication is not enabled on the edge serving accelerator, and at the origin server itself, then content might be accessible by anyone within the corporation. By default, an edge serving accelerator will deliver content only to users within the same subnet as the edge serving accelerator itself. If no ACLs are defined on the edge serving accelerator, then any user theoretically has access to the content housed on the edge serving accelerator. The requesting users must provide valid content URLs to gain access, unless directory browsing of the content is enabled on the edge serving accelerator.

There are alternative methods that may be used besides requiring authentication at the edge serving accelerator. If the URLs required for access to the content are housed within a portal, or protected website, then "security through obscurity" is one approach used today within enterprise networks. If the user does not know what the URL is, he cannot get to the content itself. An authenticated portal allows administrators to track who accessed the portal, and monitor which pages within the portal they are currently accessing. Differing levels of authentication and security are used in this model of control, hiding the content URLs throughout the corporate media portal.

When following an end-to-end secure content distribution model, the content hosted on the origin server is protected via authentication, the content is distributed between content acquiring and serving accelerators over an encrypted protocol, and the content is accessed by requesting clients who provide valid authentication credentials. An end-to-end model should not have any weak points along the way, regardless of the methods and services used for WAN access. Factors that might limit these security requirements include an origin server that does not have access to all of the required domains or user accounts, a distribution setting that has been improperly defined to use HTTP instead of the default of HTTPS, or an edge serving accelerator that has an authentication bypass enabled.

Content security is commonly the role of the content administrator, not the system administrator. Once the administrative roles are clearly defined, meeting the expectations of administrators and enabling their respective authentication responsibilities become much easier to accomplish.

Acquiring Content

Acquiring select content is the first major step of the content distribution process, followed by CDN-managed distribution and serving of the content to requesting clients. Taking into consideration the planning process, the function of acquiring content requires a significant amount of pre-acquisition work. Although the process may be as simple as designating a source of content and acquiring it once, content administrators must consider how often the content must be revalidated and whether to control access to the origin server beyond traditional authentication. Some origin servers might require a valid cookie for access to the content, while others might just use a secondary host, which is separate from the actual origin server that clients may access.

Content acquisition is based on a model that requires a content acquiring accelerator with access to an origin server or host via HTTP, HTTPS, FTP, CIFS, or RTSP. The origin server, system administrator, or content administrator does not place content on the content acquiring accelerator. The content acquiring accelerator fetches content from the origin server or host via an approved protocol.

Additional components involved in the acquisition process include a central management device. Optional devices include secondary content acquiring accelerators for redundancy, and any portal applications that require API access into the central management device to dispatch any content distribution processes throughout the CDN. Figure 5-8 illustrates a logical view of content acquisition components.

Figure 5-8 *Content Acquisition Components*

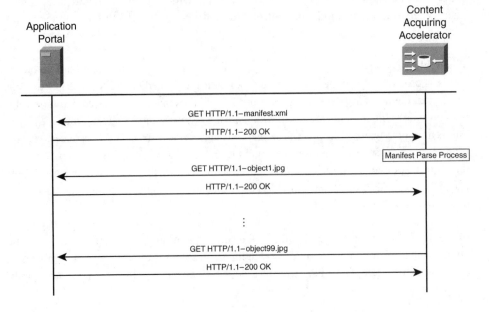

Some content might require distribution only once, and might never change after it has been acquired and distributed. Examples include long-standing documents or videos that are distributed by HR, such as a corporate logo or mission statement. Acquire-and-distribute-once processing is rarely the case; even corporate logos undergo changes throughout the life of the corporation. CDNs offer flexibility around how frequently the content should be revalidated and redistributed. The process is very simple, checking only the content headers for any changes. The content does not require a complete reacquisition prior to determining if anything new has been placed on the origin server or host. For organizations that generate frequent updates to their content, the process of discovery might occur as often as every 5 minutes. But for other groups, the process might need to be done only once a week, as a reassuring measure.

Determining how often the CDN should recheck the content that resides on the server is the responsibility of the content administrator. The system administrator carries no responsibilities in this process. The content administrator for each content group might have differing requirements. Returning to the example of the XYZ Corporation, HR's content has changed only as often as once a month. Although changes are not predictable, there have been content changes at least once per month. With such infrequent changes, the content administrators have configured the CDN to automatically rescan the HR site every 7 days. The decision to rescan the HR site every 7 days was made as both a proactive measure and a preventative measure. The CDN supports the ability to execute scans manually, which is part of the HR standard operating procedure.

Once new content has been placed on the origin server, the content administrator manually initiates the discovery process to start acquisition of the content immediately. If the administrator overlooks the initiation of the manual scan process, the content acquiring accelerator automatically initiates the process within one week's time. If 7 days is too long, the process can be adjusted to any desired time length. Automated rediscovery may occur as frequently as every 5 minutes, and as often as only once per year.

With the components identified for content acquisition, the actual content itself might have special requirements imposed by either a host server or the content owner themselves. Content and network administrators need to work together to address any of the following, which are discussed in depth in the sections that follow:

■ **Cookie-based access:** An origin server looks for a valid cookie prior to granting access to its content.

■ **Origin server content placement:** Administrative access rights are required to place content on a given origin server.

■ **Content size selection:** Administratively determine the smallest object size suitable for prepositioning.

■ **Department-managed portals:** Different departments have differing content placement needs.

Cookie-Based Acquisition

The origin server or host that the content acquiring accelerator must access might have unique safeguards to protect its content. One such method is the use of authentication cookies. Consider a web server that issues a valid cookie to a user once they have provided valid credentials to the server. It is that cookie which is required for any subsequent content requests. If the cookie is not present for subsequent requests, the user will either be prompted to reauthenticate with the server or be denied access to any additional content. When acquiring content, the cookie method of control is becoming more and more popular for large content-hosting portals. For the content acquiring accelerator to gather content from such a site, the accelerator must have the ability to present valid credentials, and also interoperate properly with the cookie that is recognized by the origin or host server.

One such method is to embed a valid and trusted cookie within the manifest file used by the content acquiring accelerator. This cookie, along with valid credentials, allows the content acquiring accelerator to place an initial authenticated request with the origin server or host, and then place subsequent content requests that include a valid cookie. Knowing that the manifest file now carries protected information, the manifest file itself must be protected from external threats. With access to the manifest file, a potential hacker would have all the needed information to gain access to the given content. For this reason, the content acquiring accelerator supports the ability to retrieve the manifest file from an external host over HTTP or HTTPS, with the inclusion of valid credentials at the time of the manifest file's fetch. A manifest file should never be placed on a given host without protection in front of the manifest file.

All information contained within the file identifies all content to be prepositioned by a given content administrator. Because each content administrator might be working with their own manifest file, several manifest files might be in use at any one time.

Origin Server Content Placement

Content that is hosted on existing corporate servers was positioned on the given server as part of an existing business process. This process is commonly a well-defined procedure. The introduction of a CDN will not disrupt this procedure. Web administrators become accustomed to specific procedures, many times including corporate security processes to place the content on a given portal.

For the XYZ Corporation, only two people within the organization have the authority to place content on the HR portal. Content posting will not take place until the content has been approved by a management team, to eliminate any potential liability concerns. The posting process is well defined, stating exactly how to transfer the content, where to place the content, and, how to enable access to the content. There is even a corporate policy defined for the process of enabling the content on the portal. These policies are not uncommon for large corporations; misplaced or inappropriate content may be costly to a corporation.

CDNs do not require that web masters and portal owners make changes to their content-posting procedures. Authenticated content acquisition and cookie-based access allow the content acquiring accelerator to interact with the origin server, web portal, or host just as any other user on the network would. CDNs should not disrupt a procedure that is known and trusted within the corporation today.

The content acquiring accelerator acquires content from two types of servers:

- The web portal or server that all users within the corporation use today

- The secondary host, which hosts the exact same content as the web portal but supports only a limited set of clients

The first, the origin server, is the most common source of content to a content acquiring accelerator. This origin server treats the content acquiring accelerator just as any other client accessing the server. The URLs associated with each acquired content item will match exactly what the users will be requesting on the network. In this case, the acquired content is served by edge serving accelerators with no URL address translation.

For content acquisition from a secondary host, the URLs will differ from those requested by the client. In many cases, the secondary host allows only a select number of users to access the host, and might even limit access to content acquiring accelerators. Content acquisition from a secondary host requires that the URLs associated with the actual origin server be defined. If the domain name associated with the actual domain is not defined within the CDN, then the CDN will have no way of matching client requests to content that has been prepositioned to edge serving accelerators.

There are benefits to implementing a secondary host to provide content to select users and the CDN. First, it allows content acquiring accelerators to interact with a defined host that has lower network and storage utilization than a production intranet portal server. Second, it provides a staging point for content prior to its availability on the corporate intranet server. A staging site allows for the site and associated content to be tested prior to being enabled in a live production environment. Staging sites are also used by corporations that require limited or restricted external access to internal intranet sites. If CDNs have been implemented outside of the corporation, for either the public Internet or subsidiary corporations, then the staging site may be the only source of content for those external content consumers.

Content Size Considerations

Acquired content consumes disk space. Some acquired content will undoubtedly be larger than other content. For example, video on demand consumes large amounts of space per file. Smaller content, such as text files, might require very little disk space. Content owners should evaluate several key factors when defining a size limit for content that is to be distributed throughout the

CDN. It is common for the lower limit to range between 50 and 100 KB in size. Content sized less than the limit will be suitable to traverse the WAN for each user's individual request. When content distribution and accelerator functions coexist within the network, the smaller objects will become reactively cached. Only a single request to populate the nonprepositioned items at the edge is required.

For larger content, objects are commonly less than 2 GB in size. Objects larger than this are usually recovery images for desktop systems, or VoD content that uses a high encoding rate and has a long running time.

System administrators are not responsible for defining object size standards, but they must be involved in allocating any storage space that the content administrator requires.

XYZ Corporation's departments each have differing storage needs. Human resources requires at least 10 GB of storage space on each edge serving accelerator, marketing requires 25 GB of storage space on each accelerator, and sales requires 75 GB of storage on each accelerator. In total, 110 GB of storage space is required on each edge serving accelerator to meet all three departments' needs. Storage space cannot overlap, so the system administrator must allocate a total of 110 GB of space on each system for prepositioned content. It is recommended that the system administrator add 25 percent additional space for content "growth," in the event a given department's needs change. Figure 5-9 illustrates the differing space needs for static objects placed at an edge serving accelerator.

Figure 5-9   *Static Object Storage Needs*

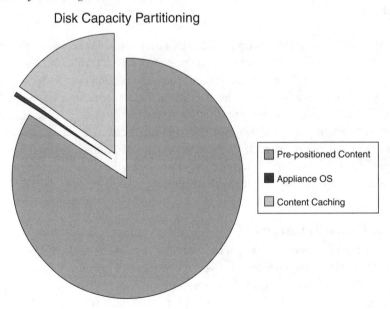

Disk Capacity Partitioning

Pre-positioned Content

Appliance OS

Content Caching

Department-Managed Portals

Content acquisition for each of sales, marketing, and HR will function independently of content acquisition for the other departments, all while accessing the same centralized management device. Content administrators from each group have access to and control over their own group's content processes through their own dedicated portals. If HR makes changes to its manifest file and initiates a manual rediscovery of content on its origin server, sales' and marketing's manifest files will not be accessed. Content administrators have the ability to define which content items carry a higher priority than other items within their given group.

Content administrators do not have control over when the acquired content will be distributed out to the edge locations. The time-of-day and bandwidth settings are owned by the system administrator. Separation of system and content administrator responsibilities becomes much more logical when considering that all three different departments within the XYZ Corporation might be competing for shared storage and distribution bandwidth. Although each group works for the same corporation, the well being of each group's content is the respective group's primary concern. If HR had the ability to set a higher priority for its content than what is set for the content of sales and marketing, the overall CDN would become a focal point of corporate political unrest. The system administrator controls the priority levels of each group's distribution process. HR most commonly has the highest priority during the acquisition and distribution processes, followed by sales and then marketing.

Understanding CDN Distribution Models

Once content acquisition has been completed, a CDN provides two different models for distribution of the acquired content:

- **Direct fetch:** Each edge serving accelerator goes directly to the origin server or a secondary host for direct fetch. This model does not use a content acquiring accelerator near the origin server or secondary host.

- **Distributed hierarchy:** A content acquiring accelerator close to the origin server or secondary host distributes the content. This model uses a tiered distribution model between the core and edge locations.

Both models have their benefits, but both models should be investigated closely to determine which is most appropriate for the content administrator and end user. Although a CDN can operate in a state that uses both models simultaneously, most corporations standardize on one model or the other.

Direct Fetch

If each edge serving accelerator in a CDN obtains its content by accessing the origin server or secondary host directly, this architecture is based on a direct fetch model. The direct fetch model requires that each edge serving accelerator operate completely independent of other content accelerators, acquiring content from origin servers in the data center. No two accelerators interact or share content. Figure 5-10 illustrates the direct fetch model.

Figure 5-10 *Simple Direct Fetch Topology*

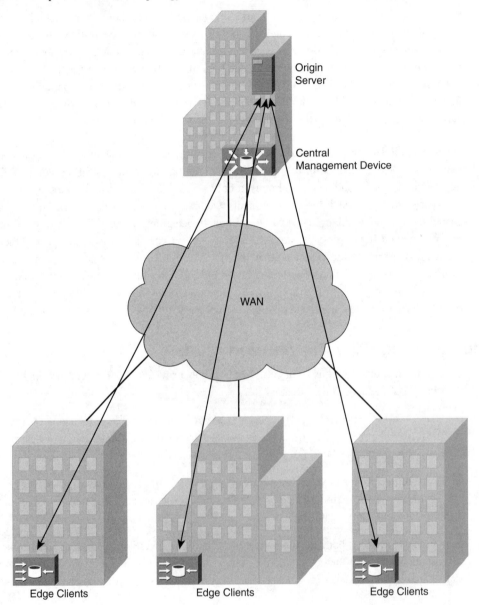

Origin Server

Central Management Device

WAN

Edge Clients

Edge Clients

Edge Clients

Allowing all edge serving accelerators to communicate directly with the origin server has positive and negative points.

Benefits of Direct Fetch

Implementing direct fetch is cheaper than implementing a distributed hierarchy and provides a simplistic approach to content distribution. For smaller networks, the direct fetch model works very well. The volume of WAN traffic is low, because traffic aggregates at the origin server or secondary host. Just as the model's name implies, each edge serving accelerator goes directly to the content source for acquisition and distribution simultaneously. For smaller networks, this model eliminates the need for content acquiring accelerators to reside near the content source, but a centralized management device must still exist. A redundant direct fetch model places the redundancy obligation on the origin server and edge serving accelerators, which inherently doubles the cost of the solution at the network edge. Redundancy may already exist for the origin server, with the use of an intelligent load balancer, but the direct fetch model is not dependent on a redundant content source.

Limitations of Direct Fetch

When implemented, the management of this model typically involves a much reduced set of functionality. Content that is to be distributed will leverage a manifest file that supports a reduced set of content variables. The transport is commonly limited to HTTP and FTP, and authentication functions are greatly reduced during the acquisition process.

Some of the limitations associated with the direct fetch model relate to the acquisition of the content, bandwidth controls, and serving of the acquired content. Content that has been acquired via the direct fetch model does not utilize an upstream parent content acquiring accelerator. When a parent-content acquiring accelerator is not used, the content cannot be distributed via an encrypted session between two accelerators. HTTP or FTP will commonly be the default protocol in this model, both being subject to network sniffing. The direct fetch model commonly lacks security-related functions, with a limited ability to present credentials during the fetch process. The lack of security continues during the distribution process, where a potential risk of origin server or secondary host traffic saturation during the distribution process may be created.

Direct fetch also lacks the ability to interoperate properly with an origin server that requires cookie support. There is no bandwidth control for the traffic that is transferred between the origin server and edge serving accelerator; there is no upstream parent accelerator to throttle the distribution of the content. Content traverses the WAN as if it were web content requested by a client using their web browser. Direct fetch is a simplistic approach to content distribution.

The direct fetch model stores content in a generic cache location on the edge serving accelerator's disk drive. If a request for content is placed with the origin server, and newer content has been found on the origin server, the newer content is reactively cached over the legacy content that has already been placed on the edge serving accelerator's disk drive. The direct fetch acquisition process lacks much of the intelligence of a distributed hierarchy model; it is a basic structure to preload content into an edge serving accelerator. Content items typically are smaller in size when using the direct fetch model, due to the lack of bandwidth control over the WAN.

Initiating preload content acquisition is a purely manual process, with timed intervals occurring manually each time. With no intelligent manifest file model, any changes to the preload content list must be done in a common location where all edge serving accelerators have access to the given file. Once the preload file has been updated, each edge serving accelerator must be accessed by a system administrator, or content administrator, to initiate a refetch of the preload content list text file.

Distributed Hierarchy

A distributed hierarchy is the foundation for a scalable CDN. With a distributed hierarchy in place, content acquisition occurs at a single location within the network and content is distributed effectively to each edge location once. If the network involves several hub-and-spoke regional data centers, each hub becomes a new layer of the CDNs' hierarchy. Figure 5-11 illustrates a sample CDN based on XYZ Corporation's corporate topology within the United States.

Figure 5-11 displays a network that is a single-level hierarchy. The origin server resides in the corporate data center, and the content acquiring accelerator resides within the same data center. This network has two remote branch locations, in Chicago and Los Angeles, which are the first level of the distribution hierarchy. In this model, content is acquired by the content acquiring accelerator, and distributed to all first-tier locations based on the time-of-day and bandwidth settings defined by the administrator. This model is an oversimplified example of how the CDN appears, but is an accurate representation of the core required accelerators.

Building upon Figure 5-11, the system administrator should consider adding additional edge serving accelerators to the remote branch office in Chicago. The office staff exceeds the capabilities of a single edge serving accelerator, so two additional accelerators have been added to this location. Several edge serving accelerators will not create additional content distribution traffic on the WAN, due to the intelligent nature of the CDN. Just as a hierarchy exists between the data center in New York City and the Chicago branch office, the CDN has the ability to create a hierarchy within a given location. Figure 5-12 provides a closer look at the hierarchy within the Chicago office. Note that one accelerator has become the parent accelerator and the other two accelerator have become children of the parent accelerator.

Figure 5-11 *XYZ Corporation Major U.S. Locations*

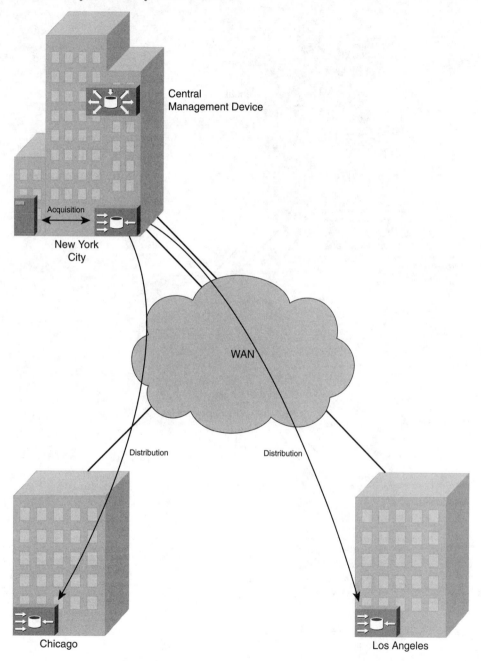

Central
Management Device

Acquisition

New York
City

WAN

Distribution

Distribution

Chicago

Los Angeles

Figure 5-12 *Location Hierarchy Model*

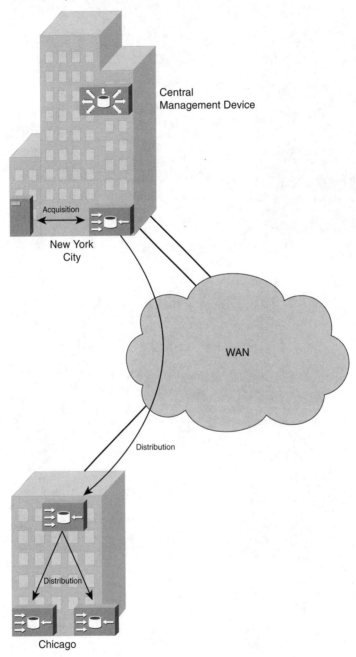

With a multitiered network established, the traffic flows in a hierarchical network gain several beneficial features. The content that is distributed between New York City and Chicago and between New York City and Los Angeles is encrypted by default. The distribution may or may not traverse the public Internet at any given point, so encryption becomes important when distributing electronic corporate assets. The administrator now has the ability to take advantage of the bandwidth throttling between accelerators, preventing WAN saturation from the content process. Time-of-day control between locations also becomes a configurable option to the administrator, allowing distribution to occur at different times, based on the differing time zones that each location resides in.

Expanding beyond XYZ Corporation's three major U.S. locations, the international map shown in Figure 5-13 illustrates the expansion of the CDN to include the corporate offices in London and Tokyo. Each regional location supports several children locations in the overall XYZ Corporation hierarchy.

Figure 5-13 *International Regional Hubs*

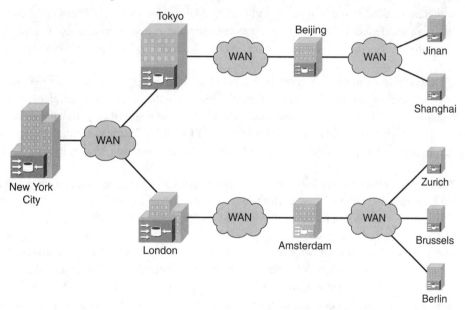

As shown in Figure 5-13, the topology map illustrates Europe's regional hub in London and related downstream branch offices. The offices in Brussels, Berlin, Zurich, and Amsterdam each feed from the regional hub via E1 connections. Although Brussels, Berlin, Zurich, and Amsterdam are all children locations of the London office, none of the children locations are aware of each other. Peer children locations are only aware of their parents, which prevents the possibility of content distribution occurring between children locations, a situation that could consume twice the desired amount of bandwidth to a given child location. They each acquire content from a common parent location, London. Multiple accelerators may reside within the data center in London, providing redundancy and scalability as needed. Even with a redundant model, a single content acquiring accelerator acquires content from New York City, sharing with all other accelerators within the London data center. Downstream locations, such as Amsterdam, Brussels, and Berlin, each acquire their content from any of the accelerators located within London. If multiple accelerators exist in a parent location, the children accelerators will load-balance across all accelerators resident in the parent's location.

If an edge serving accelerator must be replaced due to a physical failure, two options exist for populating content onto the replacement accelerator:

- Stage a replacement accelerator on the data center network, and replicate all content onto the accelerator prior to shipping to the remote location

- Allow the accelerator to repopulate the prepositioned content via the remote location's WAN

The benefit of prestaging replacement accelerators within the data center is that it allows a replacement accelerator to be fully populated prior to installation. This benefit does not come without the added cost of procuring and staging additional standby hardware in the data center. When an accelerator is shipped from the data center, the system administrator has the ability to preconfigure the replacement accelerator, making it a true plug-and-play replacement.

If an accelerator cannot be preconfigured, the installer must apply the basic configuration to the edge serving accelerator at the time of installation. Once the replacement accelerator has communicated with its central management device, all content will be populated onto the accelerator via its nearest parent. If the accelerator located in Berlin has failed, the replacement accelerator will acquire all content from the nearest parent location, in London.

The second option is commonly tied to a service contract, where the replacement accelerator is shipped directly from the vendor. Both options allow for a replacement accelerator to be used, easing the replacement process at the remote location.

Distributed hierarchies allow for regional hubs to provide content to downstream children locations, while preserving WAN bandwidth between major distribution points. Replacing an accelerator that has failed in Berlin will not consume any content distribution bandwidth between New York City and London. All content serving accelerators in the hierarchy preserve their assigned content, even if the accelerator will not be servicing content requests by any local clients.

Figure 5-14 illustrates how content that has been distributed from New York City to Tokyo resides on both locations, as well as in Beijing. The content in focus is Chinese marketing content, which originated in New York City. When building the distributed hierarchy, the content will reside on each accelerator that participates in the hierarchy. In this example, the content will reside on accelerators in New York City, Tokyo, and Beijing. Tokyo may house the content purely as part of the distribution process, and it might never be requested by a user that is local to the Tokyo data center. The offices throughout China may utilize Beijing as their regional hub for the entire country.

Figure 5-14   *Asia Distributed Hierarchy*

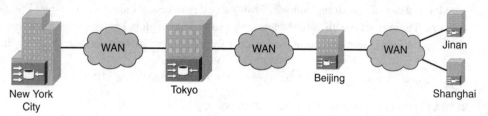

Expanding on the example in Figure 5-14, Figure 5-15 shows a fourth layer of the hierarchy, providing content from Beijing to children locations in the cities of Jinan and Shanghai.

Figure 5-15   *Fourth-Level Distribution Tier*

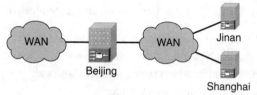

A general rule that applies to distributed networks is that IT support staff resources diminish with each additional WAN segment between the core data center and branch location. This general rule applies to XYZ Corporation as well, so the network administrators have prestaged replacement accelerators within the data center, including the regional data centers, to support expedited accelerator replacement. If an edge serving accelerator is preloaded with all content and has all network-related settings predefined, the installation in a remote location such as Jinan will be days quicker than applying a configuration to a new accelerator and waiting for the accelerator to repopulate all content from the nearest parent in Beijing. The volume of content on the accelerator will likely consume several gigabytes of space, which could involve several days of time just to repopulate the content to the replacement accelerator.

Understanding Time-of-Day Distribution

The actual distribution process of content between the parent content acquiring accelerator and children edge serving accelerators requires a network with suitable resources. During any given workday, available WAN resources will be fewer than after the workday has been completed. A system administrator controls the settings for both the allowed time of day for distributions and the available bandwidth for the distribution flows. Knowing about processes consuming the network's resources is useful to the system administrator and beneficial to the content administrator.

Time-of-day bandwidth controls are time zone aware and not limited to a single block of available time. The distributed workforce is not limited to a single time zone or country, but rather has become a global community. Some countries consider Sunday a work day, while others recognize Sunday as a day of rest; some consider Friday as a day of rest, while others consider Friday a day of work. These traits are all valid factors when supporting a global workforce for content distribution. Some common points to consider for a global workforce include the following:

- Many corporations leverage the weekend as their distribution window.

- An urgent distribution can be sent after working hours.

- Know your target audience and where they are located.

- Do not send everything everywhere, unless required.

- If some content originates in a regional data center and is destined only for children locations, consider enabling acquiring functionality on an accelerator within the regional data center.

Administrators of traditional intranet server deployments did not need to know their audience or the usage trends of the WAN. When system and content administrators know who their audience is, the network environment in which they work, and where they are geographically located, content distribution becomes much more efficient.

Know the Network

The XYZ Corporation has offices in all but a very few time zones, some with a 12-hour time zone difference from New York City. With regional data centers in New York City, Tokyo, and London, time zone based distribution is much easier to manage. Time-of-day availability can be broken up into two blocks:

- New York City to Tokyo: 11-hour difference

- New York City to London: 5-hour difference

From each regional data center to its children locations, the time-of-day windows are closer together. Bandwidth settings may be very low during overlapping working hours, but distribution will still occur. Bandwidth controls are best interpreted when the settings are being applied between locations, and not between individual accelerators. Each accelerator is assigned to a specific location. Multiple accelerators may share this location, but no accelerator can become a part of more than one location. A location may be a given floor of a building, a building itself, a city, state, or even country. A location is a logical assignment, or grouping, set by the system administrator.

Once the time-of-day windows have been established between each of the locations, bandwidth allocation settings are required. XYZ Corporation's WAN encompasses time zones that span the globe, and its system administrator must be aware of network utilization across each of the WAN links that the corporate network uses. If any of the smaller branches use offerings from their local cable company or telephone company, these links will also need to be investigated. Some links might not be active after working hours. During the content distribution process, the link must be stable and faster than a telephone-based dial-up connection.

While investigating the network's abilities, each location's network components should be well understood. Some network vendors' routers and switches are not capable of supporting multicast traffic, a limitation that could impact distribution or live streaming events. Many corporations and their networks are a collection of acquisitions and mergers, each having potentially different network hardware. If the hardware is not standardized to a common vendor, or even to a common device type for each role, understanding the network's limitations will be a time-consuming task. CDNs support mixed distribution environments, allowing for islands of multicast traffic as needed. Unlike multicast distribution, unicast requires little to no research; if the network can pass IP traffic, unicast distribution has met its only requirement.

Unicast Distribution

Unicast distribution is a one-to-one session between a content acquiring accelerator and a child accelerator. Two people that share a conversation with each other are participating in a unicast session. Unicast distribution is the most common method of distribution between accelerators, due to several different factors, including the WAN's abilities, potential licensing costs, and ease of management.

If one network device within the path of the CDN does not support multicast, that given hierarchical branch of the network must use unicast. Networks may contain mixed environments of unicast and multicast, but will most commonly establish a standard of one over the other. Unicast distribution is more common in networks that use terrestrial services, and least common in networks that use satellite services at their remote locations.

As the default method of the CDN, unicast distribution does not require any additional distribution licenses for any accelerators. Third-party vendors who provide multicast functionality require a license fee and associated key when multicast is implemented. The availability of CDNs that support license-free unicast functionality is one of the more appealing reasons why corporations select unicast over multicast within their network, even if multicast is an option to them.

The functionality of unicast distribution is based on dedicated Secure Sockets Layer (SSL) sessions between the parent and child accelerators. If SSL is not desired, then the administrator has the ability to easily switch to HTTP as an alternative. Both SSL and HTTP sessions are options with unicast content distribution. Unicast sessions are based on standard protocols, recognized today by network administrators.

There are no additional settings associated with the actual configuration of a unicast distribution setting. The SSL and HTTP protocols accommodate network latency and throughput disruptions.

System administrators can influence unicast distribution only by setting bandwidth settings higher or lower; content administrators have no control over the unicast distribution, other than selecting which content will be distributed over the CDN.

Unicast distribution applies to all types of content, including streaming media. Streaming media is classified as either video-on-demand content or live streaming media. For live streaming media, as the name implies, a unicast session is established between the parent and child accelerators, supporting a single media stream between accelerators. Unicast streams are commonly split at the edge serving accelerator, serving simultaneous users behind the accelerator. Stream splitting media over a unicast session preserves the WAN. Splitting of a unicast stream commonly involves multiple unicast streams to multiple clients that reside behind the edge serving accelerator.

Administrators must consider several factors when implementing unicast distribution. A given parent accelerator's child fan-out limitations and the impact of high-loss networks are both factors that can impact the success of the distribution process. All CDN accelerators are subject to a limitation in the number of edge serving accelerators they can directly serve via unicast. A given parent accelerator may support a fan-out of several hundred child accelerators. Consulting a vendor-authored best practices guide will prevent the architecting of a poorly designed network.

The limits of a unicast fan-out are influenced by traffic other than the content-related traffic. Administrative and system traffic all have affects the parent accelerator's ability to talk to large numbers of children accelerators. The management and monitoring traffic operates on defined timed intervals. Each of these intervals uses a default that has been determined to be optimal for a standard CDN. Each of the management and monitoring settings may be altered, for fine-tuning of the overall network's performance. For example, the default distribution monitoring setting of the central management device might establish a session every 5 minutes with each edge serving accelerator. This timed interval, when spread across 300 accelerators, might create a significant amount of traffic for the parent accelerator that all 300 accelerators communicate with. Increasing the monitoring intervals from their defaults to broader ranges will increase parent accelerator resources to allow for more content delivery functionality when large fan-out environments exist.

If a content transfer exceeds a predefined time-of-day window, a unicast session will allow the transfer to continue at the point at which the session was disrupted the day prior. The child accelerator places virtual hash marks on the content, and leverages these hash marks as the stop and start points for the distribution. Transfer fault tolerance is unique to the unicast distribution model.

Multicast Distribution

Multicast content distribution involves a single parent accelerator broadcasting bits of content to multiple child accelerators simultaneously. Each child accelerator reassembles the bits of broadcast content into the original content's form. As a analogy, the speaker at a conference presents from a podium to a seated audience of attendees. The presentation is a one-way presentation, with all persons in the audience listening to each individual word, reassembling these words into meaningful sentences.

Multicast is the best method of distribution for a single location to broadcast content destined for prepositioning simultaneously to multiple locations. Multicast is a function that adds additional costs to the CDN's purchase. The administrator must do research prior to enabling multicast to achieve a very good understanding of the network devices and their abilities. For terrestrial networks and satellite networks, the preparedness of the administrator might be the difference between a successful and failed multicast distribution of content.

Multicast distribution of prepositioned content within the enterprise network is unique. Some administrators enable multicast distribution in sections of the network, prior to enabling the distribution from end to end. Large corporations most commonly have a satellite network in place, or some form of satellite access during selected times of the day or night.

Consider a television satellite broadcast, from a corporate headquarters to remote branch offices. For video communications, this method works very well, and involves a prescheduled time of day for the event. The satellite time is reserved and the video broadcast is distributed to any remote location that has the proper satellite decoding hardware in place. For content delivery, the edge serving accelerator resides behind the satellite-enabled router or proprietary IP-enabled device. Just as employees tune into the corporate broadcast at a predefined time, the edge serving accelerator joins the multicast broadcast at an administratively defined time.

Unlike unicast distributions, which replicate content only once to each edge serving accelerator, in multicast distributions, parent accelerators will re-broadcast or "carousel" the broadcast several times to all edge serving accelerators. The reason the content is redistributed is that the initial transmission might be disrupted by factors related to the satellite link, weather, and pure timing in the network.

For example, if you were to miss the first 5 minutes of your favorite TV show, you cannot go back and watch those first 5 minutes. Consumers accept this misfortune as a fact of life. For multicast distributed content, such losses are unacceptable. If the edge serving accelerator is unable to join the initial feed of the satellite (for example, due to excessive weather at the time the broadcast started), the accelerator must have access to the content that was missed. Therefore, once a broadcast has completed a full broadcast carousel, a second carousel begins. During each carousel, any edge serving accelerators that have missed a portion of the content will communicate this fact to their broadcasting parent accelerator.

When edge serving accelerators check in with their parent accelerators, the session established between the two is an SSL-based session. Most satellite implementations support one-way broadcasts. The SSL session requires some form of terrestrial connection from the remote location and the data center where the parent accelerator resides. During these sessions, the child accelerator communicates to the parent accelerator that an additional carousel session is required for a given piece of content.

If a child accelerator cannot join a multicast broadcast within an administratively defined time frame, the child accelerator reverts to establishing a unicast session with its parent accelerator. For many corporations that use multicast, the connection timeout limit is 30 minutes. Once switched to unicast, the transfers abide by the time-of-day settings established by the system administrator. Unfortunately, the unicast session will attempt to establish a session over whatever routed path is available, many times, a link that supports throughput ratings at or below that of the satellite connection.

Some of the administratively adjustable settings include defining the address range to be used for the broadcast, setting the number of carousels to be used by the sending accelerator, and defining how many packets will be applied to an error correction block. The administrator must also determine how much bandwidth the broadcast accelerator will consume for the actual distribution broadcast.

239.0.0.0 addresses are recommended for multicast broadcasts. There are subnet ranges within the broader range of addresses that should not be used. Table 5-2 lists the IP address ranges identified as unusable for multicast broadcasts and gives the reason they should not be used. These address ranges should not be considered, due to conflicts with various operating system, hardware, and software vendors' products.

Table 5-2 *Unusable Multicast Address Ranges (Source: Cisco.com)*

Address Range	Reason
224.0.1.2/32	Known insecure service address.
224.0.1.3/32	Reserved for the discovery of resources within the administrative domain.
224.0.1.22/32	Known insecure service address.
224.0.1.35/32	Reserved for the discovery of resources within the administrative domain.
224.0.1.39/32	Reserved for the discovery of resources within the administrative domain.
224.0.1.40/32	Reserved for the discovery of resources within the administrative domain.
224.0.2.2./32	Known insecure service address.
224.77.0.0/16	Used to copy files between servers and clients in a local network.
224.128.0.0/24	Local address that maps to an Ethernet multicast address range and may overwhelm the mapping table of LAN switches.
225.0.0.0/24	Local address that maps to an Ethernet multicast address range and may overwhelm the mapping table of LAN switches.
225.1.2.3/32	Used to copy files between servers and clients in a local network.

Table 5-2   *Unusable Multicast Address Ranges (Source: Cisco.com) (Continued)*

Address Range	Reason
225.128.0.0/24	Local address that maps to an Ethernet multicast address range and may overwhelm the mapping table of LAN switches.
226.0.0.0/24	Local address that maps to an Ethernet multicast address range and may overwhelm the mapping table of LAN switches.
226.77.0.0/16	Used to copy files between servers and clients in a local network.
226.128.0.0/24	Local address that maps to an Ethernet multicast address range and may overwhelm the mapping table of LAN switches.
227.0.0.0/24	Local address that maps to an Ethernet multicast address range and may overwhelm the mapping table of LAN switches.
227.128.0.0/24	Local address that maps to an Ethernet multicast address range and may overwhelm the mapping table of LAN switches.
228.0.0.0/24	Local address that maps to an Ethernet multicast address range and may overwhelm the mapping table of LAN switches.
228.128.0.0/24	Local address that maps to an Ethernet multicast address range and may overwhelm the mapping table of LAN switches.
229.0.0.0/24	Local address that maps to an Ethernet multicast address range and may overwhelm the mapping table of LAN switches.
229.128.0.0/24	Local address that maps to an Ethernet multicast address range and may overwhelm the mapping table of LAN switches.
230.0.0.0/24	Local address that maps to an Ethernet multicast address range and may overwhelm the mapping table of LAN switches.
230.128.0.0/24	Local address that maps to an Ethernet multicast address range and may overwhelm the mapping table of LAN switches.
231.0.0.0/24	Local address that maps to an Ethernet multicast address range and may overwhelm the mapping table of LAN switches.
231.128.0.0/24	Local address that maps to an Ethernet multicast address range and may overwhelm the mapping table of LAN switches.
232.0.0.0/24	Source-specific multicast address.
232.128.0.0/24	Local address that maps to an Ethernet multicast address range and may overwhelm the mapping table of LAN switches.
233.0.0.0/8	GLOP address.
233.0.0.0/24	Local address that maps to an Ethernet multicast address range and may overwhelm the mapping table of LAN switches.
233.128.0.0/24	Local address that maps to an Ethernet multicast address range and may overwhelm the mapping table of LAN switches.
234.0.0.0/24	Local address that maps to an Ethernet multicast address range and may overwhelm the mapping table of LAN switches.

continues

Table 5-2 *Unusable Multicast Address Ranges (Source: Cisco.com) (Continued)*

Address Range	Reason
234.42.42.42/32	Used to copy files between servers and clients in a local network.
234.128.0.0/24	Local address that maps to an Ethernet multicast address range and may overwhelm the mapping table of LAN switches.
234.142.142.42/31	Used to copy files between servers and clients in a local network.
234.142.142.44/30	Used to duplicate files between clients and servers in a local network.
234.142.142.48/28	Used to copy files between servers and clients in a local network.
234.142.142.64/26	Used to copy files between servers and clients in a local network.
234.142.142.128/29	Used to copy files between servers and clients in a local network.
234.142.142.136/30	Used to copy files between servers and clients in a local network.
234.142.142.140/31	Used to copy files between servers and clients in a local network.
234.142.142.142/32	Used to copy files between servers and clients in a local network.
235.0.0.0/24	Local address that maps to an Ethernet multicast address range and may overwhelm the mapping table of LAN switches.
235.128.0.0/24	Local address that maps to an Ethernet multicast address range and may overwhelm the mapping table of LAN switches.
236.0.0.0/24	Local address that maps to an Ethernet multicast address range and may overwhelm the mapping table of LAN switches.
236.128.0.0/24	Local address that maps to an Ethernet multicast address range and may overwhelm the mapping table of LAN switches.
236.0.0.0/24	Local address that maps to an Ethernet multicast address range and may overwhelm the mapping table of LAN switches.
236.128.0.0/24	Local address that maps to an Ethernet multicast address range and may overwhelm the mapping table of LAN switches.
237.0.0.0/24	Local address that maps to an Ethernet multicast address range and may overwhelm the mapping table of LAN switches.
237.128.0.0/24	Local address that maps to an Ethernet multicast address range and may overwhelm the mapping table of LAN switches.
238.0.0.0/24	Local address that maps to an Ethernet multicast address range and may overwhelm the mapping table of LAN switches.
238.128.0.0/24	Local address that maps to an Ethernet multicast address range and may overwhelm the mapping table of LAN switches.
239.0.0.0/8	Administratively scoped address that should not be passed between administrative domains.
239.0.0.0/24	Local address that maps to an Ethernet multicast address range and may overwhelm the mapping table of LAN switches.
239.128.0.0/24	Local address that maps to an Ethernet multicast address range and may overwhelm the mapping table of LAN switches.

Carousels that the broadcast parent accelerator supports will range from one to several million carousels sessions. Most corporations will not use more than five carousels within their network, due to the amount of time required for the accelerators to access the satellite network.

Forward error correction (FEC) within a multicast environment prevents errors from occurring during the reassembly process of a content broadcast. FEC is a set of packets that represents a segment of broadcast content, calculated at the sending parent accelerator. The FEC set of packets is also used to validate the content set that the child accelerator has just received. The default number of FEC packets per broadcast is 16, but the range supported goes as low as 2 packets and as high as 128 packets. If a custom configuration is used, the settings may go as low as zero. The default setting of 16 packets is most appropriate for small to midsize child accelerator; higher settings create additional processor workload on the child accelerator.

Bandwidth settings of a multicast broadcast are independent of the distribution bandwidth settings only if the bandwidth schedule is not defined. The multicast-specific bandwidth setting is a system administrator–defined bandwidth value, which applies only to a continuous setting for 7 days per week, and 24 hours per day. If these settings must be altered, then the standard time-of-day scheduler should be used. Multicast throughput settings may be as low as 10 kbps, with the upper limitation being subject to network availability.

Licensing of edge serving accelerators requires a valid unique activation key. The process of entering the activation key involves either command-line access to the parent and child accelerators or access to the central management device. Once enabled, all functions of the multicast distribution are enabled. Centralized key management is the quickest method of applying a license key to all edge serving accelerators that will participate in the multicast distribution process. Content distribution via multicast is not the same as multicast broadcasts of live streaming media. The two technologies are not associated with each other, requiring different product licenses.

Encrypted and In-the-Clear Distribution

Two types of content distribution traffic traverse the network:

■ Encrypted

■ In the clear

Depending on the type of network that the content distribution will traverse, one setting may be required over the other. The default setting for content distribution is encrypted for all sessions. The type of network that the content traverses often is the influencing factor in determining whether to send all content encrypted or in the clear. If the network includes services exposed to the public Internet, such as a cable modem, DSL, or fiber-connected service, encryption is required. Other factors include the sensitivity of the content and its target audience. Content that contains a sensitive corporate message, for example, requires protection during the entire content distribution process, and therefore requires encryption.

Encrypted content distribution functions similar to a protected transmission session between a parent and child accelerator. During this session, the communication is encrypted via SSL, the default protection method. Only the parent and child share a valid key for the session, and no other accelerators may gain access to the communication.

Encrypted content sessions are most valuable when the communication between accelerators must traverse a network that includes the public Internet or part of a corporate network where employees might try and gain access against corporate policy. There is a common saying that there are two threats to corporate information security: those on the outside, and those that are already employed by the corporation. The default setting is encrypted content distribution, which protects the distribution sessions from both threats. The system administrator has to knowingly disable the security settings for content distribution between accelerators. Disabling the setting has no impact on the performance of the overall CDN.

The underlying protocol within the secure session is HTTPS, which allows the secure distribution to accommodate network performance disruptions. If a network disruption occurs that stops the secure distribution of content, the session is re-established when the network becomes stable again. The port numbers associated with the secure distribution differ from those of standard SSL-based traffic. SSL sessions default to port 443, whereas secure administration sessions are based on port 8443.

Insecure content distribution does not apply any encryption method to the flow between the parent and child accelerators. Content distribution traffic appears on the network just as any other HTTP traffic does. Null cipher distribution, or intentionally disabling encryption, exposes the same risks as any other nonsecure web traffic that traverses a corporate intranet. For this very reason, many corporations standardize on the default encryption method of content distribution. The system administrator must establish the setting for encrypted or insecure content distribution. At the time the system administrator establishes the properties of the content over which the content administrator will have control, encryption is defined as either enabled or disabled for all content under the control of the content administrator.

Understanding Software-Based Content Delivery Networks

Up to this point, the focus of this chapter has been appliance-based CDNs. Software-based CDN products seek to address the same business challenges addressed by appliance-based CDNs. A software-based CDN involves applications that are resident on each client's PC on a given network. The software commonly runs as a background process, monitoring a management system for any new software, media, or documents that must be distributed to all edge client computers. When the resident application observes new media that is targeted for distribution, the background process fetches the new content to the computer that the application is installed on. Software-based distribution systems work well for their intended purpose, with each vendor offering a different approach to the same content distribution problem. Some software-based CDNs have the ability to model the peer-to-peer distribution systems, while others must communicate directly with their management system for every content item. Software-based systems target the same market targeted by appliance-based systems, and are subject to many of the same obstacles that the client computer itself faces.

Unlike appliance-based CDNs, a software-based distribution model leverages the client's computer itself. An application commonly runs in the background, making its presence known via an icon located in the toolbar of the client's desktop. When the computer user opens the software-based application, they are presented with any media that has been positioned onto the computer since the last time the application was accessed. This model requires that the application reside on any computer expected to participate in the content distribution process. Any content may be prepositioned using this method, including VoD media, software applications, operating system patches, and corporate documents.

The management model of this distribution method differs from that of the appliance-based CDN. The administrator has fewer controls that are centric to the network. Whereas appliance-based CDNs place management emphasis on the CDN's interaction with the network, the software-based model places management emphasis on the client's computer. Appliance-based administration focuses on the child accelerators and any accelerators that participate in the distribution process, whereas software-based administration focuses on monitoring and managing a given installed remote application.

Corporate policies sometimes are very strict regarding client computer standards. Many corporate policies dictate exactly what version of operating system, and any related updates, must reside on a given client's computer. This might extend to controlling the exact version of a media player that must reside on each computer.

Desktop administrators also control how disk space is allocated on any given desktop computer that is under their control. The goal of the desktop administrator is to define a known and trusted standard configuration, limiting exposure to third-party applications. Their objective is to contain the desktop environment. A standardized desktop environment is the best environment for software-based content delivery systems, reducing the risk of any incompatibilities between the application and the desktop system. If all client computers are standardized, including the disk allocation of each partition, then the administrators will have the least amount of management trouble for all subscribing client computers.

Software-based CDNs face several challenges that appliance-based CDNs and accelerators do not face:

■ The software-based model has client standardization rules that do not apply to the appliance-based model.

■ Content that is distributed throughout a given network may or may not be utilized by a client, regardless of the content having been delivered and lived on the disk drive of the client's PC.

■ Client service packs or operating system patches might affect the functionality of the software-based CDN, due to incompatibilities, and streaming media updates may cause CODEC incompatibles with media that has been distributed locally to each client's desktop.

■ Software-based CDNs place requirements on the disk capacity, processor, and physical memory of the client's computer.

The traffic created during the content distribution process to software-based clients may either involve a distributed hierarchy or require that each client computer acquire content directly from a centralized server. Both models involve content distribution; some leverage standards-based protocols, while others leverage proprietary protocols. Some software-based delivery products support encrypted messaging for content delivery, while others do not.

If software-based content delivery is already in place in the network, adding an accelerator will reduce distribution traffic and optimize the software's performance when the content is not encrypted during transport. Some software-based content delivery products allow for appliance-based products to interoperate with the software-based clients, but, commonly, these two methods are seen as providing the same overall functionality. Introducing a WAN optimization appliance in each branch location will greatly reduce the traffic of the software-based CDN.

Native Protocol Playback of Streaming Media

Video-on-demand content commonly averages 30 minutes in length for most single content items. Many portals leverage a single large content item for each module or section hosted from a given content portal, leveraging time offsets within the portal. A time offset allows the client's media player to access content with a specified time designation from the beginning of the file.

If one large video contains several chapters, the portal may provide a URL that contains an offset, directing the user to join the 30-minute video at the 21-minute mark. Other functions that benefit the user include the ability to fast forward, rewind, skip, or pause the playback of content. These functions all enable the user to review content, or bypass content that they have already watched previously. In the case of Windows Media content, the RTSP protocol is desired. RTSP communications between the client's media player and the edge serving accelerator allow the client to actively interact with the media stream.

To content creators, and content administrators, digital rights management is extended to the edge serving accelerator when the native RTSP protocol is used. Credentials validation and access control are major issues to content administrators who must distribute content that contains sensitive data. Corporate announcements and company meetings are two very common subjects that media services teams must support. Digital rights management allows the corporation to both distribute the content and closely control the content at the same time. Digital rights management applies to RTSP streams of VoD content and is commonly implemented via transparent authentication with NTLM.

In a server-centric unicast environment, where all clients access a common dedicated media server in the data center, the server itself might become overloaded with client requests. The most common message a streaming media user sees is *buffering*, which indicates the server has exceeded its capacity, or cannot deliver the stream at an adequate rate. Buffering implies that the client cannot obtain the stream at a rate that is equal to the rate at which the content was encoded. In a server-centric unicast model, too many users on a common server can cause this message to be displayed within the requesting client's media player. This message might also appear on the client's media player if the WAN cannot support the number of clients requesting their own unicast streams.

The streaming traffic must coexist with other traffic traversing the same WAN link. To overcome these challenges, VoD content should be prepositioned to the edge serving accelerator. There will be fewer simultaneous content requests in the remote branch than observed on a media server that resides within the corporate data center. The barriers created by the WAN will also be eliminated, due to the edge serving accelerator's ability to serve content onto a network with significantly higher throughput abilities.

A CDN has the ability to serve hundreds or thousands of users from a single media server, by requesting a single stream from the server's publishing point. To the client, the streams occur without buffering messages, and with no disruption to the client's viewing experience. During an important live corporate broadcast, employees are more likely to participate in the entire session if there are no disruptions to the streaming service.

Network congestion increases with each client request that arrives at a Windows Media Server; the CDN establishes only a single session with the server. The single session established by the content acquiring accelerator is streamed to all subscribing accelerators, and split off to any requesting clients that reside below an edge serving accelerator. A structured distribution model allows for the streamed traffic to create a predictable amount of utilization on the WAN. WAN predictability is based on the known encoding rate of the streaming media session.

For redundancy within a given streaming media event, the content acquiring accelerator may point to a secondary publishing point for the same stream, or to a load-balancing switch with several media servers residing behind the switch. A secondary content acquiring accelerator may be enabled to provide a secondary source for all downstream content serving accelerators. The stream server software or hardware vendor might recommend a secondary publishing point, to reduce the risk of oversubscription of the primary streaming server. Some vendors support the ability to cluster several media servers behind a single common URL, while others support the ability to implement distributed media servers within the data center. The content acquiring accelerator can acquire content from any one of these media server implementations.

A load-balancing switch appears as a single media source or host to the content acquiring accelerator. A load balancer can hide the fact that several media servers reside behind the single source. It is common to use a load-balancing switch to support an increased number of client content requests, and to safeguard against a single point of failure at the media server. Load-balancing switches are not limited to streaming media, but rather include load-balancing support for all types of web content that a CDN supports.

Many corporations standardize on a specific version of media player. The version of media player deployed to all employee computers is unlikely to be the absolute latest release, but rather is commonly one or two versions old. The most common reason for using a legacy version of media player is to ensure compatibility with existing content and with the operating system installed on the employee computers. Newer versions of media players might not support legacy protocols that are deployed within the corporate network, and might contain software instabilities.

As an example of compatibility, in the latest release of Microsoft Windows Media Server and Media Player, the MMS protocol is no longer supported, unless over HTTP. Microsoft has replaced MMS with RTSP as the standardized protocol. Corporations that have thousands of links based on MMS throughout their corporate intranet pages face upgrading their URLs to reflect proper protocols, and must test for compatibility with the version of media player applied to client computers. If a media server cannot stream content over the defined protocol, the target audience might experience a disruption of service. CDNs have also made the transition from MMS to the standardized RTSP protocol, providing a streaming service that is in alignment with the broader streaming media market.

Streaming Media and Executive Demand

Demand for streaming media by corporate executives is one of the primary driving factors in its adoption today. This demand is motivated in part by increasing pressure from employees for more direct information about the status of their corporate employer. Executives are finding that their direct communication with employees improves morale and helps address employee perception of the company's initiatives. Some executive management teams provide monthly or quarterly live communications to their employees. Although most executives prerecord the live event the day before its actual broadcast, the demand is known to exist for live broadcasts to employees.

Although proper streaming media usage requires a license fee to support native protocols such as RTSP, executives recognize that paying this license fee is a worthwhile investment to achieve their communications objective. Without the required license, the stream would be disrupted, and would show poorly within the employees' media players.

The live streaming events can occur over unicast or multicast broadcast sessions, both requiring streaming licenses for all participating accelerators involved in the streaming session. License fees are structured in such a way that the system administrator must determine what the overall throughput need is of the edge serving accelerator, and license the accelerators accordingly. Licenses are not based on the number of requesting clients; licenses are based on the overall volume of content serving traffic.

Multicast broadcasts allow a single broadcast session to span the corporate network, under the guidance of distributed serving accelerators. If a corporate executive's broadcast is going to use multicast, a test session should be thoroughly tested throughout the network. Any limitations or obstacles should be addressed prior to the broadcast, with the network administrative team involved in the test session.

Sometimes multicast obstacles may be outside the control of the network administrators. For example, the network infrastructure of some service providers cannot properly handle multicast traffic. Service provider–imposed limitations typically require the streaming session to use unicast instead of multicast. Many service providers cannot quickly make changes to their infrastructure to instantly support multicast within their hosted network. The CDN allows for multicast streams to be converted to unicast streams within the accelerator. There are many corporations who do successfully use a pure multicast broadcast model today. In a hierarchical network, transition might occur within a regional data center, transitioning a unicast stream into a multicast stream, or a multicast stream into a unicast stream for network compatibility.

Unicast streaming is the most common streaming used in the corporate network today, with fewer in number supporting multicast today. Unicast streaming is not hardware or WAN dependent of the network's abilities to deliver the stream session. For a remote branch with several users, the edge serving accelerator has the ability to aggregate all users' requests for a common stream into a single WAN stream. Stream aggregation does not disrupt the service to any users located behind the edge serving accelerator. The only real limitation that users behind the edge serving accelerator may face will be LAN defined limitations set by the system administrator. Aggregate streaming prevents WAN saturation, unless the single session which the edge serving accelerator is accessing exceeds the throughput capabilities of the WAN.

Live streaming is the least likely of streaming media events for a corporate executive to use. Many executives record their live event the day before the actual event takes place. Once the live event has been encoded, the content may be placed out on all edge serving accelerators in preparation for the next day's live event. A function provided by the CDN allows the edge serving accelerator to broadcast a prepositioned content item as if it were a live event. Commonly referred to as a "live rebroadcast," the edge serving accelerators begin broadcasting the content at a predefined start time. To the clients on the LAN, the live rebroadcast appears as if an actual live event were taking place.

An alternative to a live corporate broadcast is to provide access to a prerecorded corporate event as a video on demand. Following this model, the executive will once again records their message in the days prior to the actual announcement. Once the encoded content is prepositioned to all edge serving accelerators, access to the media is restricted until a predefined date and time. Once the date and time arrives, the content becomes accessible on the edge serving accelerator. If a user requests the content prior to the defined date and time, the user may be redirected to a predetermined URL.

Content that is to be prepositioned for a live rebroadcast, or video on demand, can be encoded at a rate higher than what is supported by the WAN. When the content has been prepositioned to the edge serving accelerator, the distribution occurs over a throttled session. The throttled distribution session will have no impact on requesting clients; the distribution session is not intended for access by client media players. Corporations who preposition executive messaging to the edge of the network have an advantage in the quality of their content. Prepositioned content appears better than other video events that occur over the corporate network due to the lack of the WAN's limitations. Content which may commonly be delivered at 128 Kbps over the WAN can now be served to edge clients at rates significantly higher. The higher encoding rates allow for a significantly better viewing experience at the end user's media player.

Understanding Explicit and Transparent Proxy Modes

There are two proxy modes supported by the accelerator when deployed in a CDN. The first mode is a transparent proxy, and the second is an explicit proxy.

A transparent proxy receives content requests that are forwarded to the edge serving accelerator as they arrive at an administratively defined router. The Web Cache Communication Protocol (WCCP) facilitates communication between the router and edge serving accelerator. The router forwards specific traffic, such as all requests using port 80, to the edge serving accelerator. The edge serving accelerator processes the request to determine if the request is destined for a URL that has been prepositioned at that edge serving accelerator. Transparent proxy accelerators commonly operate within the network without the client knowing their request has been intercepted. Additional WCCP details are provided in Chapter 4, "Overcoming Application-Specific Barriers."

An explicit proxy implies that each client's web browser and media player be configured to direct all content requests toward a defined host name or IP address. When the client's request arrives at the edge serving accelerator, the target URL requested is processed to determine if the request is destined for content that has been prepositioned. Unlike a transparent proxy cache, explicit proxy settings are required at any device to direct the client to the edge serving accelerator.

Regardless of the edge serving accelerator's configured mode, the goal is to exist without the end user's knowledge. Once the client's requests are routed to a "proxy," the system administrator can implement control mechanisms such as bandwidth consumption on the LAN and WAN. Session controls may be implemented to limit the number of simultaneous sessions or the overall volume of content traffic generated by the edge serving accelerator.

Using CDN Calculation Tools

An administrator can create several spreadsheet tools to aid in calculating content distribution and storage calculations. Content storage of prepositioned content is a very straightforward calculation, but for streaming media that does not exist yet, the calculation is much more involved.

The content administrator is allocated a predetermined amount of usable space on the CDN. The system administrator makes their space allocation decision based on requests from each content administrator. All content administrators' storage assignments are independent of each other. If multiple allocations of storage are given to a specific content administrator, those assignments are also independent of each other. Storage capacity planning is important. Objects under the control of a content administrator will not require prepositioning. Effectively planning which content items will become prepositioned while others remain hosted from the origin server involves content usage awareness. If the content administrator has a good understanding of which content items will likely be the most frequently requested, the content administrator can identify those items as the most likely candidates for prepositioning.

Streaming media content will be the most space consuming of all content that is prepositioned, with the exception of operating system service packs and whole applications destined for installation. Streaming media content is created in predictable sizes, and requires special planning.

The growth of the CDN will involve increased growth and adoption of streaming media. Corporate executives are adopting streaming media in increasing numbers. Once executives seek or mandate the use of streaming media, the content administrator's capacity planning abilities will be put to the test. Proper planning at the time of the CDN's implementation will become the foundation for a successful deployment to support all users throughout the corporation. System and content administrators should not lose focus of the reason the CDN was purchased.

General Content Storage

General content explicit proxy mode (CDNs) storage is by far the easiest to calculate, due to the known static size of each object to be prepositioned. There are three methods that can be leveraged to conserve the space consumed during the calculation process:

- Determine the average object size of objects served from origin servers.

- Confirm that content has not been duplicated in multiple locations on an origin server or across multiple servers.

- Apply compression to objects that reside on the origin server.

First, only preposition content that is larger than a defined minimum size. Some corporations allow content to be served directly from the origin server if the size is less than 50 to 100 KB, whereas other corporations have a threshold that is significantly larger. The majority of content items served from a corporate intranet server are smaller than 50 KB.

Second, check to make sure that none of the content that is to be prepositioned already exists in other directories on the origin server. Even though the content is located in more than one directory, the replication of duplicate content will consume excess space on the edge serving accelerators. Web portals and intranet sites that reuse a common content item should all reference the object from a single location. By consolidating the URLs to a common single object, the CDN will distribute the object only once. For users that do not access the CDN, their local browser will benefit from an object that resides in the browser's local cache, and services subsequent page's matches.

Third, consider applying application-based compression to the objects at the origin server. Methods such as gzip allow the origin server to apply compression to objects before they are served to requesting clients or content acquiring accelerator s. This method applies to all types of content served from the origin server. Web browsers natively support decompression of gzip compressed content. Content such as Microsoft PowerPoint presentations can become excessively large when high-resolution graphics are inserted. Presentation applications support the ability to apply compression to the images that reside within the presentation itself. Oversized images and embedded objects create excessively large files that will consume the same amount of space on edge serving accelerators. Application-based compression reduces the size of the content by as much as 75 percent.

Streaming Media Storage

The three common encoding formats used within the enterprise today include

- MPEG 1

- MPEG 2

- MPEG 4

Each encoding format supports multiple rates. Table 5-3 illustrates the calculated size of a given piece of content encoded in the MPEG 1 format; calculations are based on common time lengths of an encoding session. Common encoding rates for MPEG 1 are shown for reference.

Table 5-3   *Common MPEG 1 Storage*

	5 Minutes	15 Minutes	30 Minutes	1 Hour
1.5 Mbps	56.25 MB	168.75 MB	337.5 MB	675 MB
3 Mbps	112.5 MB	337.5 MB	675 MB	1350 MB
6 Mbps	225 MB	675 MB	1350 MB	2700 MB

Table 5-4 illustrates the calculated size of a given piece of content encoded in the MPEG 2 format; calculations are based on common time lengths of an encoding session. Common encoding rates for MPEG 2 are shown for reference.

Table 5-4   *Common MPEG 2 Storage*

	5 Minutes	15 Minutes	30 Minutes	1 Hour
1.5 Mbps	56.25 MB	168.75 MB	337.5 MB	675 MB
3 Mbps	112.5 MB	337.5 MB	675 MB	1350 MB
6 Mbps	225 MB	675 MB	1350 MB	2700 MB
12 Mbps	450 MB	1350 MB	2700 MB	3375 MB
15 Mbps	562.5 MB	1687.5 MB	3375 MB	6750 MB

Table 5-5 illustrates the calculated size of a given piece of content encoded in the MPEG 4 format; calculations are based on common time lengths of an encoding session. For MPEG 4, it is important to note that not all MPEG 4 content is created equally, with each content encoder using a different compression technique. Common encoding rates for MPEG 4 are shown for reference.

MPEG 4 is the most common encoding format within the enterprise today, because nearly all employee computers' operating systems will include a media player that supports RTSP streaming, and the MPEG 4 format.

Table 5-5 *General MPEG 4 Storage*

	5 Minutes	15 Minutes	30 Minutes	1 Hour
128 kBps	4.8 MB	14.4 MB	28.8 MB	57.6 MB
300 kBps	11.25 MB	33.75 MB	67.5 MB	135 MB
512 kBps	19.2 MB	57.6 MB	115.2 MB	230.4 MB
1.5 Mbps	56.25 MB	168.75 MB	337.5 MB	675 MB
3 Mbps	112.5 MB	337.5 MB	675 MB	1350 MB

Calculating Content Delivery Times

Table 5-6 shows calculated content delivery times for four common content object sizes and eight common WAN connection throughput rates. The table provides reference timings based on availability of exactly the bandwidth rating shown. However, a WAN link rated at 1.5 Mbps (T1) typically does not allow the entire 1.5 Mbps to be consumed for the distribution process. The emphasis within the following chart focuses on fractional rates below the T1 throughput rating, representing smaller throughput ratings which the content distribution session will be allowed to consume.

Table 5-6 *Content Delivery Times*

	1 MB	5 MB	25 MB	100 MB
128 kBps	1 min, 3 sec	5 min, 13 sec	26 min, 3 sec	1 hr, 44 min, 10 sec
256 kBps	31 sec	3 min, 24 sec	13 min, 1 sec	52 min, 5 sec
512 kBps	16 sec	1 min, 18 sec	7 min, 30 sec	26 min, 3 sec
768 kBps	10 sec	52 sec	4 min, 20 sec	17 min, 22 sec
1.5 Mbps (T1)	5 sec	26 sec	2 min, 22 sec	9 min, 22 sec
2 Mbps (E1)	4 sec	20 sec	2 min, 10 sec	7 min, 29 sec
10 Mbps	1 sec	4 sec	20 sec	1 min, 20 sec
45 Mbps	.18 sec	1 sec	4 sec	18 sec

Summary

Content delivery networks have been providing corporations and service providers with an intelligent method for media distribution for many years. Intelligent CDNs go beyond a simple file replication method, adding centralized management, hierarchical distribution intelligence, distribution fault tolerance, bandwidth control and awareness, and security to the distribution process.

Centralized management provides multiple parties or departments a centralized point of control of their content's distribution state. CDNs provide visibility into the owner's content distribution and consumption statistics, becoming an end-to-end visibility tool.

With native protocol support, the integration of CDNs is a simple task for the network and content administrators. To the content consumer, access to live or on-demand streaming media and static content no longer taxes the WAN or centralized servers. The CDN provides to media owners a tool that will scale their content to the endpoints of the network.

This chapter includes the following topics:

- Understanding Transport Protocol Limitations

- Understanding Transmission Control Protocol Fundamentals

- Overcoming Transport Protocol Limitations

- Overcoming Link Capacity Limitations

CHAPTER 6

Overcoming Transport and Link Capacity Limitations

The previous chapters have discussed how to align network resources with business priority and application requirements, as well as techniques that can be applied within the network and accelerator devices to improve the overall performance of an application over the network. Techniques employed in the network, such as quality of service (QoS), can help align available network capacity with application throughput requirements or adjust queuing and scheduling for a specific application that might be latency sensitive. Application data caching, read-ahead, prediction, and CDN capabilities can help mitigate the unnecessary utilization of bandwidth for redundant object transfers and also mitigate latency by handling the majority of the workload locally or in a more optimized fashion.

You can, however, employ more generic layers of optimization, which can work across multiple applications concurrently. This type of optimization, commonly called *WAN optimization*, generally refers to functions that are commonly found in accelerator devices (such as standalone appliances or router-integrated modules) that overcome performance limitations caused by transport protocols, packet loss, and capacity limitations.

WAN optimization capabilities make the WAN a more tolerable place for applications to live by removing the vast majority of performance barriers that the WAN creates. For instance, advanced network compression can be applied to improve performance by minimizing the amount of data that needs to traverse the WAN. A secondary benefit of this is that, in many cases, fewer exchanges of data need to occur over the WAN as well, thereby mitigating the latency associated with the number of roundtrip exchanges that would have been necessary. TCP optimization, on the other hand, is commonly used to allow nodes to more efficiently use available resources and minimize the impact of loss and latency in a WAN.

This chapter examines how WAN optimization capabilities overcome performance barriers created by WAN conditions. Keep in mind that, in terms of accelerator products, you can use WAN optimization capabilities in conjunction with other optimization technologies that are application-specific, as described in Chapter 4, "Overcoming Application-Specific Barriers." Furthermore, assuming the architecture of the accelerator is transparent, you can use these optimization technologies in conjunction with network-oriented functions that provide visibility and control.

Understanding Transport Protocol Limitations

What is a transport protocol and how does it create performance limitations? Most people wonder how TCP (or other transport protocols) could ever become a bottleneck, simply because it always seems to just "work." In an internetwork, a layer must exist between applications and the underlying network infrastructure. This layer, called the *transport layer*, not only helps to ensure that data is moved between nodes, but also helps nodes understand how the network is performing so that they can adapt accordingly.

While the transport layer is an unlikely candidate for application performance woes, it can become a problem, primarily because the transport protocols in broad use today were designed in 1981. Today's application demands and network topologies differ greatly from the networks of the early 1980s. For instance, 300 baud was considered blazing fast at the time that TCP was created. Congestion was largely due to a handful of nodes on a shared network of limited scale rather than the complex, high-speed, hierarchical networks such as the Internet, which is plagued with oversubscription, aggregation, and millions of concurrent users each contending for available bandwidth. Applications in 1981 were commonly text-oriented applications (and largely terminal-oriented), whereas today even the most ill-equipped corporate user can easily move files that are tens upon hundreds of megabytes in size during a single transfer.

Although the network has changed, TCP remains relevant in today's dynamic and ever-changing network environment. TCP has undergone only minor changes in the past 25 years, and those changes are in the form of extensions rather than wholesale rewrites of the protocol. Although there are some more modern transport protocols that have roots in TCP, many are considered developmental projects only and currently have limited deployment in the mainstream.

Another important consideration relative to today's enterprise networking and application environments is the cost and available capacity of LAN technology versus declining WAN technology costs. In effect, network bandwidth capacity has steadily increased over the past 20 years; however, the cost of LAN bandwidth capacity has dropped at a rate that is more dramatic per bit/second than the rate at which the cost of an equivalent amount of WAN bandwidth capacity has dropped.

The ever-increasing disparity between WAN and LAN bandwidth presents challenges in the form of throughput. Applications and access to content have become more enabled for LAN users as LAN bandwidth has increased; however, the same level of access to those applications and content has not become more enabled for WAN users given the far different cost versus bandwidth capacity increase metrics that the WAN has undergone. Put simply, the rate of bandwidth increase found in the WAN is not keeping pace with the LAN, and this creates performance challenges for users who are forced to access information over the WAN. In this way, the LAN has enabled faster access to a much more network-intensive set of data. At the same time, the WAN has not grown to the same degree from a capacity perspective or become achievable from a price perspective to allow the same level of access for nearly the same cost.

WAN optimization techniques (discussed later in this chapter, in the section "Accelerators and Compression") are considered adjacent and complementary to the techniques presented in earlier chapters; that is, they are implemented apart from network optimization (QoS and optimized routing) and application acceleration (caching, CDN, and other optimizations such as read-ahead). For instance, an object-layer application cache can leverage compression technologies during content distribution or pre-position jobs to improve throughput and ensure that the compression history is populated with the relevant content if the transfer of the objects in question takes place over the WAN.

In the opposite direction, a user has a read-write type of relationship with an object that has been opened through an accelerator's object cache, where that object has been validated against the origin server (in the case of a cached file). If that file is saved and written back to the origin server, the compression history and protocol optimizations (such as write-back optimization) can be leveraged to improve the write performance while saving bandwidth.

Compression techniques can be leveraged to minimize the bandwidth consumed and eliminate previously seen repetitive byte patterns. This not only helps to ensure that precious WAN bandwidth is conserved but also serves to improve the performance of the user experience because less bandwidth is needed. Consequently, fewer packet exchanges must occur before the operation completes.

Coupling compression and the application acceleration techniques discussed in previous chapters with optimizations to the transport protocol ensures that the WAN is used efficiently and the user experience is significantly optimized. In many cases, WAN users experience performance levels similar to those experienced when operating in a LAN environment. WAN optimization helps to overcome the constraints of the WAN while maintaining WAN cost metrics, preserving investment, and providing a solution for consolidating distributed server, storage, and application infrastructure.

Put simply, the network is the foundation for an application-fluent infrastructure, and an optimized foundation provides the core for application performance. Transport protocol optimization and compression (that is, WAN optimization) ensure that resources are used effectively and efficiently while overcoming performance barriers at the data transmission layer. Application acceleration works to circumvent application layer performance barriers. These technologies are all independent but can be combined cohesively to form a solution, as shown in Figure 6-1.

Figure 6-1 *Application Acceleration and WAN Optimization Hierarchy*

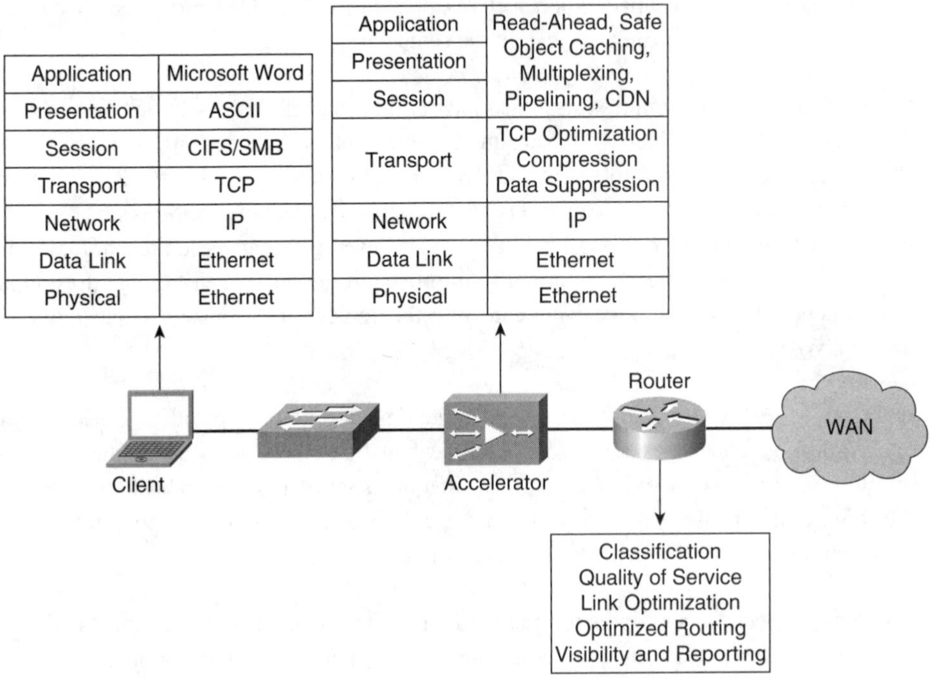

Understanding Transmission Control Protocol Fundamentals

TCP is the most commonly used transport protocol for applications that run on enterprise networks and the Internet today. TCP provides the following functions:

■ Connection-oriented service between application processes on two nodes that are exchanging data

■ Guaranteed delivery of data between these two processes

■ Bandwidth discovery and congestion avoidance to fairly utilize available bandwidth based on utilization and WAN capacity

NOTE For more information about TCP, see RFC 793, which you can access through the following link: http://www.rfc-editor.org/rfcsearch.html

Before data can be sent between two disparate application processes on two disparate nodes, a connection must first be established. Once the connection is established, TCP provides guaranteed reliable delivery of data between the two application processes.

Connection-Oriented Service

The TCP connection is established through a three-way handshake agreement that occurs between two sockets on two nodes that wish to exchange data. A *socket* is defined as the network identifier of a node coupled with the port number that is associated with the application process that desires to communicate with a peer. The use of TCP sockets is displayed in Figure 6-2.

Figure 6-2 *TCP Socket*

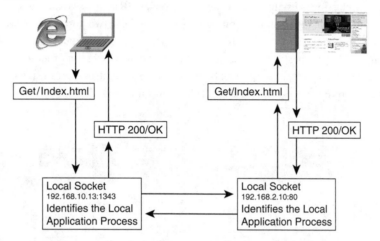

During the establishment of the connection, the two nodes exchange information relevant to the parameters of the conversation. This information includes

- **Source and destination TCP ports:** The ports that are associated with application processes on each of the nodes that would like to exchange application data.

- **Initial sequence number:** Each device notifies the other what sequence number should be used for the beginning of the transmission.

- **Window size:** The advertised receive window size; that is, the amount of data that the advertising node can safely hold in its socket receive buffer.

- **Options:** Optional header fields commonly used for extensions to TCP behavior. For instance, this could include features such as window scaling and selective acknowledgment that were not included as part of the TCP RFC but can augment TCP behavior (an authoritative list of TCP options can be found at http://www.iana.org/assignments/tcp-parameters).

For instance, if an Internet user wants to use Internet Explorer to access http://www.cisco.com, the user's computer would first have to resolve the name www.cisco.com to an IP address, and then attempt to establish a TCP connection to the web server that is hosting www.cisco.com using the well-known port for HTTP (TCP port 80) unless a port number was specified. If the web server that is hosting www.cisco.com is accepting connections on TCP port 80, the connection would likely establish successfully. During the connection establishment, the server and client would tell one another how much data they can receive into their socket buffer (window size) and what initial sequence number to use for the initial transmission of data. As data is exchanged, this number would increment to allow the receiving node to know the appropriate ordering of data. During the life of the connection, TCP employs checksum functionality to provide a fairly accurate measure of the integrity of the data.

Once the connection is established between two nodes (IP addresses) and two application process identifiers (TCP ports), the application processes using those two ports on the two disparate nodes can begin to exchange application layer data. For instance, once a connection is established, a user can submit a GET request to the web server that it is connected to in order to begin downloading objects from a web page, or a user can begin to exchange control messages using SMTP or POP3 to transmit or receive an e-mail message. TCP connection establishment is shown in Figure 6-3.

Figure 6-3 *TCP Connection Establishment*

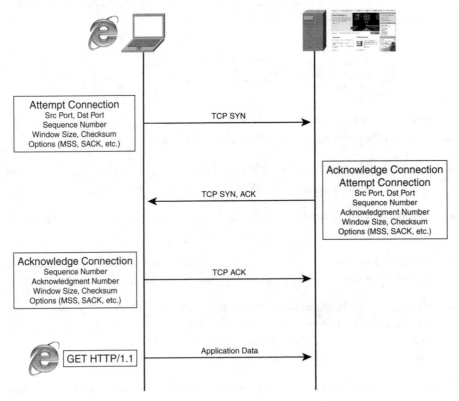

Guaranteed Delivery

Once transmission commences, application data is drained from application buffers on the transmitting process into the node's socket buffer. TCP then negotiates the transmission of data from the socket transmission buffer to the recipient node (that is, the draining of the buffer) based on the availability of resources on the recipient node to receive the data as dictated by the initially advertised window size and the current window size. Given that application data blocks may be quite large, TCP performs the task of breaking the data into segments, each with a sequence number that identifies the relative ordering of the portions of data that have been transmitted. If the node receives the segments out of order, TCP can reorder them according to the sequence number. If TCP buffers become full for one of the following reasons, a blocking condition could occur:

■ **TCP transmit buffer becomes full:** The transmit buffer on the transmitting node can become full if network conditions prevent delivery of data or if the recipient is overwhelmed and cannot receive additional data. While the receiving node is unable to receive more data, applications may be allowed to continue to add data to the transmit buffer to await service. With the blockade of data waiting in the transmit buffer, unable to be transmitted, applications on the transmitting node may become blocked (that is, momentary or prolonged pauses in transmission). In such a situation, new data cannot be written into the transmit buffer on the transmitting node unless space is available in that buffer, which generally cannot be freed until the recipient is able to receive more data or the network is able to deliver data again.

■ **TCP receive buffer becomes full:** Commonly caused by the receiving application not being able to extract data from the socket receive buffer quickly enough. For instance, an overloaded server, i.e. one that is receiving data at a rate greater than the rate at which it can process data, would exhibit this characteristic. As the receive buffer becomes full, new data cannot be accepted from the network for this socket and must be dropped, which indicates a congestion event to the transmitting node.

Figure 6-4 shows how TCP acts as an intermediary buffer between the network and applications within a node.

Figure 6-4 *TCP Buffering Between the Network and Applications*

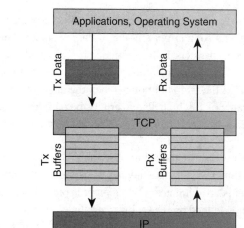

When data is successfully placed into a recipient node TCP receive buffer, TCP generates an acknowledgment (ACK) with a value relative to the tail of the sequence that has just been received. For instance, if the initial sequence number was "1" and 1 KB of data was transmitted, when the data is placed into the recipient socket receive buffer, the recipient TCP stack will issue an ACK with a value of 1024. As data is extracted from the recipient node's socket receive buffer by the application process associated with that socket, the TCP stack on the recipient will generate an ACK with the same acknowledgment number but will also indicate an increase in the available window capacity. Given that applications today are generally able to extract data immediately from a TCP receive buffer, it is likely that the acknowledgment and window relief would come simultaneously.

The next segment that is sent from the transmitting node will have a sequence number equal to the previous sequence number plus the amount of data sent in the previous segment (1025 in this example), and can be transmitted only if there is available window capacity on the recipient node as dictated by the acknowledgments sent from the recipient. As data is acknowledged and the window value is increased (data in the TCP socket buffer must be extracted by the application process, thereby relieving buffer capacity and thus window capacity), the sender is allowed to continue to send additional data to the recipient up to the maximum capacity of the recipient's window (the recipient also has the ability to send dynamic window updates indicating increases or decreases in window size).

This process of transmitting data based on the recipient's ability to receive and previously acknowledged segments is commonly referred to as the TCP *sliding window*. In essence, as the recipient continues to receive and acknowledge or otherwise notify of an increase in window size, the window on the transmitting node shifts to allow new data to be sent. If at any point buffers become full or the window is exhausted, the recipient must first service data that has been previously received and acknowledge the sender before any new data can be sent. An example of this process is shown in Figure 6-5.

Additionally, TCP provides a flag that allows an application process to notify TCP to send data immediately rather than wait for a larger amount of data to accumulate in the socket buffer. This flag, called a *push*, or PSH, instructs TCP to immediately send all data that is buffered for a particular destination. This push of data also requires that previous conditions be met, including availability of a window on the recipient node. When the data is transmitted, the PSH flag in the TCP header is set to a value of 1, which also instructs the recipient to send the data directly to the receiving application process rather than use the socket receive buffer.

Nodes that are transmitting also use the acknowledgment number, sequence number, and window value as a gauge of how long to retain data that has been previously transmitted. Each segment that has been transmitted and is awaiting acknowledgment is placed in a retransmission queue and is considered to be unacknowledged by the recipient application process. When a segment is placed in the retransmission queue, a timer is started indicating how long the sender will wait for an acknowledgment. If an acknowledgment is not received, the segment is retransmitted. Given that the window size is generally larger than a single segment, many segments are likely to be outstanding in the network awaiting acknowledgment at any given time.

Figure 6-5   *TCP Operation*

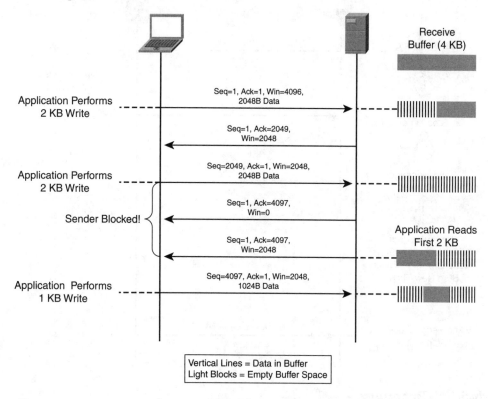

From a transport layer perspective, the loss of a segment might not prevent transmission from continuing. However, given that the application layer is really dictating transport layer behavior (for instance, an upper-layer protocol acknowledgment), the loss of a segment may indeed prevent transmission from continuing.

The purpose of this retransmission queue is twofold:

- It allows the transmitting node to allocate memory capacity to retain the segments that have been previously transmitted. If a segment is lost (congestion, packet loss), it can be transmitted from the retransmission queue, and remains there until acknowledged by the recipient application process (window update).

- It allows the original segment, once placed in the retransmission queue, to be removed from the original transmission queue. This in effect allows TCP to be continually extracting data from the local transmitting application process while not compromising the transmitting node's ability to retransmit should a segment become lost or otherwise unacknowledged.

An example of TCP retransmission management is shown in Figure 6-6.

Figure 6-6   *TCP Retransmission Management*

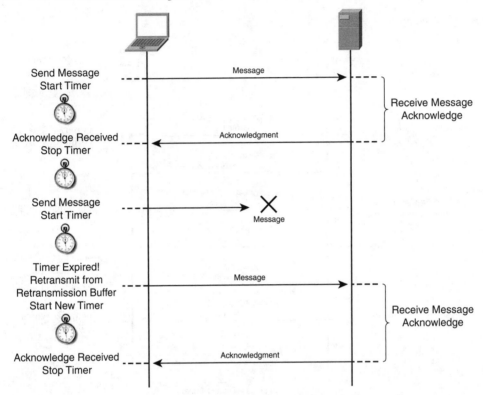

Bandwidth Discovery

The TCP sliding window can act as a throttling mechanism to ensure that transmission of data is done in such a way that it aligns with the available buffer capacity and window of the two devices exchanging data. There are also mechanisms in TCP that allow it to act as a throttling mechanism based on the capacity of the network and any situations encountered in the network.

In some cases, the nodes exchanging data are able to send more data than the network can handle, and in other cases (which is more prominent today), the nodes are not able to send as much data as the network can handle. In the case of nodes being able to transmit more data than the network is prepared to handle, congestion and loss occur. TCP has mechanisms built in to account for these situations. In this way, TCP is *adaptive* in that it bridges the gap between transmission requirements and limitations, receive requirements and limitations, congestion, and loss, for both the application process *and* the network. This throttling mechanism also provides a balancing act between applications and the network and works to continually leverage what capacity in the network is available while attempting to maximize application throughput.

Discovering the steady state for an application process, meaning the balance between available network capacity and the rate of data exchange between application processes and socket buffers, is wholly subjective because application behavior is largely dictated by the function of input, meaning the rate at which the application attempts to send or receive data from the socket buffers. Network throughput is generally more deterministic and objective based on a variety of factors (which would otherwise make it appear nondeterministic and fully subjective), including bandwidth, latency, congestion, and packet loss.

The terms congestion and loss are used separately here, even though congestion and loss are generally married. In some situations, congestion can simply refer to a delay in service due to saturated buffers or queues that are not completely full, but full enough to slightly delay the delivery of a segment of data. These factors are deterministic based on network utilization and physics rather than a set of input criteria, as would be the case with an application. In any case, applications are driving the utilization of network bandwidth, so the argument could be made that they go hand in hand.

TCP provides capabilities to respond to network conditions, thus allowing it to perform the following basic but critical functions:

- Initially find a safe level at which data can be transmitted and continually adapt to changes in network conditions

- Respond to congestion or packet loss events through retransmission and make adjustments to throughput levels

- Provide fairness when multiple concurrent users are contending for the same shared resource (bandwidth)

These capabilities are implemented in two TCP functions that are discussed in the next two sections: TCP slow start and TCP congestion avoidance.

TCP Slow Start

TCP is responsible for initially finding the amount of network capacity available to the connection. This function, as introduced in Chapter 2, "Barriers to Application Performance," is provided in a mechanism found in TCP called *slow start* (also known as *bandwidth discovery*) and is also employed in longer-lived connections when the available window falls below a value known as the *slow-start threshold*. Slow start is a perfect name for the function, even though it may appear upon further examination to be a misnomer.

Slow start uses an exponential increase in the number of segments that can be sent per successful round trip, and this mechanism is employed at the beginning of a connection to find the initial available network capacity. In a successful round trip, data is transmitted based on the current value of the congestion window (cwnd) and an acknowledgment is received from the recipient. (The cwnd correlates to the number of segments that can be sent and remain unacknowledged in the network and is a dynamic value that cannot exceed the window size of the recipient.) The cwnd value is bound to an upper threshold defined by the receiver window size and the transmission buffer capacity of the sender.

With TCP slow start, the transmitting node starts by sending a single segment and waits for acknowledgment. Upon acknowledgment, the transmitting node doubles the number of segments that are sent and awaits acknowledgment. This process occurs until one of the following two scenarios is encountered:

- An acknowledgment is not received, thereby signaling packet loss or excessive congestion

- The number of segments that can be sent (cwnd) is equal to the window size of the recipient or equal to the maximum capacity of the sender

The first case is only encountered in the following circumstances:

- The capacity of the network is less than the transmission capabilities of the sender and receive capabilities of the receiver

- A loss event is detected (no acknowledgment received within the time allocated to the transmitted segment as it is placed in the retransmission queue)

- Congestion delays the delivery of the segment long enough to allow the retransmission queue timer for the transmitted segment to expire

The second case is encountered only when the capacity of the network is equal to (with no loss or congestion) or greater than the transmission capabilities of the sender and the receive capabilities of the receiver. In this case, the sender or the receiver cannot fully capitalize on the available network capacity based on window capacity or buffer sizes.

The result of TCP slow start is an exponential increase in throughput up to the available network capacity or up to the available transmit/receive throughput of the two nodes dictated by buffer size or advertised window size. This is a relatively accurate process of finding the initially available bandwidth, and generally is skewed only in the case of a network that is exhibiting high packet loss characteristics, which may cut the slow-start process short. When one of the previously listed two cases presented is encountered, the connection exits TCP slow start, knowing the initially available network capacity, and enters the congestion avoidance mode. Slow start is never entered again unless the cwnd of the connection falls below the slow-start threshold value.

If the first case is encountered—loss of a packet, or excessive delay causing the retransmission timer to expire—standard TCP implementations immediately drop the cwnd value by 50 percent. If the second case is encountered—no loss—cwnd is in a steady state that is equal to the receiver's advertised window size. TCP slow start is shown in Figure 6-7.

Figure 6-7 *TCP Slow Start*

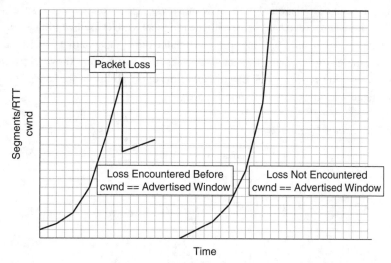

TCP Congestion Avoidance

Once the TCP connection exits slow start (bandwidth discovery), it then enters a mode known as *congestion avoidance*. Congestion avoidance is a mechanism that allows the TCP implementation to react to situations encountered in the network. Packet loss and delay signal congestion in the network, which could be indicative of a number of factors:

- **Bandwidth allocation change:** For instance, change in a variable bandwidth circuit can result in the network being able to service more or less overall throughput based on the direction and nature of the change.

- **Network oversubscription:** When a shared network connection between upstream devices is used by multiple concurrent users, it can become congested to the point of loss or delay.

- **Congestion of device queues:** Similar to network oversubscription, a shared device such as a router can have its queues exhausted to the point of not being able to accept new packets. This could also be equated to a QoS configuration that dictates maximum bandwidth utilization of a specific traffic class or drop policies for that class when congestion is encountered.

- **Overload of destination:** Destination socket buffers can become full because of an application's inability to drain data from them in a timely fashion, potentially because of the server being overwhelmed.

This list only begins to scratch the surface of why packets could be lost or otherwise delayed. The good news is that TCP was designed to work in a network that is unreliable and lossy (high levels of packet loss) and uses these events to its advantage to adequately throttle transmission characteristics and adapt to network conditions.

While in congestion avoidance mode, standard TCP continually increments the number of segments that can be transmitted without acknowledgment by one for every successful round trip, up to the point where cwnd has parity with the recipient's advertised window size. Any time a loss is detected (the retransmission timer for a segment expires), standard TCP reduces cwnd by 50 percent, thereby minimizing the amount of data that can be unacknowledged in the network (in other words, in transit), which can directly impact the ability of the sender to transmit data. TCP congestion avoidance is shown in Figure 6-8.

Figure 6-8 *TCP Congestion Avoidance*

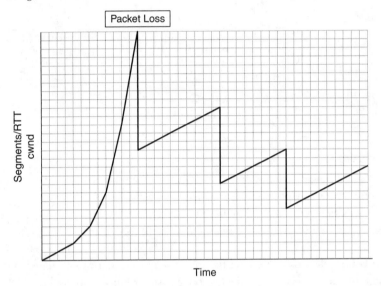

Through the use of slow start and congestion avoidance mode, TCP can discover available network capacity for a connection and adapt the transmission characteristics of that connection to the situations encountered in the network.

Overcoming Transport Protocol Limitations

Now that you understand the fundamentals of how TCP operates, you are ready to examine how TCP can become a barrier to application performance in WAN environments. If you are wondering whether TCP can also be a barrier to application performance in LAN environments, the answer is unequivocally "yes." However, given that this book focuses on application acceleration and WAN optimization, which are geared toward improving performance for remote office and WAN environments, this book will not examine the TCP barriers to application performance in LAN environments.

You may also be wondering about UDP at this point. UDP, which is connectionless and provides no means for guaranteed delivery (it relies on application layer semantics), generally is not limited in terms of throughput on the network (outside of receiver/transmitter buffers). It is also not considered a good network citizen, particularly on a low-bandwidth WAN, because it consumes all available capacity that it can with no inherent fairness characteristics. Most enterprise applications, other than Voice over IP, video, TFTP, and some storage and file system protocols, do not use UDP. UDP traffic is generally best optimized in other ways, including stream splitting for video, which is discussed in Chapter 4, or through packet concatenation or header compression for VoIP. These topics, including UDP in general, are not discussed in the context of WAN optimization in this work.

The previous section examined at a high level how TCP provides connection-oriented service, provides guaranteed delivery, and adapts transmission characteristics to network conditions. TCP does have limitations, especially in WAN environments, in that it can be a significant barrier to application performance based on how it operates. This section examines ways to circumvent the performance challenges presented by TCP, including slow start and congestion avoidance, but note that this will not be an exhaustive study of every potential extension that can be applied.

Of Mice and Elephants: Short-Lived Connections and Long Fat Networks

No, this is not a John Steinbeck novel gone wrong. "Mice" and "elephants" are two of the creatures that can be found in the zoo known as networking. The term *mice* generally refers to very short-lived connections. Mice connections are commonly set up by an application to perform a single task, or a relatively small number of tasks, and then torn down. Mice connections are often used in support of another, longer-lived connection. An example of mice connections can be found in HTTP environments, where a connection is established to download a container page, and ancillary connections are established to fetch objects. These ancillary connections are commonly torn down immediately after the objects are fetched, so they are considered short-lived, or mice, connections.

Elephants are not connection related; rather, the term *elephant* refers to a network that is deemed to be "long" and "fat." "Elephant" is derived from the acronym for long fat network, LFN. An LFN is a network that is composed of a long distance connection ("long") and high bandwidth capacity ("fat").

The next two sections describe mice connections and elephant networks, and the performance challenges they create.

Mice: Short-Lived Connections

Short-lived connections suffer from performance challenges because each new connection that is established has to undergo TCP slow start. As mentioned earlier, TCP slow start is a misnomer because it has very fast throughput ramp-up capabilities based on bandwidth discovery but also can impede the ability of a short-lived connection to complete in a timely fashion. Slow start allows a new connection to use only a small amount of available bandwidth at the start, and there is significant overhead associated with the establishment of each of these connections, caused by latency between the two communicating nodes.

A good example of a short lived connection is a Web browser's fetch of a 50-KB object from within an HTTP container page. Internet browsers spawn a new connection specifically to request the object, and this new connection is subject to TCP slow start. With TCP slow start, the connection is able to transmit a single segment (cwnd is equal to one segment) and must wait until an acknowledgment is received before slow start doubles the cwnd value (up to the maximum, which is the receiver's advertised window size). Due to TCP slow start, only a small amount of data can be transmitted, and each exchange of data suffers the latency penalty of the WAN.

Once the connection is in congestion avoidance (assuming it was able to discover a fair amount of bandwidth), it would be able to send many segments without requiring tedious acknowledgments so quickly. If the initial segment size is 500 bytes, it would take a minimum of seven roundtrip exchanges (not counting the connection setup exchanges) to transfer the 50-KB object, assuming no packet loss was encountered. This is shown in Table 6-1.

Table 6-1   *Bytes per RTT with Standard TCP Slow Start*

Roundtrip Time Number	cwnd	cwnd (Bytes)	Bytes Remaining
1	1	500	49,500
2	2	1000	48,500
3	4	2000	46,500
4	8	4000	42,500
5	16	8000	34,500
6	32	16,000	18,500
7	64	32,000	Finished!

In a LAN environment, this series of exchanges would not be a problem, because the latency of the network is generally around 1–2 ms, meaning that the total completion time most likely would be under 20 ms. However, in a WAN environment with 100 ms of one-way latency (200 ms round trip), this short-lived connection would have taken approximately 1.4 seconds to complete. The challenges of TCP slow start as it relates to short-lived connections is, in effect, what gave birth to the term "World Wide Wait."

There are two primary means of overcoming the performance limitations of TCP slow start:

- Circumvent it completely by using a preconfigured rate-based transmission protocol. A rate-based transmission solution will have a preconfigured or dynamically learned understanding of the network capacity to shape the transmission characteristics immediately, thereby mitigating slow start.

■ Increase the initial permitted segment count (cwnd) to a larger value at the beginning of the connection, otherwise known as *large initial windows*. This means of overcoming performance limitations of TCP slow start is generally the more adaptive and elegant solution, because it allows each connection to continue to gradually consume bandwidth rather than start at a predefined rate.

Using a preconfigured rate-based transmission solution requires that the sender, or an intermediary accelerator device, be preconfigured with knowledge of how much capacity is available in the network, or have the capability to dynamically learn what the capacity is. When the connection is established, the node (or accelerator) immediately begins to transmit based on the preconfigured or dynamically learned rate (that is, bandwidth capacity) of the network, thereby circumventing the problems of TCP slow start and congestion avoidance.

In environments that are largely static (bandwidth and latency are stable), rate-based transmission solutions work quite well. However, while rate-based transmission does overcome the performance challenges presented by TCP slow start and congestion avoidance, it has many other challenges and limitations that make it a less attractive solution for modern-day networks.

Today's networks are plagued with oversubscription, contention, loss, and other characteristics that can have an immediate and profound impact on available bandwidth and measured latency. For environments that are not as static, a rate-based transmission solution will need to continually adapt to the changing characteristics of the network, thereby causing excessive amounts of measurement to take place such that the accelerator can "guesstimate" the available network capacity. In a dynamic network environment, this can be a challenge for rate-based transmission solutions because network congestion, which may not be indicative of loss or changes in bandwidth, can make the sender believe that less capacity is available than what really is available.

Although rate-based transmission solutions may immediately circumvent slow start and congestion avoidance to improve performance for short- and long-lived connections, a more adaptive solution with no restrictions is available by using large initial windows. Large Initial Windows, originally defined in RFC 3390, "Increasing TCP's Initial Window," specifies that the initial window be increased to minimize the number of roundtrip message exchanges that must take place before a connection is able to exit slow start and enter congestion avoidance mode, thereby allowing it to consume network bandwidth and complete the operation much more quickly. This approach does not require previous understanding or configuration of available network capacity, and allows each connection to identify available bandwidth dynamically, while minimizing the performance limitations associated with slow start.

Figure 6-9 shows how using TCP large initial windows helps circumvent bandwidth starvation for short-lived connections and allows connections to more quickly utilize available network capacity.

Figure 6-9 *TCP Large Initial Windows*

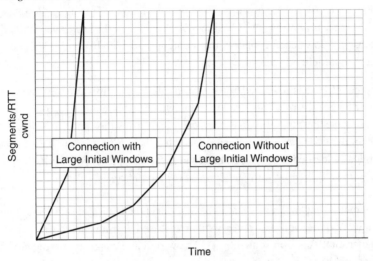

Referring to the previous example of downloading a 50-KB object using HTTP, if RFC 3390 was employed and the initial window was 4000 bytes, the operation would complete in a matter of four roundtrip exchanges. In a 200-ms-roundtrip WAN environment, this equates to approximately 800 ms, or roughly a 50 percent improvement over the same transfer where large initial windows were not employed. (See Table 6-2.) Although this may not circumvent the entire process of slow start, as a rate-based transmission protocol would, it allows the connection to retain its adaptive characteristics and compete for bandwidth fairly on the WAN.

Table 6-2 *Bytes per RTT with TCP Large Initial Windows*

RTT Number	cwnd	cwnd (Bytes)	Bytes Remaining
1	1	4000	46,000
2	2	8000	38,000
3	4	16,000	22,000
4	8	32,000	Finished!

Comparing rate-based transmission and large initial windows, most find that the performance difference for short-lived connections is negligible, but the network overhead required for bandwidth discovery in rate-based solutions can be a limiting factor. TCP implementations that maintain semantics of slow start and congestion avoidance (including Large Initial Windows), however, are by design dynamic and adaptive with minimal restriction, thereby ensuring fairness among flows that are competing for available bandwidth.

Elephants: High Bandwidth Delay Product Networks

While the previous section examined optimizations primarily geared toward improving performance for mice connections, this section examines optimizations primarily geared toward improving performance for environments that contain elephants (LFNs). An LFN is a network that is long (distance, latency) and fat (bandwidth capacity).

Because every bit of data transmitted across a network link has some amount of travel time associated with it, it can be assumed that there can be multiple packets on a given link at any point in time. Thus, a node may be able to send ten packets before the first packet actually reaches the intended destination simply due to the distance contained in the network that is being traversed. With IP, there is no concept of send-and-wait at the packet layer. Therefore, network nodes place packets on the wire at the rate determined by the transport layer (or by the application layer in the case of connectionless transport protocols) and will continue to send based on the reaction of the transport layer to network events.

As an example, once a router transmits a packet, the router does not wait for that packet to reach its destination before the router sends another packet that is waiting in the queue. In this way, the links between network nodes (that is, routers and switches) are, when utilized, always holding some amount of data from conversations that are occurring. The network has some amount of capacity, which equates to the amount of data that can be in flight over a circuit at any given time that has not yet reached its intended destination or otherwise been acknowledged. This capacity is called the *bandwidth delay product (BDP)*.

The BDP of a network is easily calculated. Simply convert the network data rate (in bits) to bytes (remember there is a necessary conversion from power of 10 to power of 2). Then, multiply the network data rate (in bytes) by the delay of the network (in seconds). The resultant value is the amount of data that can be in flight over a given network at any point in time. The greater the distance (latency) and the greater the bandwidth of the network, the more data that can be in flight across that link at any point in time. Figure 6-10 shows a comparison between a high BDP network and a low BDP network.

The challenge with LFNs is not that they have a high BDP, but that the nodes exchanging data over the network do not have buffers or window sizes large enough to adequately utilize the available link capacity. With multiple concurrent connections, the link can certainly be utilized effectively, but a single connection has a difficult time taking advantage of (or simply cannot take advantage of) the large amount of network capacity available because of the lack of buffer space and TCP window capacity.

Figure 6-10 *Comparing Bandwidth Delay Product—High vs. Low*

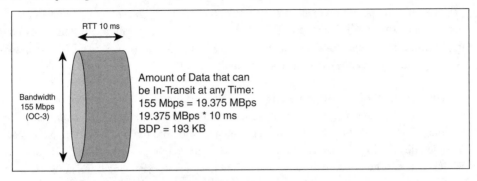

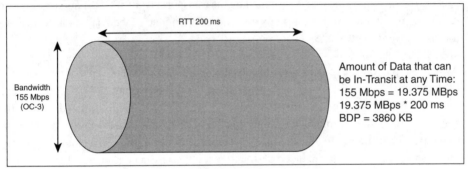

In situations where a single pair of nodes with inadequate buffer or window capacity is exchanging data, the sending node is easily able to exhaust the available window because of the amount of time taken to get an acknowledgment back from the recipient. Buffer exhaustion is especially profound in situations where the window size negotiated between the two nodes is small, because this can result in sporadic network utilization (burstiness) and periods of underutilization (due to buffer exhaustion). Figure 6-11 shows how window exhaustion leads to a node's inability to fully utilize available WAN capacity.

Figure 6-11 *Window Exhaustion in High BDP Networks*

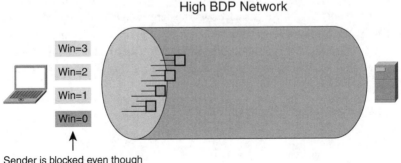

Bandwidth scalability is a term that is often used when defining an optimization capability within an accelerator or configuration change that provides the functionality necessary for a pair of communicating nodes to take better advantage of the available bandwidth capacity. This is also known as *fill-the-pipe optimization*, which allows nodes communicating over an LFN to achieve higher levels of throughput, thereby overcoming issues with buffer or window exhaustion. This type of optimization can be implemented rather painlessly on a pair of end nodes (which requires configuration changes to each node where this type of optimization is desired, which can be difficult to implement on a global scale), or it can be implemented in an accelerator, which does not require any of the end nodes to undergo a change in configuration.

Two primary methods are available to enable fill-the-pipe optimization:

■   Window scaling

■   Scalable TCP implementation

The following sections describe both.

Window Scaling

Window scaling is an extension to TCP (see RFC 1323, "TCP Extensions for High Performance"). Window scaling, which is a TCP option that is negotiated during connection establishment, allows two communicating nodes to go beyond the 16-bit limit (65,536 bytes) for defining the available window size.

With window scaling enabled, an option is defined with a parameter advertised that is known as the *window scale factor*. The window scale factor dictates a binary shift of the value of the 16-bit advertised TCP window, thereby providing a multiplier effect on the advertised window. For instance, if the advertised TCP window is 1111 1111 1111 1111 (that is, decimal 64 KB) and the window scale factor is set to 2, the binary value of the window size will have two bits added to the end of it, which would then become 11 1111 1111 1111 1111. The advertised 64-KB window size would be handled by the end nodes as a 256-KB window size.

Larger scaled windows cause the end nodes to allocate more memory to TCP buffering, which means in effect that more data can be in flight and unacknowledged at any given time. Having more data in flight minimizes the opportunity for buffer exhaustion, which allows the conversing nodes to better leverage the available network capacity. The window scale TCP option (based on RFC 1323) allows for window sizes up to 1 GB (the scale factor is set to a value of 14). Figure 6-12 shows how window scaling allows nodes to better utilize available network capacity.

Figure 6-12 *Using Window Scaling to Overcome High BDP Networks*

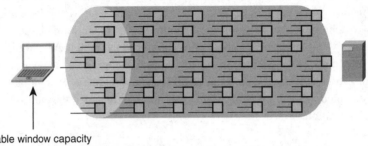

High BDP Network

Available window capacity
greater than network capacity.

Scalable TCP Implementation

The second method of enabling fill-the-pipe optimization that is available, but more difficult to implement in networks containing devices of mixed operating systems, is to use a more purpose-built and scalable TCP implementation. Many researchers, universities, and technology companies have spent a significant amount of money and time to rigorously design, test, and implement these advanced TCP stacks. One common theme exists across the majority of the implementations: each is designed to overcome performance limitations of TCP in WAN environments and high-speed environments while improving bandwidth scalability. Many of these advanced TCP stacks include functionality that helps enable bandwidth scalability and overcome other challenges related to loss and latency.

Although difficult to implement in a heterogeneous network of workstations and servers, most accelerator solutions provide an advanced TCP stack natively as part of an underlying TCP proxy architecture (discussed later in this chapter, in the "Accelerator TCP Proxy Functionality" section), thereby mitigating the need to make time-consuming and questionable configuration changes to the network end nodes. Several of the more common (and popular) implementations will be discussed later in the chapter.

The next section looks at performance challenges of TCP related to packet loss.

Overcoming Packet Loss-Related Performance Challenges

Packet loss occurs in any network and, interestingly enough, occurs most commonly outside of the network and within the host buffers. TCP has been designed in such a way that it can adapt when packet loss is encountered and recover from such situations. Packet loss is not always bad. For instance, when detected by TCP (segments in the retransmission queue encounter an expired timer, for instance), packet loss signals that the network characteristics may have changed (for example, if the available bandwidth capacity decreased). Packet loss could also signal that there is congestion on the network in the form of other nodes trying to consume or share the available bandwidth. This information allows TCP to react in such a way that allows other nodes to acquire their fair share of bandwidth on the network, a feature otherwise known as *fairness*.

Fairness is defined as a trait exhibited by networks that allow connections to evenly share available bandwidth capacity. TCP is considered to be a transport protocol that can generally ensure fairness, because it adapts to changes in network conditions, including packet loss and congestion, which are commonly encountered when flows compete for available bandwidth.

The result of packet loss in connection-oriented, guaranteed-delivery transport protocols such as TCP is a shift in the transmission characteristics to ensure that throughput is decreased to allow others to consume available capacity and also to accommodate potential changes in network capacity. This shift in transmission characteristics (in the case of TCP, decreasing the cwnd) could have a detrimental impact on the overall throughput if the cwnd available drops to a level that prevents the node from fully utilizing the network capacity.

Standard TCP implementations will drop cwnd by 50 percent when a loss of a segment is detected. In many cases, dropping cwnd by 50 percent will not have an adverse effect on throughput. In some cases, however, where the BDP of the network is relatively high, decreasing cwnd by 50 percent can have a noticeable impact on the throughput of an application.

TCP is designed to be overly conservative in that it will do its best to provide fairness across multiple contenders. This conservative nature is rooted in the fact that TCP was designed at a time when the amount of bandwidth available was far less than what exists today. The reality is that TCP needs to be able to provide fairness across concurrent connections (which it does), adaptive behavior for lossy networks (which it does), and efficient utilization of WAN resources (which it does not). Furthermore, when a loss of a packet is detected, all of the segments within the sliding window must be retransmitted from the retransmission queue, which proves very inefficient in WAN environments. Figure 6-13 shows the impact of packet loss on the TCP congestion window, which may lead to a decrease in application throughput.

When TCP detects the loss of a segment, cwnd is dropped by 50 percent, which effectively limits the amount of data the transmitting node can have outstanding in the network at any given time. Given that standard TCP congestion avoidance uses a linear increase of one segment per successful round trip, it can take quite a long time before the cwnd returns to a level that is sufficient to sustain high levels of throughput for the application that experienced the loss. In this way, TCP is overly conservative and packet loss may cause a substantial impact on application throughput, especially given that bandwidth availability is far greater than it was 20 years ago.

Figure 6-13 *Packet Loss Causing cwnd to Decrease*

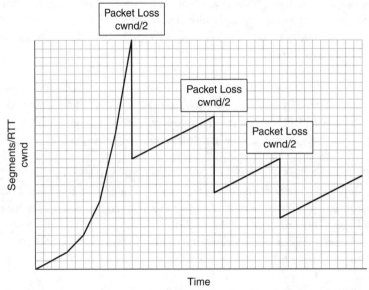

Overcoming the impact of packet loss through the use of TCP extensions in a node or by leveraging functionality in an accelerator can provide nearly immediate improvements in application throughput. Making such changes to each end node may prove to be an administrative nightmare, whereas deploying accelerators that provide the same capability (among many others) is relatively simple. There are three primary means of overcoming the impact of packet loss:

■ Selective acknowledgment (SACK)

■ Forward error correction (FEC)

■ Advanced congestion avoidance algorithms

By employing SACK, acknowledgments can be sent to notify the transmitter of the specific blocks of data that have been received into the receiver's socket buffer. Upon detecting loss, the transmitting node can then resend the blocks that were not acknowledged rather than send the contents of the entire window. Figure 6-14 shows how an accelerator acting as a TCP proxy (discussed later, in the section "Accelerator TCP Proxy Functionality") can provide SACK to improve efficiency in retransmission upon detecting the loss of a segment.

FEC is used to generate parity packets that allow the receiving node to recover the data from a lost packet based on parity information contained within the parity packets. FEC is primarily useful in moderately lossy networks (generally between .25 and 1 percent loss). Below this loss boundary, FEC may consume excessive amounts of unnecessary bandwidth (little return on bandwidth investment because the loss rate is not substantial). Above this loss boundary, FEC is largely ineffective compared to the total amount of loss (not enough parity data being sent to adequately re-create the lost packets) and therefore consumes excessive CPU cycles on the transmitting and receiving nodes or accelerators with little to no performance benefit.

Figure 6-14 *Selective Acknowledgment in an Accelerator Solution*

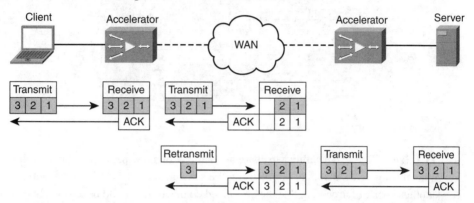

Advanced TCP implementations generally decrease cwnd less aggressively upon encountering packet loss and use more aggressive congestion avoidance algorithms to better utilize network capacity and more quickly return to previous levels of throughput after encountering packet loss. This yields a smaller drop in cwnd and faster increase in cwnd after encountering packet loss, which helps to circumvent performance and throughput challenges. Advanced TCP stacks are discussed in the next section.

Advanced TCP Implementations

The previous sections have outlined some of the limitations that TCP imposes upon application performance. Many universities and companies have conducted research and development to find and develop ways to improve the behavior of TCP (or completely replace it) to improve performance and make it more applicable to today's enterprise and Internet network environments. The result of this research and development generally comes in one of two forms: an extension to TCP (commonly applied as a negotiated option between two nodes that support the extension) or an alternative stack that is used as a replacement for TCP. For instance, SACK is an extension to TCP and is enabled based on negotiation during connection establishment. Advanced stacks, such as Binary Increase Congestion TCP (BIC-TCP), High Speed TCP (HS-TCP), Scalable TCP (S-TCP), and others, are an alternative to TCP extensions and generally require that the peer nodes be running the same TCP implementation to leverage the advanced capabilities.

Accelerator devices commonly use an advanced TCP implementation, which circumvents the need to replace the TCP stack on each node in the network. When considering an implementation with an advanced TCP stack, it is important to consider three key characteristics of the implementation:

■ **Bandwidth scalability:** The ability to fully utilize available WAN capacity, otherwise known as fill-the-pipe. Figure 6-15 shows how fill-the-pipe optimizations such as window scaling can be employed in an accelerator to achieve better utilization of existing network capacity.

Figure 6-15 *Accelerator Enables Efficient Utilization of Existing WAN*

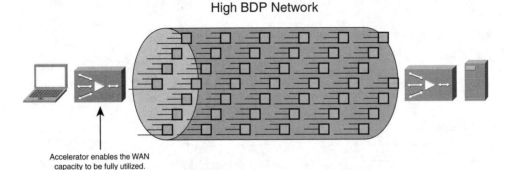

High BDP Network

Accelerator enables the WAN
capacity to be fully utilized.

- **TCP friendliness:** The ability to share available network capacity fairly with other transmitting nodes that may not be using the same advanced TCP implementation. This is another form of fairness, in that the optimized connections should be able to share bandwidth fairly with other connections on the network. Over time, the bandwidth allocated to optimized and unoptimized connections should converge such that resources are shared across connections.

Figure 6-16 shows the impact of using accelerators that provide TCP optimization that is not friendly to other nonoptimized connections, which can lead to bandwidth starvation and other performance challenges. Figure 6-17 shows how accelerators that provide TCP optimization that is friendly to other nonoptimized connections will compete fairly for network bandwidth and stabilize with other nonoptimized connections.

Figure 6-16 *TCP Friendliness—Accelerator with No Fairness*

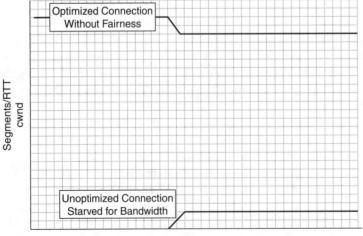

Optimized Connection
Without Fairness

Segments/RTT
cwnd

Unoptimized Connection
Starved for Bandwidth

Time

Figure 6-17 *TCP Friendliness—Accelerator with Fairness*

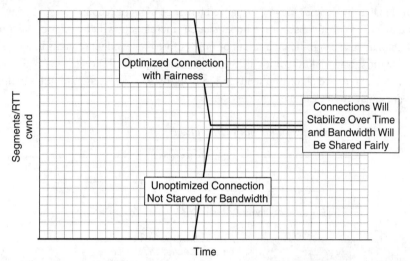

- **Roundtrip time (RTT) fairness:** The ability to share bandwidth fairly across connections even if the RTT between the two communicating node pairs is unequal. RTT fairness is another component of fairness at large.

  With RTT disparity, the nodes that are closer to one another can generally consume a larger portion of available WAN bandwidth capacity than the nodes that are more distant when sharing bandwidth. This is due to the way TCP congestion avoidance relies on acknowledgment messages to increment the cwnd, which increases the amount of data that can be outstanding in the network. This leads to the two nodes that are closer to one another being able to transmit data more quickly because acknowledgments are received more quickly and the congestion window is advanced more rapidly. Figure 6-18 shows an example of a network of nodes where RTT disparity is present.

Figure 6-18 *Roundtrip Time Differences and Fairness*

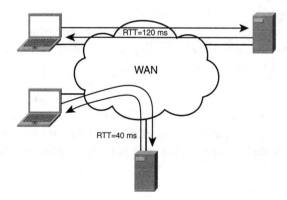

These advanced TCP implementations commonly implement an advanced congestion avoidance algorithm that overcomes the performance challenge of using a conservative linear search such as found in TCP. With a conservative linear search (increment cwnd by one segment per successful RTT), it may take a significant amount of time before the cwnd increments to a level high enough to allow for substantial utilization of the network. Figure 6-19 shows how TCP's linear search congestion avoidance algorithm leads to the inability of a connection to quickly utilize available network capacity (lack of aggressiveness).

Figure 6-19 *Linear Search Impedes Bandwidth Utilization*

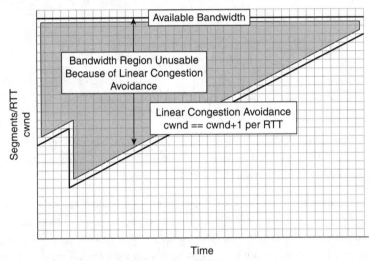

This section examines some of the advanced TCP implementations and characteristics of each but is not intended to be an exhaustive study of each or all of the available implementations.

High-Speed TCP

High-Speed TCP (HS-TCP) is an advanced TCP implementation that was developed primarily to address bandwidth scalability. HS-TCP uses an adaptive cwnd increase that is based on the current cwnd value of the connection. When the cwnd value is large, HS-TCP uses a larger cwnd increase when a segment is successfully acknowledged. In effect, this helps HS-TCP to more quickly find the available bandwidth, which leads to higher levels of throughput on large networks much more quickly.

HS-TCP also uses an adaptive cwnd decrease based on the current cwnd value. When the cwnd value for a connection is large, HS-TCP uses a very small decrease to the connection's cwnd value when loss of a segment is detected. In this way, HS-TCP allows a connection to remain at very high levels of throughput even in the presence of packet loss but can also lead to longer stabilization of TCP throughput when other, non-HS-TCP connections are contending for available network capacity. The aggressive cwnd handling of HS-TCP can lead to a lack of fairness when non-HS-TCP flows are competing for available network bandwidth. Over time, non-HS-TCP flows can stabilize with HS-TCP flows, but this period of time may be extended due to the aggressive behavior of HS-TCP.

HS-TCP also does not provide fairness in environments where there is RTT disparity between communicating nodes, again due to the aggressive handling of cwnd. This means that when using HS-TCP, nodes that are communicating over shorter distances will be able to starve other nodes that are communicating over longer distances due to the aggressive handling of cwnd. In this way, HS-TCP is a good fit for environments with high bandwidth where the network links are dedicated to a pair of nodes communicating using HS-TCP as a transport protocol but may not be a good fit for environments where a mix of TCP implementations or shared infrastructure is required. Figure 6-20 shows the aggressive cwnd handling characteristics displayed by HS-TCP.

Figure 6-20 *High-Speed TCP*

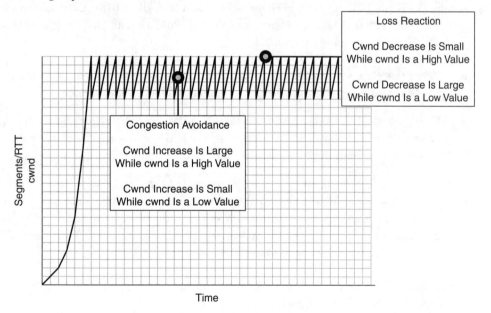

You can find more information on HS-TCP at http://www.icir.org/floyd/hstcp.html

Scalable TCP

Scalable TCP (S-TCP) is similar to HS-TCP in that it uses an adaptive increase to cwnd. S-TCP will increase cwnd by a value of (cwnd × .01) when increasing the congestion window, which means the increment is large when cwnd is large and the increment is small when cwnd is small.

Rather than use an adaptive decrease in cwnd, S-TCP will decrease cwnd by 12.5 percent (1/8) upon encountering a loss of a segment. In this way, S-TCP is more TCP friendly than HS-TCP in high-bandwidth environments. Like HS-TCP, S-TCP is not fair among flows where an RTT disparity exists due to the overly aggressive cwnd handling.

You can find more information on S-TCP at http://www.deneholme.net/tom/scalable/.

Binary Increase Congestion TCP

Binary Increase Congestion TCP (BIC-TCP) is an advanced TCP stack that uses a more adaptive increase than that used by HS-TCP and S-TCP. HS-TCP and S-TCP use a variable increment to cwnd directly based on the value of cwnd. BIC-TCP uses connection loss history to adjust the behavior of congestion avoidance to provide fairness.

BIC-TCP's congestion avoidance algorithm uses two search modes—linear search and binary search—as compared to the single search mode (linear or linear relative to cwnd) provided by standard TCP, HS-TCP, and S-TCP. These two search modes allow BIC-TCP to adequately maintain bandwidth scalability and fairness while also avoiding additional levels of packet loss caused by excessive cwnd aggressiveness:

- **Linear search:** Uses a calculation of the difference between the current cwnd and the previous cwnd prior to the loss event to determine the rate of linear search.

- **Binary search:** Used as congestion avoidance approaches the previous cwnd value prior to the loss event. This allows BIC-TCP to mitigate additional loss events caused by the connection exceeding available network capacity after a packet loss event.

The linear search provides aggressive handling to ensure a rapid return to previous levels of throughput, while the binary search not only helps to minimize an additional loss event, but also helps to improve fairness for environments with RTT disparity (that is, two nodes exchanging data are closer than two other nodes that are exchanging data) in that it allows convergence of TCP throughput across connections much more fairly and quickly.

Figure 6-21 shows how BIC-TCP provides fast returns to previous throughput levels while avoiding additional packet loss events.

For more information on BIC-TCP, visit http://www.csc.ncsu.edu/faculty/rhee/export/bitcp/index.htm

NOTE   Other advanced TCP implementations exist, including Additive Increase Multiplicative Decrease (AIMD), Fast AQM Scalable TCP (FAST), and Simple Available Bandwidth Utilization Library (SABUL). Because the focus of this book is on the advanced TCP implementations commonly found in accelerator devices, we will not discuss these additional implementations.

Figure 6-21 *Binary Increase Congestion TCP*

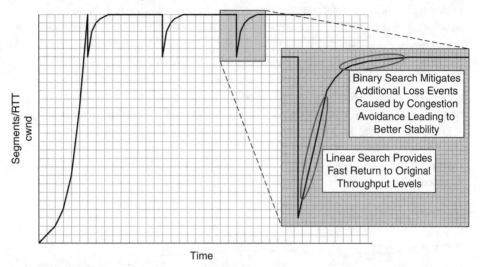

Binary Search Mitigates Additional Loss Events Caused by Congestion Avoidance Leading to Better Stability

Linear Search Provides Fast Return to Original Throughput Levels

Accelerator TCP Proxy Functionality

Most accelerator devices provide proxy functionality for TCP. This allows enterprise organizations to deploy technology that overcomes WAN conditions without having to make significant changes to the existing clients and servers on the network. In effect, a TCP proxy allows the accelerator to terminate TCP connections locally and take ownership of providing guaranteed delivery on behalf of the communicating nodes. With a TCP proxy, the accelerator manages local TCP transmit and receive buffers and provides TCP-layer acknowledgments and window management. This also allows the accelerator to effectively shield communicating nodes from packet loss and other congestion events that occur in the WAN.

Before this type of function can be employed, accelerator devices must either automatically discover one another or have preconfigured knowledge of who the peer device is. This allows existing clients and servers to retain their existing configurations and TCP implementations, and allows the accelerator devices to use an advanced TCP stack between one another for connections between communicating nodes that are being optimized. The optimized connections between accelerator devices may also be receiving additional levels of optimization through other means such as compression (discussed later, in the section "Accelerators and Compression"), caching, read-ahead, and others as described in Chapters 4 and 5.

Accelerators that use a TCP proxy terminate TCP locally on the LAN segment it is connected to and use optimized TCP connections to peer accelerators over the WAN. By acting as an intermediary TCP proxy device, an accelerator is uniquely positioned to take ownership of managing WAN conditions and changes on behalf of the communicating nodes. For instance, if an accelerator detects the loss of a packet that has been transmitted for an optimized connection, the accelerator retransmits that segment on behalf of the original node. This stops any WAN conditions from directly impacting the end nodes involved in the conversation that is being optimized by the accelerators, assuming the data remains in the socket buffers within the accelerator. The accelerator provides acceleration and throughput improvements to clients and servers with legacy TCP stacks, creating near-LAN TCP behavior while managing the connections over the WAN.

Figure 6-22 shows how accelerators can act as a proxy for TCP traffic, which shields LAN-attached nodes from WAN conditions.

Figure 6-22 *TCP Proxy Architecture*

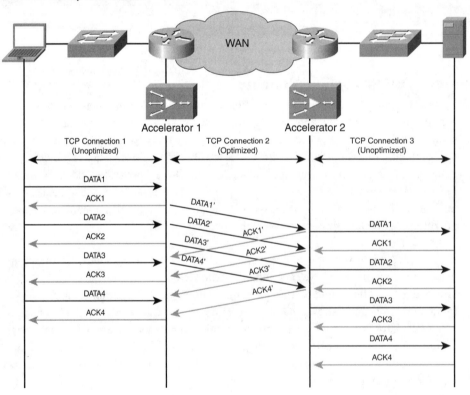

By employing accelerators in the network that provide TCP proxy functionality, clients and servers communicating over the WAN experience better performance and loss recovery. First, loss events occurring in the WAN are wholly contained and managed by the accelerators. Second, acknowledgments are handled locally by the accelerator, thereby allowing the clients and servers to achieve potentially very high levels of throughput.

When a connection is further optimized through advanced compression (as discussed later in this chapter), not only are clients and servers able to fill the pipe, but accelerators are able to fill the pipe with compressed data (or redundancy-eliminated data), which yields exponentially higher levels of throughput in many situations. Figure 6-23 shows how accelerator-based TCP optimization can be leveraged in conjunction with advanced compression (discussed later in the chapter) to fill the pipe with compressed data, providing potentially exponential throughput increases.

Figure 6-23 *TCP Optimization and Compression Combined*

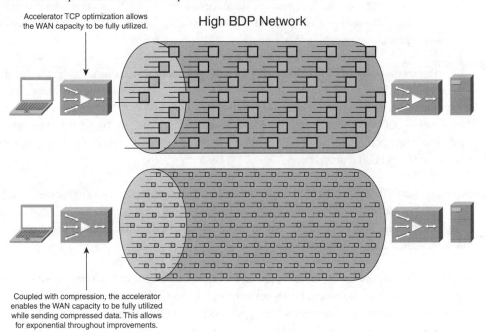

A good accelerator solution will include the TCP optimization components discussed earlier in this chapter and application acceleration capabilities discussed in Chapters 4 and 5, along with the compression techniques discussed in the next section. All of these factors combined can help improve efficiency and application performance over the WAN.

Overcoming Link Capacity Limitations

TCP optimization and advanced TCP implementations are useful to help ensure that the network resources are adequately and efficiently utilized. However, the WAN can still be a bottleneck from a performance perspective especially when considering the massive amount of bandwidth disparity that exists between the LAN and the WAN. The most common response to addressing this bandwidth disparity is to simply add more bandwidth.

There is a severe disparity in terms of available bandwidth capacity when comparing the LAN and the WAN, and a growing disparity in terms of the cost per bit of service between the two. Yet another disparity exists between the tremendous amount of latency found in WAN connections compared to the latency found in a LAN. Put simply, the cost per bit/second of low-latency LAN bandwidth is decreasing at a faster rate than is the cost per bit/second of high-latency WAN bandwidth, making it dramatically more expensive to upgrade WAN capacity than it is to upgrade LAN capacity. This problem is exacerbated when factoring in the additional service and capital expenditures that accompany a WAN upgrade.

With this in mind, many organizations are looking to accelerator solutions to bridge the divide between WAN bandwidth and performance, and most are finding that implementing accelerator solutions (which address more than just bandwidth concerns) costs far less from a total cost of ownership (TCO) perspective and provides a massive return on investment (ROI) because it [implementing accelerator solutions] enables infrastructure to be consolidated and improves productivity and collaboration.

Compression is a technology that helps to minimize the amount of bandwidth consumed by data in transit over a network and is not a new technology. Advanced compression algorithms and implementations have come about that are more effective and efficient than the simple compression algorithms that have been around for years.

This section examines compression at a high level, including the difference between per-packet implementations and flow-based compression implementations, and then provides a more detailed overview of advanced compression techniques such as data suppression. Advanced compression techniques not only compress data in flight but also reduce the frequency of the transfer of redundant data patterns. Most accelerator devices today provide some form of compression and, when coupled with TCP optimization and application acceleration, not only can improve application performance significantly, but can do so while minimizing the amount of network bandwidth required.

Accelerators and Compression

The key challenge for lower-bandwidth networks (or any WAN where there is a high amount of contention for available bandwidth) is that the device managing bandwidth disparity (that is, the router) has to negotiate traffic from a very high-speed network onto a very low-speed network. In terms of how TCP interacts with this disparity, data is sent at the rate determined by the available cwnd, and when a bandwidth disparity is present, the ingress interface queues on the router begin to fill, causing delay to a point where loss is encountered. The detection of this loss results in a decrease of the cwnd, and the transmitting node, while in congestion avoidance, attempts to stabilize at a rate that is conducive to transmission without (or nearly without) loss.

In effect, the overloaded queue (or loss in the WAN, or anything that causes loss or delay of acknowledgment) helps stimulate the transmitting node into finding the right level at which to send data. When the router receives packets into its queues, it drains the ingress queues at a rate determined by the available next-hop network capacity and any applicable QoS configuration.

The problem begins to unfold as the client is able to transmit data at a far faster pace than the router is able to forward onto the lower-bandwidth network. This results in a trickle effect whereby only a small amount of data is able to traverse the lower-bandwidth network at a given time, and ultimately the transmitting node will adjust its throughput characteristics to match this rate based on TCP congestion avoidance. This trickle of data is routed through the network and may encounter several other points of congestion and loss along the way, all of which can directly impact the transmission rate of the sender.

When the data is finally placed on the LAN at the distant location, the receiving node ultimately has the impression that it is dealing with a very slow sender. This is directly caused by the bandwidth disparity found in the network. Conversely, in the return direction, when the server is responding to the client, the same issues are encountered, thus leading both nodes to believe that the other is slow to transmit.

Figure 6-24 shows the bandwidth disparity between the LAN and the WAN and how TCP rate control stabilizes transmitter throughput to the minimum available end-to-end network capacity.

With accelerators in place and providing compression, bandwidth disparity is largely mitigated. In effect, through compression the accelerator is able to shrink the amount of data being sent across the network to minimize bandwidth consumption, and decompress the data to its original state on the other end of the network. This not only results in bandwidth savings over the WAN, but also helps to ensure that a larger amount of data can be found in the LAN. From the perspective of the client and the server, less congestion is encountered, thereby allowing them to send at higher rates, and improving the performance of the applications in use. Figure 6-25 shows the same implementation leveraging accelerators and how less congestion is encountered.

Figure 6-24 *TCP Rate Control and Bandwidth Disparity*

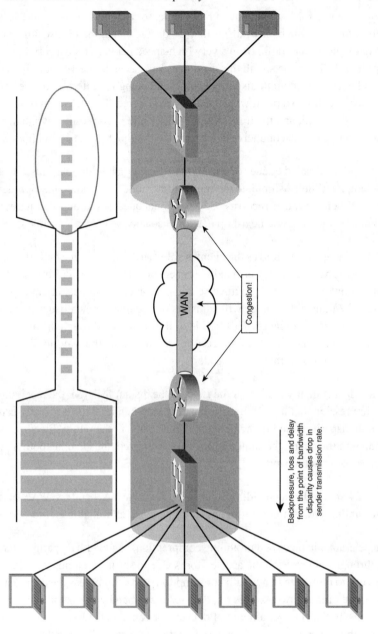

Figure 6-25 *TCP Rate Control and Bandwidth Disparity with Accelerators*

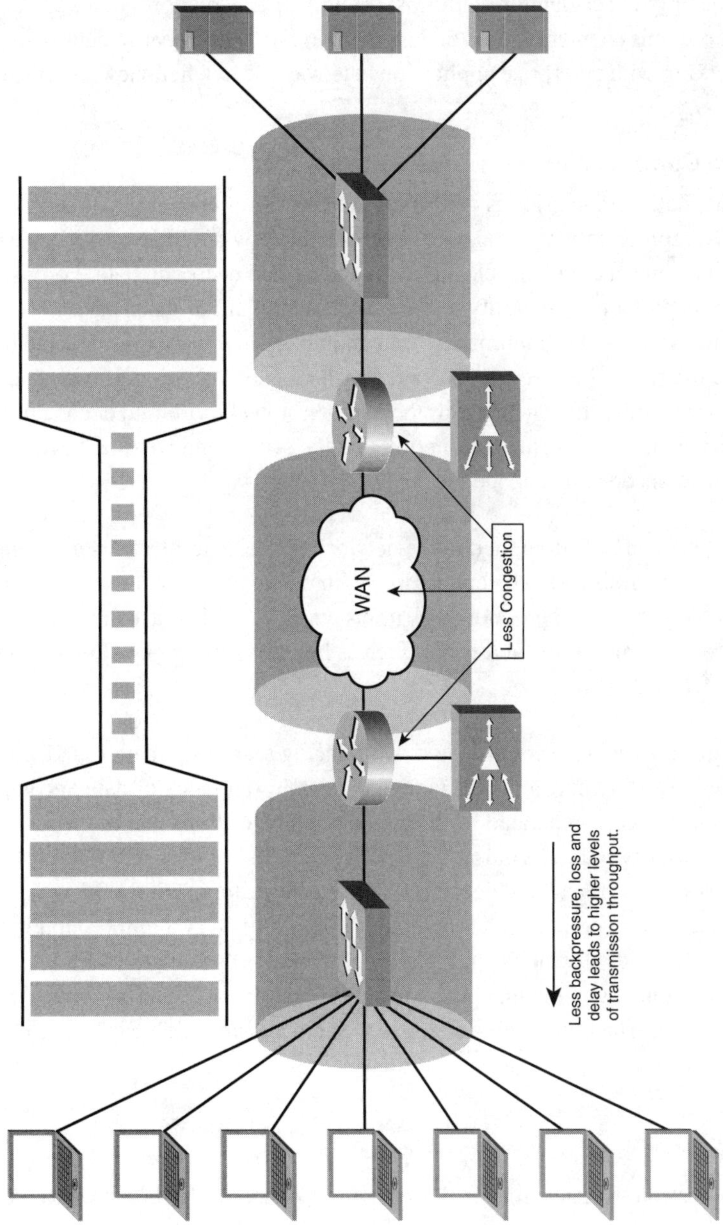

While numerous compression algorithms exist, this book focuses on the two types that are used most frequently in accelerator platforms: traditional data compression and data suppression. Furthermore, this chapter focuses on lossless compression, because data cannot be compromised when working with enterprise applications the way it can when viewing images, for example.

Traditional Data Compression

Traditional data compression is defined as the process of encoding data using fewer bits than an unencoded representation would use. This is enabled by having two devices exchanging information using a common scheme for encoding and decoding data. For instance, a person can use a popular compression utility to minimize the amount of disk space a file consumes (encoding), which in turn minimizes the amount of bandwidth consumed and time taken to e-mail that same file to another person. The person who receives the e-mail with that compressed file needs to use a utility that understands the compression algorithm to decode the data to its original form. This again relies on the assumption that the sender and receiver have explicit knowledge about how to encode and decode the data in the same way.

Data compression can be applied in the network between accelerators assuming that both accelerators are designed to be compatible with one another and have a fundamental understanding of the compression algorithms employed. Most accelerators implement a well-known type of compression algorithm, such as Lempel-Ziv (or one of its variants such as LZ77 or LZ78) or DEFLATE.

Many algorithms achieve compression by replacing sections of data found within the object with small references that map to a data table that contains an index of data encountered within the object and references generated for that data. Such algorithms commonly use a sliding window with a power-of-two fixed window size (such as 1 KB, 2 KB, 4 KB, 8 KB, 16 KB, 32 KB, or beyond) to scan through the object, identifying data patterns within the window and referencing with signatures that point back to the index table. In this way, compression is limited to the capacity of the sliding window, granularity of the patterns that are identified, and the data table structures that maintain the mapping between signatures and data structures that have been previously seen. The limit of how effective the compression itself can be is called the *compression domain*.

Data Suppression

Data suppression operates in a similar fashion to standard data compression. Unlike data compression, however, data suppression is designed to leverage a massive compression domain that extends beyond the object, packet, or session being examined. In a sense, data compression is limited to the object, packet, or session being transmitted, whereas data suppression can leverage a larger, longer-lived compression history that is specific to previous patterns seen between two accelerator devices.

Data suppression assumes that each accelerator has a storage repository that is used as a compression history. Data suppression requires that this storage repository, sometimes known as a "codebook" or "dictionary," be loosely synchronized between two accelerators that wish to provide data suppression capabilities. Some accelerators implement data suppression using memory as a storage repository for compression history. Memory-only data suppression provides high-performance I/O for compressing and decompressing data, but has a limited capacity in terms of compression history. Some accelerators use hard disk drives instead of memory, a technique that has lower I/O performance than memory-only data suppression, but has a much larger compression history capacity. Many of today's accelerators leverage a combination of both disk and memory to achieve high performance without compromising on the length of compression history for their data suppression algorithms.

Figure 6-26 shows an example of two accelerators, each deployed in separate locations, with a synchronized compression history.

Much like data compression, most data suppression algorithms use a sliding window to identify previously seen data patterns from within packets or connections. Each unique data pattern that is identified is assigned a unique signature, which is a small representation of the original data, or a reference to the entry in the compression library where the original data resides. Most signatures are typically only a few bytes in size. Given that a relatively large amount of data can be referenced by a signature that is only a few bytes in size, it is common for data suppression to be able to achieve over 1000:1 compression for a fully redundant data segment and up to 50:1 or better compression for an entire flow.

Many of the data suppression implementations available in accelerators today do not use a simple single-level data pattern identification process; rather, most use a hierarchical means of identifying data patterns. A hierarchical data pattern identification process analyzes a block of data at multiple layers. With hierarchical data pattern recognition, the accelerator is able to not only create signatures for the most basic data patterns, but also formulate additional signatures that refer to a large number of data patterns or signatures. In this way, if a greater degree of redundancy is identified within the data patterns, hierarchical data pattern recognition allows a smaller number of signatures to be used to refer to the original data being transmitted. If hierarchical data pattern recognition is not being used, one signature is required for each repeated data pattern, which may prove less efficient.

Hierarchical data pattern matching can yield far higher levels of data suppression (compression) than data pattern matching functions that are nonhierarchical. Figure 6-27 shows the difference between hierarchical and nonhierarchical data pattern recognition algorithms.

Figure 6-26 *Data Suppression and Synchronized Compression History*

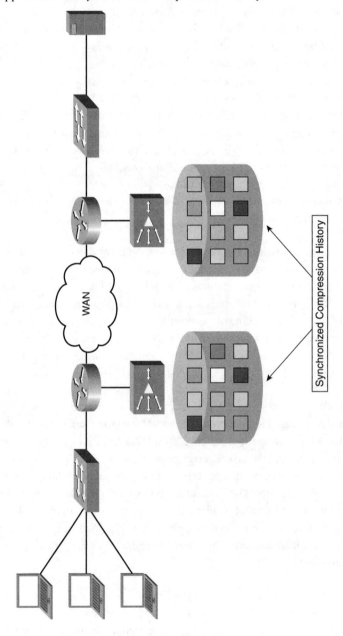

Figure 6-27 *Nonhierarchical and Hierarchical Data Pattern Recognition*

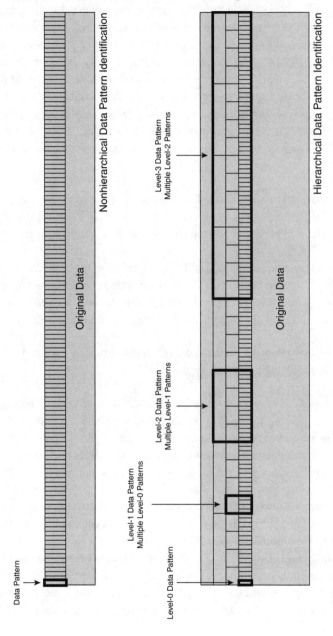

During the process of data pattern matching, a signature is generated for each identified data pattern being transmitted, and in the case of hierarchical data pattern recognition, signatures may also be generated that identify a large number of data patterns or signatures. Once the signatures have been generated, the accelerator then begins to perform a pattern-matching function whereby it compares the signature of the identified patterns (generally starting with the largest data patterns when hierarchical data pattern matching is employed) with the contents of the local compression library. This local compression library contains a database containing signatures and data patterns that have been previously recognized by the two peering accelerators, and can be built dynamically (as data is handled during the normal course of network operation) or proactively (using a cache-warming or preposition type of feature before the first user transmission is ever received).

As repeated data patterns are identified, they are removed from the message, and only the signature remains. This signature is an instruction for the distant device, notifying it of what data to retrieve from its compression history to replace the original data pattern back into the flow.

For data patterns that are nonredundant (no entry exists in the compression library for the signature), the new signature and data pattern are added to the local compression library. In this case, the newly generated signatures and data pattern are sent across the network to notify the distant accelerator that it needs to update its compression library with this new information.

Figure 6-28 shows the top-down data pattern matching function applied by an encoding accelerator when leveraging data suppression.

This entire process of suppressing data into a redundancy-eliminated message is defined as *encoding*. When peering accelerators are able to perform data suppression, the only data that needs to traverse the network is the encoded message, which includes signatures to previously seen data segments and data segments (with newly generated signatures) for data that has not been seen before, or otherwise does not exist in the local compression library.

Additionally, accelerators commonly implement data integrity protection mechanisms to ensure that the rebuild of an encoded message by the recipient accelerator is done without compromising the integrity of the original message. This commonly includes a hash calculation of the original message, called a *message validity signature*, immediately before encoding begins. In most cases, the hash calculation to generate the message validity signature includes accelerator-specific keys in the calculation or other means of ensuring that hash collisions cannot occur. Figure 6-29 shows an example of what an encoded message sent among accelerators may look like.

Figure 6-28 *Data Pattern Matching*

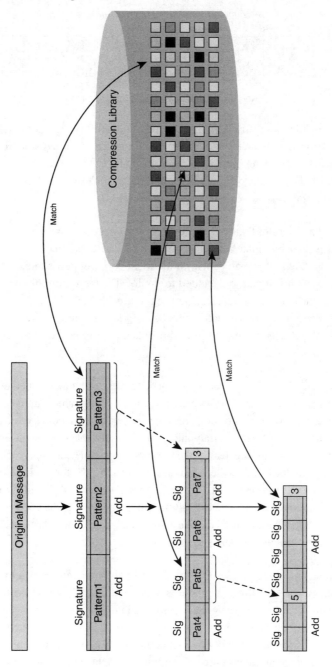

Figure 6-29 *Data Suppression Encoded Message*

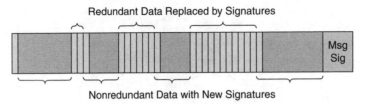

When an encoded message is received, the message validity signature attached to the encoded message is stripped and placed to the side. The remaining message contains signatures without data attached (for redundant data patterns that should exist in the compression library) and signatures with data attached (nonredundant data), which the accelerator should add to its compression library.

The receiving accelerator then begins the process of *decoding*, whereby the original message is rebuilt. This is done by replacing each signature sent without attached data with the data pattern that is identified by that signature within the local compression context. Any data pattern that has an accompanying signature is added to the local compression library and the signature is stripped from the encoded message. If any signatures is identified that was generated out of the process of hierarchical pattern matching, each of the data patterns referenced by the signature is extracted from the local compression library and put in place of the signature in the encoded message.

Once the accelerator has fully decoded the encoded message, it then generates a new message validity signature, that is, the same hash calculation using the same parameters such as accelerator-specific keys or other factors, and compares the newly generated message validity signature with the message validity signature that was supplied in the encoded message by the encoding accelerator. If the two align, the decoding accelerator then knows that the message was rebuilt with data validity and integrity guaranteed, and the decoded message can then be forwarded to its destination. If any signature referenced in the encoded message does not appear in the local compression library, the decoding accelerator can send a nonacknowledgment message to the encoder to notify the encoder that the data does not exist, thereby forcing a retransmission of the data associated with the signature that does not appear in the decoding accelerator's compression history.

Data suppression also works closely with traditional data compression in accelerators. The signatures and message validity signatures generated by the data suppression function are commonly compressible, meaning that additional layers of compression can be found above and beyond the level of compression provided by data suppression on its own. Data suppression compression libraries are generally peer-specific, and some implementations can share libraries across peers. Given that the compression library for data suppression is far larger than it is for data compression and is not tied to a packet, session, or object, it can be far more effective at freeing up available WAN capacity, and can generally be efficient in reducing redundancy even across multiple applications.

Because data suppression is commonly implemented as a WAN optimization component in the network or transport layer, it does not discriminate among applications (for example, downloading an object from a website could populate the compression library to provide significant compression for an e-mail upload with that same, or modified, object). Furthermore, a data pattern that is not deemed to be a repeated pattern can also be sent through the data compression library, which means that even though a data pattern is being seen for the first time, it may be compressible, meaning that less bandwidth is used even for those scenarios.

When deploying accelerators, a best practice is to ensure that enough storage capacity is allocated to provide at least one week's worth of compression history. For instance, if a branch office location is connected to the corporate network via a T1 line (1.544 Mbps), the amount of disk capacity necessary to support that location from a compression history perspective could be calculated. If the T1 line were utilized at a rate of 75 percent for 50 percent of each day per week, the raw compression history requirement for one week would equate to the following:

> Convert 1.544 Mbps to bytes (1.544 Mbps is approximately 192 kBps)
> 192 kBps $\times$ 60 = 11.52 MB/minute
> 11.52 MB/minute $\times$ 60 = 69.12 MB/hour
> 69.12 MB/hour $\times$ 24 = 16.59 GB/day
> 16.59 GB/day $\times$ .75 $\times$ .50 = 6.2 GB/week

Assuming that the data traversing the link from the branch office back to the corporate network is 75 percent redundant (which is conservative in most branch office scenarios), this equates to a requirement of around 1.5 GB/week of compression history required to support this particular branch office location. One week of compression history generally provides enough compression data to optimize not only immediately interactive user access requirements, but also scenarios where a user begins interacting with a working set of data that has not been touched in up to a week. This also provides sufficient coverage for multiuser scenarios—for instance, where everyone in a remote office receives an e-mail with the same attachment, even if the transmission of that e-mail happens days later.

Accelerator Compression Architectures

Most accelerators implement both data suppression and traditional data compression functions. This section examines two commonly found implementations: per-packet compression and session-based compression. This section also discusses directionality as it relates to the accelerator's compression library.

Per-Packet Compression

Per-packet compression treats each packet as a compression domain. This means that each packet is analyzed as an autonomous object and compressed as an autonomous object. With such an architecture, each packet that is received by an accelerator must be handled individually.

Given that packet sizes are largely limited by the data link layer being traversed, it is safe to assume that the compression domain for per-packet compression is generally 200 to 1500 bytes (but can certainly be larger or smaller). Given this limitation, most accelerators that implement per-packet compression also implement some form of data suppression to increase the compression history, which allows larger repeatable sequences to be identified, thus providing better compression and higher degrees of bandwidth savings. However, because the accelerator processes each packet individually, it does not have the opportunity to examine a larger amount of data, precluding it from providing higher levels of compression. Per-packet processing also creates sensitivities to data changes, which are more difficult to detect and isolate when the window of data being reduced is limited to the size of a packet.

Figure 6-30 shows how per-packet compression would be used on a fully redundant transmission of the same set of packets. In this figure, the packet stream being sent is fully redundant. The process shown in this figure follows:

1. A stream of data is sent as a series of packets.

2. The accelerator compares the contents of each packet against the compression history.

3. Redundancy is eliminated and redundant segments are replaced by signatures.

4. The compressed packet is sent across the network and intercepted by the distant accelerator.

5. The distant accelerator compares the contents of the encoded packet with the compression history.

6. The distant accelerator replaces signatures with data patterns from the compression history.

7. The distant accelerator repacketizes and reframes the original data and forwards it to the intended destination.

The challenge with per-packet compression lies in the ability of an accelerator to identify repeated data patterns that are directly associated with the position of the data pattern within the packet being received. Therefore, such forms of compression can be challenged when attempting to compress packets received from the transmission of a previously seen set of data when that set of data has undergone slight modification. The challenge is that repeated patterns are not located in the same position within the subsequently received packets after changes have been applied to the data as compared to the position where the original data was found. In this way, data does not have the same *locality* to the packet boundaries as it did before the changes were applied.

Figure 6-30   *Per-Packet Compression with Large Shared Compression History*

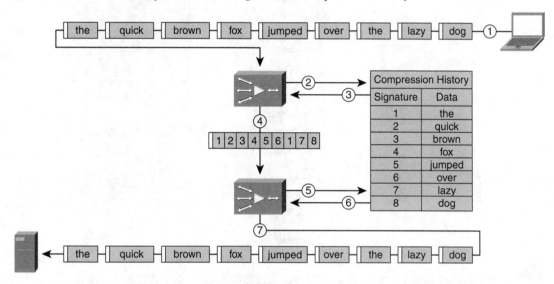

In these situations, the compression history must be augmented with the new data on both devices, which means the first transmission of the changed data can be largely considered nonredundant and, therefore, only minimal amounts of compression can be applied. The compression history from the original transfer of the data is mostly unusable in this case, which leads to excessive and inefficient use of memory and disk capacity for compression history on both accelerator devices to store the new data and the original patterns.

Figure 6-31 highlights the challenges of per-packet compression when data has been changed, causing a large number of new compression library entries to be created and thereby producing minimal compression benefits. This example shows the impact of adding the letter *a* to the beginning of the sentence used in Figure 6-30. Notice that a large number of new entries need to be added to the compression history, and little to no bandwidth savings are realized.

Figure 6-31   *Per-Packet Compression Challenges with Data Locality*

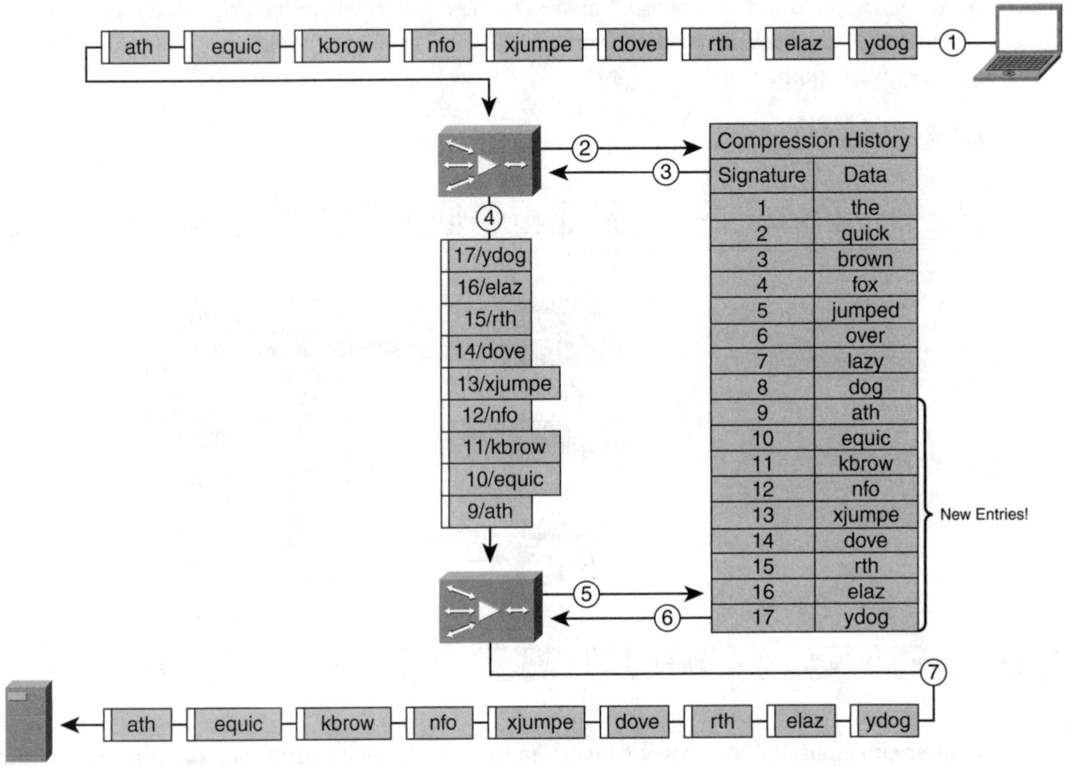

Session-Based Compression

An alternative to per-packet compression, which generally provides higher levels of compression even under significant amounts of data change, is *session-based compression*, also known as *persistent compression*. Session-based compression provides two key functions:

- The ability to leverage a compression history that extends through the life of the entire TCP connection when employing traditional data compression algorithms such as LZ or DEFLATE

- The ability to extend the compression domain for data suppression functionality by leveraging a TCP proxy as an intermediary data buffer

Extending the compression library to span the history of the TCP connection provides better overall compression because the history that can be leveraged is far greater than and not limited to the packet size.

Using the TCP proxy as an intermediary data buffer allows the accelerator to temporarily buffer a large amount of data that can then be delivered en masse to the data suppression function, which allows it to span boundaries of multiple packets when identifying redundancy. By disconnecting the data suppression function and the data from the packet boundaries, data suppression algorithms are able to better identify redundancy and isolate changes to previously encountered byte patterns. This allows for far higher levels of compression than can be provided with per-packet compression.

Figure 6-32 shows how session-based compression with hierarchical data suppression provides location-independent compression capabilities with high levels of compression. Notice how the hierarchical compression history contains signatures that reference a series of other signatures, thereby providing higher levels of compression. In this figure, a single signature represents the entire string of text being sent.

Figure 6-32 *Compression with Hierarchical Data Suppression*

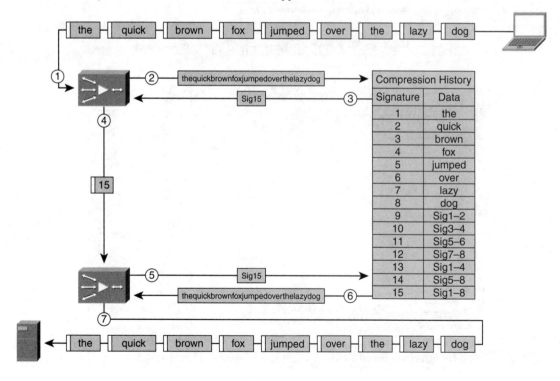

When coupled with a data suppression function that uses a content-based means of identifying data patterns and hierarchical pattern matching, this allows the data suppression function to accurately pinpoint where changes were inserted into the data stream. In essence, when changes are made to the data and the changed data is transmitted between two nodes, content-based pattern matching can isolate the new data to allow the previously built compression library entries to still be leveraged, resulting in high levels of compression even in the face of changed data. Rather than having to re-update the entire compression library on both devices, the accelerators can incrementally update the compression libraries with only the new data. This means that the challenges that plague per-packet compression are nullified.

Figure 6-33 shows that session-based compression with hierarchical data suppression capabilities provides far better identification of changed byte patterns than do per-packet compression algorithms, resulting in more efficient use of the compression library, bandwidth savings, and overall better performance.

Figure 6-33   *Session-Based Compression with Changed Data*

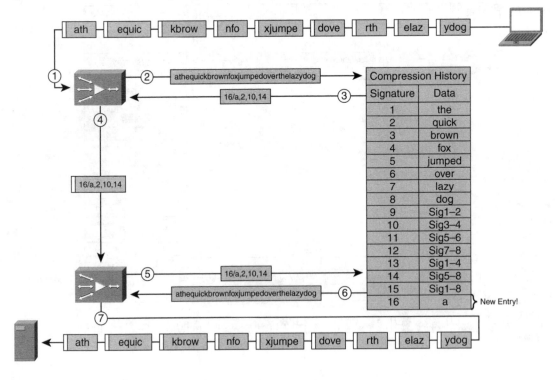

Directionality

Another subtle architectural implementation that you should consider is the directionality of the data suppression compression library. Directionality defines whether a single compression library is used regardless of the direction of traffic flow, called a *bidirectional compression library*, or whether a single compression library is used *per* direction of traffic flow, called a *unidirectional compression library*.

In the case of a bidirectional compression library, traffic flowing in one direction populates the compression library, and this same library can be used for traffic flowing in the reverse direction through the accelerators. In the case of a unidirectional compression library, traffic flowing in one direction populates one compression library, and traffic flowing in the reverse direction populates a separate compression library. With unidirectional compression libraries, there must be one library per direction of traffic flow.

Having unidirectional compression libraries introduces inefficiencies and performance limitations that need to be considered. Having a unidirectional compression library–based architecture means that when a user downloads an object, only the repeated download of that object will pass through the same library, because the traffic is flowing in the same direction. Even after an object has been downloaded, the subsequent upload (in the reverse direction) of that object passes through a completely different compression library, meaning that it will not be suppressed.

The upload of the object effectively receives no benefit from the download because two separate compression libraries are used. This not only creates the issue of having poor performance until the object has been transferred in both directions, but also means lower overall efficiency from a memory and disk utilization perspective, as the data must be stored twice. Having to store the data twice leads to a lower overall compression history. Figure 6-34 highlights the performance challenges of unidirectional data suppression libraries in scenarios where data that has been downloaded is being uploaded.

With a bidirectional compression library, the problem illustrated in Figure 6-34 is not encountered. Traffic flowing in either direction leverages the same compression library, so the download of an object can be leveraged to help suppress the repeated patterns found while uploading the same object. Furthermore, repeated patterns are not stored once per direction of traffic flow, leading to better efficiency when utilizing disk and memory resources while also extending the overall effective compression history that the accelerator peers can leverage. Figure 6-35 shows how use of a bidirectional data suppression library provides compression benefits and is agnostic to the direction of traffic flow.

Figure 6-34 *Unidirectional Data Suppression Library Challenges*

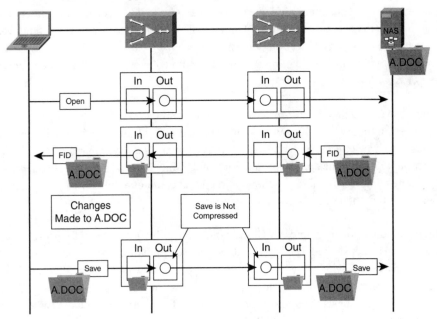

Figure 6-35 *Bidirectional Data Suppression Library*

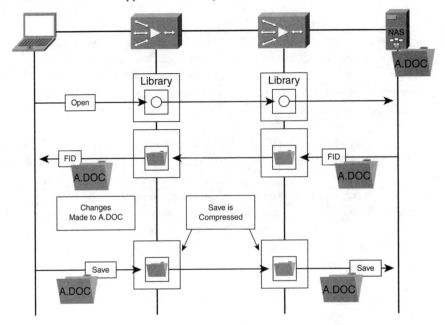

Summary

This chapter examined two of the key technologies that are provided in WAN optimization solutions: transport protocol optimization and compression. These techniques are commonly implemented in a cohesive accelerator architecture with other application-specific components and provide the foundation for overcoming WAN performance obstacles. By employing transport protocol optimization, available WAN capacity can be better leveraged and higher levels of performance can be sustained in lossy environments. Through advanced compression techniques, performance constraints related to capacity can be overcome to improve application performance while also minimizing the amount of bandwidth consumption.

WAN optimization, when combined with other acceleration techniques described in previous chapters and network control capabilities, helps to enable a globally distributed workforce with centralized I/T infrastructure, all while minimizing the impact to the existing network and mitigating costly capacity upgrades in many cases.

This chapter includes the following topics:

- Acme Data Corporation: Protecting Data and Promoting Global Collaboration

- C3 Technology LLC: Saving WAN Bandwidth and Replicating Data

- Command Grill Corporation: Improving HTTP Application Performance

- Almost Write Inc.: Implementing Content Delivery Networking

CHAPTER 7

Examining Accelerator Technology Scenarios

The previous chapters have described how accelerator technologies, including application acceleration, content delivery networking, and WAN optimization, can combine with functions within the network to help IT organizations achieve a number of goals, including the following:

- Improve application performance over the WAN

- Enable more efficient utilization of existing network capacity

- Enable consolidation of costly server, storage, and application infrastructure

- Simplify management and deployment of enterprise applications and services

- Control operational and capital costs by enabling a more intelligent architecture for application delivery

The focus of this chapter is to examine four customer scenarios where accelerator technology has been implemented to achieve these goals. Each of the customer case studies discusses the challenges faced by each customer, the accelerator solution that addressed the challenges, integration of the solution, and the impact the solution had on the environment. The following four fictional customers are examined:

- Acme Data Corporation is a data processing firm that has decided to consolidate server and application infrastructure from each of its eight remote branch offices. In the months leading up to the decision, the IT team realized that branch office backups were not happening properly. To compound the problem, a key project manager that was based out of one of those branch offices lost data when her laptop hard drive crashed and no data was available for restore.

  Acme Data is also struggling with performance of e-mail for its remote users. In addition to improving its data protection posture, the company is planning to utilize application acceleration and WAN optimization to enable infrastructure consolidation and improve performance.

- C3 Technology LLC is a producer of advanced security systems and software. C3 has two primary data centers that are geographically dispersed and needs to replicate data between the two locations while also minimizing bandwidth consumption and improving performance for users who access applications and data in the opposite data center. Application acceleration and WAN optimization are introduced into C3's network to help address these challenges.

- Command Grill Corporation is plagued by slow database application performance, which has a direct impact on the ability of customer service representatives to perform their job and maintain customer satisfaction during support calls. An accelerator solution that includes web caching is introduced into Command Grill Corporation's T1 WAN to address the inefficient design of the database application.

- Almost Write Inc. provides creative multimedia services for several customers around the world. Almost Write is no longer able to provide to its customers high-performance access to content from a single server hosted on the public Internet. Operational expenses continually increase due to a lack of cost-effective overnight courier shipping.

  The IT organization at Almost Write has determined that an acceleration solution with content delivery capabilities is the best technology to improve its content delivery services. The executives at Almost Write extended the CDN trial to include two of its international customers, creating real-world data to validate their purchase decision.

It is important to note that many acceleration solutions provide a combination of powerful features such as those discussed in previous chapters and in the use cases provided in this chapter. Some customers choose to implement a robust solution using the majority of accelerator features, and some choose to deploy for very specific tactical purposes. As the application acceleration and WAN optimization market evolves, customers will ultimately benefit as a larger degree of capability and added functionality is built into these solutions.

Acme Data Corporation: Protecting Data and Promoting Global Collaboration

Acme Data Corporation provides data processing services to a large number of companies in many different verticals including retail and technology. Acme Data has one primary data center with eight remote office locations. Each remote office location has knowledge workers and data processing employees.

When a customer outsources its data processing needs to Acme Data, the customer provides to Acme Data the requirements and the data that Acme Data should use to generate the necessary output. The project is given to a team of remote workers and one key project manager within one of the branch offices. Determining which team is engaged is based on the current utilization of each of the remote offices as individual units.

The data to be processed, along with the specified instructions and project-related information, is distributed from the data center to the remote office file server. From there, remote workers are able to perform data processing functions against the data based on the specifications and requirements supplied by the customer.

The IT organization at Acme Data recently realized that the data on the remote office servers was not being adequately protected. Simply put, backup operations were not completing successfully for a variety of reasons, one of which was that tapes were not being properly changed between backup operations. The failure to properly back up data has caused problems with one major customer in particular. When a project manager's laptop crashed, all of the data from the project manager's major customer was lost. This data could not be recovered because no backup had taken place in the remote office for weeks. As a result, Acme Data had to begin the project from scratch. By losing this important customer's data, Acme Data also lost the customer's respect. The incident cost Acme Data financially and also impacted its reputation.

Another problem Acme Data faces is the need for remote data processing employees to access shared customer data in a collaborative manner over the corporate WAN. Many of the new projects dictate that data processing teams be built from a variety of data processing workers spanning multiple remote office locations. The current project allocation system and, more importantly, the distributed server infrastructure make collaboration of a distributed team particularly difficult for users who are in locations outside of where the data physically resides.

Given the performance issues of collaborating over the WAN, many employees have turned to e-mail as a means of collaboration. However, e-mail is not performing to the degree necessary to facilitate near-real-time collaboration and is not performing well enough to allow remote office workers a decent level of productivity.

Acme Data would like to improve its data protection posture, improve e-mail performance, and enable global collaboration to allow data processing teams in distributed sites to work together in real time. Figure 7-1 shows Acme Data's network topology, including the data center and each remote office location. Notice that each of the remote office locations has a miniature carbon copy of the data center infrastructure, including file and print servers, project servers, disk storage arrays, and backup infrastructure.

Now that you understand Acme Data's objectives, application infrastructure, and issues it has encountered in the past, the next section examines some of the challenges the company has observed in implementing alternative solutions that did not fully address its requirements.

Figure 7-1 *Acme Data Corporation Network Topology*

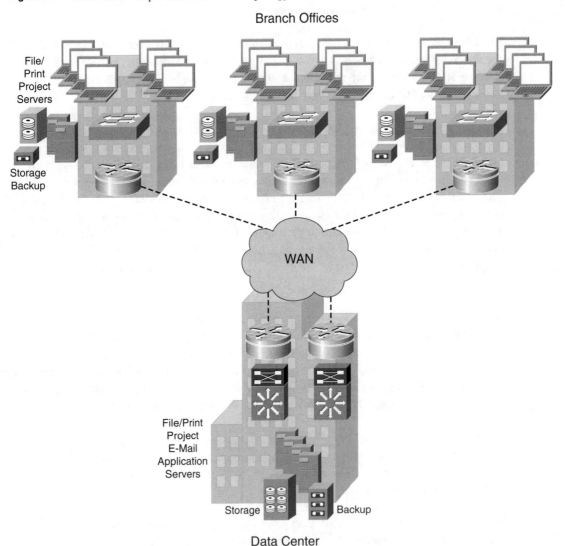

Observed Challenges

In an attempt to address its data protection, productivity, and performance issues, Acme Data changed the business process surrounding project management and productivity and moved project data to a centralized web-based portal. This centralized web-based portal is hosted and managed in the Acme Data data center at the corporate headquarters and is routinely backed up by the data center IT staff.

Although the centralized web-based portal solves the issue of global collaboration and data protection, now that all the project data is centralized, a new challenge exists. The existing WAN capacity at each remote office is no longer sufficient to support employee productivity, collaboration, or interactive communication such as Voice over IP (VoIP) and e-mail.

Also, all remote office users are now subject to the performance-limiting characteristics of the WAN, including latency and packet loss. File servers remain at each location to provide each employee with a storage repository for other administrative data, which is equally critical to the business. This data includes marketing material, price lists, customer invoices, and financial data for the location. Given that this data is not always backed up, Acme Data realizes that it is still at risk of losing precious data.

Figure 7-2 shows how Acme Data implemented portal servers in the data center to replace the project servers that were distributed throughout its network. Notice that many components had to remain in the remote offices, including file and print servers, disk storage arrays, and backup infrastructure.

Acme Data realizes that the centralized web-based portal is only a temporary fix to the larger issue of ensuring data protection and global collaboration. This solution also means that a significant portion of data is not centralized, performance is poor for all users accessing the project data, and WAN capacity needs to be increased to support the network demands of using the portal. Also, e-mail performance and voice quality are actually worse given the increase in network demands caused by all of the remote users accessing the project portal over the corporate WAN.

Accelerator Solution

Acme Data deployed an accelerator solution to address the original issues related to protecting data and promoting global collaboration as well as issues caused by deploying the centralized web-based portal. Implementing the accelerator solution results in the following:

- The advanced compression capabilities provided by the accelerator minimize WAN bandwidth consumption. The accelerator removes redundant patterns from network transmission and compresses new patterns that it learns.

- File servers can be consolidated due to the protocol acceleration and caching components of the accelerator.

- E-mail performance dramatically improves due to the newly available bandwidth capacity and protocol acceleration provided by the accelerators.

Figure 7-2 *Acme Data Challenges After Web Portal Integration*

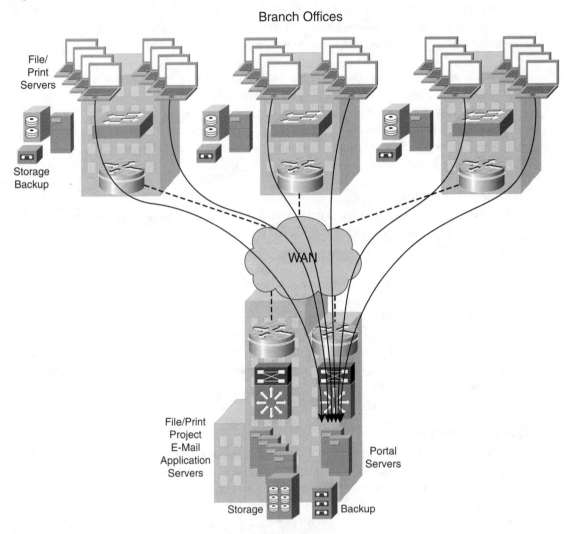

Acme Data found that by deploying the accelerator solution, global collaboration became an immediate reality. The accelerator solution provides to remote employees high-performance access to the centralized web-based portal and many other applications and services, which allows the management team to spread project workload across data processing teams in multiple locations concurrently without compromising performance or, more importantly, productivity.

Integrating the Accelerators

With three remote sites, Acme Data wants to ensure that the data center accelerator infrastructure is designed to withstand a failure and not compromise performance under any circumstance. As such, Acme Data worked with its trusted partner to design an accelerator solution that provides redundancy and load balancing in the data center. Two accelerator devices are deployed in the data center, and Acme Data selected the accelerator model based on the assumption that the full workload of all the remote offices would need to be supported by a single accelerator in a failure scenario.

Acme selected the Web Cache Communication Protocol version 2 (WCCPv2) for data center integration, because this allowed Acme Data to deploy the accelerators in an off-path fashion. With off-path deployment, if an accelerator fails, WCCPv2 goes into a "fail-through" mode, meaning no traffic is redirected to an accelerator, and network connectivity is not compromised. Using WCCPv2 also allowed Acme Data to not only provide high availability, but also fully utilize each accelerator in a load-balanced fashion, thereby improving performance.

Figure 7-3 shows how Acme Data integrated the accelerators into the data center network. The accelerator devices were attached to the distribution layer switches adjacent to the point of WAN connectivity. WCCPv2 is enabled on interfaces adjacent to the WAN routers to ensure that any traffic going to or coming from the WAN is first redirected transparently to an accelerator if one is available. If no accelerator is available, no interception occurs, thereby ensuring that connectivity is not impaired should accelerators fail.

Figure 7-3 *Acme Data: Data Center Integration Using WCCPv2*

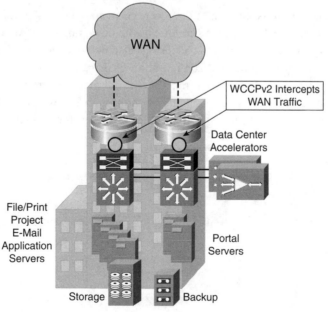

Accelerators were integrated into the remote offices based on the size of the office and the infrastructure at each office. For the larger office, which has approximately 200 users, a dedicated midrange accelerator appliance was integrated using WCCPv2, similar to the integration in the data center.

The two remaining offices each have between 30 and 100 users. Each of these offices has modular routers in place that allowed Acme Data to leverage accelerator router modules, which physically integrate into the WAN router at each of these locations. The integrated accelerators were also configured to use WCCPv2 to ensure that if an integrated network module accelerator goes offline, the network remains available in an unaccelerated state.

Acme Data realized an immediate and significant cost savings by integrating the accelerator solution into its existing routers. Acme Data's network infrastructure teams were already very familiar with the configuration, management, monitoring, and troubleshooting aspects of the network equipment in use, so adding acceleration to the portfolio was a natural fit. Combined with support costs that were covered by the maintenance contract on the router, Acme Data realized a significant total cost of ownership improvement for these locations.

Figure 7-4 shows how Acme Data integrated accelerators into each of its remote office locations. The large remote office was configured with a midrange accelerator appliance deployed using WCCPv2 in a manner similar to that of the data center. The small and medium-sized remote offices were configured with accelerator network modules in the existing modular routers.

WCCPv2 was configured in each of the locations to automatically redirect any WAN-bound TCP traffic to the accelerator to ensure that traffic traversing the WAN link was first optimized. A central management console was also deployed to allow Acme Data to use a single management system for all configuration, management, and reporting aspects associated with the accelerator solution. This central management console also integrated with Acme Data's network management system through SNMP and syslog, allowing the network operations team to provide the first-level support for problem detection and identification.

Figure 7-4   *Acme Data: Remote Office Integration*

Large Remote Office

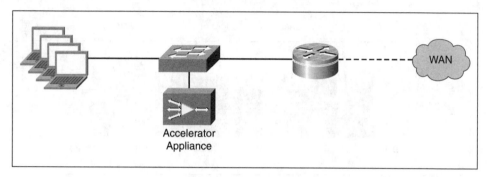

Accelerator
Appliance

Small and Medium Remote Offices

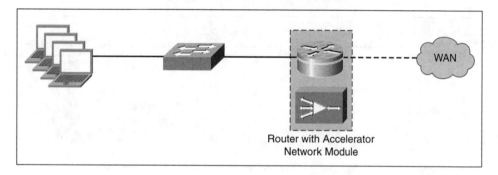

Router with Accelerator
Network Module

Features and Benefits

Once Acme Data deployed the accelerators, it noticed an immediate reduction in the amount of bandwidth being used on the WAN and dramatic improvement in performance of its portal applications and e-mail. The accelerators were able to employ a number of techniques to provide the following benefits to Acme Data:

- **WAN bandwidth savings:** Redundant data no longer traverses the WAN link due to the data suppression capabilities of the accelerator. Nonredundant data is heavily compressed by the persistent compression capabilities provided by the accelerator. Figure 7-5 shows Acme Data's WAN utilization before deploying the accelerators and after deploying the accelerators.

Figure 7-5 *Acme Data WAN Utilization Before and After*

Before Accelerators Were Deployed

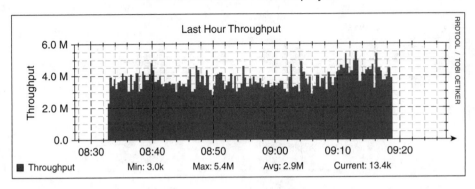

After Accelerators Were Deployed

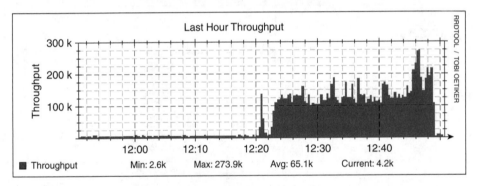

- **Application performance improvement:** The advanced compression capabilities, coupled with application acceleration and transport optimization, provided improved performance for each of the business-critical applications used by Acme Data.

- **High availability:** The accelerators were deployed using WCCPv2. Redundant devices were deployed in the data center to continue service should an accelerator fail. Failure of all accelerators within a location would not impact network connectivity, because WCCPv2 would transition into a fail-through state.

After deploying the accelerators, Acme Data was then able to begin consolidating server, storage, and application infrastructure from the remote sites into the data center. The accelerator solution Acme Data chose also provided file-caching capabilities, which allowed Acme Data to uniquely provide near-local file server performance and disconnected mode of operation without requiring confusing changes to remote office computer drive mappings. This capability also allowed Acme Data to provide better scalability for its desktop management and software distribution infrastructure, because software packages, hotfixes, service packs, and other data could be prepositioned to the edge devices and then delivered locally rather than having to be sent across the WAN for each user desktop that was to be updated.

Once the infrastructure was consolidated, Acme Data could then deploy, manage, and protect its application infrastructure from the data center. This yielded higher levels of service availability, better storage management, and increased data protection posture for Acme Data, because the staff in the data center was dedicated and highly trained.

The results of Acme Data's accelerator deployment include the following:

- Ability to move to a global team of data processing engineers spread among multiple geographic locations without compromising performance or productivity. This enabled Acme Data to plan employee productivity for upcoming projects on a per-employee basis rather than on a per-location basis, thereby allowing Acme Data to take on additional projects. This led to better efficiency, employee project mobility, and increased company revenue, and also allowed Acme Data to begin to leverage engineers in emerging markets.

- Immediate improvement in performance for all business-critical applications, including e-mail, which was historically problematic. Remote office employees noticed that there was dramatically less wait time while working with e-mail and other applications, as shown in Figure 7-6. This helped increase per-employee productivity, because common employee tasks consumed less time.

Figure 7-6   *Acme Data E-Mail Performance Before and After Accelerators*

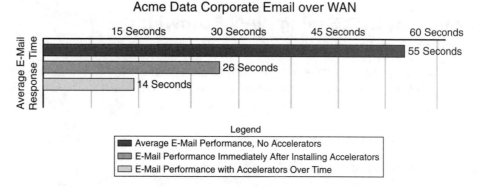

- The need for additional WAN bandwidth for each remote office location was mitigated. The product, service, and support costs of a WAN bandwidth upgrade would have been almost twice the cost of the accelerator solution, and the monthly fees would have been significant.

Coupling the costs of the WAN bandwidth upgrade, remote office file server management, server software and support, data protection infrastructure, and management, Acme Data was able to realize a return on its accelerator solution investment within six months.

Acme Data was facing a number of challenges related to data protection, application performance, and business process. After a loss of key customer data, Acme Data began searching for a solution that allowed it to consolidate project data for improved data protection.

Because Acme Data also desired to be able to assign project team members across multiple locations (in other words, global collaboration as opposed to local per-site collaboration), it chose a centralized web-portal solution for project data management. While the web-portal solution enabled global collaboration and helped improve data protection, it did not address all of Acme Data's requirements and even created new challenges. File servers were still in the branch offices, which also contained sensitive company data, and WAN link utilization immediately increased with the use of the web portal. E-mail still performed poorly, as did access to the web portal for all remote office users.

Once the accelerator solution was deployed, employees in distributed locations found that e-mail performance improved dramatically, as did access to centralized project data on the web portal. The network operations team noticed an immediate reduction in the amount of bandwidth used on the WAN. Acme Data was able to begin consolidating each of the remote office servers into the data center to ensure that data was being backed up regularly. Using the accelerator solution, Acme Data was able to realize a six-month return on investment. Furthermore, Acme Data now can globally distribute projects across multiple users from many distributed locations and no longer has application performance concerns. Employees are more productive and have better satisfaction knowing that they can work on a variety of interesting projects with a multitude of their peers in many different locations.

C3 Technology LLC: Saving WAN Bandwidth and Replicating Data

C3 Technology LLC is a producer of advanced security systems and software. Its flagship product is broadly heralded as one of the most intuitive security solutions available. The solution involves two key components:

- A hardware device, called the Infiltrator

- The software that runs the Infiltrator, called Infiltrator-OS

Over 10,000 customers globally have deployed C3's Infiltrator product and use it daily to ensure that their IT systems from end to end are safe from potential attackers, inside or outside.

C3 Technology has 2000 employees, of which approximately 600 are in hardware and software development. The rest of the employees are focused on sales, marketing, manufacturing, management, and administrative tasks. All business-critical systems are deployed in two data centers, and these data centers are approximately 1000 miles apart from each other. In most cases, users access the majority of their applications in the data center closest to them, but some applications require users to access a distant data center. Data in each of the data centers is replicated asynchronously between storage arrays to ensure that it is available in case of disaster, and this is causing high levels of utilization on the WAN connection between the data centers. VoIP traffic is also carried across the WAN connection to allow C3 to use its IP infrastructure for telephone conversations.

The engineering organization is particularly challenged by the dual data center architecture at C3. Hardware and software development teams are distributed among both data centers, and given the distance between the two data centers and WAN utilization caused by replication of data, accessing hardware blueprints or software source code and specifications in the remote data center is tedious and time consuming.

Observed Challenges

C3 is facing challenges on two fronts. First, the amount of WAN bandwidth is no longer sufficient to keep up with the replication of data between the two data centers. C3 has found that its data is becoming increasingly rich and robust in size, which has led to an increase in storage capacity requirements. Consequently, the time taken to replicate this data continues to increase.

Second, the engineering organization is spread among the two primary data center locations. Project data is spread among the two as well. Hardware and software engineers must work together, regardless of location, and routinely collaborate on the same sets of data. With many of the users attempting to access this data across an already congested WAN, productivity of the remote engineers is far less than that of the engineers who are close in proximity to the data being accessed.

Figure 7-7 shows a network diagram that includes the two primary data center locations, as well as the data access patterns of the engineers.

Accelerator Solution

C3 Technology decided to deploy an accelerator solution to free up WAN bandwidth capacity, minimize the amount of bandwidth consumed and time required to replicate data, and provide faster access to distant data for its engineering organization when working on data across the WAN. The advanced compression capabilities of the accelerator removed repeated patterns from network transmission, which provided a tangible increase in the available WAN capacity. Compression helped to ensure that nonrepeated patterns of data were shrunk to also alleviate bandwidth consumption.

Figure 7-7 *C3 Technology Engineering Data Access*

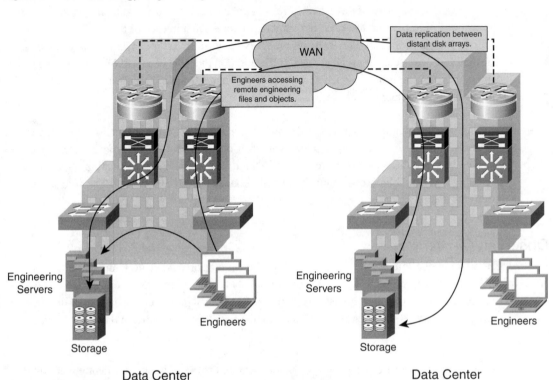

Application acceleration capabilities were employed to ensure that engineers had fast access to engineering data in the other data center. Given that C3 employs VoIP and quality of service (QoS) and its own security solution within its network, C3 opted for a transparent accelerator solution, which allowed it to retain compatibility with these services.

Integrating the Accelerators

A pair of accelerators were deployed in each of the two data centers, adjacent to the routers that terminated the WAN between the two. These accelerators were deployed off-path using WCCPv2 to provide

■ **Fail-through operation:** C3 preferred an off-path solution because such a solution would not require another "bump in the wire" between its entire data center and the WAN router, as an inline solution would. WCCPv2 provides fail-through operation such that if the accelerators become unavailable, traffic is no longer redirected and traverses the WAN connection unoptimized but also uninterrupted.

- **Automatic load balancing:** WCCPv2 provided C3 with an intelligent load-balancing mechanism to ensure that workload was spread among the accelerators, providing higher levels of performance and availability.

- **Nondisruptive addition or removal of accelerators:** If C3 needs to increase or decrease the number of accelerators in either data center, WCCPv2 allows it to add or remove devices without interrupting network flows or changing cabling.

- **Simplified control of traffic to be redirected:** C3's network operations team was highly trained on the hardware and software used in the network infrastructure and was easily able to control what traffic was and was not sent through the accelerators.

WCCPv2 was initially configured to intercept and redirect only replication traffic. This allowed C3 to see how much available WAN capacity could be gained by compressing replication data. After C3 saw the dramatic impact in replication performance and bandwidth consumption, the network operations team configured WCCPv2 to also allow the interception and redirection of other protocols that the engineers were using to access remote data.

Features and Benefits

C3 Technology's initial use of the accelerators was to improve performance of replication while minimizing the amount of bandwidth consumed on the WAN. The storage management team was shocked by the reduction in the amount of time taken to replicate data across data centers, and the network team was equally surprised by how much more bandwidth capacity the network had available due to the accelerator's advanced compression and data suppression capabilities. The accelerators employed the following techniques to immediately improve the performance and behavior of replication:

- **Advanced compression:** Repeated data sequences were removed from transmission. Nonrepeated sequences were heavily compressed. This almost immediately resulted in a 75 percent savings in WAN bandwidth utilization while also improving replication performance.

- **TCP optimization:** The optimizations applied to TCP by the accelerators helped the arrays replicating the data to more efficiently utilize the available WAN capacity. This helped mitigate the negative effects of distance and loss to move data more efficiently and quickly, thereby allowing the arrays to remain more closely synchronized.

Figure 7-8 shows the performance improvements provided by the accelerators in C3 Technology's replication environment.

Figure 7-8 *C3 Technology LLC Replication Performance with Accelerators*

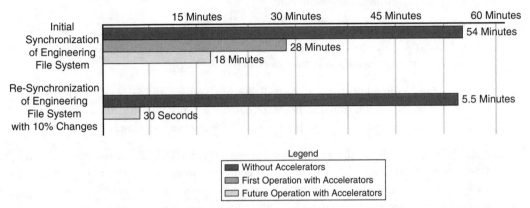

The accelerators were then configured to optimize the protocols in use by the engineers who were working with data across data centers. This traffic was optimized by the advanced compression and TCP optimizations previously mentioned, as well as by the protocol-specific application acceleration capabilities provided by the accelerators. These capabilities include

- **Object caching:** The local accelerator kept copies of engineering files (software code, libraries, documentation, hardware specifications) that engineers were accessing over the network using CIFS. If the file is accessed again and the accelerators determined that the file has not changed, the objects could safely be served locally, thereby providing huge performance gains, increased productivity, and better collaboration.

- **Protocol optimization:** The accelerators optimized the application protocols with functions such as read-ahead, message prediction, pipelining, and multiplexing to ensure that any data accessed, cached or not, provided near-LAN performance for the user.

C3 also noticed that its levels of server utilization decreased due to the deployment of the accelerator solution, as the protocol optimization and file caching capabilities mitigated a large amount of workload that the server would have otherwise needed to handle. This allowed C3 to delay a server upgrade that was pending, because C3 was now able to better scale its existing server infrastructure.

The results of C3's accelerator deployment include

- **More efficient utilization of WAN bandwidth capacity:** C3 was able to achieve higher levels of throughput over the existing WAN connection. This was caused by the accelerator's ability to intelligently suppress repeated patterns and compress nonrepeated patterns. Instead of having to upgrade WAN capacity, C3 was able to leverage accelerators to provide the same effect.

- **Improved productivity for cross-data center engineering collaboration:** By employing WAN optimization and application acceleration, C3's engineers, while working with data across the WAN, experienced far better performance, thereby leading to improved productivity, higher levels of job satisfaction, and more timely completion of engineering tasks, assignments, and projects.

- **Improved data protection:** C3 noticed that replication jobs were taking far less time and using less WAN capacity. This helped to ensure that the data at the distant data center was more closely synchronized with the source of the data. This helped C3 ensure that its exposure for data loss in the event of a disaster was minimized as the recovery point objective (RPO) and recovery time objective (RTO) were improved.

C3 examined the costs associated with a WAN infrastructure upgrade along with the tangible productivity gains. After deploying the accelerators, the next engineering release completed four weeks ahead of schedule. This allowed C3 to bring the next version of its product to market more quickly and gain a competitive advantage against its rivals, resulting in nearly immediate revenue increases and joyous sales and executive organizations. Mitigating the recurring cost of the WAN infrastructure upgrade and productivity improvements led C3 to realize a three-month return on its investment.

C3 Technology was facing challenges related to data replication and productivity of its engineers when working with data in distant data center locations. As the data sets its engineers were working with became larger in size, scope, and complexity, WAN bandwidth requirements increased to the point that its data replication was nearly unable to keep up with the rate of data change. The WAN had become congested and was creating performance challenges for its engineers. These performance challenges led to a loss of productivity, particularly when an engineer would need to work with data stored in the distant data center across the overly congested WAN connection.

C3 deployed a transparent accelerator solution to maintain compliance with the features and capabilities deployed within its network, such as QoS, Voice over IP, and its own security solution. Initially the accelerators were deployed to minimize bandwidth consumed by replication. C3 saw an immediate improvement not only in bandwidth consumption, but also in replication performance. Then, C3 utilized the accelerators to improve the performance of the applications and protocols in use by the engineering teams when accessing remote content. The accelerators were able to not only minimize the amount of bandwidth consumed on the WAN, thereby mitigating a bandwidth upgrade, but also improve performance to the degree that higher productivity levels were achieved. This gave C3 a more competitive posture in its market, allowing it to bring forth product in a more timely fashion. This led to increases in revenue and better positioning against its competitors.

Command Grill Corporation: Improving HTTP Application Performance

Command Grill Corporation provides customer service for several large retail chains throughout North and South America. As its name implies, the company provides customer support for several different brands of home gas grills. Each time a customer calls one of Command Grill Corporation's 15 support centers, the answering service agent asks the caller a series of questions to identify who the customer is and what brand and model of gas grill the customer has. The customer service agent uses an Internet browser to access a database server that resides in his corporate data center in Denver, Colorado. Command Grill Corporation's customer service centers are connected to the corporate data center via individual T1 connections.

Figure 7-9 illustrates the Command Grill Corporation's North and South America network topology.

Figure 7-9   *Command Grill Network Topology*

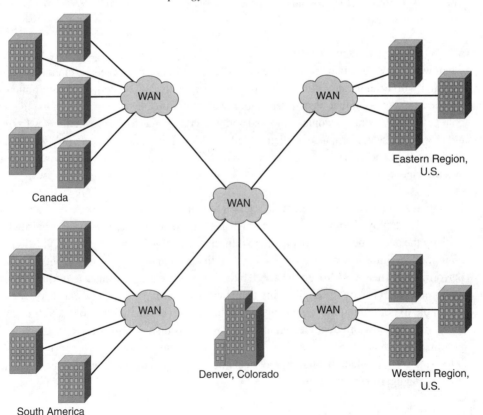

Customer service representatives have complained that access to the centralized database application has always been very slow. These delays have created customer dissatisfaction due to the increased wait times to process customer requests. The most common explanations provided to waiting callers during excessive periods of congestion include "My computer is slow" and "We are having computer problems today." The database application is only accessible via the browser and involves several large Java applets.

First Attempts to Improve Application Performance

Command Grill Corporation's information technology department was consulted by the database application team, who tried several different approaches to solve their application's slow performance. Changes ranged from adjusting settings within the client's web browser to altering the size of objects on the application server.

The first change focused on disk storage allocated to the web browser for object caching. The Java applets supporting the application used by each client equated to 250 MB of data. Only objects associated with the application framework were cached. The dynamic client information that was communicated to or from the database server, however, was not cached. Adjusting the client browser storage settings had little impact to the customer service representative, because the objects that were served to the client were marked noncacheable by the application. This prohibited the client's web browser from effectively caching the large applets, which needed to be sent to the client over the WAN frequently.

The second proposed change involved splitting the larger Java applet into two smaller Java applets. This change decreased overall application performance by requiring two individual object requests instead of one object request. Although two requests were placed, the overall quantity of bits transferred was not reduced but actually increased due to messaging overhead.

The third proposed change involved disabling the noncacheable header variable for served Java applets. The database application vendor did not allow any header changes to objects served, citing security concerns.

Accelerator Solution

Command Grill Corporation implemented an accelerator solution that provides web acceleration and caching capabilities. One accelerator appliance was installed in each of the remote branch office networks. The gains provided by the accelerator were beneficial to more than just the original database application; other, less commonly used applications and general web traffic also benefited from the gains provided by the appliance and its many other acceleration capabilities. The information technology department determined that the use of the accelerator proved to be beneficial to other applications used by remote branch users distributed throughout the corporation as well.

Integrating the Accelerators

The accelerator was deployed off-path in each branch location with WCCPv2 as a means of intercepting HTTP application traffic. Command Grill Corporation averages 100 employees at each branch location, which prohibited it from easily changing the proxy settings of each employee's web browser, which is presently a manual change within each browser. The configuration applied to each branch accelerator was the same, with the exception of the network parameters of the accelerator. Each accelerator shared a common interception configuration, storage configuration, and HTTP header manipulation settings, allowing a standardized configuration to be deployed to each branch office.

The accelerator and WCCPv2 were both configured to intercept the TCP ports used by the key applications, including TCP ports 80, 8002, and 7777. These port settings allow the accelerator to intercept traffic for a number of differing business reasons.

Interception of HTTP over port 80 allows the accelerator to cache and serve the following:

- Standard Internet-destined HTTP requests, including non-work-related general traffic

- Standard intranet-destined HTTP requests

- Any future applications that use the default HTTP port 80 but were not planned for as part of the initial evaluation

Port 8002 interception was enabled on the accelerator and router to improve performance of a legacy inventory application. This application was not considered a cause of WAN congestion until a traffic audit was performed by the network operations department. The legacy application was initially accessed via HTTP over port 80. After the authentication process was completed, the client requests were then transitioned to HTTP over port 8002. To function properly, the legacy application depended on the delivery of many large Java-based applets, each of which averaged 6.5 MB in size. During the network traffic audit, an average of seven requests per client were made for these large applets when the inventory application was accessed, causing large amounts of bandwidth utilization on the WAN.

The offending database application server hosts its HTTP application over TCP port 7777. Nonstandard port settings for transparent interception of the port 7777 traffic were required at the accelerator and associated router in each branch location. The initial login and access to the application server commenced via HTTP over TCP port 80, and then the application switched to HTTP over TCP port 7777. During the TCP port 80 login session, 4 MB of content was passed to the requesting client, followed by 14 MB of Java-based applets within a single file over TCP port 7777.

The accelerator required two additional configuration settings to allow for proper caching of database application requests. The first allows for caching many of the static HTTP objects that carry a noncacheable header variable. Instead of creating caching rules that address each object directly, a rule was configured at the accelerator to override the pragma no-cache setting for all static content served from the application server. A single rule applied against a host or domain allowed for header manipulation of all HTTP content served over any intercepted port. A single rule applied against the database server host name prevented the administrator from defining one rule for every object hosted from the database server. For content that did not carry the no-cache header variable, no changes to the content header were made, and the objects were cached as they traversed the accelerator.

The second configuration setting required at the branch accelerator involved enabling support for caching of authenticated content. By default, the accelerator will not cache content objects that require authentication. Authentication settings were observed within the object's header properties during the traffic audit process. By allowing the caching of authenticated content, the accelerator could properly cache the Java applets served by the database server. Once enabled within the accelerator's configuration, authentication will continue to function for future requests of cached Java objects, while locally delivering any authenticated requests that traverse the accelerator in the future.

The selected accelerator includes 500 GB of total disk storage, spread across two 250-GB disk drives. 128 GB of storage was allocated for HTTP caching only. The remaining storage capacity was left available for any future needs, such as streaming media, prepositioning, advanced compression capabilities, or other protocol acceleration functions. To provide maximum performance, 64 GB of storage was allocated on each physical disk, allowing for content to be written and read from both disks simultaneously as needed. When configured as individual disks, in a two-disk web accelerator, performance and throughput ratings are improved as a direct result of the number of disk spindles that can read and write data simultaneously.

Figure 7-10 illustrates the connectivity between the accelerator and peer router, including the WAN and target server. The device's storage configuration is also logically illustrated.

In the core of the network, no additional hardware is required. Each edge accelerator communicates directly with the client's target web server, with no core device required in the corporate data center to intercept edge accelerator requests. During the IT department's evaluation of needs and available options, the dedicated edge accelerator proved to be the simplest and most cost-effective approach to a given set of web-based challenges. The IT department did, however, choose an acceleration solution that also provides other capabilities such as compression and protocol acceleration. The IT department is able to leverage such capabilities with the simple addition of data center accelerators.

From the central management device, settings were applied to groups instead of to individual devices. To centrally manage all edge accelerators collectively, current and future settings reside in one key area, header manipulation via rule sets. Manually setting rules individually at each accelerator would have exposed the administrator to the risk of typographical errors, so the IT department instead opted for centrally configured rules using groupings of devices.

Figure 7-10 *Command Grill Branch Accelerator Configuration*

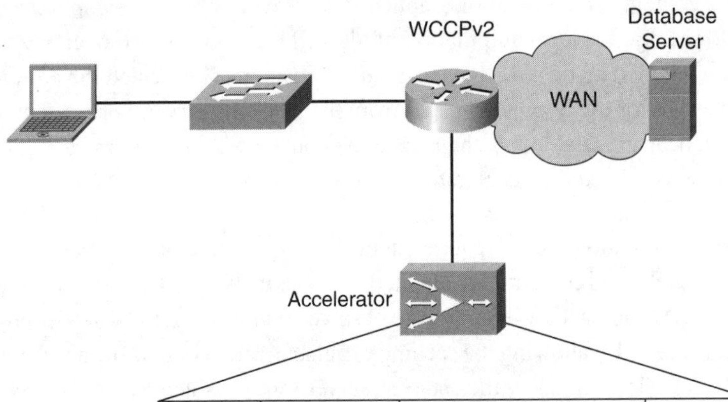

	Caching	Reserved for Future Acceleration	Total
Disk 1	64 GB	186 GB	250 GB
Disk 2	64 GB	186 GB	250 GB

Although each edge accelerator carried its own unique IP address, default gateway, and peer router for WCCP, several settings could be collectively defined against a group of devices. Authentication settings, disk allocation, transaction logging, and WCCP intercepted ports were all common settings that each edge device shared with other devices.

HTTP authentication within Command Grill Corporation's network is directed to a single domain controller in the data center, pointing all accelerators to the same host. Performance predictability throughout all branch locations became possible when all edge accelerators were configured with the same disk partitioning. Ports 80, 7777, and 8002 are intercepted via WCCP at each accelerator as a group, allowing for consistent and predictable traffic interception at all branch locations. If additional TCP ports are required in the future, new settings can be applied via the central management device against all accelerator devices. Transaction logging allows administrators to monitor the cacheability of individual objects and the usage patterns of the employees of Command Grill Corporation.

Grouped devices that are centrally managed benefit from a single reference point for edge accelerator monitoring. Two groups were given access to the central management device with read-only permissions of the performance of the edge accelerator devices. The database application administrators access the central management device to proactively monitor the cache savings created by the edge accelerator device. The network administrators monitor the network traffic patterns reported by each branch location accelerator and are provided with transaction logs on how well the accelerator is caching individual objects served by sites within and outside of the corporation's network.

Features and Benefits

After enabling acceleration in each branch location, Command Grill Corporation observed performance improvements in two key areas: the employee's computer and the database application server. For the employee, wait times were greatly reduced, because Java applets were delivered to their web browser from the accelerator instead of the database application server in the data center. A reduction in traffic was also observed at the database application server, demonstrating reduced utilization of the server's disks and network interface card. The network administrator observed reduced levels of WAN utilization, allowing for improved performance of other corporate applications and traffic.

Authentication had a direct impact on the accelerator's performance and functionality; content security was now extended to Java applets stored in the remote branch accelerator. If authentication is not enabled at an accelerator for HTTP traffic, the objects and their authentication requests merely pass through the accelerator; the accelerator becomes passive, having no way to determine if the content should be delivered to the requesting employee. Once enabled, all Java applets served by the database application and the legacy application were cached for optimized delivery in response to future employee requests.

Transaction logging was not an original requirement of the administrators during the solution selection process. During the audit process, however, transaction logging was enabled to provide traffic reports in a standardized format. These transaction logs provided a line-by-line report of every request that traversed the accelerator, including information related to cache hits or misses. During the test process, entries were recorded as a result of employees who accessed the public Internet. Although the transaction logs were not of immediate interest to the administrators, they did create significant interest within the Command Grill Corporation's information security organization.

Looking back, Command Grill Corporation faced a major performance challenge within its customer support organization: the tools provided to employees to do their job performed poorly. After evaluating several options, distributed accelerators were selected to cache the traffic hosted from a central database server that existed in Command Grill's data center. Additional value was observed throughout its network when the accelerators began caching other web-based corporate applications, in addition to traffic destined for the public Internet, resulting in significant bandwidth savings and performance improvements.

Figure 7-11 illustrates the differences between cached and noncached application objects requested at one of Command Grill Corporation's remote customer service branch offices.

In addition to increased application performance, employee performance also improved. Before the accelerators were deployed, many employees complained about application performance and would occasionally share their concerns with customers during a support call. Discussions between customers and employees that reflect negatively upon Command Grill Corporation could have an impact on future revenue for the corporation, a risk that any corporation will not tolerate.

Figure 7-11 *Observed Performance Improvements*

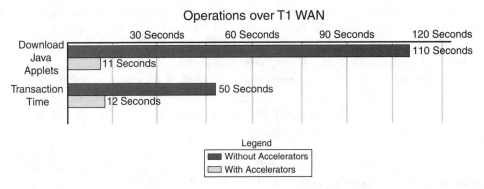

Command Grill Corporation's customer service representatives no longer wait for access to the business-critical database applications. Response times were reduced from tens of seconds to less than one second per requested object. The overall savings observed from the accelerator provided improved response times, reduced traffic on the T1 connections, and improved employee production through the customer service organization.

Almost Write Inc.: Implementing Content Delivery Networking

Almost Write Inc. provides creative content solutions for its global customers. Based in Grand Rapids, Michigan, it began business in the late 1990s, as a small dot com company, looking to tackle the world with its innovative streaming media and graphics content. As its success grew, its physical presence expanded to include locations in London, San Francisco, and Miami.

Customers gained access to Almost Write content via a secure Internet web portal, which proved to be satisfactory in the first few years of the company. However, changes in graphics and multimedia technology have caused Almost Write customers to expect a greater degree of higher-quality, higher-resolution streaming media and marketing graphics to satisfy their needs. As the demand for higher-quality rich-media content has increased, so has the size of the final product that Almost Write must deliver to its customers.

Key international customers of Almost Write reside in Munich, Germany, and Bangkok, Thailand. Figure 7-12 illustrates the Almost Write corporate network and two of its international customers' corporate headquarters.

WAN links between remote offices and the corporate office in Grand Rapids, Michigan, are all T1. The corporate office is connected to the public Internet via a T3, an interface that has increased in parallel with its customers' needs.

Figure 7-12 *Almost Write Corporate Network*

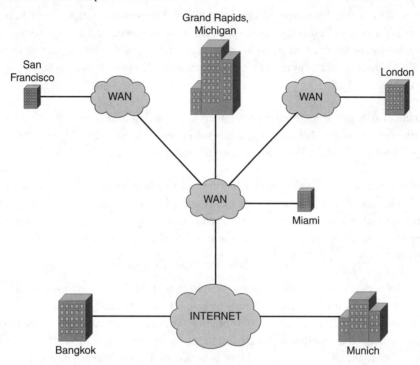

Korrekt AG, an automotive performance parts supplier based in Munich, Germany, relies upon Almost Write to create its marketing, advertising, and television commercial content. As television demands have increased, Korrekt has adjusted its needs to include video content suitable for high-definition display and electronic imaging suitable for 1600 x 1280 resolution. Korrekt's corporate office is connected to the public Internet via an E1 circuit, which has become a bottleneck between Almost Write and Korrekt's marketing department. The slow delivery of content has become a threat to Almost Write's future business transactions with Korrekt.

Khawp Khun Industries, a textile distributor based in Bangkok, relies upon Almost Write to produce its electronic catalog. Khawp Khun ships textile samples to Almost Write's San Francisco office. There, Almost Write creates scans of the textiles and then converts the scans into an electronic catalog suitable for distribution to apparel companies around the world. Khawp Khun then offers the final 600-MB catalog online or via compact disc. Unfortunately, Khawp Khun's WAN cannot reliably support the successful transfer of the catalog without disrupting other business transactions.

Observed Challenges

Almost Write's WAN is robust, offering a steady 45 Mbps of throughput. For Almost Write, this circuit is the result of evolving customer needs and a continued focus on customer satisfaction. The remote offices each connect to the corporate office via a T1 circuit, passing their traffic through this common T3 circuit. The externally accessible content portal is hosted on a web server that also shares the T3.

Content distribution from the corporate office to satellite offices has always been slow. Media distribution delays have been a problem that is frequently discussed during conference calls. Some employees have cited the WAN as a source of productivity disruption.

Historical methods of physical media distribution have become slow, insecure, and in some cases unreliable. The overnight courier is frequently relied upon as a method of overnight content delivery. Final production works were burned to CD, DAT tape, or DVD, and then packaged and shipped overnight to customers around the world who chose not to retrieve their products via the Internet.

Operational expenses were continually increasing with each new customer. Although these expenses were built into Almost Write's service offering, monthly expenses were not predictable. In an effort to reduce some courier expenses, shipping transitioned from the Grand Rapids office to the satellite office closest to the customer. This shipping method did provide some relief to the overall monthly shipping expenses, but not enough to justify a change in business process.

One unique challenge to Almost Write is its geographic location. During winter months, weather delays prevent timely courier pickup and shipment. On occasion, the local airport closes due to excessive snowfall, preventing overnight shipments from meeting customer or contact deadlines.

Internet-centric customers would frequently complain that the transfer of their purchases took too long to complete. Although Almost Write's Internet circuit was robust, many of its customers utilized Internet access over circuits far slower than Almost Write's T3. For a brief time, all completed works were compressed with popular desktop compression applications before being posted to the customers' Internet portal. Compression provided little bandwidth savings because the video content is already compressed via the use of a media encoder. Other graphics and document-based files saved approximately 50 percent but were dramatically small in comparison to the video products.

Accelerator Solution

Almost Write came to recognize its challenges through a mix of accumulating operational expenses and decreased employee and customer satisfaction. A small trial was initiated between the corporate and San Francisco offices. The trial involved the use of an accelerator at the corporate office and one deployed in the San Francisco office. The purpose of the trial was to evaluate the benefits of using the accelerators for media prepositioning to San Francisco. During the evaluation, several multigigabyte objects were distributed to the branch office during nonbusiness hours.

Integrating the Accelerators

The San Francisco office installed a large accelerator that supports just over 1 TB of storage. Traffic analysis proved that the average amount of content created for a typical customer consumes 5 GB of storage per project. The administrator allocated 800 GB of storage space for content distribution, leaving approximately 200 GB of storage for future service offerings such as compression and protocol acceleration. The accelerator was configured to use WCCPv2 as the interception method for employees accessing the accelerator via their web browser.

Figure 7-13 illustrates the connectivity between the router, client, and accelerator, including a logical representation of storage allocation.

Figure 7-13 *Almost Write Accelerator Configuration*

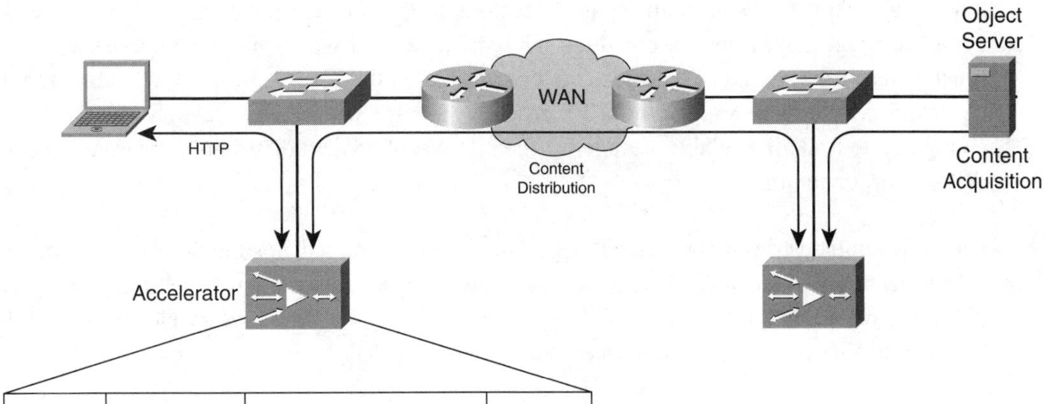

	Prepositioned Content	Remainder	Total
Disk 1	250 GB	0 GB	250 GB
Disk 2	250 GB	0 GB	250 GB

Within the corporate office, a central management device was also installed alongside the accelerator. To match the accelerator installed in the San Francisco office, just over 1 TB of storage was installed in the corporate data center accelerator. During the trial, the CDN was configured to acquire and preposition content from the existing customer-facing media portal, discovering any new content within 5 minutes of its placement on the server. The trial could not disrupt existing employee work procedures. A content distribution schedule was established, allocating 1 Mbps between 9 p.m. and 5 a.m. (2100 and 0500) EST from Grand Rapids to San Francisco.

Content administrator and network administrator accounts were configured at the central management device, allowing both departments to manage and monitor the solution's trial. The content administrator's primary concern was efficient, nondisruptive content acquisition, distribution, and serving to the employees in the San Francisco office. The network administrator's primary concern focused on the livelihood and well-being of the corporate WAN and remote branch office WAN.

Because the trial continued to provide valuable savings, Almost Write's executive management team agreed that the trial should be extended to include at least two customers. Korrekt AG and Khawp Khun Industries both agreed to participate in a limited trial, requiring the installation of at least one accelerator within their respective networks. To support the additional off-network accelerators, an additional accelerator was installed in the corporate data center. The additional accelerator acted as the parent to the accelerators installed at the Korrekt headquarters in Munich and the Khawp Khun Industries corporate office in Bangkok.

For the Korrekt network, a small 500-GB accelerator was selected. This initiative was agreed upon as a trial. The accelerator could not intercept traffic via WCCP, nor be configured to function as a browser proxy. The accelerator installed on the Korrekt network was configured to provide read-only access via the CIFS protocol. Storage within the accelerator was configured to host all available storage for the purpose of content distribution from Almost Write's corporate office.

Khawp Khun Industries was provided a midsize accelerator device, hosting 600 GB of storage. Like Korrekt's accelerator, the device became accessible by Khawp Khun Industries' employees via a CIFS read-only drive mapping. The full storage capacity of the midsize accelerator was again allocated to Khawp Khun Industries' content distribution needs.

Both Korrekt AG and Khawp Khun Industries received media during hours that they determined most appropriate to their respective time zones. Network administrators at Korrekt AG and Khawp Khun Industries defined bandwidth limitations. Both customers stated that they would monitor the activities of the accelerators installed within their networks, making sure no network disruptions occurred.

Features and Benefits

The content and network administrators of Almost Write determined that the content delivery network (CDN) did improve the distribution process of media throughout the corporate network. Content was distributed to San Francisco during off-hours, reducing the company's dependency on overnight couriers. The content and network administrators found that their working configuration required little additional administration once configured.

For Almost Write's content administrator, no changes were made to the existing media portal that existing customers accessed. The CDN could effectively acquire content from the portal server without adding any additional steps to the media creation process. The CDN became a turnkey solution once the source and destinations were configured via the central management device. During the 60-day trial, nearly 500 GB of content was successfully distributed and served by the CDN, averaging nearly 8 GB of data per day.

Almost Write's network administrator determined that the CDN distribution was within the approved time and bandwidth allocations. As a result, the administrator approved the future installation of accelerators in the Miami and London offices. Korrekt AG approved of the performance gains the edge accelerator device demonstrated in its network. Korrekt's marketing department stated that it would like to continue use of the accelerator device in the future.

The number of web-based requests made to Almost Write's customer media portal by Korrekt AG and Khawp Khun Industries has steadily declined since the accelerator was installed. Physical media shipments have reduced, improving the operational expenses incurred by Almost Write in support of its customer. The customer states that he is extremely satisfied with the new means of accessing his rich-media content.

Khawp Khun Industries' edge accelerator created a stronger relationship with Almost Write. Traditionally, Almost Write provided one compressed 600-MB object to Khawp Khun Industries. The file was decompressed, containing hundreds of smaller files. If a change was required, Almost Write would build and redistribute a new compressed file for Khawp Khun Industries, at Almost Write's expense. With the introduction of the edge accelerator, the compressed file is no longer utilized. Instead, each of the smaller files is distributed to Khawp Khun, and if a change is required, Almost Write applies its changes to the appropriate files that are distributed individually. Updates to the Khawp Khun Industries catalog now average less than 30 MB per update. The distribution process occurs in minutes, instead of days.

Operational expenses have immediately declined for courier costs to all of Almost Write's remote branch locations. Human resources, sales, and marketing all determined that the CDN would benefit their respective department's efforts as well. Almost Write's accountants observed that reduced overall operational expenses have increased profit margins with two of its international customers.

For Almost Write's customers, satisfaction improved. The turn-around time required for project adjustments reduced the overall amount of time customers like Khawp Khun Industries were required to wait for completed projects. For Korrekt AG, content delivery became a vehicle for quicker time to market of new products.

Summary

An accelerator solution provides application acceleration and WAN optimization techniques that help IT organizations solve a myriad of problems with infrastructure and business process. By combining a powerful set of application-agnostic capabilities with application-specific components, accelerator solutions enable IT departments to more intelligently deploy infrastructure in a centralized manner, leading to better manageability, stronger data protection, better collaboration, and overall lower costs of ownership. In essence, the powerful technologies found in accelerator solutions are helping make the dream of a low-cost, high-impact IT infrastructure environment a reality and changing the way business process is architected.

As discussed throughout this book, each accelerator solution includes a fundamental set of features:

- **Advanced compression:** Removes the need to transmit repeated data patterns and compresses new data patterns in flight. Advanced compression results in improved performance through packet concatenation and higher levels of throughput while also minimizing WAN bandwidth consumption.

- **Transport optimization:** Overcomes inefficiencies in the transport protocols that link application processes on disparate nodes. Transport optimizations help applications to contend fairly for available network capacity while also being able to fully utilize the network when appropriate. Transport optimizations also help to ensure that the negative effects of distance and packet loss do not severely impact the throughput obtained between two nodes that are exchanging application data.

- **Application acceleration:** Protocol-specific and application-specific optimizations mitigate application layer latency and bandwidth consumption. These techniques include caching, content delivery, read-ahead, message prediction, pipelining, and multiplexing.

These fundamental features coexist in a solution that allows the right level of optimization to be applied at the appropriate time to best improve performance for the user.

Other factors must also be considered when examining an accelerator solution. An accelerated network must be provisioned in such a way that aligns with business priority and application requirements. Furthermore, the network should be visible and manageable, providing the IT organization with insight into how the network is being utilized, thereby enabling granular control. Simply put, network resources should be provisioned using network-centric capabilities such as QoS. Because the network is the common foundation that all business process traverses, it is the best choice for where such control and provisioning should occur.

Accelerators that integrate transparently will naturally support such capabilities. However, nontransparent accelerators, which manipulate control information such as packet headers, might defeat these capabilities.

In short, while accelerators provide the capabilities necessary to improve application performance, minimize bandwidth consumption, and radically change the way the IT business process model is deployed, a complete solution will involve not only accelerators, but also components in the network. It is only in this way that a true end-to-end application-optimized network infrastructure can be realized.

Common Ports and Assigned Applications

This appendix provides a quick reference that highlights many of the port numbers commonly used by applications in a network environment. This helps you identify what applications are using the network, thereby allowing you to configure acceleration services, quality of service (QoS), security, or monitoring. You can then optimize, control, or generate reports about how applications are utilizing your network.

The port numbers are divided into three ranges:

- **Well-known ports:** The ports from 0 through 1023.

- **Registered ports:** The ports from 1024 through 49151.

- **Dynamic and/or private ports:** The ports from 49152 through 65535. The range for assigned ports managed by the IANA is 0 through 1023.

The list of ports in Table A-1 is not complete or exhaustive. The list that follows is a subset copied from the full list maintained by IANA and contains many of the most common protocols and applications found in today's enterprise and commercial networks. The list in this book should not be considered authoritative or up-to-date; for a complete and up-to-date list of port assignments maintained by IANA, please visit IANA at the following URL:

http://www.iana.org/assignments/port-numbers

Table A-1 *Port Assignments*

Keyword	Decimal	Description
ftp-data	20/tcp	File Transfer [Default Data]
ftp-data	20/udp	File Transfer [Default Data]
ftp	21/tcp	File Transfer [Control]
ftp	21/udp	File Transfer [Control]
ssh	22/tcp	SSH Remote Login Protocol
ssh	22/udp	SSH Remote Login Protocol
telnet	23/tcp	Telnet

continues

Table A-1 *Port Assignments (Continued)*

Keyword	Decimal	Description
telnet	23/udp	Telnet
smtp	25/tcp	Simple Mail Transfer
smtp	25/udp	Simple Mail Transfer
name	42/tcp	Host Name Server
name	42/udp	Host Name Server
nameserver	42/tcp	Host Name Server
nameserver	42/udp	Host Name Server
nicname	43/tcp	Who Is
nicname	43/udp	Who Is
tacacs	49/tcp	Login Host Protocol (TACACS)
tacacs	49/udp	Login Host Protocol (TACACS)
domain	53/tcp	Domain Name Server
domain	53/udp	Domain Name Server
whois++	63/tcp	whois++
whois++	63/udp	whois++
covia	64/tcp	Communications Integrator (CI)
covia	64/udp	Communications Integrator (CI)
tacacs-ds	65/tcp	TACACS-Database Service
tacacs-ds	65/udp	TACACS-Database Service
sql*net	66/tcp	Oracle SQL*NET
sql*net	66/udp	Oracle SQL*NET
bootps	67/tcp	Bootstrap Protocol Server
bootps	67/udp	Bootstrap Protocol Server
bootpc	68/tcp	Bootstrap Protocol Client
bootpc	68/udp	Bootstrap Protocol Client
tftp	69/tcp	Trivial File Transfer
tftp	69/udp	Trivial File Transfer
gopher	70/tcp	Gopher
gopher	70/udp	Gopher
finger	79/tcp	Finger
finger	79/udp	Finger

Table A-1 *Port Assignments (Continued)*

Keyword	Decimal	Description
http	80/tcp	World Wide Web HTTP
http	80/udp	World Wide Web HTTP
Kerberos	88/tcp	Kerberos
Kerberos	88/udp	Kerberos
npp	92/tcp	Network Printing Protocol
npp	92/udp	Network Printing Protocol
objcall	94/tcp	Tivoli Object Dispatcher
objcall	94/udp	Tivoli Object Dispatcher
hostname	101/tcp	NIC Host Name Server
hostname	101/udp	NIC Host Name Server
rtelnet	107/tcp	Remote Telnet Service
rtelnet	107/udp	Remote Telnet Service
pop2	109/tcp	Post Office Protocol - Version 2
pop2	109/udp	Post Office Protocol - Version 2
pop3	110/tcp	Post Office Protocol - Version 3
pop3	110/udp	Post Office Protocol - Version 3
sunrpc	111/tcp	SUN Remote Procedure Call
sunrpc	111/udp	SUN Remote Procedure Call
auth	113/tcp	Authentication Service
auth	113/udp	Authentication Service
sftp	115/tcp	Simple File Transfer Protocol
sftp	115/udp	Simple File Transfer Protocol
sqlserv	118/tcp	SQL Services
sqlserv	118/udp	SQL Services
nntp	119/tcp	Network News Transfer Protocol
nntp	119/udp	Network News Transfer Protocol
ntp	123/tcp	Network Time Protocol
ntp	123/udp	Network Time Protocol
epmap	135/tcp	DCE endpoint resolution
epmap	135/udp	DCE endpoint resolution

continues

Table A-1 *Port Assignments (Continued)*

Keyword	Decimal	Description
netbios-ns	137/tcp	NETBIOS Name Service
netbios-ns	137/udp	NETBIOS Name Service
netbios-dgm	138/tcp	NETBIOS Datagram Service
netbios-dgm	138/udp	NETBIOS Datagram Service
netbios-ssn	139/tcp	NETBIOS Session Service
netbios-ssn	139/udp	NETBIOS Session Service
imap	143/tcp	Internet Message Access Protocol
imap	143/udp	Internet Message Access Protocol
sql-net	150/tcp	SQL-NET
sql-net	150/udp	SQL-NET
bftp	152/tcp	Background File Transfer Program
bftp	152/udp	Background File Transfer Program
sgmp	153/tcp	SGMP
sgmp	153/udp	SGMP
sqlsrv	156/tcp	SQL Service
sqlsrv	156/udp	SQL Service
snmp	161/tcp	SNMP
snmp	161/udp	SNMP
snmptrap	162/tcp	SNMPTRAP
snmptrap	162/udp	SNMPTRAP
print-srv	170/tcp	Network PostScript
print-srv	170/udp	Network PostScript
vmnet	175/tcp	VMNET
vmnet	175/udp	VMNET
bgp	179/tcp	Border Gateway Protocol
bgp	179/udp	Border Gateway Protocol
irc	194/tcp	Internet Relay Chat Protocol
irc	194/udp	Internet Relay Chat Protocol
at-rtmp	201/tcp	AppleTalk Routing Maintenance
at-rtmp	201/udp	AppleTalk Routing Maintenance
at-nbp	202/tcp	AppleTalk Name Binding

Table A-1 *Port Assignments (Continued)*

Keyword	Decimal	Description
at-nbp	202/udp	AppleTalk Name Binding
at-3	203/tcp	AppleTalk Unused
at-3	203/udp	AppleTalk Unused
at-echo	204/tcp	AppleTalk Echo
at-echo	204/udp	AppleTalk Echo
at-5	205/tcp	AppleTalk Unused
at-5	205/udp	AppleTalk Unused
at-zis	206/tcp	AppleTalk Zone Information
at-zis	206/udp	AppleTalk Zone Information
at-7	207/tcp	AppleTalk Unused
at-7	207/udp	AppleTalk Unused
at-8	208/tcp	AppleTalk Unused
at-8	208/udp	AppleTalk Unused
qmtp	209/tcp	The Quick Mail Transfer Protocol
qmtp	209/udp	The Quick Mail Transfer Protocol
ipx	213/tcp	IPX
ipx	213/udp	IPX
CAIlic	216/tcp	Computer Associates Int'l License Server
CAIlic	216/udp	Computer Associates Int'l License Server
dbase	217/tcp	dBASE Unix
dbase	217/udp	dBASE Unix
imap3	220/tcp	Interactive Mail Access Protocol v3
imap3	220/udp	Interactive Mail Access Protocol v3
rsvp_tunnel	363/tcp	RSVP Tunnel
rsvp_tunnel	363/udp	RSVP Tunnel
rpc2portmap	369/tcp	rpc2portmap
rpc2portmap	369/udp	rpc2portmap
clearcase	371/tcp	Clearcase
clearcase	371/udp	Clearcase
ldap	389/tcp	Lightweight Directory Access Protocol

continues

Table A-1 *Port Assignments (Continued)*

Keyword	Decimal	Description
ldap	389/udp	Lightweight Directory Access Protocol
netware-ip	396/tcp	Novell Netware over IP
netware-ip	396/udp	Novell Netware over IP
https	443/tcp	http protocol over TLS/SSL
https	443/udp	http protocol over TLS/SSL
microsoft-ds	445/tcp	Microsoft-DS
microsoft-ds	445/udp	Microsoft-DS
appleqtc	458/tcp	apple quick time
appleqtc	458/udp	apple quick time
exec	512/tcp	remote process execution
ncp	524/tcp	NCP
ncp	524/udp	NCP
timed	525/tcp	timeserver
timed	525/udp	timeserver
irc-serv	529/tcp	IRC-SERV
irc-serv	529/udp	IRC-SERV
courier	530/tcp	rpc
courier	530/udp	rpc
conference	531/tcp	chat
conference	531/udp	chat
netnews	532/tcp	readnews
netnews	532/udp	readnews
nmsp	537/tcp	Networked Media Streaming Protocol
nmsp	537/udp	Networked Media Streaming Protocol
klogin	543/tcp	
klogin	543/udp	
kshell	544/tcp	krcmd
kshell	544/udp	krcmd
appleqtcsrvr	545/tcp	appleqtcsrvr
appleqtcsrvr	545/udp	appleqtcsrvr
dhcpv6-client	546/tcp	DHCPv6 Client

Table A-1 *Port Assignments (Continued)*

Keyword	Decimal	Description
dhcpv6-client	546/udp	DHCPv6 Client
dhcpv6-server	547/tcp	DHCPv6 Server
dhcpv6-server	547/udp	DHCPv6 Server
afpovertcp	548/tcp	AFP over TCP
afpovertcp	548/udp	AFP over TCP
rtsp	554/tcp	Real Time Stream Control Protocol
rtsp	554/udp	Real Time Stream Control Protocol
nntps	563/tcp	nntp protocol over TLS/SSL (was snntp)
nntps	563/udp	nntp protocol over TLS/SSL (was snntp)
whoami	565/tcp	whoami
whoami	565/udp	whoami
banyan-rpc	567/tcp	banyan-rpc
banyan-rpc	567/udp	banyan-rpc
banyan-vip	573/tcp	banyan-vip
banyan-vip	573/udp	banyan-vip
philips-vc	583/tcp	Philips Video-Conferencing
philips-vc	583/udp	Philips Video-Conferencing
keyserver	584/tcp	Key Server
keyserver	584/udp	Key Server
password-chg	586/tcp	Password Change
password-chg	586/udp	Password Change
submission	587/tcp	Submission
submission	587/udp	Submission
http-alt	591/tcp	FileMaker, Inc. - HTTP Alternate (see Port 80)
http-alt	591/udp	FileMaker, Inc. - HTTP Alternate (see Port 80)
eudora-set	592/tcp	Eudora Set
eudora-set	592/udp	Eudora Set
http-rpc-epmap	593/tcp	HTTP RPC Ep Map
http-rpc-epmap	593/udp	HTTP RPC Ep Map
ipcserver	600/tcp	Sun IPC server

continues

Table A-1 *Port Assignments (Continued)*

Keyword	Decimal	Description
ipcserver	600/udp	Sun IPC server
syslog-conn	601/tcp	Reliable Syslog Service
syslog-conn	601/udp	Reliable Syslog Service
compaq-evm	619/tcp	Compaq EVM
compaq-evm	619/udp	Compaq EVM
passgo-tivoli	627/tcp	PassGo Tivoli
passgo-tivoli	627/udp	PassGo Tivoli
ipp	631/tcp	IPP (Internet Printing Protocol)
ipp	631/udp	IPP (Internet Printing Protocol)
ldaps	636/tcp	ldap protocol over TLS/SSL (was sldap)
ldaps	636/udp	ldap protocol over TLS/SSL (was sldap)
lanserver	637/tcp	lanserver
lanserver	637/udp	lanserver
dhcp-failover	647/tcp	DHCP Failover
dhcp-failover	647/udp	DHCP Failover
mac-srvr-admin	660/tcp	MacOS Server Admin
mac-srvr-admin	660/udp	MacOS Server Admin
nmap	689/tcp	NMAP
nmap	689/udp	NMAP
msexch-routing	691/tcp	MS Exchange Routing
msexch-routing	691/udp	MS Exchange Routing
kerberos-adm	749/tcp	kerberos administration
kerberos-adm	749/udp	kerberos administration
iscsi	860/tcp	iSCSI
iscsi	860/udp	iSCSI
rsync	873/tcp	rsync
rsync	873/udp	rsync
ftps-data	989/tcp	ftp protocol, data, over TLS/SSL
ftps-data	989/udp	ftp protocol, data, over TLS/SSL
ftps	990/tcp	ftp protocol, control, over TLS/SSL
ftps	990/udp	ftp protocol, control, over TLS/SSL

Table A-1 *Port Assignments (Continued)*

Keyword	Decimal	Description
telnets	992/tcp	telnet protocol over TLS/SSL
telnets	992/udp	telnet protocol over TLS/SSL
imaps	993/tcp	imap4 protocol over TLS/SSL
imaps	993/udp	imap4 protocol over TLS/SSL
ircs	994/tcp	irc protocol over TLS/SSL
ircs	994/udp	irc protocol over TLS/SSL
pop3s	995/tcp	pop3 protocol over TLS/SSL (was spop3)
pop3s	995/udp	pop3 protocol over TLS/SSL (was spop3)

The registered ports, as shown in Table A-2, are in the range 1024 through 49151.

Table A-2 *Registered Ports*

Keyword	Decimal	Description
activesync	1034/tcp	ActiveSync Notifications
activesync	1034/udp	ActiveSync Notifications
adobeserver-1	1102/tcp	ADOBE SERVER 1
adobeserver-1	1102/udp	ADOBE SERVER 1
adobeserver-2	1103/tcp	ADOBE SERVER 2
adobeserver-2	1103/udp	ADOBE SERVER 2
mini-sql	1114/tcp	Mini SQL
mini-sql	1114/udp	Mini SQL
hpvmmcontrol	1124/tcp	HP VMM Control
hpvmmcontrol	1124/udp	HP VMM Control
hpvmmagent	1125/tcp	HP VMM Agent
hpvmmagent	1125/udp	HP VMM Agent
hpvmmdata	1126/tcp	HP VMM Agent
hpvmmdata	1126/udp	HP VMM Agent
saphostctrl	1128/tcp	SAPHostControl over SOAP/HTTP
saphostctrl	1128/udp	SAPHostControl over SOAP/HTTP
saphostctrls	1129/tcp	SAPHostControl over SOAP/HTTPS
saphostctrls	1129/udp	SAPHostControl over SOAP/HTTPS

continues

Table A-2 *Registered Ports (Continued)*

Keyword	Decimal	Description
kvm-via-ip	1132/tcp	KVM-via-IP Management Service
kvm-via-ip	1132/udp	KVM-via-IP Management Service
omnivision	1135/tcp	OmniVision Communication Service
omnivision	1135/udp	OmniVision Communication Service
iascontrol	1157/tcp	Oracle iASControl
iascontrol	1157/udp	Oracle iASControl
dbcontrol-oms	1158/tcp	dbControl OMS
dbcontrol-oms	1158/udp	dbControl OMS
oracle-oms	1159/tcp	Oracle OMS
oracle-oms	1159/udp	Oracle OMS
olsv	1160/tcp	DB Lite Mult-User Server
olsv	1160/udp	DB Lite Mult-User Server
cisco-ipsla	1167/tcp	Cisco IP SLAs Control Protocol
cisco-ipsla	1167/udp	Cisco IP SLAs Control Protocol
cisco-ipsla	1167/sctp	Cisco IP SLAs Control Protocol
mysql-cluster	1186/tcp	MySQL Cluster Manager
mysql-cluster	1186/udp	MySQL Cluster Manager
kazaa	1214/tcp	KAZAA
kazaa	1214/udp	KAZAA
shockwave2	1257/tcp	Shockwave 2
shockwave2	1257/udp	Shockwave 2
opsmgr	1270/tcp	Microsoft Operations Manager
opsmgr	1270/udp	Microsoft Operations Manager
emc-gateway	1273/tcp	EMC-Gateway
emc-gateway	1273/udp	EMC-Gateway
bmc_patroldb	1313/tcp	BMC_PATROLDB
bmc_patroldb	1313/udp	BMC_PATROLDB
pdps	1314/tcp	Photoscript Distributed Printing System
pdps	1314/udp	Photoscript Distributed Printing System
icap	1344/tcp	ICAP
icap	1344/udp	ICAP

Table A-2 *Registered Ports (Continued)*

Keyword	Decimal	Description
lotusnote	1352/tcp	Lotus Note
lotusnote	1352/udp	Lotus Note
netware-csp	1366/tcp	Novell NetWare Comm Service Platform
netware-csp	1366/udp	Novell NetWare Comm Service Platform
ibm-mqseries	1414/tcp	IBM MQSeries
ibm-mqseries	1414/udp	IBM MQSeries
novell-lu6.2	1416/tcp	Novell LU6.2
novell-lu6.2	1416/udp	Novell LU6.2
autodesk-lm	1422/tcp	Autodesk License Manager
autodesk-lm	1422/udp	Autodesk License Manager
blueberry-lm	1432/tcp	Blueberry Software License Manager
blueberry-lm	1432/udp	Blueberry Software License Manager
ms-sql-s	1433/tcp	Microsoft-SQL-Server
ms-sql-s	1433/udp	Microsoft-SQL-Server
ms-sql-m	1434/tcp	Microsoft-SQL-Monitor
ms-sql-m	1434/udp	Microsoft-SQL-Monitor
ms-sna-server	1477/tcp	ms-sna-server
ms-sna-server	1477/udp	ms-sna-server
ms-sna-base	1478/tcp	ms-sna-base
ms-sna-base	1478/udp	ms-sna-base
sybase-sqlany	1498/tcp	Sybase SQL Any
sybase-sqlany	1498/udp	Sybase SQL Any
shivadiscovery	1502/tcp	Shiva
shivadiscovery	1502/udp	Shiva
wins	1512/tcp	Microsoft's Windows Internet Name Service
wins	1512/udp	Microsoft's Windows Internet Name Service
orasrv	1525/tcp	oracle
orasrv	1525/udp	oracle
prospero-np	1525/tcp	Prospero Directory Service non-priv
prospero-np	1525/udp	Prospero Directory Service non-priv

continues

Table A-2 *Registered Ports (Continued)*

Keyword	Decimal	Description
pdap-np	1526/tcp	Prospero Data Access Prot non-priv
pdap-np	1526/udp	Prospero Data Access Prot non-priv
tlisrv	1527/tcp	oracle
tlisrv	1527/udp	oracle
coauthor	1529/tcp	oracle
coauthor	1529/udp	oracle
rdb-dbs-disp	1571/tcp	Oracle Remote Data Base
rdb-dbs-disp	1571/udp	Oracle Remote Data Base
oraclenames	1575/tcp	oraclenames
oraclenames	1575/udp	oraclenames
shockwave	1626/tcp	Shockwave
shockwave	1626/udp	Shockwave
isis-am	1642/tcp	isis-am
isis-am	1642/udp	isis-am
isis-ambc	1643/tcp	isis-ambc
isis-ambc	1643/udp	isis-ambc
groupwise	1677/tcp	groupwise
groupwise	1677/udp	groupwise
firefox	1689/tcp	firefox
firefox	1689/udp	firefox
rsvp-encap-1	1698/tcp	RSVP-ENCAPSULATION-1
rsvp-encap-1	1698/udp	RSVP-ENCAPSULATION-1
rsvp-encap-2	1699/tcp	RSVP-ENCAPSULATION-2
rsvp-encap-2	1699/udp	RSVP-ENCAPSULATION-2
l2tp	1701/tcp	l2tp
l2tp	1701/udp	l2tp
h323gatedisc	1718/tcp	h323gatedisc
h323gatedisc	1718/udp	h323gatedisc
h323gatestat	1719/tcp	h323gatestat
h323gatestat	1719/udp	h323gatestat
h323hostcall	1720/tcp	h323hostcall

Table A-2 *Registered Ports (Continued)*

Keyword	Decimal	Description
h323hostcall	1720/udp	h323hostcall
pptp	1723/tcp	pptp
pptp	1723/udp	pptp
oracle-em2	1754/tcp	oracle-em2
oracle-em2	1754/udp	oracle-em2
ms-streaming	1755/tcp	ms-streaming
ms-streaming	1755/udp	ms-streaming
tftp-mcast	1758/tcp	tftp-mcast
tftp-mcast	1758/udp	tftp-mcast
www-ldap-gw	1760/tcp	www-ldap-gw
www-ldap-gw	1760/udp	www-ldap-gw
nmsp	1790/tcp	Narrative Media Streaming Protocol
nmsp	1790/udp	Narrative Media Streaming Protocol
oracle-vp2	1808/tcp	Oracle-VP2
oracle-vp2	1808/udp	Oracle-VP2
oracle-vp1	1809/tcp	Oracle-VP1
oracle-vp1	1809/udp	Oracle-VP1
etftp	1818/tcp	Enhanced Trivial File Transfer Protocol
etftp	1818/udp	Enhanced Trivial File Transfer Protocol
ibm-mqseries2	1881/tcp	IBM WebSphere MQ Everyplace
ibm-mqseries2	1881/udp	IBM WebSphere MQ Everyplace
ecsqdmn	1882/tcp	CA eTrust Common Services
ecsqdmn	1882/udp	CA eTrust Common Services
ibm-mqisdp	1883/tcp	IBM MQSeries SCADA
ibm-mqisdp	1883/udp	IBM MQSeries SCADA
vrtstrapserver	1885/tcp	Veritas Trap Server
vrtstrapserver	1885/udp	Veritas Trap Server
can-nds	1918/tcp	IBM Tivole Directory Service - NDS
can-nds	1918/udp	IBM Tivole Directory Service - NDS
can-dch	1919/tcp	IBM Tivoli Directory Service - DCH

continues

Table A-2 *Registered Ports (Continued)*

Keyword	Decimal	Description
can-dch	1919/udp	IBM Tivoli Directory Service - DCH
can-ferret	1920/tcp	IBM Tivoli Directory Service - FERRET
can-ferret	1920/udp	IBM Tivoli Directory Service - FERRET
macromedia-fcs	1935/tcp	Macromedia Flash Communications Server MX
macromedia-fcs	1935/udp	Macromedia Flash Communications server MX
tivoli-npm	1965/tcp	Tivoli NPM
tivoli-npm	1965/udp	Tivoli NPM
unisql	1978/tcp	UniSQL
unisql	1978/udp	UniSQL
unisql-java	1979/tcp	UniSQL Java
unisql-java	1979/udp	UniSQL Java
hsrp	1985/tcp	Hot Standby Router Protocol
hsrp	1985/udp	Hot Standby Router Protocol
licensedaemon	1986/tcp	cisco license management
licensedaemon	1986/udp	cisco license management
tr-rsrb-p1	1987/tcp	cisco RSRB Priority 1 port
tr-rsrb-p1	1987/udp	cisco RSRB Priority 1 port
tr-rsrb-p2	1988/tcp	cisco RSRB Priority 2 port
tr-rsrb-p2	1988/udp	cisco RSRB Priority 2 port
tr-rsrb-p3	1989/tcp	cisco RSRB Priority 3 port
tr-rsrb-p3	1989/udp	cisco RSRB Priority 3 port
stun-p1	1990/tcp	cisco STUN Priority 1 port
stun-p1	1990/udp	cisco STUN Priority 1 port
stun-p2	1991/tcp	cisco STUN Priority 2 port
stun-p2	1991/udp	cisco STUN Priority 2 port
stun-p3	1992/tcp	cisco STUN Priority 3 port
stun-p3	1992/udp	cisco STUN Priority 3 port
snmp-tcp-port	1993/tcp	cisco SNMP TCP port
snmp-tcp-port	1993/udp	cisco SNMP TCP port
stun-port	1994/tcp	cisco serial tunnel port
stun-port	1994/udp	cisco serial tunnel port

Table A-2   *Registered Ports (Continued)*

Keyword	Decimal	Description
perf-port	1995/tcp	cisco perf port
perf-port	1995/udp	cisco perf port
tr-rsrb-port	1996/tcp	cisco Remote SRB port
tr-rsrb-port	1996/udp	cisco Remote SRB port
gdp-port	1997/tcp	cisco Gateway Discovery Protocol
gdp-port	1997/udp	cisco Gateway Discovery Protocol
x25-svc-port	1998/tcp	cisco X.25 service (XOT)
x25-svc-port	1998/udp	cisco X.25 service (XOT)
tcp-id-port	1999/tcp	cisco identification port
tcp-id-port	1999/udp	cisco identification port
cisco-sccp	2000/tcp	Cisco SCCP
cisco-sccp	2000/udp	Cisco SCCP
hsrpv6	2029/tcp	Hot Standby Router Protocol IPv6
hsrpv6	2029/udp	Hot Standby Router Protocol IPv6
isis	2042/tcp	isis
isis	2042/udp	isis
isis-bcast	2043/tcp	isis-bcast
isis-bcast	2043/udp	isis-bcast
dls	2047/tcp	
dls	2047/udp	
dls-monitor	2048/tcp	
dls-monitor	2048/udp	
nfs	2049/tcp	Network File System - Sun Microsystems
nfs	2049/udp	Network File System - Sun Microsystems
event-port	2069/tcp	HTTP Event Port
event-port	2069/udp	HTTP Event Port
ah-esp-encap	2070/tcp	AH and ESP Encapsulated in UDP packet
ah-esp-encap	2070/udp	AH and ESP Encapsulated in UDP packet
autodesk-nlm	2080/tcp	Autodesk NLM (FLEXlm)
autodesk-nlm	2080/udp	Autodesk NLM (FLEXlm)

continues

Table A-2 *Registered Ports (Continued)*

Keyword	Decimal	Description
kdm	2115/tcp	Key Distribution Manager
kdm	2115/udp	Key Distribution Manager
navisphere	2162/tcp	Navisphere
navisphere	2162/udp	Navisphere
navisphere-sec	2163/tcp	Navisphere Secure
navisphere-sec	2163/udp	Navisphere Secure
ddns-v3	2164/tcp	Dynamic DNS Version 3
ddns-v3	2164/udp	Dynamic DNS Version 3
jps	2205/tcp	Java Presentation Server
jps	2205/udp	Java Presentation Server
mysql-im	2273/tcp	MySQL Instance Manager
mysql-im	2273/udp	MySQL Instance Manager
giop	2481/tcp	Oracle GIOP
giop	2481/udp	Oracle GIOP
giop-ssl	2482/tcp	Oracle GIOP SSL
giop-ssl	2482/udp	Oracle GIOP SSL
ttc	2483/tcp	Oracle TTC
ttc	2483/udp	Oracle TTC
ttc-ssl	2484/tcp	Oracle TTC SSL
ttc-ssl	2484/udp	Oracle TTC SSL
citrixima	2512/tcp	Citrix IMA
citrixima	2512/udp	Citrix IMA
citrixadmin	2513/tcp	Citrix ADMIN
citrixadmin	2513/udp	Citrix ADMIN
citriximaclient	2598/tcp	Citrix MA Client
citriximaclient	2598/udp	Citrix MA Client
patrol-mq-gm	2664/tcp	Patrol for MQ GM
patrol-mq-gm	2664/udp	Patrol for MQ GM
patrol-mq-nm	2665/tcp	Patrol for MQ NM
patrol-mq-nm	2665/udp	Patrol for MQ NM
extensis	2666/tcp	extensis

Table A-2 *Registered Ports (Continued)*

Keyword	Decimal	Description
extensis	2666/udp	extensis
alarm-clock-s	2667/tcp	Alarm Clock Server
alarm-clock-s	2667/udp	Alarm Clock Server
alarm-clock-c	2668/tcp	Alarm Clock Client
alarm-clock-c	2668/udp	Alarm Clock Client
banyan-net	2708/tcp	Banyan-Net
banyan-net	2708/udp	Banyan-Net
vrts-at-port	2821/tcp	VERITAS Authentication Service
vrts-at-port	2821/udp	VERITAS Authentication Service
citrix-rtmp	2897/tcp	Citrix RTMP
citrix-rtmp	2897/udp	Citrix RTMP
webmethods-b2b	2907/tcp	WEBMETHODS B2B
webmethods-b2b	2907/udp	WEBMETHODS B2B
njfss	3092/tcp	Netware sync services
njfss	3092/udp	Netware sync services
bmcpatrolagent	3181/tcp	BMC Patrol Agent
bmcpatrolagent	3181/udp	BMC Patrol Agent
bmcpatrolrnvu	3182/tcp	BMC Patrol Rendezvous
bmcpatrolrnvu	3182/udp	BMC Patrol Rendezvous
isns	3205/tcp	iSNS Server Port
isns	3205/udp	iSNS Server Port
netwkpathengine	3209/tcp	HP OpenView Network Path Engine Server
netwkpathengine	3209/udp	HP OpenView Network Path Engine Server
fcip-port	3225/tcp	FCIP
fcip-port	3225/udp	FCIP
iscsi-target	3260/tcp	iSCSI port
iscsi-target	3260/udp	iSCSI port
msft-gc	3268/tcp	Microsoft Global Catalog
msft-gc	3268/udp	Microsoft Global Catalog
msft-gc-ssl	3269/tcp	Microsoft Global Catalog with LDAP/SSL

continues

Table A-2 *Registered Ports (Continued)*

Keyword	Decimal	Description
msft-gc-ssl	3269/udp	Microsoft Global Catalog with LDAP/SSL
mysql	3306/tcp	MySQL
mysql	3306/udp	MySQL
ms-cluster-net	3343/tcp	MS Cluster Net
ms-cluster-net	3343/udp	MS Cluster Net
ms-rdp	3389/tcp	MS Remote Desktop Protocol
dsc	3390/tcp	Distributed Service Coordinator
dsc	3390/udp	Distributed Service Coordinator
ifcp-port	3420/tcp	iFCP User Port
ifcp-port	3420/udp	iFCP User Port
websphere-snmp	3427/tcp	WebSphere SNMP
websphere-snmp	3427/udp	WebSphere SNMP
ov-nnm-websrv	3443/tcp	OpenView Network Node Manager WEB Server
ov-nnm-websrv	3443/udp	OpenView Network Node Manager WEB Server
prsvp	3455/tcp	RSVP Port
prsvp	3455/udp	RSVP Port
ibm3494	3494/tcp	IBM 3494
ibm3494	3494/udp	IBM 3494
ibm-diradm	3538/tcp	IBM Directory Server
ibm-diradm	3538/udp	IBM Directory Server
ibm-diradm-ssl	3539/tcp	IBM Directory Server SSL
ibm-diradm-ssl	3539/udp	IBM Directory Server SSL
can-nds-ssl	3660/tcp	IBM Tivoli Directory Service using SSL
can-nds-ssl	3660/udp	IBM Tivoli Directory Service using SSL
can-ferret-ssl	3661/tcp	IBM Tivoli Directory Service using SSL
can-ferret-ssl	3661/udp	IBM Tivoli Directory Service using SSL
eserver-pap	3666/tcp	IBM eServer PAP
eserver-pap	3666/udp	IBM eServer PAP
infoexch	3667/tcp	IBM Information Exchange
infoexch	3667/udp	IBM Information Exchange
adobeserver-3	3703/tcp	Adobe Server 3

Table A-2 *Registered Ports (Continued)*

Keyword	Decimal	Description
adobeserver-3	3703/udp	Adobe Server 3
adobeserver-4	3704/tcp	Adobe Server 4
adobeserver-4	3704/udp	Adobe Server 4
adobeserver-5	3705/tcp	Adobe Server 5
adobeserver-5	3705/udp	Adobe Server 5
tftps	3713/tcp	TFTP over TLS
tftps	3713/udp	TFTP over TLS
radius-dynauth	3799/tcp	RADIUS Dynamic Authorization
radius-dynauth	3799/udp	RADIUS Dynamic Authorization
netboot-pxe	3928/tcp	PXE NetBoot Manager
netboot-pxe	3928/udp	PXE NetBoot Manager
opswagent	3976/tcp	Opsware Agent
opswagent	3976/udp	Opsware Agent
opswmanager	3977/tcp	Opsware Manager
opswmanager	3977/udp	Opsware Manager
wafs	4049/tcp	Wide Area File Services
wafs	4049/udp	Wide Area File Services
cisco-wafs	4050/tcp	Wide Area File Services
cisco-wafs	4050/udp	Wide Area File Services
pcanywheredata	5631/tcp	pcANYWHEREdata
pcanywheredata	5631/udp	pcANYWHEREdata
pcanywherestat	5632/tcp	pcANYWHEREstat
pcanywherestat	5632/udp	pcANYWHEREstat
msdfsr	5722/tcp	Microsoft DFS Replication Service
msdfsr	5722/udp	Microsoft DFS Replication Service
openmail	5729/tcp	Openmail User Agent Layer
openmail	5729/udp	Openmail User Agent Layer
openmailg	5755/tcp	OpenMail Desk Gateway server
openmailg	5755/udp	OpenMail Desk Gateway server
x500ms	5757/tcp	OpenMail X.500 Directory Server

continues

Table A-2 *Registered Ports (Continued)*

Keyword	Decimal	Description
x500ms	5757/udp	OpenMail X.500 Directory Server
openmailns	5766/tcp	OpenMail NewMail Server
openmailns	5766/udp	OpenMail NewMail Server
s-openmail	5767/tcp	OpenMail Suer Agent Layer (Secure)
s-openmail	5767/udp	OpenMail Suer Agent Layer (Secure)
openmailpxy	5768/tcp	OpenMail CMTS Server
openmailpxy	5768/udp	OpenMail CMTS Server
vnc-server	5900/tcp	VNC Server
vnc-server	5900/udp	VNC Server
wsman	5985/tcp	WBEM WS-Management HTTP
wsman	5985/udp	WBEM WS-Management HTTP
wsmans	5986/tcp	WBEM WS-Management HTTP over TLS/SSL
wsmans	5986/udp	WBEM WS-Management HTTP over TLS/SSL
wbem-rmi	5987/tcp	WBEM RMI
wbem-rmi	5987/udp	WBEM RMI
wbem-http	5988/tcp	WBEM CIM-XML (HTTP)
wbem-http	5988/udp	WBEM CIM-XML (HTTP)
wbem-https	5989/tcp	WBEM CIM-XML (HTTPS)
wbem-https	5989/udp	WBEM CIM-XML (HTTPS)
wbem-exp-https	5990/tcp	WBEM Export HTTPS
wbem-exp-https	5990/udp	WBEM Export HTTPS
x11	6000-6063/tcp	X Window System
x11	6000-6063/udp	X Window System
bmc-grx	6300/tcp	BMC GRX
bmc-grx	6300/udp	BMC GRX
bmc_ctd_ldap	6301/tcp	BMC CONTROL-D LDAP SERVER
bmc_ctd_ldap	6301/udp	BMC CONTROL-D LDAP SERVER
repsvc	6320/tcp	Double-Take Replication Service
repsvc	6320/udp	Double-Take Replication Service
gnutella-svc	6346/tcp	gnutella-svc
gnutella-svc	6346/udp	gnutella-svc

Table A-2   *Registered Ports (Continued)*

Keyword	Decimal	Description
gnutella-rtr	6347/tcp	gnutella-rtr
gnutella-rtr	6347/udp	gnutella-rtr
kftp-data	6620/tcp	Kerberos V5 FTP Data
kftp-data	6620/udp	Kerberos V5 FTP Data
kftp	6621/tcp	Kerberos V5 FTP Control
kftp	6621/udp	Kerberos V5 FTP Control
mcftp	6622/tcp	Multicast FTP
mcftp	6622/udp	Multicast FTP
ktelnet	6623/tcp	Kerberos V5 Telnet
ktelnet	6623/udp	Kerberos V5 Telnet
bmc-perf-agent	6767/tcp	BMC PERFORM AGENT
bmc-perf-agent	6767/udp	BMC PERFORM AGENT
bmc-perf-mgrd	6768/tcp	BMC PERFORM MGRD
bmc-perf-mgrd	6768/udp	BMC PERFORM MGRD
pmdmgr	7426/tcp	OpenView DM Postmaster Manager
pmdmgr	7426/udp	OpenView DM Postmaster Manager
oveadmgr	7427/tcp	OpenView DM Event Agent Manager
oveadmgr	7427/udp	OpenView DM Event Agent Manager
ovladmgr	7428/tcp	OpenView DM Log Agent Manager
ovladmgr	7428/udp	OpenView DM Log Agent Manager
opi-sock	7429/tcp	OpenView DM rqt communication
opi-sock	7429/udp	OpenView DM rqt communication
xmpv7	7430/tcp	OpenView DM xmpv7 api pipe
xmpv7	7430/udp	OpenView DM xmpv7 api pipe
pmd	7431/tcp	OpenView DM ovc/xmpv3 api pipe
pmd	7431/udp	OpenView DM ovc/xmpv3 api pipe
oracleas-https	7443/tcp	Oracle Application Server HTTPS
oracleas-https	7443/udp	Oracle Application Server HTTPS
ovbus	7501/tcp	HP OpenView Bus Daemon
ovbus	7501/udp	HP OpenView Bus Daemon

continues

Table A-2 *Registered Ports (Continued)*

Keyword	Decimal	Description
ovhpas	7510/tcp	HP OpenView Application Server
ovhpas	7510/udp	HP OpenView Application Server
cfs	7546/tcp	Cisco Fabric service
cfs	7546/udp	Cisco Fabric service
sncp	7560/tcp	Sniffer Command Protocol
sncp	7560/udp	Sniffer Command Protocol
http-alt	8080/tcp	HTTP Alternate (see port 80)
http-alt	8080/udp	HTTP Alternate (see port 80)
sqlexec	9088/tcp	IBM Informix SQL Interface
sqlexec	9088/udp	IBM Informix SQL Interface
sqlexec-ssl	9089/tcp	IBM Informix SQL Interface - Encrypted
sqlexec-ssl	9089/udp	IBM Informix SQL Interface - Encrypted
davsrc	9800/tcp	WebDav Source Port
davsrc	9800/udp	WebDav Source Port
davsrcs	9802/tcp	WebDAV Source TLS/SSL
davsrcs	9802/udp	WebDAV Source TLS/SSL
ndmp	10000/tcp	Network Data Management Protocol
ndmp	10000/udp	Network Data Management Protocol
scp-config	10001/tcp	SCP Configuration Port
scp-config	10001/udp	SCP Configuration Port
dicom	11112/tcp	DICOM
dicom	11112/udp	DICOM
vnetd	13724/tcp	Veritas Network Utility
vnetd	13724/udp	Veritas Network Utility
bpcd	13782/tcp	VERITAS NetBackup
bpcd	13782/udp	VERITAS NetBackup
nbdb	13785/tcp	NetBackup Database
nbdb	13785/udp	NetBackup Database
nomdb	13786/tcp	Veritas-nomdb
nomdb	13786/udp	Veritas-nomdb
vrts-tdd	14149/tcp	Veritas Traffic Director

Table A-2 *Registered Ports (Continued)*

Keyword	Decimal	Description
vrts-tdd	14149/udp	Veritas Traffic Director
vad	14154/tcp	Veritas Application Director
vad	14154/udp	Veritas Application Director
cisco-snat	15555/tcp	Cisco Stateful NAT
cisco-snat	15555/udp	Cisco Stateful NAT
ovobs	30999/tcp	OpenView Service Desk Client
ovobs	30999/udp	OpenView Service Desk Client
filenet-powsrm	32767/tcp	FileNet BPM WS-ReliableMessaging Client
filenet-powsrm	32767/udp	FileNet BPM WS-ReliableMessaging Client
filenet-tms	32768/tcp	Filenet TMS
filenet-tms	32768/udp	Filenet TMS
filenet-rpc	32769/tcp	Filenet RPC
filenet-rpc	32769/udp	Filenet RPC
filenet-nch	32770/tcp	Filenet NCH
filenet-nch	32770/udp	Filenet NCH
filenet-rmi	32771/tcp	FileNET RMI
filenet-rmi	32771/udp	FileNet RMI
filenet-pa	32772/tcp	FileNET Process Analyzer
filenet-pa	32772/udp	FileNET Process Analyzer
filenet-cm	32773/tcp	FileNET Component Manager
filenet-cm	32773/udp	FileNET Component Manager
filenet-re	32774/tcp	FileNET Rules Engine
filenet-re	32774/udp	FileNET Rules Engine
filenet-pch	32775/tcp	Performance Clearinghouse
filenet-pch	32775/udp	Performance Clearinghouse
filenet-peior	32776/tcp	FileNET BPM IOR
filenet-peior	32776/udp	FileNET BPM IOR
filenet-obrok	32777/tcp	FileNet BPM CORBA
filenet-obrok	32777/udp	FileNet BPM CORBA
idmgratm	32896/tcp	Attachmate ID Manager
idmgratm	32896/udp	Attachmate ID Manager

Ten Places for More Information

The following list of ten information resources is most useful to network administrators and those seeking additional technical information about protocols and products. Sources include hardware and operating system vendors, application vendors offering tools to aid administrators, and IEEE-controlled resources. A description for each resource was obtained from within the resource's respective website.

1: Cisco IOS Technologies

Cisco IOS Software is the world's leading network infrastructure software, delivering a seamless integration of technology innovation, business-critical services, and hardware platform support. Cisco IOS technologies include NetFlow, Quality of Service, IP Service Level Agreements, and many other value-added, network-oriented capabilities that provide foundational components for ensuring application-fluent networks.

Learn more about Cisco IOS Technologies at http://www.cisco.com/en/US/products/ps6537/products_ios_sub_category_home.html

2: Cisco Product Documentation

Cisco product documentation is a comprehensive library of technical product documentation. The online documentation enables you to access multiple versions of installation, configuration, and command guides for Cisco hardware and software products. With the online product documentation, you have access to HTML-based documentation. Certain products also have PDF versions of the documentation available.

Download documentation at the following URL: http://www.cisco.com/public/support/tac/documentation.html

3: NetQoS Network Performance Management Tools

NetQoS provides network performance management products and services that optimize the performance of enterprise networks. Information is tailored to the needs of network engineering, operations, and management. NetQoS products help IT organizations optimize their network infrastructure.

Visit NetQoS at http://www.netqos.com/

4: BIC TCP

Binary Increase (BIC) TCP is one of many advanced TCP implementations that addresses performance problems associated with TCP in WAN environments as well as high-speed networks. BIC uniquely provides bandwidth scalability while also providing connection fairness among numerous packet loss ranges and scenarios where there is a latency disparity among connections.

Learn more about BIC TCP at http://www.csc.ncsu.edu/faculty/rhee/export/bitcp/

5: Low Bandwidth File System

The Low Bandwidth File System (LBFS) is a network file system that helps to improve performance and minimize network utilization between clients and servers. LBFS leverages cross-file similarities to minimize bandwidth consumption by using content chunking and indexing, thereby removing the need to transmit data that has been previously seen.

You can find the home page for LBFS at http://www.fs.net/sfswww/lbfs/index.html

6: Locating a Request for Comment

The Requests for Comments (RFC) contain technical and organizational notes about the Internet and the applications and protocols used on the Internet.

Visit the following website to search for a specific RFC: http://www.rfc-editor.org/rfcsearch.html

7: Microsoft TechNet

Microsoft TechNet is a program that provides comprehensive technical resources and information about Microsoft products, along with solution design, implementation, management, and troubleshooting.

Learn more about TechNet at the TechNet home page: http://technet.microsoft.com/en-us/default.aspx

8: Hewlett-Packard Product Documentation

Hewlett-Packard's website allows users to search for, browse, and print the latest technical documentation for many HP software and hardware products. The website provides two main ways to access documentation: by topic area or OS release.

Access HP technical documentation at http://docs.hp.com/

9: Red Hat Product Documentation

Red Hat documentation is available in HTML, HTML tarball, and PDF formats. Some of the latest manuals are also available in RPM format for easy installation.

Access Red Hat product documentation at http://www.redhat.com/docs/

10: Registered TCP and UDP Port Numbers

IANA's list is used in RFC 793 to name the ends of logical connections that carry long-term conversations. For the purpose of providing services to unknown callers, a service contact port is defined. This list specifies the port used by the server process as its contact port. The contact port is sometimes called the "well-known port." This list is updated frequently.

Access the list at http://www.iana.org/assignments/port-numbers

Index

Numerics

A

U-V

W-X-Y-Z

Cisco Press

3 STEPS TO LEARNING

STEP 1 **STEP 2** **STEP 3**

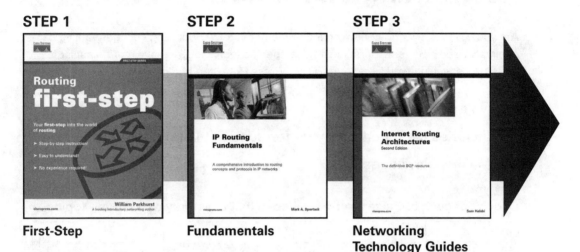

First-Step **Fundamentals** **Networking Technology Guides**

STEP 1 **First-Step**—Benefit from easy-to-grasp explanations. No experience required!

STEP 2 **Fundamentals**—Understand the purpose, application, and management of technology.

STEP 3 **Networking Technology Guides**—Gain the knowledge to master the challenge of the network.

NETWORK BUSINESS SERIES

The Network Business series helps professionals tackle the business issues surrounding the network. Whether you are a seasoned IT professional or a business manager with minimal technical expertise, this series will help you understand the business case for technologies.

Justify Your Network Investment.

Look for Cisco Press titles at your favorite bookseller today.

Visit **www.ciscopress.com/series** for details on each of these book series.

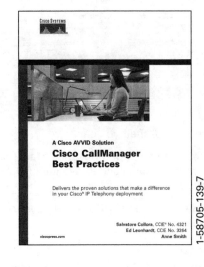

SEARCH THOUSANDS OF BOOKS FROM LEADING PUBLISHERS

Safari® Bookshelf is a searchable electronic reference library for IT professionals that features more than 2,000 titles from technical publishers, including Cisco Press.

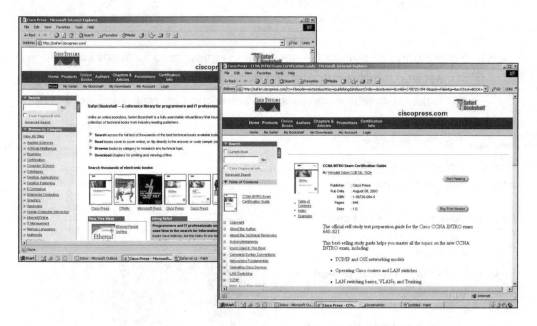

With Safari Bookshelf you can

- **Search** the full text of thousands of technical books, including more than 70 Cisco Press titles from authors such as Wendell Odom, Jeff Doyle, Bill Parkhurst, Sam Halabi, and Karl Solie.

- **Read** the books on My Bookshelf from cover to cover, or just flip to the information you need.

- **Browse** books by category to research any technical topic.

- **Download** chapters for printing and viewing offline.

With a customized library, you'll have access to your books when and where you need them—and all you need is a user name and password.

TRY SAFARI BOOKSHELF FREE FOR 14 DAYS!

You can sign up to get a 10-slot Bookshelf free for the first 14 days.
Visit **http://safari.ciscopress.com** to register.

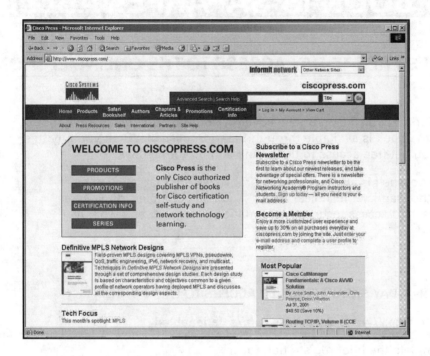
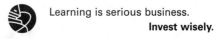

THIS BOOK IS SAFARI ENABLED

INCLUDES FREE 45-DAY ACCESS TO THE ONLINE EDITION

The Safari® Enabled icon on the cover of your favorite technology book means the book is available through Safari Bookshelf. When you buy this book, you get free access to the online edition for 45 days.

Safari Bookshelf is an electronic reference library that lets you easily search thousands of technical books, find code samples, download chapters, and access technical information whenever and wherever you need it.

TO GAIN 45-DAY SAFARI ENABLED ACCESS TO THIS BOOK:

- Go to **http://www.ciscopress.com/safarienabled**

- Complete the brief registration form

- Enter the coupon code found in the front of this book before the "Contents at a Glance" page

If you have difficulty registering on Safari Bookshelf or accessing the online edition, please e-mail customer-service@safaribooksonline.com.